ABDULAZIZ SACHEDINA is Francis Myers Ball Professor of Religious Studies at the University of Virginia.

Islamic Biomedical Ethics

Islamic Biomedical Ethics

Principles and Application

ABDULAZIZ SACHEDINA

OXFORD
UNIVERSITY PRESS
2009

OXFORD
UNIVERSITY PRESS

Oxford University Press, Inc., publishes works that further
Oxford University's objective of excellence
in research, scholarship, and education.

Oxford New York
Auckland Cape Town Dar es Salaam Hong Kong Karachi
Kuala Lumpur Madrid Melbourne Mexico City Nairobi
New Delhi Shanghai Taipei Toronto

With offices in
Argentina Austria Brazil Chile Czech Republic France Greece
Guatemala Hungary Italy Japan Poland Portugal Singapore
South Korea Switzerland Thailand Turkey Ukraine Vietnam

Published by Oxford University Press, Inc.
198 Madison Avenue, New York, New York 10016

www.oup.com

Library of Congress Cataloging-in-Publication Data
Sachedina, Abdulaziz Abdulhussein, 1942–
Islamic biomedical ethics : principles and application / Abdulaziz
Sachedina.
p. cm.
Includes bibliographical references and index.
ISBN 978-0-19-537850-4
1. Medical ethics—Religious aspects—Islam.
2. Bioethics—Religious aspects—Islam. I. Title.
[DNLM: 1. Bioethical Issues. 2. Ethics, Medical. 3. Islam. WB 60
S121i 2009]
R725.59.S33 2009
174'.957—dc22 2008028322

9 8 7 6 5 4 3 2 1

Printed in the United States of America
acid-free paper

To my grandsons, Maysam Ali son of Rahela and Alireza Sachedina and Matteen Jean-Baptiste son of Morwarid and Muhammadreza Sachedina, beacons of hope and prosperity

Foreword

This is a most welcome book—the result of many years of deep and broad study of Islam's fundamental beliefs and principles and their applications to novel biomedical technologies and practices as well as to more conventional problems in medical ethics.

As a scholar steeped in Islam, his own religious tradition, Abdulaziz Sachedina has also been a conversation partner with scholars in other religious and nonreligious traditions of ethical reflection, as well as in debates about public policy in a pluralistic society. For instance, at the University of Virginia, Sachedina co-taught, with another colleague and me, a seminar on Christian, Jewish, and Islamic perspectives on taking human life, which addressed important questions in bioethics, such as abortion, suicide, and euthanasia, as well as questions about killing in self-defense, capital punishment, and warfare. That is just one of the many contexts in which he has engaged colleagues—locally, nationally, and internationally—in rigorous examinations of comparative religious ethics.

In debates about public policies, Sachedina has been called upon time and again to present Islamic perspectives on such topics as human reproductive cloning and human embryonic stem cell research. Through his testimony before the National Bioethics Advisory Commission and congressional committee hearings, for instance, policymakers have learned much from Sachedina's unfailingly clear and illuminating portrayals of Islamic principles and juridical decisions. His presentations have enabled government officials and advisory committees to understand and consider Islamic views in their deliberations. He has also been an important spokesman on the international scene, for example, in conferences sponsored by the World Health Organization (WHO) and other international bodies.

In public policy fora, as well as in the academy, Sachedina is able to communicate Islamic positions clearly and effectively. He is able to do so both because he has lived and studied his tradition so thoroughly and because he understands as well the views of other religious and secular traditions. This understanding enables him to communicate at once what is shared and what is distinctive about Islamic perspectives and positions and to contribute significantly to on-going scholarly and public discourse.

As Islam has become an increasingly important voice in conversations about bioethics in the West, its interpreters have often addressed particular issues or problems, such as the moral status of the fetus. While these particular contributions have greatly enhanced our understanding of Islamic bioethics, we have long needed a more systematic and comprehensive articulation of Islamic bioethics, one that also connects Islamic juridical decisions to broader theological-ethical beliefs. This need has now been met in Sachedina's *Islamic Biomedical Ethics*, a remarkably clear, illuminating, and reliable guide. It not only portrays the Islamic tradition's bioethical views; it also contributes to the tradition's on-going development.

We are deeply indebted to Sachedina for this rich and masterful work.

James F. Childress
The John Allen Hollingsworth Professor of Ethics
University of Virginia

Contents

Islamic Biomedical Ethics

1

Introduction

As a monotheistic tradition Islam shares its spiritual, moral, and cultural genome with Judaism and Christianity. The word *islām*, which designates the last of the Abrahamic religions, literally means "submission to God's will." Muḥammad (born 570 CE), the Prophet of Islam and the founder of its public order, proclaimed Islam in the seventh century CE in Arabia. The beginning of Islam in 610 CE was marked by a struggle to establish a monotheistic faith in the polytheistic Arab tribal culture, with a clear departure from its divisive and violent tendencies, in order to create an ethical public order embodying divine justice and mercy. Muḥammad as a statesman instituted a series of reforms to create his unified community, *umma*, on the basis of religious affiliation.

Muḥammad's religious-political leadership and the universalizing mission for his community to spread Islam provided the major impetus for the expansion of the Muslim community beyond Arabia. Within a century of his death in 632, Muslim armies had conquered the region from the Nile in North Africa to the Oxus in Central Asia up to India. The political success of the Muslim armies and the territorial expansionism that ensued did not quell the internal struggle that was brewing among different powerful groups that vied for the leadership of the nascent community in the aftermath of the Prophet's death. The question of succession to Muḥammad was already on the minds of some of his prominent followers in the last days of Muḥammad's illness. One of the major issues that divided the community into the Sunni and Shīʿa was the post-Muḥammadan leadership. The most powerful group supported the candidacy of Abū Bakr (d. 634), an elderly associate of the Prophet, as the successor to the Prophet's political leadership. Those who paid allegiance to Abū Bakr and his successors came to be known as the Sunnis (followers of communal "tradition"). Another equally influential group that included prominent members of the Prophet's family contested Abū Bakr's leadership. According to them, the Prophet had actually appointed his cousin and son-in-law, ʿAlī b. Abī Ṭālib (d. 660) as the leader of the community during his farewell pilgrimage before his death in 632. Those who refused to accept Abū Bakr and instead paid allegiance to ʿAlī and his descendants as the rightful successors of the Prophet in both his spiritual and temporal functions formed the minority group, known as the Shīʿa ("partisans" of ʿAlī). Today almost eighty percent of the Muslims are Sunnis. Hence, they form the majority of the community.

The dispute on leadership in the community was more than political. It had profound implications beyond politics. The Qur'an's persistent injunctions of obedience to the Prophet endowed him with enormous personal prestige and power in shaping the public order and the future course of comprehensive Muslim life. In the post-prophetic period the dispute over the ideal leadership and the course of Muslim history left the community endlessly searching for a paradigmatic authority whose obedience could lead to this-worldly and the other-worldly prosperity. The Sunnis located that authority in the "tradition" (*sunna*) and the "community" (*jamāʿa*);[1] whereas the Shīʿites found it in the charismatic person of an infallible Imam.[2] Both the Sunna and the personal authority of the learned Imam have shaped the practice and attitude of the community in the area that this book intends to explore: Islamic biomedical ethics.

The Sharīʿa: Islamic Legal-Ethical Tradition

Epistemically, inquiry about the new issues connected with modern biomedical advancements is situated in Islamic legal-ethical studies. Since biomedical issues occur both in the area of interhuman as well as human-divine relations, Islamic juridical inquiries tend to be comprehensive. They comprise every possible case of conscientious decision-making as well as evaluation of consequences of one's action. In the context of biomedical ethics this inquiry covers practical aspects of clinical and research related decisions. Much of the juridical inquiries arose from settling more formal interpersonal activities that affected the morals of the individual in the context of the community as a whole. For instance, what was the obligation of the physician when it was clear that prolongation of life in the case of a patient in a persistent vegetative state (PVS) put enormous financial and psychological burden on the close family members? Or, in a case of a spousal dispute over the continuation of a pregnancy that was dangerous to the health of the woman, what was the right course of action in the matter of allowing or terminating early life of the fetus that enjoyed inviolability, at least, after the first trimester?

Islamic law covers all the actions humans perform, whether toward one another or toward God. The Sharīʻa is the norm of the Muslim community. It grew out of Muslim endeavors to ensure that Islam pervaded the whole of life. Two essential areas of human life define its scope: acts of worship, both public and private, connected with the pillars of faith; and acts of public order that ensure individual and collective justice. The first category of actions, undertaken with the intention of seeking God's pleasure, is collectively known as "ritual duties" toward God (*ʻibādāt,* literally "acts of worship"). These include all religious acts such as daily prayers, fasting, almsgiving, and so on; the second category of actions, undertaken to maintain a social order, is known as "social transactions" (*muʻāmalāt,* literally "social intercourse"). The religious calibration of these two categories depends upon the meticulous division of jurisdiction based on the ability of human institutions to enforce the Sharīʻa and provide sanctions for disregarding its injunctions. In Islam all actions should be performed to secure divine approval, but human agency and institutions have jurisdiction only over the social transactions that regulate interpersonal relations. The acts of worship are exclusively within God's jurisdiction since they are performed simply as part of one's relation to God. Consequently, God alone reserves the right of judging their final merit and reward. Human courts, however, are empowered to enforce the laws that govern interpersonal relations in society. Remarkably, from the early days of Islam, the Sharīʻa recognized the functional secularity of human institutions without presuming to meddle in the God-human relationship. This distinction between the two areas of jurisdiction allowed Muslims to adopt local cultures and institutions to enhance the administration of newly conquered regions of the world. It also secured a better understanding of the Qur'anic principle of coexistence among diverse communities.

The Qur'an, as the main revelatory source, provided paradigm cases regarding the sanctity of human life and certain situational aspects that might serve as referent points to resolve specific instances that affected human well-being under various conditions. For example, the Qur'an advised Muslims to write down all interhuman contractual agreements in matters of financial obligations. Muslim jurists have used this paradigm case to develop a detailed section in the jurisprudence to extrapolate all necessary rulings to ensure that no injustices could occur between two or more parties in matters that involve reciprocal claims and responsibilities. Hence, as I shall discuss in the book, surrogate motherhood that involved such a reciprocal financial as well as social claim and responsibility, has received much attention in the new rulings that allow a certain form of legally and religiously approved surrogacy. Whether in the civil or criminal cases, the Qur'an laid down an ethical standard of conduct from which jurists have extracted legal rulings in the realm of social interaction to ensure that justice and fair practice prevail in all human dealings.

In order to create such an all-comprehensive legal system founded upon revealed texts, Muslim scholars went beyond the Qur'an to the person of the founder and the early community. The Qur'an required obedience to the Prophet and those invested with authority, which included the idealized community made up of the elders among the first and second generations. In this way the Qur'an opened the way for extending the normative practice beyond the Prophet's earthly life. Such an understanding of the normative tradition was theoretically essential for deriving the legal system that saw its validity only in terms of its being extracted from the Prophet's own paradigmatic status. Clearly, for the Qur'an there could be no community without the Prophet. Hence, the Prophet's life as understood and reported by the early community became an ethical touchstone for what the Muslims call the Sunna, the Tradition. The word *sunna* strictly meant a legal precedent from which later jurists could derive further laws for the growing needs of the community. Hence, in this book I will use the term "Tradition" (with a capital "T") for the Sunna to indicate the information that was handed down to posterity—a *ḥadīth*-report, collected and compiled to form the basis for legal-ethical rulings. The Tradition in religious sciences is composed of major compilations of the *ḥadīth*-reports, which include the six officially recognized collections of the *ṣaḥīḥ* ('sound' traditions) among the Sunni Muslims, and the four *Kutub* ("books") among the Shī'ites. The intellectual activity surrounding the interpretation of God's will expressed in the Qur'an and the evaluation of the *ḥadīth*-reports that were ascribed to the Prophet and the early community became the major religious-academic activity among Muslims, laying the foundation for subsequent juridical deliberations—what became known as *fiqh* ("understanding"), or jurisprudence.

By the ninth through the tenth centuries every jurist was affiliated with one or the other leading scholars in the field of juristic investigation. The legal school that followed the Iraqi tradition was called "Ḥanafī," after Abū Ḥanīfa (d. 767), the "imām" (teacher) in Iraq. Those who adhered to the rulings of Mālik b. Anas (d. 795), in Arabia and elsewhere, were known as "Mālikis." Al-Shāfi'ī, who is also credited as being one of the profound legal thinkers, is the founder of a legal school in Egypt whose influence spread widely to other regions of the Muslim world. Another school was associated with Aḥmad b. Ḥanbal (d. 855), who compiled a work on *ḥadīth*-reports that became the source for juridical decisions of those who followed him. Shī'ites developed their own legal school, the Ja'farī school, whose leading authority was Imam Ja'far al-Ṣādiq (d. 748). Normally, Muslims accepted the legal school prevalent in their region. Most of the Sunnis follow Ḥanafī or Shāfi'ī, whereas the Shī'ites follow the Ja'farī school. In the absence of an organized "church" and ordained "clergy" in Islam, determination of valid religious practice was left to the qualified scholar of religious law—collectively known as ulema. Hence, there emerged a living tradition, with different interpretations of the

Qur'anic laws and prophetic traditions, giving rise to different schools of the juridical practice.

Understanding Juridical-Ethical Discourse

Muslim legal theorists were thoroughly aware of the moral underpinnings of the religious duties that all Muslims were required to fulfill as members of the faith community. In fact, the validity of their research in the foundational sources of Islam (the Qur'an and the Tradition) for solutions to practical matters depended upon their substantial consideration of different moral facets of a case that could be discovered by considering conflicting claims, interests, and responsibilities in the precedents preserved in these authoritative sources. What ensured the validity of their judicial decision regarding a specific instance was their ability to deduce the universal moral principles like "there shall be no harm inflicted or reciprocated" (*lā ḍarar wa lā ḍirār*)[3] that flowed downward from their initial premise to support their particular conclusion without any dependence on the circumstances that would have rendered the conclusion circumstantial at the most. In their appraisal of a network of conflicting moral considerations in the new case that required a legal solution, theoretical arguments embedded in primary sources to derive a resolution functioned more as *ratio legis* (*'illa*) or the attribute common to both the new and the original case. The rule or the principle (*qā'ida* or *aṣl*) was attached to the original case, which due to similarity between the two cases was transferred from that case to the new case. As such, more attention was paid to the original rule and the *ratio legis* that also became the source of much debate among Muslim jurists and formed an important part of the procedures used to resolve earlier problems and reapply them in the new problematic situations.[4] Practical solutions based on earlier precedents carry the burden of proof on how closely the present case resembles those of the earlier paradigm cases for which this particular type of argument was originally devised. However, the power of these conclusions depended on the ethical considerations deduced from the rules that were operative in the original cases and the agreement of the scholars about analogical deduction that sought to relate the new case to the original rationale as well as rules.

In Islamic jurisprudence ethical values are integral to the prescriptive action guide that the system provides to the community. No legal decisions are made without meticulous analysis of the various factors that determine the rightness or the wrongness of a case under consideration. The universal major premise provided by the scriptural sources—the Qur'an and the Tradition—that serves as known is part of the divine commandments regarding the good that must be obeyed and the evil that must be avoided. There is an inherent correlation between God's command in the revelation and the moral reasoning that undergirds the command that is acknowledged by reason as being good. The metaphysical backdrop of the Sharīʿa is the discovery of God's purposes for humanity. Human reason is God's endowment to enable human intellect to fathom the supernatural by exploring the meanings of the revealed message through the Prophet.

Whereas I am a believer in universal moral values that have application across cultures, human conditions in specific social and political cultures demand searching for principles and rules that provide culture-specific guidance in Muslim societies to resolve practical quandaries. My working assumption in this book is that praxis precedes search for principles and rules. Customarily, when faced with a moral dilemma deliberations are geared toward a satisfactory resolution in which justifications are based on practical consequences, regardless of applicable principles. For instance, in deciding whether to allow dissection of the cadaver to retrieve a valuable object swallowed by the deceased, Muslim jurists have ruled the permission by simply looking at the consequence of forbidding such a procedure. The major moral consideration that outweighs the respect for the dignity of the dead is the ownership through inheritance of the swallowed object for the surviving orphan. Dissection of the cadaver is forbidden in Islam; and, yet, the case demands immediate solution that is based on consequential ethics. Or, in the case of a female patient who, as prescribed in the Sharīʿa, must be treated by a female physician, in an emergency situation the practical demand is to override the prohibition because the rule of necessity (*ḍarūra*) extracted from the revealed texts outweighs the rule about sexual segregation extracted from rational consideration. Hence, the rule of necessity determines the teleological solution and provides the incontestable rationale for the permission granted to a Muslim female patient to refer to a male physician not related to her. There are numerous instances that clearly show the cultural preferences in providing solutions to the pressing problems of health care in Muslim societies in which the highly rated principle of autonomy in the West takes a back seat, while communitarian ethics considers the consequence of any medical decision on the family and community resources.

The major objective of this chapter is to introduce Islamic ethical discourse in the context of newly emerging field of bioethics in the Muslim world. The ethical doctrines that undergird the legal tradition in Islam hold the potential for an inclusive universal language that can engage secular bioethics that epistemically determines the direction of the international deliberations on several biomedical and biotechnical issues. What is critically needed in the Muslim context is to demonstrate to the religious scholars that Islamic ethics shares a common moral terrain with secular bioethics that can provide an opportunity to dialogue with international organizations like WHO or UNESCO to protect human dignity and to advance human physical and psychological health. Bioethics in the Muslim world is a relatively new field of inquiry and, hence, there has never been any serious attempt at defining the epistemic parameters of the field as it relates to Muslim culture. Commonly, until recently, bioethical issues have been raised in the Muslim world without much interest in the native cultural sensibilities about human wellness and illness. Universalization of medical education has led to an erroneous assumption among healthcare professionals and institutions in Muslim societies that the solutions offered to moral dilemmas in the Western secular setting apply across other cultures. However, the growing interest in specifically Islamic solutions among a largely religiously sensitive population has required healthcare institutions and professionals to take people's moral and religious sensibilities more seriously to provide culturally sensitive solutions in medical practice and research.

After spending much time in the centers of Islamic juridical sciences, gathering rulings about new problematic areas in patient-physician relations or new medical treatments that have generated moral and religious dilemmas for Muslims, I quickly realized that in order to sit in conversation with secular or other religion-based bioethicists, I needed to take my research beyond the usual study of the juridical opinions in those areas. In particular, I needed to explore Islamic social ethics to understand the underpinnings of these rulings in their social and cultural contexts. In my studies of Islamic jurisprudence I was aware that although Islamic juridical methodology was firmly founded on some moral principles like rejection of harm and promotion of public good in deriving solutions that Muslims encountered in their everyday life, gradually, the judicial opinions were formulated without any reference to ethical dimensions of the cases under consideration. In general, ethical inquiry connected with moral epistemology or moral ontology is underdeveloped in the Muslim seminarian curriculum which is, in large measure, legal-oriented. This lack of interest in the theological-ethical underpinnings of the juridical methodology that deduces rulings in all areas of human activity is a major drawback of seminary education in the major centers of Islamic higher learning. A number of Western scholars of Islamic legal tradition, following the anti-rational attitude of mainly Sunni jurists have erroneously excluded any organic relationship between theological and legal doctrines in shaping the legal methodology and application. In contrast, Shīʿite legal tradition has not severed its epistemic correlation with, for instance, the theological question whether good and evil are objective categories that can be known intuitively by divinely endowed reason to the agent or not. The moral consequences of raising such questions about ethical epistemology are enormous since they lead to larger issues about human ability to comprehend justice and to assume moral agency to take the responsibility to effect changes in social and political realms. Moreover, the fact is that theological-ethical deliberations have led to moral categorization of human acts in jurisprudence based on rational understanding of one's duties and reciprocal responsibilities. Legal categorization has simply followed what was intuitively estimated as necessary, recommended, or forbidden. More importantly, investigation in the rulings that dealt with biomedical issues confirmed my suspicion that the categorical language of the rulings ruled out necessary revisions in the final decision about the right course of action that depended upon unfolding of different facets of the case in its day-to-day context of clinical research and information.

During my research in biomedical ethics in the Muslim centers of juridical studies I often raised questions about theological ethics in Islam that dealt with ontology of human action and determined its goodness or otherwise, providing scriptural as well as rational justifications for the right course of action. But based on the prevalent juridical methodology, it was evident that while the judicial decisions were made with proper reference to the scriptural sources there was very little interest in the morality of biomedical practice and research that investigated the action based on human volition and cognition. During my several sojourns in Jordan and Iran, for instance, I raised the prospects of examining modern medical advancement from ethical, more specifically social-ethical, perspectives. In the course of my lectures in medical universities I conceptually distinguished ethical from juridical in Islamic religious sciences. However, it was not until 2005, when I spent the entire year in Iran, researching and teaching bioethics, that my proposal to analyze ethical dimensions of problematic cases in clinical situations began to be taken seriously, both in medical schools and religious seminaries.

My major concern with bioethics in the Muslim world today is that it has severed its partnership with faith communities in providing solutions to the moral problems that have arisen in clinical situations as well as public health around the world. International bodies like WHO and UNESCO, which support local efforts in developing culturally sensitive bioethical curriculum, still appear to be unaware of the essentially religious nature of bioethical discourse in the Muslim world and the need to engage religious ethics in the Muslim context to better serve the populations whose cultures take religion more seriously. In a number of UNESCO and WHO sponsored conferences that I have participated in Iran and in Pakistan, it was obvious to me that those who presented Muslim bioethics were least informed about the local cultures and their religious ingredients and least able to speak with necessary acumen and sensitivity about how bioethics can find a legitimate native voice without simply mimicking the Western secular bioethics, which does not fully resonate with the local and regional Muslim values.

My other aim in pursuing the ethical foundation of Islamic juridical tradition is to emphasize the human dimension of the juridical enterprise in Islam so that the normative essentialism attached to the interhuman relationships in the juridical corpus of the classical heritage is understood in its historical and relative cultural and social contexts. There is no dearth of conceptual resources in theological ethics, as I shall demonstrate in chapter 2, for deriving universal moral principles to guide the life of a person who needs to be treated fairly in terms of allocation of limited resources. Not surprisingly, the neglect of Islamic ethical resources to work toward an inclusive, universal morality has impacted upon different human rights articles promulgated in Cairo Declaration of 1994 in which fundamental human rights are guaranteed in accordance with the provisions of Sharī'a, which determines the "insider/outsider" as well as gender distinctions and differentiations that have actually led to discrimination at different levels of access to public health in Muslim societies. For instance, Article 24 of the 1994 Cairo Declaration is very explicit in asserting that "All the rights and freedoms stipulated in this Declaration are subject to the Islamic Sharī'a." More pertinently, Article 25 asserts the absolute role of the Islamic Sharī'a as "the only source of reference for the explanation or clarification of any of the articles of this Declaration" (Cairo, 14 Muharram 1411/5 August 1990). Not unlike the Cairo Declaration, the history of legal reforms in the Muslim world is replete with examples that needed internal response from Muslim jurists to develop an expansive legal methodology that could go beyond the classical legal theory to offer solutions within the larger context of a new social and political reality of a modern nation-state that must treat all its citizens equally. Without articulating and recognizing the moral worth of all humans based on Islamic revelation, it is ludicrous to speak about inherent human dignity and inalienable human rights.

The neglect of the ethical presuppositions of Islamic juridical tradition has become endemic among Muslim jurists in dealing with the Muslim-non-Muslim distinction in all spheres of interpersonal justice. Bioethics as a subfield of social ethics requires investigation of morally problematic areas in medical practice. Without fully accounting for rationally and scripturally derived justifications for a certain moral course of action to determine the permissibility or otherwise of a questionable medical procedure does injustice to the moral values that undergird healthcare in Muslim societies—in the Muslim world as well as in countries where Muslims have migrated in large numbers. Ultimately, the function of ethical inquiry is to recommend a course of action in congruence with universal moral values that have application across cultures. Can Muslims develop that universal language that is firmly derived from their religious or cultural sources?

Having taught bioethics in Muslim societies for a number of years I have come to this academic conclusion: Translation or grafting of the secular Western bioethics to the Muslim medical and healthcare institutions is unproductive without first investigating native epistemic and cultural resources to teach and disseminate bioethics in Muslim societies. Taking into consideration what Muslim societies need in terms of developing a fresh approach to morality and, in particular, professional and healthcare ethics, I have endeavored to develop both a relevant epistemology and historically anchored bioethics in a Muslim healthcare environment.

The present work is a study in religious resources of the Islamic legal-ethical tradition as well as an application in Muslim culture-friendly bioethics. On the one hand, the overall purpose is to further a dialogical discourse that would initiate an important consideration that seems to be missing in the Muslim societies, namely, the patient's empowerment vis-à-vis healthcare institutions. In the absence of consensual politics in the majority of Muslim countries, healthcare policies are, in large measure, formulated without public debate over proper assessment of Islamic moral and cultural resources and without respect of human dignity and accruing human rights in furthering public and private health. On the other hand, the study will enable Muslim jurists working in the area of biomedical ethics to engage in bioethical discourse with other faith communities, who struggle, like them, to preserve their religious and moral values in the largely agnostic culture of medical practice. The juridical decisions that are given to the modern biomedical problems demonstrate the role of both revealed texts and the underlying ethical principles in deriving a moral-legal decision. Nevertheless, these revealed sources were produced in history and require a constant reference to establish the religious validity of modern decisions.

The task of moving back and forth between juridical and ethical traditions in Islam is challenging. It is not always possible to intellectually engage historical Islamic juridical methodology to appreciate and elicit modes of moral reasoning that undergirds rulings in the area of bioethics. There is a lack of general interest in theological ethics as a separate discipline, and yet organically connected to jurisprudence, among scholars of Islamic law in the West as well as the Muslim world. In the West, Islamic theological ethics began to be taken seriously after George F. Hourani and Majid Fakhry's published works on the subject drew attention to the richness of the subject and its organic relation to Christian-Hellenistic natural and rational theologies. What passes for Islamic ethics in Muslim countries is mostly Aristotelian ethics, and not the theological ethics introduced by Hourani's groundbreaking study on the Mu'tazilite theologian, Qāḍī 'Abd al-Jabbār (d. 1025).[5] Aristotelian ethics as taught in the Muslim world deals with development of virtuous life as part of one's spiritual and moral discipline. Consequently, what has been circulating as "Islamic bioethics" has very little to say about ethics as a discipline that endeavors to understand the moral reasoning behind ethical decisions.

This is not surprising. The majority of the articles and studies on biomedical issues in the Muslim world have been written by Muslim medical practitioners whose interest in these issues is sparked through the ongoing international debates on bioethics. More recently, there has been a growing interest in the international community, especially WHO, to learn about Islamic perspectives. It is important to keep in mind that it was in the West that autonomy as an overriding right of a patient found institutional and legal-ethical support. Western notions of universal human rights rest on a secular view of the individual and of the relations between such individuals in a secularized public sphere. The idea of individuals as bearers of something called rights presupposes a very particular understanding and reading of the self essentially as self-regulating agent. The modern idea of the autonomous self envisions social actors as self-contained matrixes of desires who direct their own interests. In Islamic communitarian ethics autonomy is far from being recognized as one of the major bioethical principles. The Islamic universal discourse conceives of a spiritually and morally autonomous individual incapable of attaining salvation outside the nexus of community-oriented Sharī'a, with its emphasis on an integrated system of law and morality. The Sharī'a did not make a distinction between external acts and internal states because it did not regard the public and the private as unrelated in the totality of individual salvation. Islamic communal discourse sought to define itself by legitimizing individual autonomy within its religiously based collective order by leaving an individual free to negotiate his/her spiritual destiny, while requiring him/her to abide by a communal order that involved the play of reciprocity and autonomy upon which a regime of rights and responsibilities are based in the Sharī'a. In the context of Islamic communitarian ethics, then, the central question is how to preserve the system of reciprocity and responsibilities at the individual as well as collective levels. Moreover, in the Muslim world, like many developing world countries, medical practice continues to remain essentially authoritarian and paternalistic, depriving patients and their families of any substantial role in determining the pros and cons of a treatment in critical care where ethical dilemmas predominate. Hence, Islamic perspectives that are included in the studies conducted by these medical professionals based on prescriptive rulings in their original Arabic or Persian or their translations, lack any intellectual engagement with ethical analysis that requires training in the normative contents of Islamic legal sciences or theological ethics to evaluate their relevance and application. In the absence of essential information about the underlying ethical principles that guide the juridical research in Islamic law, the literature in English that I have examined thus far suffers from sweeping, immature judgments about Islamic positions. In some cases, "Islamic" is used simply to legitimize the ascription of the contents to Islam with no indication, whatsoever, that normative sources of Islamic ethical reflection provide a variety of options and resolutions to each ethical dilemma in biomedicine. These articles and studies, although important in their own right, can hardly form the backbone of Islamic bioethics. Instead, as this study undertakes, this emerging discipline needs to define its epistemic parameters and develop both a methodology and a justificatory mechanics of moral reasoning that explore and open venues for deriving ethical "recommendation (*tawṣīya*)" rather than "judicial opinion (*fatwā*)" on issues that confront human health and medical research in Muslim societies.

To underscore the importance of the normative sources that validate fresh rulings, Islamic biomedical ethics cannot ignore judicial opinions and the sources that provide their legitimization as being Islamic. Actually, judicial opinions function as raw material for further inquiry into the moral reasoning that undergirds these rulings. In other words, the *fatwā*-literature needs be investigated for the purpose of exploring and understanding the legal reasoning behind the rulings. Such an investigation would unfold the rational-textual methodology (*al-ijtihād al-sharʿī*) and enable the researcher to identify operative principles and rules that Muslim jurists employ in their resolution of new cases.

There are a number of Muslim scholars in the Muslim world, both trained in jurisprudence or in medicine, who have undertaken to author books and articles on bioethical issues of international interest. In a number of these published works in Arabic and Persian, it is possible to gauge the spirit of Islamic juridical discourse founded upon extrapolating a fresh ruling on the subject. However, in the absence of any ethical discussion this published literature hardly provides the frame of reference for comparative study between Islamic and, for instance, secular or other religion-based bioethics. At this time, Islamic bioethics in a comparative mode still awaits calibrations.

"Islam" and "Muslims" in This Study

Throughout this work I use the word "Islam" and "Muslim(s)" as multilayered terms that identify different trends of Islamic thought and practice in diverse social and political contexts. In general, I use "Islam" to identify three variable categories of Islamic tradition that appear to be prevalent in the community at large:

(1) Islam as a civilization and its influence as a culture throughout the regions of the world where it spread as a religious tradition. Muslims with strong nationalistic religiosity regard Islamic civilization as one of the highly successful civilizations and one of the major global cultural traditions, founded upon justice and inclusive-egalitarian spirituality. As a world-embracing tradition, Islam in this sense inspires and sustains a public theology based on concern for others. It continues to motivate moral conduct through its normatively founded emphasis on equality in creation, thereby establishing the norms for the universal human cultural heritage.[6] As a significant force in shaping the presuppositions of universal world civilization and as a cultural tradition that has shaped and adjusted its own moral understandings in different social and political environments, this Islam seeks guidance from its own history. In the process, it steers away from raising historical contingencies to the status of authoritatively normative models and accepts the role of time and place in interpretive relativism as part of general progress toward relevant appropriation of Islamic beliefs and practices.[7] Indeed, by stepping back from many of the traditional cultural prohibitions (empowerment of women in general, including their becoming medical practitioners and licitness of their caring for patients of opposite sex, and other related issues), as well as by not insisting on literal adherence to traditional Islamic notions (the doctrine of soul and body for the

sake of avoiding becoming organ donors), this form of Islam tends to reduce the judicial and the dogmatic to the mystical (different forms and orders of Sufi affiliations and communal celebrations that encourage humanitarianism and altruism); cultural public rituals (fasting of Ramadan and other festive public celebrations that teach sharing and caring for less privileged); and well-staged public rituals (Friday and festival worship attended by rulers and public officials, and, now the annual pilgrimage to Mecca, as a show of Muslim unity and power in the divided world of nation-states with implications for providing public health care for all during the ḥajj).

(2) Islam as a religious-moral system for contemporary secularized societies. This is the sense in which modern educated people acknowledge Islam, yet with much deeper religious commitments and responsibilities. For them Islam possesses the fullness of God's revelation to humankind, offering unique insight into the importance of God's merciful justice and concern for humanity. Though the revelation is particularistic and addressed to a specific community in their language, the grounds for moral conduct and the substantive moral discernment is available to all human beings through their natural constitution created by the Almighty and All-compassionate God. Since a good moral life is taken to be a sufficient condition for attaining this-worldly and other-worldly prosperity (*falāḥīya*), this Islam does not regard itself as the only repository of human salvation, and, in this sense, it does not make exclusivist claims (e.g., the claim that Islam is the only privileged way to the divine truth and salvation). Furthermore, because ethical knowledge is grounded in human nature informed by intuitive reason, Islamic morality shares moral sensibilities with all other human beings equally endowed with that divinely ordained nature (*fiṭra*). Islamic morality develops its moral principles guided by conventional wisdom and moral insight discerned by living with others in society.

The provocative thesis of this genre of Islam is that because the rationality of Islamic ethics is held to be the same rationality shared by moral secular viewpoints this Islam shares general secular progress in moral insights that advances religious insights as being compatible with public reason. Since this genre of Islam affords centrality to the overlapping consensus in the matter of moral commitments that affect not only communal bonds but also advance intercommunal relations in the public forum, the moral premises and rules of evidence are culturally inclusive and capable of advancing received moral commitments for the public good.[8]

(3) Islam as the unique and exclusive experience of the Truth. This genre of Islam is popular among Muslim seminarians and Muslim masses. Islam, according to this account, is the only complete revelation of God to humankind. Islam not only offers a special motivation for moral conduct, but the full content of the religious life which, if properly lived, could lead to salvation. In order to be saved, one needs the right belief, which should precede right conduct. Living a good moral life for virtue's sake is recognized as insufficient

for salvation, in that salvation requires obedience to God's revealed guidance. Human prosperity in this and the world to come is achieved by bringing the world to affirm what is disclosed by revealed reason, not merely that disclosed by secular reason acting independent of divine guidance. Moral progress is achieved insofar as secular morality comes to conform to religious morality (e.g., by protecting human life from all kinds of detriment as required by the Sharī'a). This account of Islam is the traditional Islam upheld in the seminaries and among large sectors of the society in the Muslim world that looks for religious guidance from the ulema who represent this culture.

This traditional Islamic perspective appreciates that moral theological truth is the result of neither sensory empirical evidence nor discursive reason. Truth as a rightly ordered relationship with transcendent God is beyond discursive rationality. As a result, its traditional commitments cannot be brought into question by supposed moral theological progress grounded in developments in philosophical and metaphysical reflection. Finally, this traditional form of Islam recognizes the external forms of religious practices—the rituals—as secure and sufficient means to affect salvation without any need to relate them to moral progression of the individual or the community.

These three categories are not in any sense exhaustive. They simply underscore the religious plurality in Muslim communities when it comes to apply religious values in matters of healthcare institutions and public health. When it comes to the condemnation and prohibition of homosexual relations or affirmation of men's dominant position as the sole decision-maker in the family, it is the traditional perspective that poses the most significant challenge to public health policies that aspire to bind persons apart from any religious commitments. More to the point, in the context of this study, in order to advance the public good and protect the human rights of women, children, and the downtrodden in matters affecting their healthcare in the Muslim societies there is a need to sit in dialogue with the kind of Islam that regards religious considerations as critical in shaping the public policies and its discourse. It is important to keep the context of the secular demand for public reason in building the overlapping consensus in the public discourse. Obviously, traditional interpretation of Islam cannot achieve that consensus in a religiously oriented society without transforming religious discourse into an expression of appropriate reciprocal human relations. This was a historical struggle for Muslim societies, which needed to develop an inclusive morality that was normative and that aimed at inculcating in persons civic virtues that gave rise to the centrality of moral reasoning in public domain.

The Present Work

The research for this book began in earnest during the winter of 1996, when I was at the School of Oriental and African Studies, University of London. In the early stages of this research there were few works in Arabic or Persian exclusively on biomedical issues; today there are a number of monographs on different aspects of biomedical topics available in almost all Islamic languages. Most of these provide an array of juridical opinions (*fatāwā*) compiled on the authority of various scholars representing different schools of legal thought in Islam. The subjects include organ transplant, abortion, technically assisted reproduction, euthanasia, and so on. The audience for these publications is, in most cases, healthcare professionals and the Muslim public. However, as indicated earlier, there is a conspicuous absence of any discussion about the principles or the rules that govern such legal-ethical decisions in Islamic law.

Contemporary moral discourse has been aptly described as a minefield of incommensurable disagreements. Such disagreements are believed to be the result of secularization marked by a retreat of religion from the public arena. Privatization of religion has been regarded as a necessary condition for ethical pluralism. The essentially liberal vision of community founded on the radical autonomy of the individual moral agent runs contrary to other-regarding communitarian values of shared ideas of justice and of public good. There is a sense that modern, secular, individualistic society is no longer a community founded on commonly held beliefs of social good and its relation to responsibilities and freedoms in a pluralistic society.[9] To provide the fundamentals of the Islamic ethical discourse that ultimately must guide our search in the complexity of bioethical pluralism in the Muslim world, in this book I have explored distinctly Islamic, and yet cross-culturally communicable, principle-rule based deontological-teleological ethics. The deontological ethical norm determines the rightness (or wrongness) of actions without regard to the consequences produced by performing such actions. By contrast, the teleological norm determines the rightness (or wrongness) of actions on the basis of their consequences produced by performing these actions. Deontological norms can further be subdivided into objectivist and subjectivist norms: objectivist because the ethical value is intrinsic to the action independently of anyone's decision or opinion; subjectivist because the action derives value in relation to the view of a judge who decides its rightness (or wrongness).[10] Deontological-teleological ethics undergirds Muslim legal-moral culture in assessing moral dilemmas in Islamic biomedical ethics.

As soon as I launched my research, I faced the problem of redefining the conceptual boundaries of Islamic biomedical ethics. The Iranian scholars use *akhlāq-i pizishkī*, which literally means "virtues of the medical profession." Under this rubric they speak about the moral virtues that must be cultivated by Muslim physicians. Obviously, one cannot use this rubric for juridical decisions that affect Muslim medical practice. A new term has now entered the medical education in Iran, namely, *akhlāq-i zīstī*, which is the translation of "bioethics," which fundamentally deals with judicial rulings on biomedical issues rather than ethics of medical practice. A better designation of this kind of literature has now received the Arabic appellation, namely, *fiqh al-ṭabīb* ("jurisprudence affecting medical professionals") that has found currency in the Arabic speaking world under *qaḍāya fiqhīya wa ṭibbīya mu'āṣira* ("Modern Juridical and Medical Issues") or *aḥkām* ("rulings or judicial opinions"). From time to time one also finds the Arabic translation of "bioethics" (*akhlāqiyāt al-ṭibīya*), again, without substantially taking up ethical dimensions of the issues. In fact, most of the Arabic and Persian works treat biomedical ethics as a subspecialty of applied Islamic jurisprudence. Juridical rulings, as pointed out above, do not undertake to explicate the theoretical and practical ethical issues connected with human conscience. Simply stated, the goal of Islamic jurisprudence is to derive legal rulings that state only the permissibility or prohibition of a particular medical practice or procedure. Discussion about the reasons why it is morally permissible or forbidden is beyond its scope of the inquiry. Nevertheless, an ethical inquiry must seek the moral foundations of an act before it can prescribe or proscribe it in practice.

Governments all over the Muslim world have established committees or commissions to obtain Muslim scholarly opinions on various issues in medical practice that have implications for public policy. In 1995, for instance, the Iranian parliament debated the transplantation of organs taken from a Muslim cadaver or from a brain-dead person; there was a dispute among the members whether permission for such procedures had been granted by the late Ayatollah Khomeini and other high-ranking jurists. More importantly, the parliament wanted to enact policy guidelines for the Ministry of Health and the Iranian Medical Association on such matters. Predictably, the bill was not approved, and the Islamic juridical establishment was criticized for having failed to undertake adequate research to provide Islamic responses to the newly advanced criteria in support of the validity of brain death.

The subject of brain death has elicited clashing views among Sunni and Shī'ite scholars that reflect the deep rift between medical professionals and the religious establishment. The religious establishment in the Muslim world has failed to take into consideration the change in the situational aspects of biomedical cases. More importantly, they have failed to articulate ethical values and justifications that are necessary to understand the moral dilemmas that face healthcare professionals and Muslim patients and their families today. The juridical literature examined for this study reveals the inadequacy of these judicial decisions to provide moral justification and guide to moral action in dealing with newly emerging medical cases. Ethical issues today demand meticulous application of moral reasoning based on understanding human conditions to arrive at a realistic solution. In the recent decades medical advancements have ushered enormous changes and development in the social and biotechnical structures that govern human life. These advancements in medical treatment have transformed human relationships and the manner in which humans view their relationship to God, to nature and to their religious faith. These far-reaching, ever-accelerating changes in the way humans see their health and illnesses demand rulings from

Muslim jurists that are informed by extensive evaluation of Islamic moral values and justificatory processes that are in place in Islamic jurisprudence to guide contemporary experts in medical profession. Seminarian juridical studies with their limited interest in Islamic theological ethics cannot expect to provide the necessary moral guidance that these new cases demand. These ethical inquiries need to go beyond the historical legal tradition. A majority of judicial decisions on bioethics-related issues studied for this book evince the disjuncture between situational exigencies and doctrinal-ethical tradition. Islamic law faces the challenge of knowledgeably incorporating the changed circumstances of today's society in the overall context of social ethics if it is to remain a relevant guide for Muslims in fulfilling their religious and ethical responsibilities.

There are two varieties of situational realities that Islamic jurisprudence needs to deal with in contemporary rulings on biomedical topics:

1. Substantial transformation: Sometimes the social or cultural situation changes so radically that it no longer bears any resemblance to previous circumstances. This kind of substantial change is known as "transformation" or "transmutation" (*istiḥāla* or *qalb*) in jurisprudence. Such a transformation leads to a change in the ruling. Take for example, the Muslim-non-Muslim composition of citizenry in the modern Muslim states. Whereas the classical rulings of the Sharī'a retained the distinction in its treatment of non-Muslim protected peoples, today these rulings would be construed as violation of equal human rights of all citizens in a modern nation-state. Hence, any discriminatory healthcare policy based on the classical rulings would be incompatible to the bioethical principle of justice.
2. Functional transformation: Sometimes the situational aspects do not show change in their external, conventional form but rather in their social function. By "social function" I mean the modes of their utilization in society. Situational transformation of social function occurs when the past function becomes inapplicable and is either replaced by a new social function or generates new functions alongside the old ones. Here the example of gender discrimination in the historical jurisprudence shows explicitly the change in the social function of a woman as breadwinner and her responsibilities and rights along with man in furthering public health in all its dimensions.

Further example is provided by traditional Islamic law's interdiction regarding the buying and selling of blood. Many jurists have based this prohibition on the idea that blood is unclean and has no beneficial or rationally recognized use. This view conforms to that which prevails in a number of traditions that clearly prohibit the buying and selling of ritually unclean materials. Such a view is understandable given the inability to use blood for transfusion in the early days of Islam. Blood in the pre-Islamic Arabian culture was used to treat certain kinds of ailments or was consumed as a food in folk medicine to treat some diseases. Islam, however, emphasized the harm that resulted from these procedures and banned the sale of blood.

Today blood is known to have beneficial, even life-saving uses in transfusions. Hence the buying and selling of blood—even giving it as a gift—has been deemed permissible by some Muslim jurists. Among the Shīʻites donation of blood during the annual commemoration of the martyrdom of Imam Ḥusayn, the grandson of the Prophet, is encouraged and is regarded highly meritorious. Today blood can be preserved in most sterilized conditions and can be transported where needed without causing any harm to the recipient of a transfusion. In other words, with changes and development in society and culture, substances that were once regarded as harmful or useless are now regarded as critical and indispensable to human life. Hence past juridical rulings have been changed to accommodate these functional transformations.[11]

There are many other examples of the impact of situational change on doctrinal tradition. These transformations are evident in the changes in Sharīʻa that have been spurred by social and cultural change—for example, it is now permissible to transplant organs retrieved from a dead person or through donation. It is worth keeping in mind that there are those jurists who oppose these rulings, and, in most cases, their prohibition is based on a lack of relevant technical information or simply strict adherence to the letter of the law.

My research is prompted by the need to undertake a careful analysis of the juridical-ethical literature to unearth the kind of reasoning, whether legal or moral, that has gone into formulating opinions in the field of biomedical ethics among both of Sunni and Shīʻite Muslims. I have attempted to explore the situational transformations in important areas of biomedicine in order to delineate a set of rules and principles to guide Muslim ethical deliberations and responses.

The most critical part of this research is definitely the search for specifically Islamic principles and rules for biomedical ethical deliberations and resolutions. I began treating Islamic bioethics as a subfield of Islamic social ethics rather than Islamic jurisprudence. Consequently, my investigation of morally problematic areas in medical practice had to fully account for rationally and scripturally derived justifications in Islamic tradition. The two major principles of Islamic social ethics, namely, "Public Good" and "No harm, no harassment" and a number of subsidiary rules that were commonly cited as justification in the numerous rulings that had been published on various biomedical and biotechnological issues in the last two decades resonated with some of the principles that had been identified in secular bioethics in the West. Despite its communitarian aspects, what prompted me to argue for specifically Islamic and yet cross-culturally applicable principles of bioethics was the common moral language that existed between secular and Islamic ethics. The theoretical foundation for the Islamic bioethics in this study, on the one hand, can engage other religious or secular bioethics in a meaningful conversation, and, on the other, can provide healthcare providers ways of assessing moral dilemmas and determining rationally and religiously acceptable solutions.

This study is in many ways a pioneer effort in defining and constructing Islamic biomedical ethics. I have very little to stand on in terms of primary sources in the field of applied ethics except juridical theories and applications dealing with religious laws in the area of God-human and interhuman relations. Hence, the following points are important to keep in mind:

1. There are very few sources in Arabic or Persian devoted to biomedical issues, whether from the classical or modern period. Hence, the research has many rough edges that will, I hope, prompt other Muslim ethicists to pursue further research.
2. I make no claim that the present work is definitive in any sense. It is simply an attempt to lay the foundation of biomedical ethics in Islamic studies in order to help future scholars of biomedical ethics to refine both the methodology and practical applications.
3. This book is not meant to be a collection of rulings (*fatāwā*). It is a discussion of the rulings and the reasoning that underlay these opinions. Accordingly, even when it specifies rulings on specific issues, the book avoids advocating one or the other position as categorical, especially in matters that are open to varying interpretations and judgments. However, it does not mean that I do not take a moral stance on some morally sensitive issues. My concern is to indicate that juridical inquiry by its emphasis on culminating its investigation in deriving a ruling is epistemically insufficient to generate necessary confidence in the final resolution of a moral dilemma.

To emphasize the subtle methodological differences between legal and ethical forms of deliberation and decision-making, with which this study is concerned, I provide the following two figures. The first schematizes the legal methodology for deducing a new legal ruling from authoritative precedent; the second figure shows the ethical methodology for reaching a reasonable tentative recommendation.

As shown in figures 1.1 and 1.2, both legal and ethical deliberations search for a precedent in the normative source (*aṣl*), which includes a search in the juridical corpus, to derive a resolution for a new case (known as *nazīla* or *far'*). The search for a paradigm case is interactive, in the sense that it moves back and forth from normative to present case, from history to modernity. The resolution in the legal case is the *ḥukm*, which carries the authority of being implemented, whereas the resolution in the ethical case is a provisional conclusion to provide a recommendation that could change as the case begins to unfold in its complexity, seeking a justifiable course of action.

It is this distinction between legal and ethical decision-making that makes this study unique and hard to classify as a strictly legal or moral study of Islamic

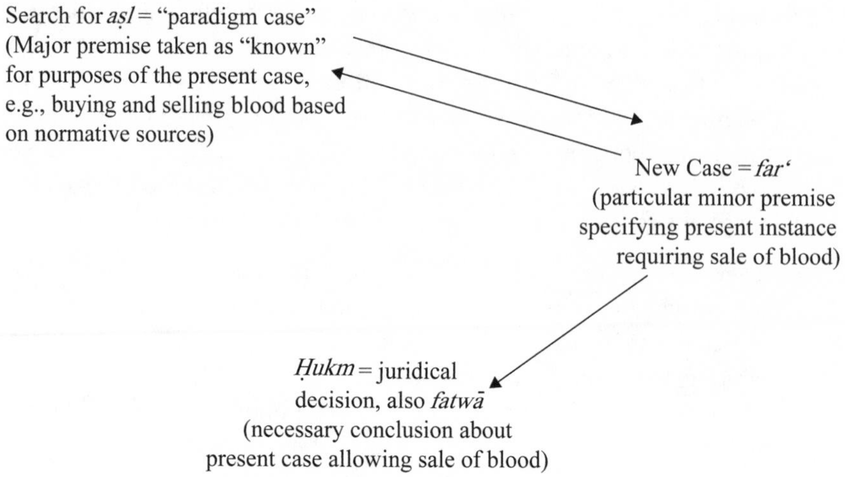
Search for *aṣl* = "paradigm case"
(Major premise taken as "known"
for purposes of the present case,
e.g., buying and selling blood based
on normative sources)
New Case = *far'*
(particular minor premise
specifying present instance
requiring sale of blood)
Ḥukm = juridical
decision, also *fatwā*
(necessary conclusion about
present case allowing sale of blood)

FIGURE 1.1. Patterns of Legal Decision-making

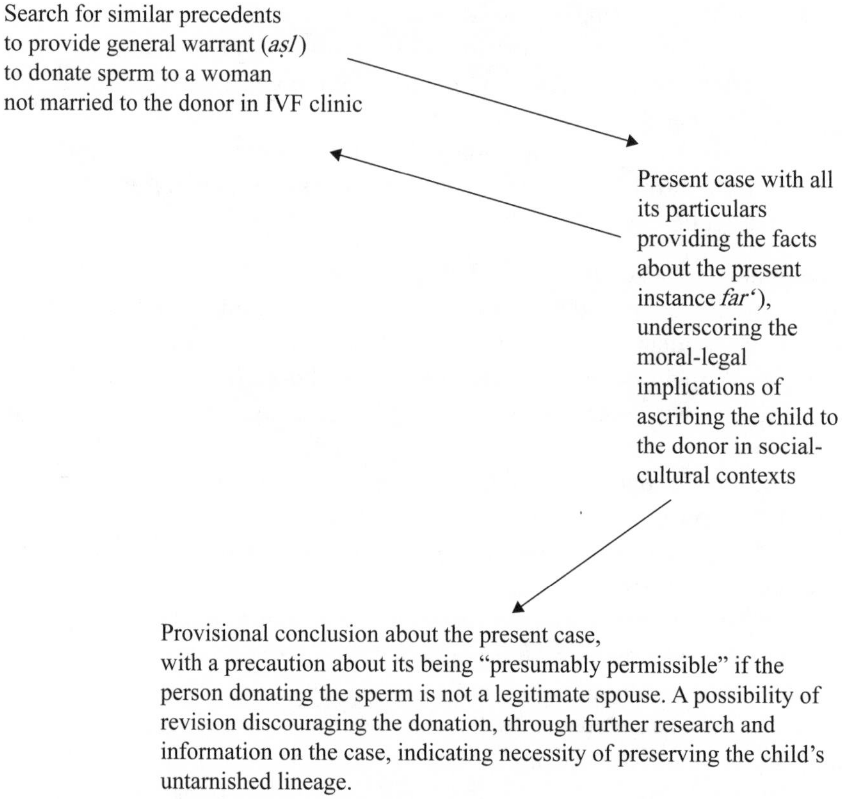
Search for similar precedents
to provide general warrant (*aṣl*)
to donate sperm to a woman
not married to the donor in IVF clinic
Present case with all
its particulars
providing the facts
about the present
instance *far'*),
underscoring the
moral-legal
implications of
ascribing the child to
the donor in social-
cultural contexts
Provisional conclusion about the present case,
with a precaution about its being "presumably permissible" if the
person donating the sperm is not a legitimate spouse. A possibility of
revision discouraging the donation, through further research and
information on the case, indicating necessity of preserving the child's
untarnished lineage.

FIGURE 1.2. Patterns of Ethical Decision-making

biomedical ethics. To further elaborate the methodological foundation of the study chapter 2 underscores that Islamic ethical discourse is founded upon the human ability to know right from wrong. Through God's special endowment for the entire humanity each and every person on earth is endowed with the nature (*fiṭra*), the receptacle for intuitive reason, that guides humanity to its spiritual and moral well-being. Moral cognition, in this notion of divine endowment, is innate to human nature and because of it human beings are capable of discerning moral law. The discussion of ethics in Islam is not confined to the legal concerns of Sharī'a. The Muslim tradition is steeped in lively theological discussions about God's will and action as they relate to human responsibility and accountability in fulfilling the divine plan for humanity. Ethical epistemology in Islam is anchored in theology: in what does the inherent goodness or evil of an act consist, and how does a human know about it?

Chapter 3 deals with theological dimensions of human suffering in the context of human illness. Biomedical research and medical practice have the ultimate goal of relieving human beings from illness—a form of suffering and affliction that asks ultimate questions about the reasons why humans suffer. The discussion in this chapter simply raises questions that have been part of Islamic theological discourse and points to the plausible explications of how Muslims handle the question of unrequited suffering. Chapters 4, 5, and 6 then embark on the human life cycle: from the beginning to the end of life, touching upon all possible manifestations of issues related to early termination of embryonic life to the determination of the brain death criteria. Chapter 7 takes up the ethics of human ownership or stewardship of bodily organs. It discusses issues related to organ retrieval and donation and ultimate human responsibility toward one's physical body and toward the bodies of others. The religious-cultural importance of the issues covered in these four chapters is underscored by the fact that my search for solutions to the modern issues in both the historical as well as modern juridical literature constitutes a fundamental justificatory process to uncover the ethical dimension of various judicial decisions.

Chapter 8 engages in recent developments in the biomedical field and their impact upon ethical and religious sensibilities of modern societies in general and Muslim societies in particular. In some noticeable ways, this chapter does not anchor the modern discussions of the issues like human cloning or stem cell research in the juridical heritage to provide Islamic reasoning for these issues that have little or no allusion in the revealed texts except through modern interpretation. Accordingly, the chapter undertakes to discuss the ethical issues in recent biotechnical advancements using the universal moral discourse that has been articulated by different religious traditions that Islam shares with these religious-moral traditions. In the last chapter, which serves as an epilogue to this complex study, I once again endeavor, like I did in the introductory chapter, to smooth out the rough edges of relating theory with practice in Islamic biomedical ethics.

2

In Search of Principles of Healthcare Ethics in Islam

Islam, as a comprehensive religious-moral system, does not divide the public space into spiritual and secular domains with separate jurisdictions. Rather it strives to integrate the two realms to provide total guidance about the way human beings ought to live with one another and with themselves in both the private and public realms. Islam regards the whole array of human institutions—whether cultural, religious, or political—as instruments of a single goal: subserving the purposes of God, the Merciful, the Compassionate. Muslim ethics tries to make sense of human moral instincts, institutions, and traditions in order to provide a foundation of rules and principles that can govern a virtuous life. Its judgments are ethical in the sense that they seek to elaborate criteria for making basic moral distinctions such that reasonable people can agree on what is good and bad, praiseworthy and blameworthy, in human relationships and human institutions. This ethical philosophy encompasses the most important issues of human life: suffering, illness, and death; reproduction and abortion; law and justice; and so on. As God's creatures, humans' welfare and conduct ultimately fall under his divine governance as mediated and interpreted by his earthly exponents.

How do Muslims solve their ethical problems in biomedicine? Are there any distinctive theories or principles in Islamic ethics that Muslims apply in deriving moral judgments in bioethics? Is the revealed law, the Sharīʿa, as an integral part of Islamic ethics, the only recognized source of prescriptive precedents in Islam? Can it serve as a paradigm for the moral experience of contemporary Muslims living in changing social and cultural contexts? Do human experience and/or intuitive reasoning have a legitimate role in Islamic moral reflection?

I begin with these questions in the hope of verifying the validity of a poignant observation made by Edmund D. Pellegrino:

> Culture and ethics are inextricably bound to each other. Culture provides the moral presuppositions and ethics the formal normative framework, for our moral choices. Every ethical system, therefore, is ultimately a synthesis of intuitive and rational assertions, the proportion of each varying from culture to culture. There is also in every culture an admixture of the ethnocentric and the universal, of that which is indissolubly bound to a particular geography, history, language, and ethic strain, and that which is common to all humans as humans.[1]

In this chapter I will explore the applicability of Pellegrino's observation to Muslim cultures and Islamic ethics. I will examine the nature of Islamic ethical discourse in order to demonstrate that ethical judgments in Islam are an amalgam of the empirical—the relative cultural elements derived from the particular experience of Muslims living in a specific place and time—and the a priori—the timeless universal norms derived from the scriptural[2] sources.

In the recent years attempts have been made to engage Muslim scholars in the continuing debates about biomedical ethics in the West. At the center of this debate is the role of ethical principles and rules in the evaluation of an action from multiple perspectives, including those of the agent, the act itself, the end, and the consequences. Many disputes in biomedical ethics in the West stem from disputes about the extent to which normative principles in this domain can be generalized throughout various cultures such that certain actions can be universally acknowledged as required, prohibited, or permitted.[3]

I have examined several articles written by Muslim scholars[4] that attempt to show the compatibility between the principles of biomedical ethics used in the West and the ethical precepts of Islam without exploring the nature of moral-theological discourse[5] that informed the development of the Islamic legal-ethical system, the Sharī'a. For example, in the recently published volume *Principles of Health Care Ethics*, G. I. Serour's article, "Islam and the Four Principles" and K. Zaki Hasan's article, "Islam and the Four Principles: A Pakistani View"[6] have catalogued the four principles and their supposed Islamic equivalents without attempting to analyze the foundational claims of Islamic ethical resources and their underlying moral reasoning. In other words, their descriptive rather than analytical approach to the debate about the principles of biomedical rulings in Islam does not deal with Islamic theological-philosophical ethics and the way it has affected medical jurisprudence in the modern times. More importantly, none of the authors, because of their lack of training in actual application of the legal-moral principles and rules that undergird many practical judgments in bioethics, are interested in demonstrating the combination of cultural and universal factors that contribute to moral philosophy in Islam and the West. The ethical questions in contemporary discussions require attention to larger questions about what constitutes ethical conduct in Islam rather than the mere presentation of the legal rulings (*fatāwā*) as regards issues like abortion, organ donation, and so on. There is no consensus among Muslim jurists of various schools of Islamic law on any of these issues. In the cross-cultural context of bioethics, the work of Muslim scholars would be significantly enhanced by systematic investigations into the underlying principles and rules of practical ethical guidance in the Islamic tradition.[7]

The Nature of Islamic Juridical-Ethical Discourse

The Islamic juridical tradition seeks to address and accommodate and reconcile the demands of justice and public good. Without adequate training in the legal sciences, especially legal theory, one cannot pinpoint the principles and the rules that Muslim jurists use to justify and assess moral-legal decisions within their own cultural environment. In dealing with immediate questions about autopsy, organ donation, dignity of the dead, and so on, Muslim jurists draw on legal doctrines and rules in addition to analogical reasoning based on paradigm cases. The practical judgments or legal opinions, known as *fatāwā*, reflect the insights of a jurist who has been able to connect cases to an appropriate set of linguistic and rational principles and rules that can provide a basis for a valid conclusion of a given case.

The enunciation of underlying ethical principles and rules that govern practical ethical decisions is crucial for making any religious perspective an intellectually insightful voice in the contemporary debate about a morally defensible cross-cultural biomedical ethics. All cultures share certain moral principles (beneficence, compassion, honesty and so on), all require rules like truthfulness and confidentiality as essential elements in regulating a responsible physician-patient relationship, yet major global controversies persist on issues such as the right of a woman to abortion, discrimination against ethnic and religious minorities, respect for individual autonomy against competing moral considerations of the community. What kind of ethical resources do different traditions possess that might lead to a common ethical discourse about, and perhaps even a resolution of, global controversies in biomedicine?[8]

Muslims have often been guilty of shirking an unsparing, critical assessment of the normative resources of their faith that might contribute to a resolution of contemporary biomedical ethical dilemmas. This uncritical approach to the normative sources has deep roots in the theology of revelation in Islam. There are two major trends concerning the meaning and relevance of revelation for Muslims. According to one, Islamic revelation in its present form was "created" in time and space and, as such, reflects historical circumstances of that original divine command. According to the other, the revelation was "uncreated" and hence its current form is not conditioned by place and time. Most Sunni Muslims reject any hints that the revelation's interpretation is a cultural or historical variable. Quantitative and qualitative changes in the modern Muslim world have raised questions about the relevance of traditional readings of the revelation to contemporary ethical and social exigencies.

Little wonder, then, that so few Muslim scholars in theology and jurisprudence of bioethics have made significant contributions to debates over controversial biomedical issues, whether internationally or within various Muslim nation-states. In Muslim countries religious scholars, the ulema, are passive participants in day to day deliberations about formulating modern national health policies within the moral and legal framework provided by Islamic scriptural sources. Advanced Western medical technology is imported with little heed taken for its potential impacts on the political, economic, communal, social, and individual lives of the population. Unquestionably, the impact of medical technology and its attendant moral dilemmas transcends geographical or cultural boundaries. Some issues confronting contemporary biomedical ethics in the West have found their way to the Islamic world, where strong paternalism and the physician's undisputed authority have led to a harmful medical authoritarianism and a loss of respect for individual and family wishes and choices.[9]

The Question of Cultural Relativism in Ethical Values

Ethical values seek cultural legitimacy by adapting themselves to prevailing economic and political circumstances. Accordingly, these values arise in a climate of cultural relativity. Since human reason depends on the data of experience to make correct ethical judgments, moral presuppositions interact with the specific social experiences to yield culturally conditioned moral justifications.[10] In fact, even objectivist ethical theories, which presuppose a transcultural validity for moral standards, include a certain aspect of social or conventional relativism. In the highly politicized debates about the applicability of the International Bill of Human Rights, cultural relativism figures prominently in the arguments advanced by non-Western nations concerning the charter's ethnocentric language that undermines its universalistic aspirations.[11] Similar arguments against the universalizability of a single bioethical theory in an inherently pluralistic ethical discourse are commonly heard in national and international biomedical ethics conferences.

However, there is already an intellectual movement to search for a "metacultural" ethics that can overcome the ethical antinomies of cultural relativism in the areas of human rights as well as medical ethics. There is a growing consensus in the international community that seeks to adopt a transcultural framework of ethical principles and rules that could engage theologians, scholars, and policy makers in the health professions in fruitful dialogue.

An academic venture that holds much promise for the timely development of a cross-cultural principle-based bioethics is epitomized in *Principles of Biomedical Ethics* by Tom L. Beauchamp and James F. Childress.[12] Although the historical and cultural context of the work is Western (mainly American), the moral reflections and justifications covered in this volume suggest their applicability to the experiences and cultural expectations of non-Western societies. More pertinently, *PBE* demonstrates that through the universalizability of morally relevant human conditions rather than moral norms, it is possible to speak about "metacultural" moral principles and rules for moral assessment and judgment in other traditions and ethical systems. Metacultural ethical systems can speak to the world community across socio-political and cultural barriers to communicate concern about the moral rights of patients, their unusual vulnerability as sick persons, and their dependence on the physician's knowledge.

In this chapter, then, my purpose is not merely to search for Islamic equivalents of the primary principles of autonomy, nonmaleficence, beneficence (including utility), and justice, but also to make a strong case for a distinctly Islamic yet metaculturally communicable and principled deontological-teleological ethics[13] that could aid in the assessment of moral problems in Islamic biomedical ethics.

The process has already begun in Egypt and Iran, where religious scholars, medical professionals, and the government are searching for ontological foundations of Islamic law to enable them to reconcile Islamic teachings with the demands of modern clinical medicine and biomedical research. I mention Egypt and Iran only because these are the only Muslim countries where religious scholars, the ulema, are engaged in formulating national policies related to health care. In Iran one can even observe the relative independence enjoyed by the religious scholars from governmental interference in formulating their judicial decisions. Accordingly, there the function of the ulema is not merely to provide endorsement of the decisions made by the government, as so often happens in Saudi Arabia or to a lesser extent in Egypt. In these latter countries, since the religious authority is under the direct control of the government, usually the dissenting opinion against the *fait accompli* is repressed. In the case of Pakistan, as indicated by K. Zaki Hassan,[14] there seems to be a wide gulf between medical professionals and religious scholars.

Even when the source of normative life was believed to have been revealed by God in the Sharī'a, the procuring of a judgment (*ḥukm*) and its application was dependent upon reasons used in moral deliberation. This moral deliberation took into account particular human conditions. In other words, Islamic law developed its rulings within the pluralistic cultural and historical experience of Muslims and non-Muslims living in the different parts of the Islamic world. The Sharīʿa recognized the autonomy of other moral systems within its sphere of influence, without imposing its judgments on peoples with different cultural beliefs and practices. More importantly, it recognized the validity of differing interpretations of the same revealed system within the community, thereby giving rise to different schools of legal thought and practice in Islam. In the absence of an organized "church" or a theological body authorized to speak for the entire tradition or the community, Islam has remained inherently discursive and pluralistic in its methods of deliberation and justification of moral actions. Hence, when it comes to the particular application of principles and rules to emerging ethical issues, like a woman's right to abortion following rape or incest, it is possible to observe differing judicial opinions.

The Nature of Islamic Ethical Discourse

When one considers the normative sources for standards of conduct and character it becomes obvious that besides scriptural sources, Muslim scholars have recognized the value of decisions derived from specific human conditions as an equally valid source for social ethics in Islam. Early on, the theologian-jurists conceded that the scriptural sources could not easily cover every situation that might arise, especially when Muslim political rule required rules for urban life, commerce, and government in advanced countries. How exactly was human intellectual endeavor to be directed to discover the rationale (*ʿilla*), the philosophy and the purpose behind certain paradigm rulings (known as *al-aṣl*, plural *uṣūl*) provided in God's commandments, in order to formulate principles for future decisions?

The question had important implications for the administrators of justice, who were faced with the practical necessity of making justifiable, nonarbitrary legal rulings. There was a fear of reason in deriving the details of law. The fear was based on the presumption that if independent human reason could judge what is right and wrong, it could rule on what God could rightly prescribe for humans. However, it was admitted that although revealed law can be known through reason and aid human beings in cultivating the moral life, human intelligence was not capable of discovering the reasons for a particular law, let alone demonstrating the truth of a particular assertion of the divine commandment. In fact, as these theologian-jurists asserted, the divine commandments to which one must adhere if one is to achieve a specific end prescribed in the revealed law are not objectively accessible to human beings through reason. Moreover, judgments of reason are deemed arbitrary since they often contradict each other and can simply reflect the personal desire of the legal expert.

One problem, then, was resolving the substantive role of reason in understanding the implicit rationale of a paradigm case and elaborating the juridical-ethical dimension of revelation as it relates to the conduct of human affairs in public and private spheres. Another problem was situating credible religious authority empowered to provide validation to the ethical-legal reasoning associated with the philosophy behind legal rulings. On the one hand, following the lead of the Sunni jurists like Muḥammad b. Idrīs al-Shāfi'ī (d. 820) and Aḥmad b. Ḥanbal (d. 855), Sunni Islam located that authority in the Qur'an and the Tradition. These scholars represented the predominant schools of rationalist-traditionalist theology, which held that questions of Islamic law, to a large extent, could be resolved from the working out of an adequate system based on a juridical elaboration of the scriptural sources. On the other hand, following the line of thought maintained by the Shī'ite Imams, Shī'ite Islam located that authority in the rightful successors to the Prophet. The Shī'ite Imams maintained that there was an ongoing revelatory guidance available in the expository ability of human reason in comprehending the divine revelation. It is exemplified by the solutions offered by the Shī'ite leadership.

In general, Muslim theologian-jurists paid more attention to God's creation than God's nature per se. In addition, they discussed human beings' relation to God as the creator, lawgiver, and judge. They were also interested in the extent of God's power and human freedom of will as it affected the search for a right prescription for human behavior. In view of the absence of the institutionalized religious body that could provide the necessary validation of the legal-moral decisions on all matters pertaining to human existence, it proved difficult to elucidate the sacred lawgiver's intent in juridical rulings that had direct relevance to the social life of the community. The intellectual activity related to Islamic juridical-ethical tradition can be summed up as the attempt to relate specific moral-legal rulings (*aḥkām*, singular *ḥukm*) to the divine purposes expressed in the form of norms and rules in the Qur'an and the Tradition, notwithstanding the tangle of ambiguities that impeded the task. Given the incomplete state of knowledge about the present circumstances and future contingencies, the jurists proceeded to make ethical judgments with a cautious attitude on the basis of what seemed most likely (*ẓann*) to be the case. Such ethical judgments were normally appended with a clear, pious statement that the ruling lacked certainty. Only God was knowledgeable about the true state of affairs.[15]

In due course, the jurists were able to identify two methods of understanding the justification behind a legal-ethical decision. Sometimes the rationale was derived directly from the explicit statements of the Qur'an and the Tradition that set forth the purpose of legislation. At other times, human reason discovered the relationship between the ruling and the rationale. The jurists admitted and determined the substantive role of human reasoning in grounding the legitimacy of a legal or moral decision. Moreover, human reason's role depended upon the jurist's comprehension of the nature of ethical knowledge and the means by which humans can access information about good and evil. In other words, it depended upon the way the human act was defined in terms of human ethical discernment about good and evil and the relation of human act to God's will. Any advocacy of reason as a substantive rather than formal source for procuring moral-legal verdicts required authorization derived from sources like the Qur'an and the Tradition. It is possible to read the Qur'an as advancing a teleological view of human beings as endowed with the ability to use reason to discover God's will, especially when the revelation itself endorses reflection on the reasons for revealed laws as well sheer obedience to them. All the jurist-theologians, whether Sunni or Shīʿite, maintained that without the endorsement of revelation reason could not become an independent source of moral-legal decisions.

This precautious attitude toward reason has its roots in the belief that God's knowledge of the circumstances and of the consequences in any situation of ethical dilemma confronted by human existence is exhaustive and infallible. Whereas the Qur'an and the Tradition had provided the underlying justification for some moral-legal rulings when declaring them obligatory or prohibited, on a number of issues the rulings were expressed as divine commands which had to be obeyed even if the reasons behind them remained unfathomable to human reason. Thus, for instance, the effective cause for the duty of seeking medical treatment is to avoid grave and irremediable harm to oneself, whereas the reason for prohibition against taking human life is the sanctity of life as declared by the revelation. The commandments were simply part of God's prerogative as the creator to demand unquestioning obedience to them. To act in a manner contrary to divine commands is to act both immorally and unlawfully. The major issue in legal thought, then, was defining the admissibility and the parameters of human reasoning as a substantive source for legal-moral decisions. Can reason discover the divine will in confronting emerging legal-ethical issues without being eclipsed by human self-interest?

The Rationalist and Traditionalist Ethical Reasoning in the Revealed Law

The use of "rationalist" and "traditionalist" in this section conforms to the general identification of the two major trends in Islamic theological-ethical discourse above. Based on their cautious attitude toward reason as a substantive source for ethical-legal judgment, Sunni-Muʿtazilites (followers of the rationalist-naturalist theology that privileged human reason the ability to know moral truth) and Shīʿites fall into the rationalist group. In contrast, due to their emphasis on revelation, especially the Tradition, Sunni-Ashʿarites (followers of the traditionalist theology that privileged the divine command in the form of revealed text as the only valid source for ethical knowledge) fall into the traditionalist group. The process of formulating the methodology for deriving sound ethical-legal decisions was undertaken with a clear view of providing principles and rules for extrapolating predictable judgments in all matters of interpersonal relationships. Central to this discussion was the analytical treatment of the twin concepts of justice (*'adāla*, usually defined as "putting something in its appropriate place") and obligation (*wujūb*, sometimes defined as "promulgation of divine command and prohibition"). The concept of justice provided a theoretical stance for the question of human obedience to divine commands and the extent of human capacity in carrying out the moral-religious obligations (*takālif shar'īya*). The concept of obligation defined the nature of divine command and provided deontological grounds for complying with it. The commandments have reasons of their own that can be explained in terms of the function that they fulfill for the good of humankind.

Gradually, two responses emerged to the pressing need of providing consistent and authentic guidance in the matter of social ethics. Some prominent jurists of the tenth and eleventh centuries CE maintained that in deciding questions on which there was no specific guidance available from the normative sources of Islamic law and ethics, judges and lawyers had to make their own rational judgments independently of the revelation. This was certainly the case when the law, being stated in general terms, did not provide for the particularity of situations. This was, obviously, the rationalist group. Other jurists disapproved of this rational method as not being adequately anchored in the normative sources. They insisted that no legal or moral judgment was valid if not based on the revelation, both the Qur'an and the Tradition. There was no way for humanity to know the meaning of justice outside the divine revelation. In fact, the traditionalists contended, justice is nothing but carrying out the requirements of the revealed law. It was the revealed law, the Sharī'a, that provided the scales for justice in all those actions that were declared morally and legally obligatory (*wājib, farḍ*). At the end of the day, the latter traditionalist thesis became the standard view held by the majority of the Sunni Muslims. Some Sunni-Mu'tazilite and the majority of the Shī'ite Muslims, on the other hand, maintained the rationalist thesis about the fundamentality of reason in ethical epistemology with some adjustment in conformity to their doctrine about supreme religious authority of the Imam, who could and did arbitrate in cases that confounded human intellect in offering a resolution.

However, the role of ethical principles in deriving moral judgments was articulated in greater detail by the theologians who, too, were divided along the same lines as the jurists: those who supported the substantive role of reason in knowing what is right and obligatory; and those who argued in favor of the revelation as the primary source of ethical knowledge. In other words, ethical reasoning is directly related to religious epistemology in Islamic thought. Ethical objectivism or deontological theory, with its thesis that human beings can know much of what is right and wrong because of the intrinsic goodness or badness of actions is connected with the rationalist ethicist Sunni-Mu'tazilite theologians; whereas ethical voluntarism, the traditionalist ethics, which denied that anything objective in human acts themselves would make them right or wrong, is connected with Sunni-Ash'arite theologians.[16]

The Ash'arite reactions to the rationalist ethics were reflected in the jurists' reluctance to cite rational grounds for reaching judicial decisions. The arbitrariness of human reason, as the traditionalists pointed out, could not guarantee an objective and right solution to the complex moral dilemmas faced by human beings in everyday situations. Moreover, if reason was capable of reaching ethical judgment unaided by revelation, then what need is there for God's guidance? Hence, according to the upholders of traditionalist ethics, it was more accurate to maintain that the divine command in the form of revelation is not only the primary source of the moral law; it is also the sole guarantee for avoiding the contradictory claims of competing lines of rational thought that seek to supersede the function of revelation.[17]

This cautious, even negative, evaluation of reason in traditionalist ethics had a parallel in the systematization of juridical theory among the Muslim jurists. The juridical problem-solving device was in search of a fundamental principle that could function as a template for the formulation of emerging legal-moral decisions. The expansion of Muslim political rule beyond Arabia raised questions about the application of the rulings provided by the revelation. The jurists were quick to realize such absolute application without considering the specific social and cultural context of these rulings was not without problems. After all, the rulings provided by the revelation emphasized specific human conditions related to custom, everyday human behavior, and ordinary language used to convey moral precepts and attitudes to life in Arabian society. Even when the moral law is wholly promulgated through divine legislation in the form of the Qur'an and the Tradition, such a law is objective because of the diversity that can be observed among human beings.

Very early on scholars of jurisprudence were led to distinguish between duties to God (*'ibādāt* ="ritual duties") and duties to fellow human beings (*mu'āmalāt* = "social transactions"). "Ritual duties" were not conditioned by specific human conditions and hence were absolutely binding. "Social transactions" were necessarily conditioned by human existence in specific social and political contexts and hence were adjustable to the needs of time and place. It was in the latter sphere of interpersonal relations that the jurists needed to provide fresh rulings generated by changing human conditions. The entire area of social ethics in Islam falls under the *mu'āmalāt* sections of jurisprudence. However, authoritative decisions in matters of social ethics could not be derived without first determining the nature of human acts under obligation (*taklīf*). The divine command, understood in terms of religious-moral obligation (*taklīf*), provided the entire ethical code of conduct and a teleological view of humanity and the world. More pertinent, violation of divine command, as Muslim jurists taught, is immoral on the grounds that it interferes with the pursuit of the human goal of achieving perfection that would guarantee salvation in the hereafter. Ultimately, human salvation is directly connected with human conduct—the subject matter of legal-theological ethics.

Legal and Theological Ethics in Islam

Islamic law is concerned with human conduct. It pertains to the total welfare of human beings. Human perfection involves having a correct belief and a noble moral quality. This perfection guarantees a good end in this world and the next. In this latter sense, human perfection is salvific since it strengthens the bond between God and humanity. Hence, the revealed law of Islam is concerned with apprehending divine wisdom through the study of rules derived from revelatory sources for the acts of people under legal-moral obligation.

Every category of act, whether classified as incumbent (*wājib*), recommended (*mandūb*), permitted (*mubāḥ*), disapproved (*makrūh*), or forbidden (*ḥarām*) in the Sharīʻa, is founded upon explicit or implicit rules in the Qur'an or the Tradition. Thus, Sharīʻa, as a religious-ethical system, is theoretically able to discover the divine judgment in every category of human act in the area of "ritual duties" and "social transactions". However, Sharīʻa also investigates the revelatory sources—the Qur'an, the Tradition, and the juristic consensus (*ijmāʻ*)—for their admission as evidence in deducing fresh cases occurring in different contexts. This part of the juridical studies is concerned with legal principles (*uṣūl al-fiqh*) or jurisprudence. Islamic jurisprudence is an inquiry into the principles of normative ethical judgments on external human acts. The philosophical aspects of the ethics of action are concerned with fundamental questions about whether reason (*ʻaql*) on its own can rule (*ḥākim*) things necessary (*wājib*), good (*ḥāsan*) or evil (*qabīḥ*).[18]

Muslim Scheme of Classification of "Necessary," "Good," or "Evil" Acts

To understand the impact of moral epistemology as worked out by the rationalist and traditionalist scholars, we need to see the way obligation or duty is defined and applied in practice. The derivation of ethical judgments (obligatory, recommended, and so on) is related to the ontology of good and evil in human acts. Ultimately, any valuation of divine or human acts is dependent upon the way relevant categories are constructed in theology first and then in law.

In Islamic ethics the categories of value terms resemble the categories of the Sharīʻa law, but their definition depends on the way the nature of human agency is perceived doctrinally. All the Sharīʿa categories (obligatory, recommended, permitted, disapproved, and forbidden) are defined in relation to actual divine command and prohibition, the rewards and punishments by God in the next life. In contrast, among Sunni-Muʿtazilite and Shīʿite jurists, legal-ethical categories are defined in terms of their relation to whether action is possible from the agent as a result of his/her power to do it or as a part of his/her nature that is predetermined by God.

The Ashʿarite ethics roots ethical values in the commands and prohibitions of God. This was the divine command theory of ethics maintained by the majority of the Sunni theologians. For them an obligatory (*wājib*) act is that which is commanded, and a prohibited act is that which is evil (*qabīḥ*). The rules governing an ethical judgment are neither in the acts themselves nor in their properties. They are grounded simply in what God commands or prohibits. The ontological reference of an evil act is God's prohibition and not reason's intuitive judgment.[19]

In contrast, Muʿtazilite ethics asserted that a command or prohibition, even by God, is insufficient to make the act itself obligatory or evil. The obligatoriness (*wujūb*) or evilness (*qubḥ*) is characteristic of the act as such. The ontological reference is either to an act's essence or category or to the circumstantial mode of its occurrence. The agent is regarded morally responsible for the act as he or she simply caused it to come into being, or knowingly and intentionally caused it to occur in a particular way. Hence, these characteristics have to be indicated by words other than just command or prohibition. Accordingly, the command or prohibition statement should read, "Do it *because* it is obligatory" and "Don't do it *because* it is evil."[20] The commands and prohibitions that are admittedly part of the Sharīʿa possess ethical properties of their own over and above being commanded and forbidden by God.[21]

Muslim jurists define "necessary" or "prudentially necessary" in terms of the juridical category of the obligatory act from the standpoint of the self-interest of the agent, who reasons that action would be preferable to some harm that might arise from inaction.[22] Thus, an act is necessary when it is obligatory for the agent to do it if he or she is to avoid such harm. It is also prudential because the act serves the practical interest of the agent. Expected harm in this life may be recognized by reason, whereas expected harm in the next life is known only by revelation.[23] The ethical character of this concept becomes evident when one considers the objective-subjective aspects of a necessary act. An act's objective aspect is determined by the facts of the world regardless of the opinion of some judge or observer. This sense, this type of ethical knowledge, is autonomous and self-validating, having been established by reason as necessary.[24] On the other hand, an act's subjective aspect is determined by the opinion of some judge or observer. Reason does not determine anything morally or religiously necessary, nor are goodness and badness generic or essential qualities of action that can be known through reason. Rather, divine command and prohibition determine an act as good or bad, respectively.[25]

The Mu'tazilite rationalist definition of "necessary" looks at the relation of praise and blame to the agent for the act. Accordingly, "necessary" as applied to an act is that for whose omission the agent deserves (*mustaḥiqq*) blame (*dhamm*).[26] For instance, when a person suffers pain because of having donated a kidney, the two steps of donating a kidney and suffering pain are connected by a relation of praise. At the same time, while the two steps are empirical facts, the relation of praise that the donor "deserves" is not so in any obvious way. "Deserving praise" suggests the appropriateness (*mulā'ama*) of the two successive events. This appropriateness is objective because "deserves" introduces a fact, which is truly or falsely predicated regardless of anyone's opinions.[27] This was the doctrine firmly held by the Shī'ite legal-ethical theorists.[28] The Ash'arites, conversely, denied that an obligatory act was an attribute of certain types of acts in themselves. God's commanding of certain types of acts was itself the essential characteristic that made them obligatory.[29]

The Ash'arites denied the Mu'tazilite thesis that an obligatory act had an ontological reference in human reason because reasonable, intelligent, and honest people often disagree on the degree to which certain acts should be deemed obligatory.[30] This was the doctrine that served as the fundamental characteristic of theistic subjectivism or voluntarism among the Sunni jurist-theologians, more particularly, by the Sunni law schools of Shāfi'ī and Aḥmad b. Ḥanbal. For them an obligatory act is that for which there is a threat of punishment and a forbidden act is that whose omission is necessary, as prescribed by the revealed law.[31]

It is important to note that the Qur'an distinguishes objective ethical concepts from God's acts of commanding and forbidding. It was only through the development of Islamic jurisprudence—more specifically, its adoption of the limited senses of ethical concepts of the Qur'an and their transformation into expanded meanings of legal categories of the Sharī'a—that good and evil were tethered to the notions of commandment or prohibition. Gradually, the Sharī'a categories—for instance, terms such as "act of disobedience" (*ma'ṣiya*)—were widened and came to substitute for the original ethical terms themselves. This widening gave rise to ethical subjectivism, which equated objective ethical terms like good and evil to God's commanding and forbidding, respectively.

The thrust of the argument in the Ash'arite theory of ethics about an obligatory act is that the conditions that control what is necessary in the actual world are created by the will of God. Such conditions include the idea that human behavior is always predestined (*muqaddar*) and that a person's direction in life is governed by superior forces (*majbūr*).[32] It is God who decides and commands what acts it is necessary for humans to do to achieve their predestined ends. This is the prescriptive theory of ethics, which relates ethical values to divine commands and prohibitions. Moreover, God imposes the sanctions that make such acts necessary for humans. Hence, there is no attribute that renders acts necessary for humans other than their having been commanded by God.[33]

Accordingly, obedience to God's commands is *wājib* (obligatory) in that it is necessary for serving one's own long-term interest. The Mu'tazilites contended that certain acts of God are *wājib* for God because of the benefit they confer on his creatures. For example, God must send prophets in order to inform human beings of the conditions of life to come and prepare them accordingly through the adherence to moral behavior. As humans are obligated to do what is right and obligatory, so God is obligated to reward them for fulfilling their moral obligations.[34] In contrast, the Ash'arites did not regard *wājib* as that which contains benefit to others, since there is no benefit to God in benefiting others. Since it is impossible to explain God's command in terms of any purpose or end, there is no reason or purpose for human voluntary conformity to his command. The ultimate moral perfection of a human being is simply to obey without any expectation of reward in the next life.[35]

Ḥasan in general means "agreeable" or "fitting to an end" and although translated as "good," its connotation is broader than the English "good." In relation to acts *ḥasan* is "that for which the agent does not deserve blame."[36] The purpose of undertaking a *ḥasan* act may be that of the agent, as in the commonest usage, or that of other persons, or that of the agent in one respect or one time but not others. Thus *ḥasan* is relative to the end or purpose specified, and what is good for John may not be so for Jack, or even for either of them in different respects or times. Thus, an irreligious person may call adultery good because he approves of it.[37]

The essential technical meaning of *ḥasan* is whatever is fitting for any end in this life. However, the Sunni Muslims have adopted the second, technical meaning, which is what is fitting only for the ends of the next life. The ends and the means are assigned to everyone by revelation, not by individually chosen ends. *Ḥasan* can be extended to cover anything that agents are permitted to do.[38] The Mu'tazilites define *ḥasan* with reference to acts as "that for which [by its very nature] the agent does not deserve blame."[39]

Qabīḥ, "evil," is in many ways symmetrical with good in its various meanings. Thus, in the general sense, the Ash'arites view *qabīḥ* as whatever is repugnant or inappropriate to an end. But the evil of an act is determined by divine command and not by any inherent blameworthiness.[40] These definitions of good and evil resemble that of *wājib* (obligatory). Instead of referring to what is necessary to do for this life or the hereafter, as in *wājib*, *ḥasan* refers simply to what is serviceable to an end; *qabīḥ* refers to what hinders attainment of an end.

Mu'tazilite belief in the autonomy of the human intellect, its ability to discern good and evil unaided by the directives of revealed law, led to the objection that the meaning of good in common usage is not restricted to what promotes an end, nor the meaning of evil to what hinders attainment of an end. For people perform some acts as good on their intrinsic merits, when they cannot possibly foresee any advantage to themselves, and likewise they avoid other acts as evil even when they can see no disadvantage to themselves. For example, someone gives help and comfort to a dying person with no expectation of reward; she does it simply because it is good in itself to help others in distress. As an instance of intrinsic evil avoided, a physician without belief in religion, and thus in no fear of punishment in the hereafter, refuses to help a terminally ill patient to commit suicide, even under threat of execution for his refusal; such a physician regards suicide as evil not merely in relation to ends but as evil in itself.

The Ash'arite belief that good and evil have no objective value is not deterred by such examples. They explain the first instance by natural sympathy between human beings, love of praise, or by an association of ideas that leads one to do in an abnormal situation what would serve an end in a normal one—in this case, where the patient would be expected to live and show gratitude. Hence, they reject the explanation about a rational desire for good. They explain the second instance by the agent's love of praise for not succumbing to the pressure, or by association of ideas—taking a life, however indirectly, through physician-assisted suicide, is normally followed by harmful consequences. Hence, they rule out a rational avoidance of evil. In other words, Ash'arites look for self-interested or emotional causes for the acts mentioned in order to avoid admitting attributes of good and evil intrinsic to the acts themselves by the light of reason alone.[41] Their view of ethics is based on extrinsic relations of acts to good and evil. That is to say, an act is good when it promotes human ends; moreover, it does so not by direct instrumental causation but because God has decided upon rewards for certain acts and punishment for others.

Such a view is coherent with the occasionalist theory of God's relation to the world.[42] According to this theory, the end of a human as an individual is the attainment of happiness, and happiness is to be found overwhelmingly in the next life. This is known from the revelation. The primary means to the end are of two kinds: external acts of obedience to the rules of conduct, revealed in scripture, and internal cultivation of the virtues of the soul. External acts are helpful both because obedience is rewarded directly for its own sake and because these acts contribute to the acquisition of virtues. But the inner state of the heart is more important than any external acts in the eyes of God and more conducive to reward. None of the relations just described is causal. Acts do not cause virtues; they do not cause rewards in the next life. Even virtues do not cause rewards. In all cases, God, through his grace, bestows the rewards of moral progress. Here once again God is the only cause, and he is under no obligation. Religious enlightenment consists largely in understanding these revealed truths.[43]

The secondary means—knowledge and motivation—are necessary for the effectiveness of the primary means to happiness. The mission of the prophets is designed to provide these aids, for scripture gives both guidance and inspiration, both to acts of obedience and to the virtues. Finally, the Muslim community, when it is working properly, sustains the individual in various ways through its organization and leaders.[44]

Corresponding to the two human means to happiness are two practical sciences mentioned previously: *fiqh* (law), the ethics of action, and *akhlāq* (virtues), the ethics of character. The Sunni-Ash'arite theory of the ethics of action is a form of the theory of ethical voluntarism (or theistic subjectivism). The core of that theory is that the evaluative terms applied to action, such as "necessary," "good," and "evil," have no meanings in themselves, hence their application to action cannot be known by the human intellect. However, since these terms acquire meaning when related to the commands (*awāmir*, plural of *'amr*) and prohibitions (*nawāhī*, plural of *nahy*) of the Sharī'a, their application can be learned exclusively by studying that law.

The targets of this outlook were the Sunni-Mu'tazilites and the Shī'ites with their objectivism and rationalism. The objectivist position was the commonsense understanding of ethical terms in all or most cultures and their languages. Most people think that when they describe someone else as "just," "wicked," and so on, they are describing a real quality of that person (however hard to analyze), not merely some relation of obedience or disobedience to a social group or even to God. The presumption is that a common ethical language is being used, understood clearly and in the same way by the speaker and the addressed parties. Such a language could not depend on their prior acceptance of the particular scripture being delivered by the speaker. Many of the terms used have definite objective meanings as far back as can be traced. Mu'tazilite principles of ethics, as Hourani explains, resemble those of British intuitionism and can be understood by any rational person. Yet this rationalism incorporates an indispensable role for revelation in determining important evaluative truths that would lie beyond the grasp of unaided reason.[45]

From an early time Muslims who understood the overwhelming power of God as the chief message of the Qur'an could not admit that human beings could ever work out by their own reason, without aid from scripture, what was right and what was wrong in the world, much less what was obligatory for God to do or not to do with his creation. The traditionalists naturally felt this way since the Mu'tazilite claim undermined the utility of their collections of the *ḥadīth*-reports that were used as paradigm cases for moral-legal deliberations. More substantially, the schools of law increasingly inclined in this direction until voluntarism as a theory of jurisprudence was worked out with the most thoroughgoing logic by Shāfi'ī, who insisted that the entire legal-ethical system could be derived from the revelation, that is, the Qur'an and the Tradition, without resorting to reason in the form of *al-ra'y* ("sound opinion" of a jurist). On the side of theology, voluntarism, with its theistic subjectivism, found a champion in Ash'arī (873–935) and his successors. In the sphere of ethics, the conservative spokesmen of Islam, who referred themselves as "the people of tradition and the community" (*ahl al-sunna wa al-jamā'a*), continued to react against Mu'tazilite rationalism. The main reason is probably that the Mu'tazilite theory was the only articulate theory that could be set in contrast to the prevailing trend of Islamic thought on ethics in theological and juristic circles.

Knowledge of Ethical Necessity

How can the individual acquire knowledge of morally and legally necessary acts? Bearing in mind the definitions of these terms and the ends and the means of human action as explained earlier, it is possible to see that these are questions about an individual's knowledge of his or her true interests and ends. What should he or she do and become in this world to attain prosperity in the life of the next world? Moreover, these questions can be posed either with regard to a particular choice or with regard to a long-range plan of life.

Ethical reflection, both with regard to general rules that are invoked to derive ethical directions and to particular actions, whether public or private, belongs to the discipline of jurisprudence and the study of its sources. Regardless of whether one accepts the rationalist-objectivist Mu'tazilite position or the theistic-subjectivist Ash'arite one, the Muslim jurist has to relate legal-moral decisions to normative sources. The intellectual undertaking in jurisprudence, as a consequence, is concerned with identifying the rules in their generality and their application in particular legal-moral cases. The search for practical solutions begins with procuring evidence in the normative sources for the derivation of a practical rule that regulates the conduct of the agent under moral obligation.

Each act and attitude is brought under a general rule—a judgment of normative value for a type of act or attitude—so that a system of such rules to cover all occasions is readily available to a jurist engaged in formulating legal-moral decisions. This juridical inquiry into reasons and ends demands that one possess the rules of the moral-legal system—the Sharī'a—in their generality and know how to apply them to particular human situations. The exposition of basic procedures to relate theoretical doctrines derived from the normative sources to the requirements of a particular case in a deductive mode[46] forms the essential scope of the discipline of jurisprudence. This intellectual activity is undertaken to justify a ruling derived inferentially by taking into consideration relevant facts of a case and supporting it by reference to the scriptural sources through deduction. For instance, in the case of organ donation, about which normative sources have very little to say directly, it is possible to justify a permission to do so by reference to the Qur'an that regards saving human life as meritorious. Muslim jurists discuss this scope in terms of a choice between two large sources that encompass all methodological alternatives: independent reason and revelation. By "independent" reason they mean precisely any reasoning that proceeds as a result of a prior conviction that revelation is true and it is the major source of knowledge of the duties of the Sharī'a. This is *'aql*, meaning "reason." In juridical-theological sciences "reason" is contrasted with "tradition."[47] The latter covers revelation in its direct and derivative forms whose elaboration leads to the formulation of transmitted judgments. But reason also has dependent uses, when it serves to draw out implications from the tradition in certain ways to be specified below. The main emphasis of the Sunni ethical-legal theory of knowledge can be stated in two short sentences: Ethical-legal knowledge is not derivable from independent reason; it is derivable entirely from revelation. The Sunni intellectual circle denied that ethical rules could be known by independent reason because this issue implied a rationalist threat to the position of the Qur'an and the Tradition as the unique and indispensable sources of all ethical knowledge.

The objectivist theories of Islamic philosophers and the Mu'tazilites commonly fall into teleological and deontological theories of ethics. In a teleological theory the true value of acts is determined by the consideration of their efficacy in promoting ends. According to Hourani, ancient Greek philosophers from Socrates onward took as their starting point the ends of individuals and concentrated on their good, with little attention to obligation. They assumed that there is a natural comprehensive end for everyone—happiness—and attempted to show how all less comprehensive ends were either constituents of happiness or means to it. The main thrust of their argument was that virtuous living is the key to happiness, but not because of any direct external rewards it gives—experience shows the contrary—but because constant activity of this sort purifies the soul and makes it delight in such activity more and more.[48]

The core of Greek ethics is an attempt to demonstrate causal relations, showing how certain ways of life directly cause certain changes in the subject (as well as in other people through education and corruption); and such explanations are extended, with some hesitation, to the states of souls in the next life. The entire construction is based on the assumption of natural causality, which was shared by all the Greek and Muslim philosophers. On the other hand, Sunni-Ash'arite theologians who followed the occasionalist theory to explain divine action rejected natural causality and applied this rejection to every stage in the chain of means and ends that led to ethical action. Hence, in the absence of the knowledge about causal connections, which can be acquired only through scripture, no process of independent teleological reasoning can reveal the way in which human acts conduce to divine favor or disfavor.

Both the Sunni-Mu'tazilites and the Shī'ites avoid teleology by defining an act deontologically in terms of its character without reference to consequences. Although the main terms of their ethics affirmed human ability rationally to know which acts are good and which evil, and to attain practical certainty about the means to ends, they explain "necessary," "good," and "evil' not entirely in relation to ends. "Necessary" (*wājib*) as an attribute of acts is defined as "that for the omission of which the agent deserves blame," "evil" (*qabīḥ*) as "that for doing of which the agent deserves blame," and so on. The blame can be known by any person with sound reason, as in cases of suicide and infanticide, without reference to consequences. This sharp turn from teleology to deontology in Mu'tazilite ethical theory was probably marked by the new prominence of obligation in Islamic legal-ethical thinking.

The prominence of obligation in the revelation is underscored by the requirements of the Sharī'a, the sacred law. These duties, as the Sharī'a explains, must be performed by virtue of a contractual agreement between God and humanity. As God's creatures, human beings must serve divine purposes by obeying God's commands. In return for this obedience God promises rewards. Hence, judged on the basis of divine scales of justice provided in the Sharī'a, every human will receive what he or she deserves.[49] In such a contractual relation between God as the benefactor and humans as the servants, obligation occupies a central role. The Mu'tazilites and the Shī'ites, thus, did not explain obligation wholly in terms of the interest of the subject and its good consequences. Rather, they were concerned to show the essence of the deontological perspective in ethics. Actions become obligatory because of the characteristic of "obligatoriness" in them (i.e., fidelity to promises, truthfulness, and justice).

Their central position on ethics is that a human being of sound mind can know in an immediate intuition that certain acts are good or evil prior to and without the aid of scripture. Ethical predicates refer to objectively real attributes and characteristics of actions they describe. However, ethical judgment should be based merely on *prima facie* values of actions. Before arriving at a final decision, different aspects of an act should first be appraised separately; then these aspects should be weighed against each other to deduce an overall judgment. This process will lead to varying conclusions because of the variability of the circumstances under consideration. Ethical deliberations in certain classes of acts, despite having an invariable value character, regardless of other *prima facie* aspects, do not necessarily lend themselves to the derivation of a clear-cut final judgment. For example, all ethically good or bad acts are known to be such by all humans of sound mind. Still, it is in principle possible to derive from these absolute characteristics of a moral act a full set of universal rules such that one can know the ethical value of any act in any given situation by systematic reflection upon the objective facts of value.[50]

Some Sunni-Ash'arite theologians did not deny the feature of objectivity in the Mu'tazilite ethical concepts. They concentrated instead on opposing the partial and inessential feature of absoluteness in some of the rules. The main thrust of their attack is that ethical rules are grounded neither in the acts themselves nor in their rationally accessible properties. In other words, in moral cognition they turned their attention to relativism versus absolutism, whereas for the Mu'tazilites the issue was one of subjectivism versus objectivism. While some acts are essentially good or evil and agreed on by all people of sound mind without regard to relative conditions, Ash'arites insisted that there could be relativistic definitions of good, evil, and so on.

The debate about moral epistemology remains contested by both Sunni and Shī'ite scholars in their contemporary discussions about the modern project of searching for universal and absolute moral values, independent of revelation. Such a universal and autonomous claim is difficult to sustain without due emphasis on intuitive human reasoning in knowing good and evil objectively. Hence, it remains unacceptable to the majority of Sunni jurist-theologians today. This rejection has led to epistemological crisis in juridical-ethical deliberations in matters that are beyond the scope of traditional jurisprudence. In fact, a majority of the issues related to social ethics in Muslim societies worldwide remains unresolved because of the conservative spirit that permeates juridical-ethical studies in the seminaries. Recent scholarship to resolve this crisis (mostly undertaken by modern educated Muslims) is considered a dissident, secularist approach to social ethics in Muslim societies. Undoubtedly, nothing less than the reinstatement of reason as a substantive partner of revelation will bring back Qur'anic ethical discourse to the center stage of religious revival among Muslims.

The Principles and Rules in Islamic Juristic Ethics

Theological debates about ethical evaluation of human actions and of the nature of human being as moral agents were foundational in the development of Islamic jurisprudence. The consideration of ethical good and prevention of evil as self-evident to the sound mind made the legal doctrines adaptable to contemporary legal problems and issues. The ultimate purpose of the legal deliberations entailed doing justice and preserving people's best interests on earth and in the hereafter. How was that purpose to be fulfilled when all possible human contingencies in the future were not covered in the revelation, whether the Qur'an or the Tradition?

Here paradigm cases (preserved in the form of a *ḥadīth*) played a critical role as discoverers of divine purposes for human institutions. Contrary to commonsense expectations that the application of judicial decisions must be posterior to the prior elaboration of legal theory, Islamic jurisprudence actually antedated the genre of paradigm cases. Muslim scholars were able to appropriate these paradigm cases to resolve more immediate cases because these cases had the backing of the consensus built upon the practice of the community. The legal decisions preserved in the paradigm cases mark a transition point wherein the cumulative tradition, the Sunna, was utilized to document substantive law. As precedents for subsequent legal decisions, these cases indicated the underlying rationale (*'illa*) upon which depended the final judgment in those cases. Such cases became the sources for the development of juridical principles and rules. The novel issues were then settled through the evocation of these principles and rules.

At other times principles like justice and equity that were stated directly and in most general terms in the revelation were to be applied to concrete situations in the Muslim society to determine the level of culpability in cases of violation of justice. The intellectual responsibility of a Muslim legal expert included providing the definition of the nature of religiously prescribed justice and its determination in the given context of a particular case, whether it was distributive or corrective. Moreover, he had to determine whether the scale of violation necessitated financial or other forms of compensation recognized in the penal system. Undoubtedly, a major part of a Muslim jurist's training dealt with learning these principles and rules in the context of the Qur'an and the Tradition to offer new methods of approach to problem solving in the society. In the context of this book we need to determine the most important juridical doctrines and principles that have been evoked in the contemporary situation to provide the necessary solutions for novel issues in biomedicine.

Islamic Principles of Bioethics

In our discussion about the ethical theories known among Muslims, human reason and its substantive role in deriving legal-ethical decisions, whether through the references to the relevant principles or prescriptive precedents, occupied a central place. Sunni Muslim ethicists assigned minimal and, to a certain extent, formal role for reason to discover the correlation between divine command and human good. Here, precedents derived from the revelation, both the Qur'an and the Tradition, served as paradigmatic cases for casuistic decisions. Moreover, ethical reflection occurred within the Tradition as a process of discernment of principles that were embedded in propositional statements in the form of rulings (*fatāwā*) as well as approved practice of the earlier jurists. The relationship between legal-ethical judgments and the principles in such cases is overshadowed by reference to revelation, however far-fetched it might appear. It is important to keep in mind that for Sunni Muslims, knowledge of rules of law and ethics is anchored in divine revelation and not in human intuitive reason (*'aql*). The process of deriving rules from the revelation is founded upon the interpretation of texts. In this sense, Islamic law is a body of practical rules by virtue of the formulations of jurists based on the revealed texts rather than the dictates of their own intuition. The exposition of law depended on a text-oriented approach, although a great deal of positive law in the area of interpersonal relations was derived from individual discretion in employing intuitive reasoning.

The substantive role for reason was propounded by Muslim ethicists belonging to the Sunni-Mu'tazilite and Shī'ite schools of thought who saw human reason capable of not only discovering the divine purposes for human society, but also establishing the correlation (*mulāzama*) between human moral judgment and divine commandments. They identified the major principles and rules ensuing from both revelation and rational sources that could be used to make fresh decisions in all areas of interpersonal relationship. In other words, these principles and rules became general action guides to determine the ethical valuation of an act and declare it as incumbent or necessary (*wājib*), prohibited (*ḥarām*), permitted (*mubāḥ*), recommended (*mustaḥabb*), or reprehensible (*makrūh*) in the context of specific circumstances. But the process of ethical reflection did not necessarily involve unchanging norms from which other rules or judgments were deduced. Rather, it involved a dialectical progression between the insights and beliefs of the jurists and the paradigmatic cases in the revelation that embedded principles and rules for solving particular cases. Nevertheless, there were certain principles that transcended relative circumstances in history and tradition and which became the source for solving contemporary moral problems.

However, there was no unanimity among the representatives of four major Sunni legal schools of thought (Mālikī, Ḥanafī, Shāfi'ī, and Ḥanbalī) regarding these principles nor that these principles were derived from foundational, rationalistically established moral theories from which other principles and legal-moral judgments were deduced. Rather, scholars from different legal schools identified several principles, often but not always the same ones. Since the language of Sharī'a is the language of obligation or duty, the primary principles (*qawā'id uṣūl*) and rules (*qawā'id fiqhī*) in Islamic ethics are stated as obligations and their derivatives, respectively. Some jurists have identified principles to encompass both principles and rules and have indicated the primary and the subsidiary distinction in their application to particular cases.

Two such intellectual sources in Muslim jurisprudence were *istiḥsān* (prioritization of two or more equally valid judgments through juristic practice) and *istiṣlāḥ* (promoting and securing benefits and preventing and removing harm in the public sphere). These represented independent juristic judgments of expedience or public utility. However, the legitimacy of employing these rationally derived principles depended upon their authentication extracted from the normative sources.

Thus, for instance, the duty to avoid literal enforcement of an existing law that might prove detrimental in certain situations has given rise to the principle of "juristic preference" (*istiḥsān*).[51] This juridical method of prioritization of legal rulings, which takes into account the concrete circumstances of a case at hand, has played a significant role in providing the necessary adaptability to Islamic law to meet the changing needs of society. However, the methodology is founded upon an important principle derived from the directive of "circumventing of hardship," stated in the Qur'an in no uncertain terms: "God intends facility for you, and he does not want to put you in hardship" (2:185). This directive is further reinforced by the tradition that states, "The best of your law (*dīn*) is that which brings ease to the people." In other words, the principle of "juristic preference" allows formulating a decision that sidesteps an established precedent in order to uphold a higher obligation of implementing the ideals of fairness and justice without causing unnecessary hardship to the people involved. The obvious conclusion to be drawn from God's intention to provide help and remove hardship is that the essence of these principles is their adaptability in meeting the exigencies of every time and place on the basis of public interest. In the absence of any textual injunction in the Qur'an and the Tradition, the principle that "necessity overrides prohibition" furnishes an authoritative basis for deriving a fresh ruling.

The scope of this work does not permit an exhaustive identification of all the principles that are applicable to juridical decisions in various fields of interpersonal relations in Islamic law. What seems to be most useful and feasible is to identify a number of fundamental Islamic principles that are in some direct and indirect ways discerned through the general principle of *maṣlaḥa*, that is, "public good." This principle is evoked in providing solutions to the majority of novel issues in biomedical ethics. The rational obligation to weigh and balance an action's possible benefits against its costs and possible harms is central to social transactions in general and biomedical ethics in particular. As stated earlier, Islamic juridical studies are undertaken to understand the effective causes (*'ilal*, plural of *'illa*) that underlie some juridical decisions that deal with primary and fundamental moral obligations. The principles to be elaborated in this chapter are not necessarily the same in priority or significance as those recognized, for instance, in Western bioethics, namely, respect for autonomy, nonmaleficence, beneficence (including utility), and justice. In comparison, Islamic principles overlap in important respects but differ in others. For instance, the two distinct obligations of beneficence and nonmaleficence in some Western system are viewed as a single principle of nonmaleficence in Islam on the basis of the overlapping of the two obligations in the famous Tradition: "In Islam there shall be no harm inflicted or reciprocated" (*lā ḍarar wa lā ḍirār fī al-islām*). This is the principle of "No harm, no harassment." Moreover, the principle of "Protection against distress and constriction" (*al-'usr wa al-ḥaraj*) applies to social relations and transactions, which must be performed in good faith but are independent of religion. There are also a number of derivative rules that are an important part of the Islamic system but are underemphasized in secular bioethics. Thus, among the derivative obligations is the rule of consultation (*shūrā*), a feature of Islamic communitarian ethics, against the dominant principle of autonomy that is based on liberal individualism.

Moreover, although this research is based on the rulings compiled from four major Sunni legal schools and one Shīʿite school, I have attempted to identify only the most common principles or rules in biomedical jurisprudence without necessarily attributing them to one or the other school except when there has been fundamental disagreement on their inclusion in one or the other legal theory. These are the principles that have made possible the derivation of fresh rulings in bioethics by seeking to identify and balance probable outcomes in order to protect the society from harm.

In the last two decades jurists belonging to all the Muslim legal schools have met regularly under the auspices of ministries of health of their respective countries to formulate their decisions as a collective body. Some of these new rulings have been published under the auspices of *Majmaʿ al-fiqhī al-islāmī* (the Islamic Juridical Council) of the World Muslim League in Mecca, Saudi Arabia. A close examination of the juridical decisions made in this council reveal the balancing of likely benefits and harm to society as a whole. In addition, these decisions indicate the search for proportionality (*tanāsub*) between individual and social interests of the community and the need, in certain cases, to allow collective interests to override individual interests and rights. The inherent tension in such decisions is sometimes resolved by reference to a critical principle regarding the right of an individual to reject harm and harassment ("no harm, no harassment"), which constrains unlimited application of the principle of common good.

Al-Maṣāliḥ al-mursala in the Lexicon and as a Technical Term

In the Arabic lexicon, the term *maṣlaḥa* means "considerations that promote benefit and prevent and remove harm."[52] But, according to Abū Ḥāmid Muḥammad al-Ghazālī (d. 1111), an Ashʿarite theologian-jurist, this is not the sense in which the term is used in the law. There it simply means considerations that preserve the goals of the Sharīʿa.[53] Fakhr al-Dīn Muḥammad al-Rāzī (d. 1210) has defined *maṣlaḥa* as the concern that leads to an action approved by the members of the community as a reasonable one, whether that action promotes their good or defends them against harm. In addition, *maṣlaḥa* can refer to actions that customarily agree with what reasonable people do. The first part of this definition, as Rāzī tells us, is accepted by those who analyze God's injunctions in terms of people's welfare and their defense against harm, whereas the second part is based upon the opinions of those who have rejected the first opinion.[54] In other words, there is a consensus among scholars about the admissibility of the considerations that lead to the derivation of fresh rulings in society's interests.

The second part of the term, that is, *al-mursala*, means "to be free." Technically, *al-mursala* means "extra-revelatory," that is, not requiring scriptural proof.

When used with *maṣlaḥa,* the phrase signifies seeking the good of the people without any reference to a particular text in the revelation. For this reason *maṣlaḥa* has been linked to the term *istiṣlāḥ,* that is, "to seek to promote and secure the common good." This connotation implies that *maṣlaḥa,* being the "public good," is self-evident and hence "free" from the required textual proof that would support its validity. Moreover, because its purpose (being good) is discernible by God-given intuitive reason, from the divine lawgiver's point of view, it has God's approval too, because in general there is a correlation between reason and revelation in matters of the common good.[55] Sources cite another reason for this appellation of "public good that is free from textual evidence," namely, that promoting the public good is rationally derived. It is a positive obligation that requires people to act beneficently whenever possible, and hence, is not in need of scriptural proof.

Istiṣlāḥ, then, is a kind of a guiding principle, formulated on the basis of sound opinion through which its public utility is inferred. Yet it requires the jurist to provide justification for a ruling by appealing to principles and rules that are established in the legal theory. These principles are utilized in all situations about which the Sharī'a has neither ruled explicitly nor provided any relevant precedents. In other words, in matters on which the law has not ruled, any moral-legal judgment that falls outside the framework of general rules derived from *maṣlaḥa* does not have the force of law. The verse "God commands justice and good deeds," (Q. 27:90) and the tradition "No harm, no harassment" are rules that flow from the principle of "common good."[56]

Ghazālī, who, as an Ash'arite, believed in divine-command ethics, was opposed to the sense in which the term *maṣlaḥa* was used by the Mu'tazilites to indicate an independent, extra-revelatory source of law. After giving the lexical meaning to the word as "bringing about benefit (*manfa'a*) or forestalling harm (*maḍarra*)," he understandably adds his objection and affirmation of the position that good and evil are not rational categories that could be discerned through the moral cognition implanted by God in human nature (*fiṭra*): "We do not consider [*maṣlaḥa*] in the meaning of bringing about benefit or forestalling harm as part of [God's] purposes for the people or [God's] concern for the people, in order for them to achieve those purposes." Rather, *maṣlaḥa* is a principle derived from the scriptural sources to serve God's ends in the revelation (*al-shar'*). He goes on to mention the five things for the protection of which the revelation institutes legal injunctions: to protect the right to religion, life, reason, lineage, and property.[57]

The Concept of Public Interest/Common Good (*Maṣlaḥa*)

Consideration of public interest or the common good of the people has been an important principle for Muslim jurists in accommodating new issues confronting the community. *Maṣlaḥa* has been admitted as a principle of reasoning to derive new rulings or as a method of suspending earlier rulings out of consideration for the interests and welfare of the community. However, its admission as an independent source for legislation has been contested by some Sunni and Shī'ite legal scholars. To be sure, *maṣlaḥa* is based on the notion that the ultimate goal of the Sharī'a necessitates doing justice and preserving people's best interests in this and the next world. But who defines justice, and what is most salutary for the people? Here theological ethics defines the scope of *maṣlaḥa*.

Looking at the majority of the Muslims who follow the Sunni-Ash'arite school of thought in their understanding of God's plan for humanity, one needs to pay close attention to their doctrine of *maṣlaḥa* in order to gauge what they regard to be the best for the people. The Ash'arites, who maintained the divine-command ethics (theistic subjectivism), confined the derivation of *maṣlaḥa* to being from the revelatory sources, that is, the Qur'an and the Tradition. Ghazālī elucidates this position in his legal theory:

> *Maṣlaḥa* is actually an expression for bringing about benefit (*manfa'a*) or forestalling harm (*maḍarra*). We do not consider [*maṣlaḥa*] in the meaning of bringing about benefit or forestalling harm as part of [God's] purposes for the people or [God's] concern for the people, in order for them to achieve those purposes. Rather, we take *maṣlaḥa* in the meaning of protecting the ends of the Revelation (*al-shar'*). The ends of the Revelation for the people are five: To protect for them (1) their religion, (2) their lives (*nufūs*), (3) their reason (*'uqūl*), (4) their lineage (*nasl*), and, (5) their property (*māl*). All that guarantees the protection of these five purposes is *maṣlaḥa* and all that undermines these purposes is *mafasada* (a source of detriment).[58]

Hence, justice, according to the Ash'arites, lies in the commission and application of what God has declared to be good and the avoidance of that which God had forbidden in these sacred sources. Moreover, ruling an action good or evil depends on the consideration of the general principles laid down in the revelation. Consequently, human responsibility is confined to the course ordained by God by seeking to institute what God declares good and shunning what God declares evil. Moreover, as far as the derivation of fresh rulings is concerned, the Ash'arites maintain that the principle of *maṣlaḥa* is internally operational in the rulings that reveal with certainty that in legislating them God has the welfare of humankind in mind.[59]

The estimation of the Sunni-Mu'tazilite thinkers, who maintained objectivist rationalist ethics, was understandably at variance with the Ash'arites. Their thesis was founded upon human reason as capable of knowing *maṣlaḥa*—the consideration of public interest that promoted benefit and prevented harm. For them, *maṣlaḥa* was an inductive principle for the derivation of fresh decisions in areas for which the scriptural sources provided little or no guidance at all, and in which judgments had to depend upon an evolving moral life that takes into consideration previous moral struggles and reflections derived from particular cases and circumstances.

In the context of matters connected with social ethics, which deal with everyday contingencies of human life, it is important to keep in mind that whether the principle of common good originates internally in the scriptural sources or externally through intuitive reason, no jurist questions the conclusion that legal-ethical judgments are founded upon concern for human welfare and in order to protect people from corruption (*mafāsid*) and harm (*ḍarar*). In other words, they maintain that God provides guidance with a purpose of doing the most beneficial for people, even when the exact method of deducing this general principle is in dispute.[60]

Some jurists have, for all intent and purposes, related all the ordinances back to the principle of common good by employing case-based reasoning that compares cases and analogically deduces moral-legal conclusions. Hence, for example, Shāṭibī (d. 1388 CE) maintains that the promulgation of the ordinances took place by referring to the paradigm cases in the scriptural sources like the Qur'an and the Tradition that took into consideration the welfare of the people (*li-maṣāliḥ al-'ibād*) in this world and the next. This assertion that God has the interest of the people in mind is dependent upon an authoritative proof that could determine the validity of the claim that the paradigm case reflects an underlying doctrine that God is bound to do the most beneficial for his creatures. However, as Shāṭibī correctly points out, regardless of the doctrinal aspects of the principle of common good treated in theology proper (*'ilm al-kalām*), it is important to emphasize that the application of this principle in legal theory (*uṣūl al-fiqh*) permits and even fosters new moral insights and judgments in the Sharī'a. The majority of contemporary jurists maintain the latter view and have produced evidence in their works on legal theory in support of the specific legal decisions analogically derived on the basis of the principle of public good.[61]

Shāṭibī provides several examples of ordinances from the Qur'an and the Tradition that were instituted by God in keeping with his aim of achieving the highest good for people in this and the next world. Thus in justifying the rules of purity and ablutions, God says in the Qur'an: "God does not intend to make any impediment (*ḥaraj*) for you; but he desires to purify you, and that he may complete his blessings upon you" (Q. 5:6). In addition, the scriptural sources have made the corrupting aspects of this world and the next known to humanity so that people can protect themselves from them. If one investigates the Tradition, one will find nothing but the fact that all religious and moral duties (*takālīf al-shar'īya*) point to God's concern for the welfare of humanity.[62]

In the works on Islamic legal theory (*uṣūl al-fiqh*), the principle of public good is identified as *al-maṣāliḥ al-mursala*, that is, the public good attained by rules that arise on the basis of intuitive reason that interacts with guidelines inspired by a cultural matrix external to the Qur'an or the Tradition. This standpoint is close to the Sunni-Mu'tazilite and Shī'ite view of objective good and evil that enables an agent to apply moral judgments to particular situations. In addition, the historical record of precedents provide foundational and absolute principles like the one about rejection of probable harm (*daf' al-ḍarar al-muḥtamal*). It is evident that the application of this principle requires a reason-based approach, even when its application is not independent of scriptural proofs derived from paradigm cases. The antecedent provides a broad and extra-revelatory interpretation of these precedents in order to permit moral insights and conclusions that conform to the general norms in the scriptural sources even when they appear to have been derived independently of them.

The Validity of "Public Good" as a Legal Principle

Since its admission in legal methodology, the issue of the public good—*maṣlaḥa*—has raised a number of questions about its authoritativeness (*ḥujjīya*) in deducing fresh rulings, depending on how one defines the principle. Some hold that the principle falls outside the scope of the kind of legal documentation that is admissible as a proof for a ruling. Moreover, the classification of public good into general and particular kinds has raised doubts about the notion's applicability to a variety of circumstances, especially those open to a wide range of interpretations. Two significant views about *maṣlaḥa* as a proof for a ruling are as follows:

1. One view unconditionally rejects the principle of public good as having evidentiary value in legal-ethical decision-making. According to Taqī al-Dīn al-Subkī (d. 1355), a Shāfi'ī jurist, the majority of the Sunni legal scholars hold this opinion about *maṣlaḥa*.[63]
2. Another view accepts the principle of public good unreservedly as having evidentiary value in legal-ethical decision-making. This view has been ascribed to Mālik,[64] Imām al-Ḥaramayn al-Juwaynī (d. 1085), jurist-theologian, Shāfi'ī,[65] and Aḥmad b. Ḥanbal. Some Ḥanafī scholars have also accorded sympathetic treatment to the principle of public good.[66]

Those who do not admit the public good principle as a source for legal-ethical decision-making point to the lack of any textual endorsement of the principle in the Qur'an or the Tradition. Moreover, they maintain that decisions made by reference to *maṣlaḥa* are necessarily based on conjecture, which is not a permissible way to derive religious ordinances.[67] Some object to this principle simply because they reject the doctrine that God's injunctions are based on their good and bad consequences. It is only human actions that are based on such considerations. In fact, they contend, human beings always weigh benefit and harm in undertaking or avoiding an action. God's actions are not limited by such considerations. They furthermore argue that the analogical deduction founded upon human and divine actions leads to a false doctrine about God's actions: namely, that they are informed by ends. God does not act in accordance with a good or bad end. God, being omnipotent and omniscient, does not need to evaluate divine acts in terms of their good or bad consequences for humankind. It is also possible to see that there is nothing in the world of contingencies that rules out the conclusion that what is good for one is harmful for another. Hence, God is not bound to do the best or the worst for humankind. God simply does what God wishes to do absolutely and immutably. More pertinently, if one were to believe that God works in the interest of humanity based on public good to protect people from possible harm, the possibility of such speculation and its application in the matter of divine ordinances could lead any ruler or scholar to change or commit an error in these ordinances.[68]

On the other side of the spectrum are those scholars who have unconditionally supported the doctrine of *maṣlaḥa* and have defined its legal and ethical scope as a source of fresh rulings. They have appealed to reason in order to argue for its authoritativeness. In fact, they contend, the divine lawgiver himself has granted recognition to the interests of humanity in all the laws of the Sharīʿa. Even when it is deduced conjecturally that in doing *x*, *y* benefit will accrue, it is valid to admit *maṣlaḥa* as an important means of investigating the level of benefit. Such a conjecture is necessary, and it is only through this process that one can evaluate and calculate what should be done, considering the needs of everyone affected by such a ruling. This is what the term *istiṣlāḥ*, meaning, "to seek to maximize benefit and minimize harm" conveys. This has been regarded as one of the two arguments that support the public good as outlined by Mālik.[69]

The other argument is the one in which supporters of *maṣlaḥa* have undertaken to assess the greatest good with such rigor that the concept can withstand the most exacting critical scrutiny. Ostensibly, this goal can be achieved only if the conjectural process can find support in the revelation. The revelation endorses all human endeavors that lead to the attainment of maximal good and the protection of the people from harm. Hence, when a jurist derives a ruling by taking into consideration, however conjecturally, maximal good and minimal harm, the conjectural aspect of the ruling is overcome. This kind of ruling is rendered authoritative by the revelation. To act on such a conjecture is obligatory because any sound mind weighs the preponderance of good over harm and sanctions the maximal good. This method has support in the Tradition, in which the Prophet says, "I judge on what is apparent."[70]

The supporters of the *maṣlaḥa* have also pointed out the problems of formulating rulings with the flexibility needed to cope with communities living under different conditions. Although the Qur'an and the Tradition provide theoretical guidelines for relevant rulings, these rulings must reflect the needs of people living under concrete and evolving conditions. The supporters of *maṣlaḥa* have also resorted to the notion of abrogation of the pre-Qur'anic revelations to argue for gradual legislation of the divine law. This argument is, however, inadequate to allow later generations to make a case for the principle of chronological evolution and thereby support the flexibility that is needed to respond to the changing circumstances of each generation. The reason is that the law of Moses was abrogated because it had lost relevance for later generations and not because the need for the flexibility in applying the same for the following generations. Islam was founded to provide relevant guidance and prescriptions for communities living under changed circumstances.

This chronological argument also applies to rulings in Islamic jurisprudence. The need to respond to people's religious and worldly interests is consonant with the belief that God's guidance for humanity in Islamic revelation applies to all times and places. Hence, they assert, what applies to the arguments about the abrogation of the pre-Qur'anic revelation also applies to the admission of *maṣlaḥa* as a divinely sanctioned principle to improve the lives of people at all times. This view implies that the laws enacted with an eye to the welfare of the community are necessarily mutable. There is an intrinsic relationship between public good and the most effective and just formulation of laws.[71]

There are numerous examples in the early history of Islam to show that at different times the Prophet and the caliphs made necessary adjustments to their rulings by taking into consideration changed circumstances and needs of the people. In one such instance, the Prophet sent 'Alī b. Abī Ṭālib on a mission with clear instructions and asked him to assess the situation before implementing the terms of his instructions. If need be, the Prophet instructed, 'Ali should make necessary adjustment to accommodate the situation as he assessed it. In other words, the Prophet's instructions to 'Alī provide a precedent for going beyond the letter of the revelation in order to rationally deduce its spirit in the best interest of the people.[72] On another occasion the Prophet instructed his army not to apply the legal punishment against a soldier found guilty of theft—cutting off his hand—because the soldier might seek refuge with the enemy and endanger the Muslim army.[73]

Even more to the point is 'Alī's statement about the Prophet's instruction about dyeing one's beard with henna to avoid appearing like Jews, who, apparently, did not dye their beards. 'Ali was asked about the applicability of the Prophet's ruling, to which he replied: 'The Prophet of God (may God's mercy and salutations be upon him) gave this instruction when there were few Muslims. Now that Islam has become widespread and has attained firmer ground on its own, people can do [with their beard] what they want."[74]

There is enough evidence to suggest that *al-maṣāliḥ al-mursala*—that is, the principle of public good beyond what had been already prescribed in the revelation—had a long history before legal scholars began to discuss its authoritativeness as a source for ethical and legal decisions. In fact, it is correct to surmise that the proofs, whether textual or rational, in support of the principle are far more logical and convincing than those against it. Most of these proofs that deny any validity to the public good argument are inconsistent with the spirit of legislation for the good of the people. If the purpose of the divine lawgiver is to guide people in building a just and ethical society, then to rule out the principle of public good as invalid is to question the very essence of God's guidance being for all people in all ages.

The Types of Issues Covered Under the Principle of Public Good

In view of the above explanation about "public good principle," this principle consists of each and every benefit that has been made known by the purposes stated in the divine revelation (*al-shar'*),[75] and because some jurists have essentially regarded public good as safeguarding the divine lawgiver's purposes,[76] they have discussed the principle in terms of both the types and the purposes they serve. Some have classified public good in terms of types, while others have resorted to purposes for classification. For instance, among the Sunni jurists, the Mālikī jurist from Andalusia, Abū Isḥāq al-Shāṭibī (d. 1388) has treated the principle and its corollaries in great detail in his legal theory by pointing out that religious duties (*al-takālīf al-shar'īya*) have been imposed on people for their own good in view of the fulfillment of God's purposes for them. In fact, the entire Sharī'a is instituted in the interests of Muslims, whether these interests pertain to this life or to life in the hereafter. In order to safeguard these interests and achieve God's purposes for humanity the Sharī'a seeks to promote three universal goals. The three goals are discussed under the following universal principles whose authority is based on a number of probable instances and supporting documentation in the revelation:

(1) **The Essentials or the Primary Needs (*al-ḍarūriyāt*):** These are indispensable things that are promulgated for the good of this and the next world, such as providing health care to the poor and downtrodden. Such actions are necessary for maintaining public health and the good of people in this life and for earning a reward in the next. Moreover, without them, life would be threatened, resulting in further suffering for people who cannot afford even the basic necessities of life. According to Muslim thinkers, the necessity to protect the essentials is felt across traditions among the followers of other religions, too. The good of the people is such a fundamental issue among all peoples that there is a consensus among them that when one member of a society suffers, others must work to relieve the afflicted.[77] Some jurists have claimed unanimity among all religions, in that among the essentials of each is the protection of the five indispensable things (religion, life, reason, lineage, and property)

that human beings need to maintain an orderly existence and the prohibition against ignoring them. In other words, without them one cannot acquire the benefits (*al-maṣāliḥ*) of carrying out the rulings that are necessary for maintaining order in this life and gaining a reward in the next. Moreover, without them existence would be chaotic, resulting in the loss of life and property.[78]

(2) **The General Needs (*al-ḥājiyāt*)**: These are things that enable human beings to improve their life and to remove those conditions which lead to chaos in one's familial and societal life in order to achieve high standards of living, though these needs do not reach the level of essentials. These benefits are such that, if not attained, they lead to hardship and disorder, but not to corruption. According to Shāṭibī, this kind of common good is materialized in matters of religious duties (*'ibādāt*), everyday life situations (*'ādāt*), interpersonal relationships (*mu'āmalāt*), and a penal system (*jināyāt*) that prevents people from causing harm to others. As an example of the religious duties, the Sharī'a exempts a sick person or a traveler from performing certain obligations under those conditions; under the category of everyday situations the law permits one to undertake transactions that are beneficial for one's advancement in life; under the category of interpersonal relationships the law allows all those dealings that are justly executed; and under the penal system, the law imposes various penalties that deter people from committing crimes that hurt one and all.[79] Muslim jurists of various schools disagreed on the admission of the category of "needs" as a source of legal decisions. Some have even argued against its authoritativeness in deriving legal rulings.[80]

(3) **The Secondary Needs (*al-taḥsīnāt*)**: These are the things that are commonly regarded as praiseworthy in society, which also lead to the avoidance of those things that are regarded as blameworthy. They are also known as "noble virtues" (*makārim al-akhlāq*).[81] In other words, although these things do not qualify as "primary" or "general" needs, their goal is to improve quality of life, to make these needs easily accessible to an average member of a society, and even to embellish these noble virtues in order to render them more desirable.[82]

In terms of the public good principle's application, when a number of beneficial or corruptive aspects converge or when public good and corruption appear in the same instance, it gives rise to disagreement. For example, one of the issues in the Muslim world is sex selection in assisted reproduction. Sex selection is any practice, technique, or intervention intended to increase the likelihood of the conception, gestation, and birth of a child of one sex than the other. In the Muslim world, some parents prefer one sex above the other for cultural or financial reasons. Some jurists have argued in favor of sex selection, as long as no one, including the resulting child, is harmed. However, others have disputed the claim that it is possible for no harm to be done in sex selection. They point to violations of divine law, natural justice, and the inherent dignity of human beings. More important, permitting sex selection for nonmedical reasons involves or leads to unacceptable discrimination on grounds of sex and disability, potential psychological damage to the resulting children, and an inability to prevent a slide down the slippery slope toward permitting designer babies. In such cases it becomes critical to assess the important criteria for the public good, or to lead the jurists to prioritize criteria that lead to public good or corruption, before providing the requisite ruling.[83]

Shāṭibī and other jurists are careful not to extend the principle of public good as a basis for legal decisions in matters relating to human welfare in the hereafter. The reason is that such matters are known through the authority of the revelation only, whereas intuitive reason can estimate the good of this world. In other words, intuitive reason has no place in determining the benefits of the next world.[84] Actually, all rulings connected with the God-human relationship (*'ibādāt*) are related to the good of the next world and are covered in the revelation. In this area, then, the principle of public good does not serve as the basis of the rulings. However, in the area of interpersonal relationships, the principle of "seeking the common good (*istiṣlāh*)," serves as an important source of legislation that requires a rational investigation of all aspects of benefit and harm that are included in the three goals of the Sharī'a. This consideration is evident in four of the five purposes stated in justification of the principle of the public good—those that cover transactional laws and penal system. These matters fall under the category of "Secondary Needs" (*ḥājiyāt*), as described above.

The principle of public good has also been examined in terms of collective or individual goodness. When the juristic rule of *istiḥsān* (i.e., choosing between two possible solutions of a case within the context of recognized sources of Islamic law) is evoked to justify a legal-ethical solution, the actual rationale for the decision is based on considerations of common welfare that is unrestricted and that reaches the largest number. However, it is sometimes likely that an individual benefit could become the source for a ruling that could clash with another ruling that entails morally superior consequences. To put it differently, the only criterion for legislation on the basis of public good is that the ruling must lead to the common good even when it is prompted by a specific individual good. The underpinning of primary ordinances (e.g., saving human life or maintaining just order) in the revelation is this kind of good. However, the consideration of individual welfare is provided by the change of context for a ruling from absolutely needed to not needed to such an extent when accommodating reality allows relaxing the stringent requirement, (e.g., prolongation of life without any hope for cure), so that it can benefit that particular individual in that particular situation. To be sure, the elimination of the absolutely needed ordinance that requires saving life and its change to a less than absolutely needed ruling that allows discontinuing extraordinary care takes place in the context of a particular situation. In this sense, common interests function as criteria for legislation, whereas individual interests function as the context for derivative rulings. This change from common to individual good causes disagreement among Muslim jurists in determining the benefits and harm of the situation under consideration.[85]

The Religious-Social Dimensions of Public Good

Discussion about the extent of public good in matters related to people's religious and social life takes place under one of the following rubrics:

(1) **"Public Good" in Legislation Promulgated by the Divine Lawgiver**

Consideration of the public good occurs when the divine lawgiver has determined the common good in laws enacted in the interest of the people regardless of whether these laws are related to God-human or interhuman relationships or are simply related to social customs or whether this good is determined by human reason. Hence, common good, in this sense, is assumed in all matters related to the religious or social dimensions of life without requiring that reason must discover the criteria and the merit of public good or of forbidden activities. This is where the public good principle takes on a theological dimension—through an evaluation of God's actions and laws to determine whether they are necessary or granted as a special favor in the interest of humankind. This dimension brings to mind the rule about the "correlation" (*mulāzama*) between rules derived by revelation and those derived from reason.

In general, moral reasoning in Islam is founded upon the divine endowment of ethical cognition through the creation of innate dispositions (*fiṭra*) in humankind. This ethical cognition is capable of evaluating and judging the moral aspects of human action. The same cognition is also granted the ability to fathom the correlation between God's guidance through revelation and human intuitive reason in all ethical matters. However, the acknowledgement of the authority of revelation is based on one's faith in God's power of guidance. The revelation covers God's guidance comprehensively; yet it is in the area of interpersonal justice in particular that human reason can engage in the ethical evaluation of human acts. The principle of correlation (*mulāzama*) intuitively discovers the congruity between the judgment of reason and revelation to determine the rightness or the wrongness of an act. As a result, in assessing the scope of public good, which covers all areas of public activity, the jurist rationally establishes the correlation between the dictates of revelation and reason.

The inquiry about public good and public corruption (*mafsada*) is important for understanding the reasons behind ethical requirements in Islam today, just as the discussion about instituting good (*'amr bi al-ma'rūf*) and preventing evil (*nahy 'an al-munkar*) was central to the classical juridical tradition. Muslim governments in power had the duty of instituting good and preventing evil; the extent of this power was determined by the juridical authority of the Muslim jurists. Today, the authority to determine the public good has become one of the most fiercely contested areas of conflict between Muslim jurists and nominally Muslim governments.

(2) **"Public Good" in the Rulings Deduced by Human Agents**

This is one of the most contested areas in Muslim social ethics today: Who can determine what is good for the people: the pragmatic political leaders or the traditional religious keepers of the revelation? The problem is further complicated by the fact that the religious leadership in the Muslim world is known for its conservative and narrow-minded attitude toward any changes that threaten the perceived sanctity of the tradition. In contrast, Muslim governments are obliged to make policy in the face of modern technical advancements that complicate definitions of the public good. To be sure, Muslim peoples have very little faith and confidence in the workings of their mostly autocratic political systems. Under these circumstances the responsibility of guiding the community to its spiritual and moral goals has fallen on the shoulders of Muslim legal scholars, who go through rigorous training in Islamic jurisprudence. However, only some jurists have responded to the challenge of making Islamic teachings relevant today. Those who have undertaken to promote the public good in everyday life through their deliberations on Islamic juridical resources have relied heavily on the principle of public good and other rationally derived rules.

Muslim jurists have extended the scope of public good to cover a wide range of topics arising from novel social circumstances. Biomedical issues, like all other matters related to human relationships, are treated from the standpoint of the public good. This type of legal-ethical reasoning gives a pivotal role to the doctrine of "considerations of public good (*istiṣlāḥ*)." Some jurists have criticized such rulings as not being sufficiently grounded in the sacred texts. In so doing, such critics have called into question the reliance on considerations of public good as a juristic practice. Public good, according to these scholars, appears to be too arbitrary and inductive if each jurist may formulate a response based on his personal assessment of the situational aspects of a case.

As discussed above in the typology of public good, sometimes the good is collective and general, and at other times individual and specific. When public good is admitted as a valid source for the derivation of a new decision, consideration of sheer necessity (*ḍarūra*), which in some cases renders a prohibited act permissible, cannot be evoked as a justification in the same ruling. The reason is that since the ruling is based on the rationally derived principle of public good it is open to further discussion in order to determine the extent to which it arises out of concern for the public good or from necessity. If it is determined that individual well-being is at stake, then the secondary consideration that admits promotion of common good is upgraded to qualify as a primary consideration in the derivation of final ruling. The jurist at this stage is engaged in discovering the secondary consideration related to the special circumstance of the case. Hence, he could rule, for instance, that if a specific medical treatment is harmful for a particular individual, then he/she may be allowed to reject that treatment. Such an opinion raises the question whether he/she should abstain from receiving the treatment in order to reject harm as required by the Sharīʿa under its principle of avoiding probable harm (*dafʿ al-ḍarar al-muḥtamal*). It is important to keep in mind that although the ruling pertains to the welfare of the person involved, it is made independent of this consideration. What actually ends up being inferred on the basis of the principle of common good is the secondary consideration, which gives the person a right to reject harm (*dafʿ al-ḍarar*), and the application of this consideration in this specific situation in which he/she knows that doing otherwise is not in his/her best interest. It is for this reason that the jurists, who are opposed to invoking the subsidiary rule about necessity (*ḍarūra*), which renders a forbidden act permissible under certain critical conditions, regard the appeal to the rule of necessity as a justification for rejecting harm beyond the scope of the principle that seeks to promote the good. Nevertheless, if the ruling in an individual case transcends the individual in its impact by reaching the collectivity and thereby attains universal recognition, then the individual good is regarded as having attained the level of common good and is thus valid in its claim to authoritativeness. The principle of public good is applicable as a basis for legal-ethical decisions in all those cases in which the welfare of all the people is under consideration. However, this criterion applies only to social, interpersonal transactions and cannot be admitted in matters that pertain to the God-human relationship.

The Change of *Maṣlaḥa* and the Change of Rulings

One of the consequences of considering the public good is the inevitable change of laws in accordance with changes of social circumstances that require reassessment of what serves the people's interests and what causes corruption among them. Many precedents in the early history of the community, which serve as documentation in support of the public good, and which have been used as paradigm cases by jurists to extrapolate fresh decisions, are rooted in this principle. If it is accepted that religious ordinances are based on considerations that lead to increasing positive value and minimizing evil, especially in matters that deal with social transactions, then we must regard these ordinances as being relative to the situation, mutable, and hence specific to the logic of time and space. A number of prominent jurists have accepted this relative dimension of the ordinances dealing with all matters connected with interpersonal relationships. They have also asserted that alteration and adaptation are permissible, even if they go against the apparent sense of religious texts or if there is an agreement among the jurists advocating a position contrary to the terms of the text. However, an even larger number of jurists permit modification and adaptation in the ordinances dealing with specific topics about which there does not appear to be a textual proof or an agreement among the scholars.[86]

In general, Sunni jurists were connected with the day-to-day workings of the government. Accordingly, they were required to provide solutions to every new problem that emerged in society. In order to do this they devised methodological stratagems based on analogical reasoning (*al-qiyās*), sound opinion (*al-ra'y*), efforts to promote the good of the people (*istiṣlāḥ*), the selection of the most beneficial of several rulings (*istiḥsān*), the removal of obstruction to resolving a problem (*sadd al-dharāyi'*), conventions and customs of the region (*'urf*), and, different forms of reasoning. Through these methodological tools they were, to a large extent, able to respond to the situations that arose in the medical practice. The Shī'ite jurists did not admit that ensuring the public good was a principle of problem resolution until more recently. Not until the Iranian revolution in 1978–79 did Shī'ite jurists take up the question of admitting the public good principle as an important source for legal-ethical decision making. The direction followed by these jurists in Iran is not very different from the one followed by their Sunni counterparts throughout the political history of Sunni Islam. The relatively late acceptance of *istiṣlāh* by Shī'ites is likely because unlike the Sunni, they were a minority and thus did not have to provide the practical guidance needed by the government or the people in everyday dealings. During the period of their Imams since the Imams themselves could resolve any difficulties there was little need for them to engage in intellectual approaches to ethical and legal matters.[87]

Shi'ite Jurisprudence and the Principle of *al-maṣāliḥ al-mursala*

Among Shī'ite jurists, opinions about *istiṣlāḥ* (seeking the maximal positive value) and *al-maṣāliḥ al-mursala* (going beyond the revelation to do what is best for the people) vary according to the criteria set for achieving the maximum good by minimizing evil. The most common contemporary Shī'ite position in connection with 'seeking the maximal positive value' is that it is not a valid source for the derivation of legal-ethical rulings. It is for this reason that in their jurisprudence during the classical age (ninth to eleventh centuries), there is no discussion of this topic.[88] Some Sunni jurists have criticized Shī'ite jurists for having rejected analogical reasoning and for nonetheless finding themselves obliged to use the principle of public good in generating new decisions.[89]

Other scholars have attributed to the pre-Revolution Shī'ites a middle position. Such is the view taken by Muḥammad Taqī al-Ḥakīm (d. 2002), a Shī'ite jurist and professor of Islamic law in Mustanṣiriya University of Baghdad, who maintains, based on his research on the lexical and technical uses of the principle, that there is no evidence to suggest that the Shīʿites absolutely rejected the idea of going beyond the revelation or seeking the maximal positive value. Hence, if one accepts the source for the admission of the public good to be revelatory texts as well as the general obligation for jurists to consider the welfare of the people, then any consideration of the good of the people beyond the revealed texts must be linked to the Tradition, the second major source after the Qur'an. Here the Tradition functions as the minor premise that might prompt reason to reexamine the major premise of a syllogism. When the major premise becomes evident, then one can search for its conformity with minor premise. But if one is not able to establish the principle through any scriptural text, then it has to be based solely on reason. In this latter case, its authoritativeness and its type will depend on the way in which it is assessed by the investigator. If its assessment is thorough and comprehensive enough to yield a certain derivation for the ruling, then the principle of public good can be admitted as authoritative. However, if this assessment is not comprehensive—if it cannot resolve any contrariety that confronts the positive value or if the perceived positive value cannot satisfy all the conditions to generate necessary confidence—then the principle will lack authoritativeness and will require revelatory proof for admission as a source. Of course, this question about the validity of public good principle applies when one does not have any scriptural proof to establish its validity in the first place.[90] Al-Ḥakīm points out that even if one might wish to treat public good principle as a source, it cannot be regarded as an independent source for legislation beside reason (*al-ʿaql*); rather, it can function as a minor premise for a reason-based syllogism.[91]

Another prominent Shīʿite legal theorist who has discussed the principle of public good is Mīrza Abū al-Qāsim al-Qummī (d. 1816), author of *Qawānin al-uṣūl* (*Laws that Regulate the Principles*). He explains three kinds of public good:

1. Public good founded upon revelation: This type of public good is admissible as a source for deducing a fresh ruling, even when this admissibility is established inferentially from the common element in the revelation that aims for the attainment of the good of the people as revealed in God's law. The positive value, free from any evil, in protecting one's religion, life, property, and lineage is derived rationally, and confirmed by the revelation that affords positive value to the good that protects these values from becoming corrupted.
2. Public good based on practical considerations: This type of public good has no basis in the revealed texts. Nevertheless, the revelation provides grounds for regarding religious requirements as a source of ease rather than hardship. As such, it provides practical solutions to the problem of neglect in the performance of religious and moral duties. Hence, for instance, although revelation prescribes definite ways in dealing with the outbreak of an epidemic, practical considerations

make it necessary to introduce preventive measures to protect public health in ways that are not covered in revealed texts.

3. Public good founded on time-honored norms: This type has neither been validated nor invalidated by the revealed texts. It simply holds sway because it is free from any evident affront to widely accepted values. This is the kind of public good that has been endorsed and been regarded as authoritative by a number of Sunni jurists. But other Sunni scholars and the Shīʻites have rejected it. The reason is that there is no textual or rational proof to support the admissibility of some positive values as good and the rejection of others as corruptive.[92]

Among the Shīʻite jurists who wrote their juridical corpus in the classical age, one finds Muḥaqqiq al-Ḥillī (d. 1277) discussing the Sunni-Muʻtazilite take on objective evil. According to Ḥillī, Muʻtazilites regarded evil as something that causes harm without promoting any good or benefit. In addition, they regarded wrongdoing as self-evidently evil. However, it is important to bear in mind that this statement was based on the principle of correlation between reason and revelation, which, according to later generations of jurists, was the basis for the inclusion of reason as a substantive source of legal and ethical decisions beside the revealed texts.[93]

The Rulings Based on Custom (*ʻurf*) and the Problem of Time and Place

One of the fundamental issues confronting the Muslim jurists is the role of time and place in the formulation of Sharīʻa rulings. To be sure, the principle of public good gives rise to the relativity of the rulings in the area of interpersonal relations. The more one emphasizes the contextual aspect of a case, the more one is led to base the ruling on considerations stemming from the relativity of the situation. Hence, while the jurists have maintained the prohibition of abortion at any time, they have regarded a threat to the mother's life as a legitimate exception. There are many such issues that raise questions about the source of this change in the rulings given at different times. Since the use of considerations about the public good as an important source for change of rulings at times depends on *ʻurf*—local custom and convention—Muslim jurists have also discussed *ʻurf* in the context of legal methodology. Can custom serve as a source for legal-ethical decision-making?

Custom was not one of the formal sources of law in classical jurisprudence. In practice, however, custom was frequently drawn on as a material source of law. Eventually, in the sixteenth century, it gained something close to formal recognition; but before that time attempts were made to incorporate custom in the law without granting it formal recognition, particularly by the Sunni jurists in the Ḥanafī school. Unlike the public good criteria, custom had the potential to prevail over a written text. Some jurists regarded this as unacceptable. However, the tension was resolved by practical incorporation of custom through *istiḥsān*, that is, the personal preference of a jurist. In these cases the jurist could incorporate a customary practice into the law by exercising juristic preference. At other times, the principle of necessity (*ḍarūra*) provided justification for incorporating custom.[94]

Among the Shīʿite jurists, custom, like the public good, cannot prevail over a revealed text. Hence, integrating custom into jurisprudence as a source has been problematic. However, there was recognition of the fact that custom could become part of the Tradition by finding expression in the *ḥadīth*. Hence, there was no need to accept custom as a formal source of law. In spite of that, they could not ignore the question of the influence of temporal conditions on legal rulings.

In fact, Some Shīʿite jurists speak about the variability of rulings according to changes of time and place. Muḥammad b. Makkī, known as al-Shahīd al-Awwal (d. 1384), has maintained that it is acceptable that the ordinances should change in tandem with circumstances and customs.[95] He mentions several examples to support his statement. For example, he cites the amount of maintenance that is due a divorced woman. He maintains that the amount has not been fixed in the Tradition. If there is any reference in this matter in some traditions, it is based on the customs of that society. In another instance, Shahīd al-Awwal mentions a claim that a woman makes about not having received her bridal gift (*mahar*). It was customary during the days of the Imams that women received their bridal gift before the marriage was consummated. Therefore, she could claim that she had not received her gift, but she had to provide evidence. In later periods, when Shahīd al-Awwal was writing his corpus, the custom changed. Women at this time did not claim any right to the bridal gift until after the marriage was consummated. Thus, if they claimed that they had not received their gift, the burden of the proof was on the man to show that he had given it. This shows that with the change of custom the ordinance also changed. Such an explanation by Shahīd al-Awwal resembles the arguments made by the Sunni jurists who maintain the validity of custom as one of the important sources for rulings. The Shāfiʿī-Sunni jurist Jalāl al-Dīn al-Suyūṭī (d. 1505) regards custom as one of the five major sources for rulings mentioned in the Tradition.[96] Among the Shīʿite jurists, from time to time, one finds that leeway was given for the precedence of necessity over traditional rules in the following matters:

1. Forcing the merchant who hoards to sell his goods as ruled by Muḥaqqiq al-Ḥillī.[97]
2. Giving the ruler the discretion to fix the amount of poll tax as he saw fit. This ruling is reported in the Sunni and Shīʿite sources. Muḥaqqiq

mentions the ruling and adds that the poll tax 'Alī had fixed was specific to his time.[98]

3. Making it mandatory on a husband to pay spousal maintenance. Shaykh al-Ṭūsī (d. 1068) has ruled to this effect.[99]
4. Giving legal authority to a qualified jurist to dissolve the marriage of a woman whose husband has disappeared beyond the accepted waiting period.

Aside from these instances there are many cases whose resolution is governed by custom. These cases show the evolution of the legal-ethical decisions and their connection to the period and place in which they occurred. In the modern period Ayatollah Khomeini's legal thought has been foundational in acknowledging time and place and admitting custom (*al-'urf*) as a valid source in reaching rulings that are relevant to the everyday life of people.[100] He states most explicitly that time and place are two most important elements in defining the scope of the independent reasoning of a jurist. The change of circumstances in people's social and economic life forces the jurist to take into consideration the circumstances of the period in which the earlier legal-ethical decision was formulated. Khomeini takes up the question of ownership and its limitations, land and its distribution, public wealth and its protection, new financial structures, exchange and banking, foreign and domestic trade, cultural issues, environmental issues, biomedical issues connected with organ transplantation and related matters, women's participation in public life, individual freedoms and responsibilities in the context of nation building, and so on. All these and numerous other issues have been tackled by Khomeini with due care based on the following considerations:

1. Cultural change in modern times leading to a search for new principles and stretching the already existent intellectual sources of legal decision making.
2. The need to make relevant decisions that speak to the everyday needs of the people living under completely changed circumstances.
3. The creation of new social and cultural institutions based on the public good and new ways of organizing modern society.

Since most ethical decisions in bioethics represent general moral considerations related to the principle of public good in its ordinary sense (that is, the obligation to seek and promote good [*manfa'a*] and prevent and remove evil [*maḍarra*]), I have begun by discussing this principle and its subsidiary principles and rules. Overall, the principle includes obligations not to harm others, including not killing them or treating them cruelly, obligations to take full account of proportionality in order to produce a net balance of benefits over harm, and obligations to honor contractual agreements. Islamic bioethics regards this principle of beneficence and nonmaleficence as central in the

Islamic conceptions of health care. More importantly, the moral duty to work for the common good of society renders the subsidiary twin principle of beneficence and rejection of harm as the derivatives of the fundamental doctrine of rational good and evil, accessible to all reasonable people. The theological justification for the principle derives its validity from the doctrine that all God's acts are founded upon specific purposes. Since it is inconceivable that God's purpose can be evil, responsibility for the act with a purpose other than beneficence reverts to the human agent. All human actions are undertaken with a purpose to either promote the benefit or avert the harm of the agent. In both cases the benefit or harm could be connected to this or the next world. Religious ordinances in Islam are derived on the basis of assessing benefit and harm. Each religious ordinance that has a major purpose connected with the next world, whether it promotes benefit or prevents harm, is known as *'ibāda* ("service to God"); whereas any religious ordinance that has a major purpose connected with this world, regardless whether it promotes benefit and prevents harm, or whether promotion of the benefit and prevention of harm are related primarily or secondarily to this worldly purpose, is known as *mu'āmala* ("social transaction"). These purposes connected with the necessities of life are five in number: life, religion, reason, lineage, and property. In fact, all religious ordinances are directly connected to these five necessities, which are indirectly linked to politics and the administration of justice.

The Rule of "No Harm, No Harassment"

The rule of "No harm, no harassment" (*lā ḍarar wa lā ḍirār fī al-islām*) is regarded as one of the most fundamental rules for deducing rulings dealing with social ethics in Islam. While Shī'ite jurists have discussed and debated the validity of this principle because it is regarded as one of the critical proofs in support of numerous decisions that were made in different periods of juridical development, Sunni jurists have limited their juridical discussion to the tradition, which is the source of their reference to the principle of public good (*maṣlaḥa*) in their legal deliberations. The importance of the rule is underscored by its serving as a justificatory principle among all jurists to deduce fresh rulings. Moreover, what makes the rule authentic is its ascription to the Prophet himself. Jurists belonging to different legal schools are in agreement that the rule was set by no less a person than the founder of Islam.[101] For example, Sulaymān b. 'Abd al-Qawī al-Ṭūfī (d. 1316), the Ḥanbalī legal theorist, in providing the justification for the principle of the public good, affirms the ascription of the tradition on "No harm, no harassment" to the prophet and regards it as one of the most important sources in the area of social transactions.[102] Hence, whether from the point of transmission or from the congruity in the sense conveyed by it, the jurists have endorsed its admission among the rules that are employed in making decisions that pertain to the social and political life of the community. In fact, the Shāfi'i-Sunni jurist al-Suyūṭī regards "No harm, no harassment" as one of the five major traditions that served as authoritative sources for the derivation of the rules on which depended the deduction of legal-ethical decisions in the Sharī'a.[103] In addition, he affirms that the majority of juridical rubrics were founded on the principle of "No harm, no harassment," and that closely related to this principle are a number of other rules, among them this one: "Necessities make the forbidden permissible, as long as it does not lead to any detriment."[104] However, Shī'ite jurists have taken up the rule in their works on legal theory, analyzing it in much detail to render it as one of the foundational principles in social ethics. In what follows, I have basically followed the theoretical exposition of the rule by Shī'ite jurists, with a clear emphasis that there is a consensus among all Sunni and Shī'ite jurists that the principle serves as a major source for resolving contemporary issues in medical practice.

According to Shahīd al-Awwal, "No harm, no harassment" is among the five major rules that shaped the new rulings in the area of interpersonal relations. These are as follows:

1. "Action depends upon intention." This rule is deduced from the tradition related by the Prophet: "Indeed, actions depend upon intentions."
2. "Hardship necessitates relief." This rule is inferred from the tradition that says: "No harm should be inflicted or reciprocated."
3. "One needs certainty." To continue an action requires linking the present situation with the past. This rule is rationally deduced on the basis of a juristic practice that links present doubtful condition to the previously held certain situation to resolve the case.
4. "Harm must be rejected." This rule is deduced on the basis of the need to promote benefit and institute it in order to remove causes of corruption or reduce their impact upon the possibility of having to choose the lesser of the two evils.
5. "Custom determines course of action." The rule acknowledges the need to take local custom into account when making relevant rulings.[105]

Defining the Rule of "No Harm, No Harassment"

There are two key terms in the rule that require careful examination. Both these terms have implications for its application in deriving ethical-legal judgments. The first term in the famous tradition that I have translated as "harm" is *ḍarar*. Its lexical meaning consists of "detriment, loss," the opposite of "benefit." The term connotes any detriment or loss suffered by a person to himself, his property, dignity, or personal interest. Moreover, whether intentional or unintentional, it is an act committed by one person against another. The second term is *ḍirār* which I have translated as "harassment." Its lexical meaning conveys "harming, injuring, or hurting in return." According to some lexicographers, it is synonymous with *ḍarar* and is added in the tradition as a corroborative. However, the precise translation of the rule based on the lexical sense of the two key terms is as follows: "There shall be no harming, injuring or hurting, of one man by another, in the first instance, nor in return, or requital."[106]

The next part of the tradition that needs clarification is the negative particle *lā*. The particle "no" negates a thing and connotes absence of that thing which it negates. In a sentence like "There is no man in the house," the negation rules out the possibility of such existence in that house. However, this type of negation is not intended in this tradition, because we know that harm does exist in the world and people do experience it in their everyday contact with one another. It is for this reason that jurists have endeavored to give reasons for the negation of harm in this tradition. Certainly, in this case, the negation does not mean absence; it simply means that one should not inflict harm or evil, which is the result of a specific, unjustified, intentional or unintentional action committed by one party to another. Taken in this sense, the negation communicates that any command by the sacred lawgiver must be free of harm in its execution. For instance, if taking certain kinds of medication proves to be detrimental, then, according to this rule, it is obligatory to stop taking it even though it is normally considered curative or beneficial. In other words, the negation is actually applied to the ruling about harm, which is omitted in the tradition by the Prophet. Thus interpreted, the negative command should read, "There shall be no [ruling that will lead to] harming of one man to another."

However, others have pointed out, perhaps correctly, that the negation actually has a bearing on the final judgment that incorporates the subject of harm. It resembles the negation in the following: "The one who doubts too often must ignore the doubting because his doubt is no doubt at all." Since the person experiences constant doubt, this situation produces a changed negative ruling, requiring the person to ignore his/her doubt, based on the harm that is caused by frequent doubt. Another way of putting this is to consider the ruling that says: "It is obligatory for a physician to administer medication when a patient is ill." However, if for some reason giving that treatment causes more harm than good, then the obligation to administer that medicine will change to prohibition. Accordingly, the negative command in the Prophet's tradition would read, "There shall be no [adopting of a course of action that leads to] harming of one man to another." In other words, the negation in the tradition applies to a course of action that might cause harm. The situation determines the course of action. Hence, in the above example, it is not the ruling that requires administering the medication that is negated; rather the situation that causes harm is negated.[107]

In the light of the above, one can say that the negative particle in the tradition does not convey prohibition; it conveys rejection. Moreover, the harm is not limited to the person of the agent; it is general and inclusive of all kinds of harm, including violating someone's rights or causing a setback to someone's justifiable interests. In addition, one can conclude that the tradition unmistakably conveys that harm has no legitimacy in Islam. The Prophet's statement explicitly forbids and removes harm from any consideration. Hence, the statement sets up the laws that provide protection from harm in all aspects of human interaction, more particularly, in those instances where one person's action may cause harm to another.

More importantly, the rule impinges on all primary obligations, which under certain situations become suspended because of the harm that accrues to the agent and to others in society. Since "No harm, no harassment" functions both as a principle and a source for the rule that states "hardship necessitates relief," it connotes that there can be no legislation, promulgation, or execution of any law that leads to the harm of anyone in society. For that reason, in derivation of a legal-ethical judgment the rule is given priority over all primary obligations in the Sharī'a. In fact, it functions as a check on all other ordinances to make sure that their fulfillment does not lead to harm. In the case of dispute in any situation, the final resolution is derived by applying the rule of "No harm, no harassment." For instance, the primary obligation of seeking medical treatment becomes prohibited if it aggravates the affliction suffered under certain medical conditions.

It is important to keep in mind that "No harm, no harassment" functions most effectively when a rule that recognizes the absolute "right of discretion" (*taslīṭ*) of an owner over all his possessions is in competition with the "No harm" rule. Simply stated, the problem is how to protect the owner's interests when exercising one party's discretion leads to thwarting another's interests. In situations in which the lack of owner's discretion may harm his interests, the jurists bypass the rule of "No harm" and simply adhere to the rule of "Right of discretion." However, if one party's overriding discretion leads to hindering another's interests, then the jurists are faced with competing and conflicting interests. In such a case, admitting the "Rule of discretion" to the exclusion of the rule of "No harm" actually results in promoting the owner's interests only. If this occurs, some jurists prioritize the "Rule of discretion" in order to rule in favor of the owner's right to promote his legitimate interests. At the same time, the rule of "No harm" also becomes pertinent in promoting the owner's interests by considering the probable harm that can occur if the right of discretion is denied.

For instance, a person has a right of discretion over his bodily organs and can decide to donate a kidney to save someone's life. However, if he were to do that without any consideration of the harm this may cause to his personal health, this right of discretion can be restricted by the rule of "No harm." On the other hand, if the right of discretion is invoked for the legitimate objective of saving, for example, the life of one's own child, and even if there is a probability of causing harm to oneself, the rule of the "Right of discretion" prevails over the rule of "No harm." In a large number of complicated clinical cases, because the prognosis of the treatment is not always predictable with certainty, the jurists tend to give priority to the rule of "No harm"; they avoid applying the rule of "Right of discretion." However, if exercising one party's discretion (donating a kidney) thwarts another's interests (an entire family might suffer if any harm were to befall the donor), then admitting the "Right of discretion" to the exclusion of the principle of "No harm" actually results in promoting the owner's interests. In such cases some jurists have given precedence to the "Right of discretion," thereby favoring the owner's right to promote his legitimate interests. The rule of "No harm" indirectly becomes pertinent in promoting the agent's interests by taking into account the probable harm that can occur if the right of discretion is denied (e.g., donating a kidney to one's child). Moreover, the application of the rule about the owner's absolute discretion becomes necessary in situations where it is obvious that the lack of the agent's discretion may cause harm to his interests. Hence, in the first instance, exercise of discretion promotes the agent's legitimate interests, whereas in the second instance, it thwarts his legitimate interests, thereby causing harm.

One more instance of competing interests is a case in which the owner exercises his discretion without any justification to promote or prevent benefit. He simply undertakes something for amusement. Here the rule of "No harm" becomes preponderant in providing the ruling, regardless whether that action causes or reciprocates harm. Actually the tradition that bears the rule narrates a story of a man who had a legitimate right to pass through his own property in order to get into the garden where the neighbor's house was located. But this passing through, done frequently and even in the exercise of his own discretion over his property, invaded the privacy of his neighbor, making it uncomfortable for that family. The case was referred to the Prophet for judgment because the owner of the property refused to comply with simple courtesy of announcing his arrival before entering the garden. Several alternative solutions were presented to the owner, which he turned down by the mere fact of his claim to the right of discretion. Hence, the Prophet sidestepped the "Right of discretion" and pointed to the fact of harm caused by this intrusion in the privacy of the neighbor, setting the precedent that prompted the exercise of the principle of "No harm, no harassment." In other words, the rule of "Right of discretion" in this story is made ineffective by "No harm" because exercise of discretion is restricted by consideration of harm and harassment. Any unreasonable exercise of discretion, which neither promotes nor thwarts the agent's interests, is forbidden. But who defines what is reasonable or unreasonable in the matter of the exercise of discretion? At this point, custom and culture provide the guidelines.

In the Sharī'a, the definition of harm and harassment in a negative sense depends upon custom (*al-'urf*), which determines its parameters. Custom also establishes whether harm to oneself or to another party has been done in a given situation. If custom does not construe a matter to be harmful, then it cannot be admitted as such by applying the rule itself, nor can it be considered as forbidden according to the Sharīʿa, even if the matter is lexically designated as "harmful." It is important to keep in mind that ultimately it is the sacred lawgiver who defines the parameters of harm. However, if custom regards as harmful something for which revelation offers no specific evidence against, the harm in that situation becomes more broadly defined as conditions that lead to injustice and the violation of someone's rights. Moreover, harms differ as to who is causing the harm, as with self-harm and harm caused by another party. Hence, one's social status, culture, and the time in which one lives play a role in defining harm. Harm is relative to the person who experiences it. Therefore, what appears to be wrong *prima facie* and is regarded by one party as a harmful act may not be considered wrong or unjustified by another. Human experience, although subjective, attains considerable importance in the evaluation of the kind of harm that is to be rejected in the rule of "No harm, no harassment." The context in which the Prophet gave the rule clearly leaves the matter of harm to be determined by the situation. In the report that speaks about the harm caused by an inconsiderate neighbor who violated the privacy of his neighbor, it was a case of harmful invasion by one party of another's interest. To be sure, the rule of "No harm, no harassment" allows for the ruling that one must not become a cause for harm.[108]

The application of the ruling to reject harm has no bearing on the assessment of the actual situation when a person is going through setbacks to his interests. Nor does the lawgiver's admission of harm in certain situations as a contributing cause for some rulings that require reparation or compensation. In the final analysis, it is the personal assessment of harm that functions as an important consideration in determining related obligations. Hence, for instance, when a person is sick, she determines whether she can keep the fast of Ramadan as required by the Sharīʿa in consideration of the harm that fasting can cause. Regardless of the criteria one applies to determine the level of harm, whether it is less or more, once custom establishes its existence, then the Sharīʿa endorses it as equally so, even when there might be a difference of opinion as to what forms of harm are more detrimental. In any case, when such a difference of opinion occurs, the law requires following the decision that leads to least harm and that causes the least damage to one's total well-being.

A number of subsidiary rules are related to the rule "No harm, no harassment," including the second rule, "Hardship necessitates relief," which becomes almost part of this rule. In addition, a number of traditions and verses of the Qur'an are cited to support its admission as a source of legal-ethical decision-making in order to seek benefits and avert sources of harm, or to choose the lesser of two plausible evils. In general, Muslim jurists mention subsidiary rules in various other contexts dealing with interpersonal relations to correlate the establishment of good with the prevention of malevolence. Moreover, they provide guidelines that govern situations in which a person has to choose between two evils that appear to be equal, or a situation in which one of the two equal evils has preponderance because of external or internal causes. It is important to keep in mind that although the jurists do not mention or allude to any traditions in support of the rule directly, in different contexts of applying the five rules they assert that these are figured out on the basis of the four principal sources of Islamic jurisprudence: the Qur'an, the Tradition, consensus, and arguments based on reason.[109] Moreover, some jurists justify the rule "Hardship necessitates relief" on the basis of the same tradition that sets up the rule "No harm, no harassment," that is, "No harm shall be inflicted nor reciprocated."[110]

However, the question remains as to when the rule can be promoted to the status of a principle that had wider application in matters related to social ethics. The problem in applying the rule was connected with the determination of actual harm. Was this harm objective enough to overcome subjective assumptions about it? As discussed above, the tradition uses the word "harm" in its broadest sense to include any setback suffered by a person, whether physical or psychological. Hence, in the case of terminally ill patient, if the medical decision to prolong life leads to more harm for the patient and his immediate family, then to start him on life-saving equipment is regarded as causing further harm to the patient's and his family's well-being and hence is forbidden. However, once the person is already on the life-saving equipment, then stopping the treatment is non-permissible unless the prognosis is based on certainty. At the same time, the human experience of harm is key to its actual assessment as such. However, there is evidence in the juridical assessment of the concept that suggests that even when certain acts appear *prima facie* to be wrong and unjustifiable, it is not possible to attach absolute meaning to them. Obviously, there are acts that are regarded as being detrimental, which stop being so as soon as their negative aspect is overcome. This was particularly true in matters that dealt with acts that were classified as being harmful in the area of both God-human and interhuman relationships.[111] Following this difficulty in determining its reality as harmful, there was another difficulty arising from consideration that the divine lawgiver does not legislate anything harmful to people. In other words, God does not require people to do anything that would necessitate inflicting harm on oneself or on others. There are two verses in the Qur'an that refer to the rule as a negative injunction, in the situation related to conflict between two harms or between harm and benefit, and the lawgiver's giving preponderance to the weightier among them: "They will question you concerning wine and arrow-shuffling. Say: 'In both is heinous sin (*ithm*), and uses (*manāfi'*) for men, but the sin in them is more heinous than the usefulness'" (Q. 2:219) and "If it had not been for certain men believers and certain women believers whom you know not, lest you should trample them, and there befall you guilt unwittingly on their account. . . ."(Q. 48:25) These two passages are interpreted to convey the negative injunction against inflicting or reciprocating harm. There is no normative ranking proposed in them. In cases of conflict, not harming is given preponderance, but the guidelines vary with circumstances, providing no a priori rule that requires avoiding harm over providing benefit. They simply require weighing an action in a circumstance of conflict in terms of its potential for preventing and removing harm and promoting good.

Some Shīʿite jurists regard the tradition that states the rule "No harm, no harassment" as the source for a juristic principle. They report several other traditions that speak about negation of harm in all matters related to human interaction to support this view.[112] In fact, as these scholars maintain, since the tradition "No harm, no harassment" is reported by all schools of thought among Muslims, it should be accorded the status of one of the most important principles (*aṣl*) that is a source of a large number of ordinances regarding intersubjective relationships.[113]

Other Shīʿite scholars have permitted carving out a precedent by including the rule about rejection of harm in their discussion about legal theory. They have afforded it a prominence that is enjoyed by other principal sources like the Qur'an and the Tradition in deriving new rulings. The question of compensation looms large in the rulings that regard the person causing harm as being responsible for providing appropriate compensation. Once legal authority establishes that harm has occurred, the application of a rule that relieves a person of responsibility for compensating the victim becomes pointless, especially when the person is definitely responsible for causing the harm and the payment of compensation. Using a rational argument, these jurists have contended that it is reasonable and even natural to expect the person who has caused the harm to another be held responsible for the compensation. In fact, both causing harm and reciprocating it require restitution in the Sharīʿa. In other words, one cannot escape paying the compensation by resorting to the rule of "Relief from responsibility" when the rule of "No harm" holds one responsible for compensation. In line with the necessity to compensate the victim of harm, some Shīʿite jurists have ruled that although causing any kind of harm to oneself or to another person is forbidden, one should definitely avoid those harms in which the victim cannot be compensated, as specified in the sacred law. The responsibility to compensate in cases of harm and harassment is ingrained in human nature and confirmed by the sacred lawgiver, who has not ruled anything that might cause harm without taking into consideration due compensation. For various situations in which an agent might suffer a setback to his interests the Sharīʿa has determined a fixed level of compensation. And, in situations that are not covered there, the Sharīʿa has permitted a fair settlement through arbitration as long as the validity of the claim is indisputable.[114]

In sum, most jurists have accepted the rule of "No harm, no harassment" as being one of the principal sources of legal-ethical decision-making. Some others have regarded the rule being closely related to another rule that states, "No constriction, no distress," regardless of whether constriction or distress is caused by God or by human being. They mention three significations of the tradition "No harm, no harassment":

1. It simply signifies the proscription (*al-nahy*).
2. It simply signifies proscription of harm without compensation.
3. It means that God does not wish harm for his creatures, neither from him nor from human beings.

The third meaning is regarded as being closest to what the tradition denotes and to what reason and the practice of the community indicate. Many jurists base their decisions on the "No harm, no harassment" rule. They also mention the traditions that support the use of this principle in the juristic method of deduction. "No harm, no harassment" is a well-established enduring principle, validated by long-standing traditions and the practice of scholars, who have viewed it as a valuable aid for promoting tolerance and averting social harm and hardship.

An obligation not to inflict harm (*nafy al-ḍarar*) has been closely associated in Muslim ethics with an obligation to promote good (*istiṣlāḥ*). As a matter of fact, obligations of nonmaleficence and beneficence are treated under a single principle, *istiṣlāḥ* (promoting good). Obligations to promote good cannot be fulfilled without taking stringent measures not to harm others, including not killing them or treating them cruelly; without fulfilling one's obligations to take full account of proportionality in order to produce net balance of benefits over harms; and without fulfilling one's obligations to honor contractual agreements. Accordingly, Islamic bioethics regards the principle of "No harm, no harassment" as central to the Islamic conceptions of health care. It is for this reason that there is constant evaluation of the situation to prioritize obligations of preventing harm in order to make a final ethical decision. In cases of conflict between probable harm and probable benefit, each individual case of such a conflict requires careful weighing of the rule that states, "Preventing or removing harm has a priority over promoting good." To be sure, the principle of "No harm, no harassment" has as its source in both the revelation and reason. Reasonable people are capable of recognizing the sources of good life in the sacred texts and human intellect.

However, whether the obligation not to inflict harm can be regarded as one of the principles or rules of the bioethical system is contested by the Muslim jurists. To be sure, even the rationalist-objectivists, that is, the Shī'ites and the Sunni-Mu'tazilites, who regard human reason to be the sole judge in determining harm or benefit, have debated the centrality of this obligation in ethical deliberations in all fields of human interaction, including biomedical conditions.

In almost 90 percent of cases confronting healthcare providers in the Muslim world, the issue of inflicting or reciprocating harm is at the heart of the ethical deliberations. In the cases studied for the present work, the jurists almost unanimously provided reasons for their rulings based on the obligation not to inflict harm. For example, in the rulings against human cloning, most jurists refer to the infliction of harm on the well-being of an offspring who would be deprived of normal parentage, regarded as a necessary condition for the healthy upbringing of a child. Or in the rulings against population control through abortion, the references all point to the harm that could be done to the moral fabric of society through the legalization of abortion.

As a subsidiary rule, "Preventing harm has a priority over promoting good" also provides the jurists with the principle of proportionality. This principle is a source for the careful analysis of harm and benefit when, for example, a medical procedure prolongs the life of a terminally ill patient without advancing a long-term cure. The principle also allows for reasoned choices about appropriate benefits in proportion to costs and risks for not only the patients but also their family. It is well known that in many complicated cases, decisions about the most effective medical treatments are based on probable benefits and harms for the patients and their families. Islamic bioethics requires that medical professionals and healthcare providers ascertain the implications of a given course of medical procedure for a patient's and the patient's family's overall well-being by fully accounting for the probable harm or benefit. The principle of "no harm, no harassment" thus is critical in clinical settings where procedural decisions need to be made in consultation with all parties to a case and with a sense of humility in the presence of God: There is nothing for humans to do but to strive to do their best.

3

Health and Suffering

No affliction befalls, except it be by the leave of God. Whosoever believes in God, he will guide his heart. And God has the knowledge of everything.

—Qur'an 64:12

The problem of suffering in the context of death and disease is an existential rather than a theological problem. All religions have responded to the question of suffering as a form of evil, in both its moral and physical manifestations. But the challenge of physical suffering as a form of teleological evil, with its psychological and cultural overtones, has loomed large among healthcare professionals, who often face patients who are seeking to understand why they have been subjected to such pain. A closer look at the ways a cultural-religious tradition handles moral and physical evil might aid in the quest to understand the reasons for human suffering and pain.

Moral evil is an instance of intentional ill will or wrongdoing perpetrated by a free human agent—or agents—that results in some harm or violation either to the agent, to an entity external to the agent, or both. In such cases the responsibility rests with the individual(s) who willfully committed the act. The act may give rise to an inner existential struggle with pangs of conscience occasioned by the violation of some moral standard. Such bouts of remorse are often attended by feelings of sin and guilt that may strike the evildoer as the retributive or punitive measures of a superior power that mysteriously controls human destiny.

Physical or natural evils, on the other hand—for example epidemics, storms, and earthquakes—arise from physical, biological, or even social causes but are not instigated by a human agent. Most religious traditions regard illness, whether individual or collective (e.g., great epidemics), as a kind of physical evil, experienced as an aggression from mysterious sources over which individuals have no control. In contrast, a disease or debility resulting from bad habits—such as a heart attack caused by overeating or an injury suffered because of reckless driving—is considered an instance of both moral and physical evil, combining personal culpability with circumstances beyond human control.

In Islam, naturally caused evil is a grim reminder of human fragility and mortality, whether the source of misfortune is an external power like God or the internal agency of human fallibility. The suffering that attends such natural or physical evils is often regarded as some sort of divine punishment, a divinely sanctioned evil inflicted to teach humanity in general—as opposed to a particular person—a lesson in humility. By contrast, the guilt and suffering that attend the evil perpetrated by a free human agent are often viewed as the just deserts of the wrongdoer. Here the correlation is drawn between the freely committed evil and the personal suffering endured by the human author of the evil.

Because suffering can result from either natural or moral evil, we are obliged to examine the concept of good health in Islam, especially insofar as this is regarded as part of a person's obligation to avoid undue pain and suffering. The Arabic word *ṣiḥḥa* ("sound" or "health") is rich in connotations. Like the word *salāma* (also "sound" or "health"), it conveys the wholeness and integrity of a being that generates a sense of security. Further, it connotes a life of balance and moderation that avoids behavioral extremes. Disturbing this balance of *ṣiḥḥa* causes a physical ailment. The Qur'an lays down the golden rule about moderation: "O children of Adam, . . . eat and drink the good things you desire, but do not become wasteful" (Q. 7:31). Imbalance or overindulgence in the enjoyment of God's bounty will lead to both physical and moral suffering. In the moral sense, human volition may result in the overconsumption of certain foods because of sensual indulgence rather than attention to good health. The Prophet is reported to have advised his disciples to avoid overeating and recommended that one stop eating before feeling full.[1] Another tradition traces all sickness to a lack of moderation in eating. On this view, physical or psychological conditions beyond one's own control dictate lifestyle adjustments in the interests of physical well-being.

The Qur'an, as we shall see below, prescribes the pursuit of self-knowledge as a part of maintaining good health. Physical and psychological health cannot be taken for granted—they are a divine benefaction that depends on human moderation in food and drink and regular physical activities, including swimming and horse riding, as the Prophet instructed his followers.[2] Yet there are people who suffer from illnesses that are genetically inherited, in which case they have exercised no choice whatsoever. It is this kind of suffering that raises questions about God's will and the existence of evil in the world. Who is the actual author of this suffering? Is it God's determination? Or do human choices somehow play a role? And, as a human endures suffering, what is the role of faith in God and the belief in the hereafter, the final abode of all humans, where there is freedom from all pain and suffering?

These troublesome questions constitute a major challenge to the belief in God's justice and goodness. Muslims, like other peoples of faith, have struggled to reconcile God's omnipotence with the persistent evils of the world, including the pain and suffering that attend illness. I do not wish to treat the problem of theodicy beyond the context of Islamic biomedical ethics. Moreover, the purpose of raising the issue of suffering in the context of disease and death is not to provide a definitive solution to the problem, nor is it to absolve God of responsibility for evil by granting it a separate ontological status. My objective in this chapter is to demonstrate the importance of understanding religious and cultural attitudes among Muslims that influence their choices in healthcare and medical treatment. None of the recently published works on Islamic biomedical ethics have addressed the relationship between theology and medicine in Islam to probe the sociological and psychological dimensions of the problem of suffering as it relates to a bioethical principle such as, "No harm, no harassment." This principle, as discussed in the last chapter, has become the major source of bioethical decisions in the Muslim community and obliges an active response to unparalleled medical advancements in prolonging the lifespan of terminally ill patients.

Given the predominance of a strong theological belief in predestination among the majority of Sunni Muslims, it is refreshing to observe a transformation from thoroughgoing fatalism to choice-oriented human action. This shift from the hardcore deterministic orthodoxy to naturalist-rationalist theology is subtle, yet noticeable in the areas of biomedical ethics and human rights. The classical notions of resignation and submission in the face of death and suffering have yielded to a growing awareness of the possibilities offered by modern medicine. In addition, modern education, with its assertive operational agnostic culture, has minimized the influence of superstitious beliefs about the human body and its ailments; yet, even today the perceived impact of hidden maleficent powers still plagues large sectors of Muslim rural populations that lack access to adequate healthcare facilities.

Suffering in Religious Thought

People with different backgrounds approach suffering with a wide range of deeply entrenched cultural and religious attitudes about its causes and consequences. Sometimes these attitudes undermine the efficacy of treatments that require the patient to summon the will to fight the disease. A holistic medical approach, which treats both psychosomatic and physical conditions, obliges clinicians to be aware of the patient's emotional condition and cultural background in order to formulate an accurate diagnosis and successful treatment plan.[3] What should the healthcare worker know about a Muslim patient's religious and moral presuppositions about the nature of suffering?

Promoting such sensitivity to the patient's presuppositions requires an investigation of illness viewed as a form of evil. Such an inquiry should seek to furnish objective criteria by which serious medical conditions are perceived as evil. Such criteria will enable healthcare providers and ethicists to understand, articulate, and address preconceptions that foster despair and loss of confidence in the fight against life-threatening diseases. Usually a situation that is negatively described as evil refers to an objective state of affairs ("It is unbearable!") and the subjective response ("It is harmful for the patient!") of a judging individual. In other words, assessing suffering as a form of evil, either objectively or subjectively, requires a recognition of the agent, the act of suffering, and any potential harm, all of which can influence a positive or privative understanding of evil. When both subjective and objective elements are present in an illness, the resulting suffering is sometimes deemed to be undesirable and maleficent. Both physically and morally, such judgments posit an objective standard that can be tragically harmful to the agent, quite apart from any reference to any ontology or complex metaphysical or theological explanation.

I regard this to be the meeting point for religious and medical views of illness—the point at which the metaphysical and physical dimensions of medical care come to terms with the human condition and the limitations of human endeavors to alleviate suffering. The difference between the religious and medical assessment of the situation is stark. Whereas religion teaches humility and reveals human limitations in comprehending the ways of the powerful God who gives and takes life, medicine, taking the responsibility for removing the evil of pain and suffering, seeks a cure or at least a prolongation of life, irrespective of the wishes or intentions of any divine agency. This stark difference is further underscored by the religious approach to illness, which inculcates faith in God's goodness and an acceptance of suffering as part of the overall divine plan for humanity's spiritual and moral development. Medicine, on the other hand, displaces God and empowers humanity to take charge of its destiny, to seek to overcome suffering rather than to passively accept it as a divinely ordained fate. Religion emphasizes the finitude of human life and reminds humanity not to defy God's will to take life at a predetermined time known to God alone. In contrast, medicine today seemingly unburdens God by taking the entire responsibility for determining a patient's lifespan through technological intervention. The everyday human condition, as witnessed by all of us at one time or another, is too concrete to deny as we see our loved ones departing this life, having suffered untold misery, loneliness, and vulnerability, while the medical team struggles to save that life. In the traditional view, when the time comes for the person to depart, then she has to leave everything behind: family, wealth, and status: "All that dwells upon the earth shall perish; except the face of thy Lord, majestic and splendid" (Q. 55:26).

The reality of human suffering and the endeavors to overcome that suffering make religion and medicine partners in serving humanity. Hence, religion and medicine must work together in understanding moments of suffering and death and collaborate in providing explanations for those who are especially troubled by the suffering of the innocent. Throughout recorded history religious leaders and medical practitioners have collaborated in trying to understand why human beings suffer. This quest to explain suffering is rooted in the human mind's inherent tendency to question the discrepancy between the ideal and the real, especially in glaring cases such as the suffering of children and the poor, or the prosperity of the wicked. Such meditations have given rise to theodicy, the attempt to justify the omnipotence of God in the face of earthly evil and suffering.

Medical science seeks to cure or attenuate the illnesses that cause pain and suffering. The relief of human suffering through curing and healing is the main justification for investing large sums of money in healthcare institutions. Because all humans will experience illness at some point in their lives, both physicians and nurses are obliged to approach suffering with the requisite cultural-religious sensitivity. Modern bioethics, deeply rooted in the dominant intellectual culture marked by a radical reduction of the religious to the moral, tends to ignore theological questions connected with understanding the evil of human suffering, whether divinely ordained or humanly acquired. For a bioethics rooted in a religious or sacred tradition such as Islam, ethical issues are bound up with God's will. While both secular and religious bioethics seek to reduce pain within ethical boundaries, religious bioethics goes further in nurturing hope and trust in God in the face of incurable illness. Hence, in the case of physician-assisted suicide, while both secular and religious ethicists object to PAS as a resolution of human suffering, religion raises a fundamental question about granting such prerogatives to humans, who are viewed as stewards rather than owners of their bodies. Some objections to physician-assisted suicide are prudential: PAS may compromise the public's confidence in the doctor's healing role. Humanitarian treatment of terminally ill patients is a deeply ingrained aspect of religious traditions of compassion and mercy. Accordingly, biomedical ethics dovetails with a religious tradition in a way that should promote greater understanding between secular medical science and theodicy, which recognizes death as a station on the path toward eternal life.

Understanding suffering is central to Islamic bioethics. In Muslim theology, human suffering in any form raises the question of God's knowledge of and power over human beings. The belief in God's omnipotence is the most important idea in Muslim theology. Muslim theologians differentiate between God's attributes of essence and action. Unity of God is an essential attribute (*ṣifa dhātīya*) of the divine being; whereas God's power and justice are part of God's attributes of action (*ṣifa fi'līya*) that impact upon human well-being. What raises serious questions about human suffering, consequently, reverts to the doctrine of divine omnipotence and justice rather than to God's unity. God is the creator of all things, including human destiny (*qadar*) on earth and rewards and punishments in the hereafter. Such a deterministic concept of human action gives rise to the problem of reconciling divine predetermination of human action with divine justice, which entails God's punishment of the wicked and his rewarding of the righteous. This aspect of the problem of theodicy, as I will show presently, arose out of statements from the Qur'an and the Tradition. In the context of health care, the idea of God's omnipotence has enormous implications, breeding a quietism that discourages the ill from prying into God's unfathomable ways and encourages resignation to suffering.[4] With modern medicine's enormous strides in healing the sick and alleviating suffering, the inexorability of God's decrees provides little comfort to those who want to see an end to agonies of incurable diseases.

Muslim theologians have striven to comprehend the rationale of the suffering of innocents—for instance, of children and even animals. Explanations of the suffering of bad people, even though unconvincing, have been easier because of the evident link between sin as cause and suffering as effect. But how, then, does one account for the suffering of innocent children? There will be ample opportunity to discuss the suffering of children in the chapter on reproductive technologies and genetics and the unprecedented devaluation of defective fetuses. At this point, I will discuss general responses offered by Muslim theologians.

Some readers may be looking for an "official" Islamic position on doctrinal matters that bear on medical practice. In the absence of an officially organized and recognized theological body such as the Vatican Council in Catholicism, it is important to keep in mind that such an "official" position is nothing more than a provisional claim. It is not helpful for outside observers to think of Islamic opinions in monolithic terms on any theological or ethical matter.[5] In fact, plurality in matters of belief and practice is inherent in Islam, which, like Rabbinical Judaism, invests the power of interpretation and decision-making not in an institution like a church but in the experts of religious-juridical matters, the ulema. Hence, for the sake of brevity and clarity in expounding Muslim views on health and suffering, I will not dwell on distinguishing views as being strictly Sunni or Shī'ite. As we shall see in this chapter, it is not unusual to find contrary views about freedom of will and predetermination within a single school of thought. Moreover, although it is not impossible to identify certain theological trends as being generally espoused by the Sunnis or Shī'ites, it is misleading to insist on their dogmatic uniformity, even within the same school. Though it is common to describe the Sunni position on human suffering as being predeterminist, the Sunni-Mu'tazilites believed in human responsibility for suffering. My sole purpose in clarifying Muslim theological positions is to speak to medical practitioners and remind them to attend to a patient's beliefs as an integral part of the healing process; the Muslim views of God's justice matters to their practice. In addition, I speak to Muslim theologians and encourage them to continue working on theodicy questions, for they are not merely speculative concerns.

Suffering in Arabic Lexicon and Thought

The Arabic word *muṣība*, which connotes suffering or affliction caused by events that lead to some form of harm or loss (*ḍarr or ḍurr*), relates to Muslim beliefs about the omnipotence and omniscience of God. Closely related to the issue of affliction and harm is the everyday expression in Muslim culture that connects the occurrence of suffering to God's "permission" (*idhn*). It is common to express one's sympathy for someone's loss or illness saying, *bi idhni-llāh* or *bi mashīyati-llāh:* It happened with God's "permission" or God's will—that is, God decreed the causal links that led to the loss of health, and, if he did so, it must have been for the best. However, such a statement creates two distinct theological problems: either imputing evil to God or upholding an extreme voluntarism, that is, predeterminism, which would lead one to doubt causal connections between sin and undeserved suffering.

Unmerited suffering is likely to make people doubt God's goodness, even if such suffering turns out to be the cause of some greater good. In a similar vein, the promise of the future reward of the righteous in the hereafter does little to placate a righteous person's fear of earthly misery and suffering. The idea of predetermined suffering implicates God in the authorship of an act that seems to cause both physical and moral evil. More critically, the problem of undeserved physical evil generates a struggle between hope and despair—an inner conflict that arises often in the face of the grim reality of inherited diseases like cancer. In their endeavor to absolve God from any blame for concocting physical evil, Sunni-Ash'arite theologians defended God's goodness, asserting that whatever happens, "happens for the best." They devoted a great deal more attention to God's omnipotence than to human freedom, pushing the problem of evil deep into the realm of theology, thereby pushing ethics and psychology aside. Ironically, the more they conflated the problem of evil with God's absolute will, the more they absolved humans of responsibility for moral evil. Ash'arite theology lost its importance because of this emphasis on God's will. The neglect of the human, psychological dimension of evil had ramifications in the field of education, where human behavior is scrutinized in terms of human intention and the capacity to execute a plan and to perform an action, good or bad. The Sunni-Mu'tazilites and the Shī'ites therefore undertook to explain the ethical and psychological dimensions of human action and individual responsibility for moral evil.

The scriptural sources of Islamic thought do not always provide theologically consistent accounts of the existence of evil in the world. Amid these ambiguities a diversity of scholarly interpretations has flourished. The cryptic nature of some of the scriptural language about God's role in creating or "permitting" evil in the world contributes to the problem of understanding evil. Moreover, one can detect an unofficial state theology at work in furthering an unquestioning submission to the all-powerful God that engenders a kind of psychological numbness on the question of evil in society. The result is a quietism and acceptance of adverse social and political conditions that fails to hold the authorities responsible for their unjust behavior. There is overwhelming historical evidence to show that under the Umayyad rulers (660–748 CE), the state policy was to perpetrate a belief in the absolute will of God that predetermined all human action, including the evil conduct of those in power, in order to contain growing discontent and opposition to the dynasty.[6] Selected verses of the Qur'an were cited to inculcate the belief that human suffering is a form of divine punishment to be accepted passively, without questioning. Everything is the best that it could be because it is willed by God. Hence, there is no need to do anything about suffering. In fact, an active response aimed at combating suffering in society might be deemed impious. In the recent case of inoculation against polio in Nigeria, religious authorities discouraged Muslims from getting inoculated because, they contended, the program was a Western conspiracy to make Muslims sterile and a defiance of the will of God, who had determined that the Muslim community should become more numerous than other faith communities.[7] In the developing world it is not uncommon to observe such conspiracy theories, which often generate passivity and resignation among the most desperately poor and diseased peoples of Africa and the Middle East. The increase in the number of AIDS victims in African countries has been blamed on the religious attitudes that propagate a deterministic, quietist theology based on the sin-suffering doctrine.

Does God Permit Natural Evil?

The Qur'an is the foundation of Muslims' belief system.[8] Accordingly, Muslims regard the Qur'an as an indisputable, authentic authority. The Qur'an, however, is not a systematic work of Muslim theology. There is no methodical exposition of any doctrine in it. In fact, creedal issues are treated in the form of short responses offered piecemeal, as circumstances dictated, throughout the twenty-three years of the prophetic mission. This feature of the Qur'an makes it imperative to discern historical context in order to interpret the intent of the wording of relevant passages. The task is not easy because classical commentaries do not always record the occasions of specific responses. There are passages in the Qur'an that suggest that there must have been a discussion of a particular instance of naturally caused human suffering in which the authorship of the evil was at issue: Was it God? A human being? The responses are recorded in the verse, depending on the case that was presented to the Prophet.

The subject matter is of utmost importance to the faithful even today: if God is all-powerful and all-merciful, then why does natural evil exist? It is self-evident that the most difficult task of any religion is to reconcile faith in God's benevolence with the suffering of innocents. One classic argument based on traditional theodicy—that we need to suffer pain and disease in order to appreciate the blessing of good health—appears to be incompatible with the scriptural descriptions and assurances of God's goodness and justice. Religious traditions often appear to justify the existence of evil in any form as a sort of divinely instituted punishment for humanity's moral and spiritual failures—perhaps for religious disobedience or lack of human response to divine calling. However, even a cursory understanding of the historical conditions in seventh-century Arabia suggests a far more complex picture.

The context of the scriptural references must be decoded to explain the apparent contradiction regarding the authorship of evil as explained in two separate verses in the Qur'an: in one it declares good and evil to be from God (Q. 57:22); in the other it imputes evil to human beings (Q. 4:67). A further complication that obscures this decoding is the ideological and sectarian exegesis of the verses under investigation. If a researcher is unaware of the exegete's sectarian affiliation, then she may end up generalizing and attributing universalizing opinions that are maintained only by a specific school of thought.

A meticulous reading of the sections of the Qur'an that deal with self-inflicted miseries points to the vulnerability of human life in the difficult conditions of living near the desert. The intricate interaction between humanity and a harsh physical environment often gives rise to the natural evils that human beings face. In addition to natural causes of physical evil, the Qur'an speaks about affliction that "your own hands have earned" (Q. 42:29). In one place the Qur'an addresses the suffering that occurs on the battlefield, reminding the faithful that they did not suffer anything more than what they had suffered before they became Muslim or joined the Prophet in his struggle against the hostile unbelievers of Mecca:

> Why, when an affliction visited you, and you had visited twice over the like of it, did you say, "How is this?" Say [to them O Muhammad]: "This is from *your own selves* (emphasis added); surely God is powerful over everything; And what visited you, the day the two hosts encountered, was by God's leave, and that he might know the believers; and that he might also know the hypocrites when it

> was said of them, 'Come now, fight in the way of God, or repel!'" They said, "If only we knew how to fight, we would follow you." (Q. 3:166–67)

The passage provides the context in which the question about the source of affliction was raised and the response was, "This is from your own selves." Apparently, the Prophet's followers believed that as believers they were immune from the suffering caused by combat, but the Qur'an countered that their battlefield affliction was their own doing; moreover, they had also suffered something similar before they joined the community. Such a contextual reading is essential to understanding the Qur'anic statement about human affliction as a matter of human agency. Clearly, the source of this affliction is the human being. In fact, the Qur'an emphatically absolves God from committing any wrongdoing, which is squarely blamed on human beings. "God wronged them not, but themselves they wronged" (Q. 3:117). Since human beings are endowed with cognition and the freedom to choose their course of action, they carry the responsibility of its consequences. This freedom of choice is also the source of moral evil. God does not will evil for human beings. Actually, as the Qur'an reminds human beings, if God "should hasten unto men evil as they would hasten good, their term would be already decided for them. But we leave those, who look not to encounter us, in their insolence wandering blindly" (Q. 10:11).

In describing the evil conduct of the Pharaoh's army that was pursuing the Children of Israel as they were crossing the Red Sea, not believing that they would encounter God for their wrongdoing, the Qur'an declares, "Surely they were an evil people, so we drowned them all together" (Q. 21:76). Consequential affliction as something that the agent deserves does not in itself give rise to the historical problem of theodicy in the Qur'an. However, as soon as the Qur'anic verse attributes both good and evil to God as in this particular verse 'Every soul shall taste of death; and we try you with evil and good for a testing' (Q. 21:35), the Qur'an becomes entangled in the quandaries of traditional theodicy.

The Qur'an offers no explanation or defense of God's ways of dealing with human existence. Hence the resolution of theodicy that arises because of affliction that exists "by leave of God" requires an insight into the concept of life to come, the hereafter (*al-ākhira*), and the kind of moral responsibility it generates for reasonable people, regardless of their religious affiliations. The belief in the accountability for one's conduct in the world to come provides the ethical impulse for weighing the ethical pros and cons of one's decisions. Faith in the world to come sustains the idea of a just, rewarding God who will compensate the righteous for what they have endured in this world. Faith in a transcendent God rather than the rational understanding of the philosophy of evil brings about necessary confidence in divine wisdom—the basic argument used in traditional theodicy.

The Sin of Disobedience and Its Consequences

In Islam, physical or mental suffering is regarded as a divine penalty for those who disobey God's commandments. The Qur'an also speaks of God's punishment for those who disbelieve, disobey, and spread corruption on earth. It is not so much disbelief per se, but rather disbelief that leads to destructive and harmful behavior that leads to divinely ordained suffering. The Qur'an does not deny the existence of either moral or natural evil. It simply connects the evil of suffering to the sin of ungrateful disobedience, the source of which is human rejection of belief in God. In this sense, sin, which causes suffering, refers to the act of disobedience (*ma'ṣiya*).

The gravity of a sin of disobedience varies with the eminence of the authority that has been flouted. Because God is the highest authority, disobedience toward God is a mortal sin. Offences against equals are not as grave as those committed against a higher authority. In this sense, disobedience toward God always constitutes a grave sin (*kabīra*) that incurs divine punishment in this world, the next, or both, unless the sinner has atoned for the wrongdoing; by contrast, noncompliance with due obedience in relation to one's equal, even though a sin, constitutes a minor sin (*ṣaghīra*) which incurs divine disapproval and requires seeking forgiveness. The most serious sins are transgressions of boundaries set by God's commandments; lesser sins are omissions of something required or recommended by the Tradition. Until the act of transgression takes place, no sin exists. Sin has no ontological reality because it has no existence prior to its being performed. Once it is performed, then it constitutes an act with religious implications—negative for disobedience, positive for those sins that lead to spiritual and moral maturity and acts of obedience.

Clearly, Islam regards many forms of evil as a product of human behavior, with a theologically defined hierarchy of judgments and punishments. But does God commit evil? Since God owes no obedience to anyone and is bound by no commandment, no evil can be imputed to God. In contrast, humans are bound to the limits set by the revelation, and evil can be imputed to them as soon as they transgress those limits and defy the commandments. Evil has no external existence beyond disobedience. In this sense, evil is not evil in and of itself. In fact, the evil of things is not a true or absolute attribute; it is a relative one. Goodness in the Qur'an is identical with being, and evil is identical with nonbeing; wherever being makes its appearance, nonexistence is also implied. Thus, privative states such as poverty, ignorance, or disease imply their opposites—wealth, knowledge, and health—which actually have a positive existence. Thus poverty is simply not having wealth, ignorance is the absence of knowledge, and disease is loss of health. In this sense poverty and ignorance have no tangible reality; they are defined as the nonexistence of their logical correlates. The same is the case with afflictions and misfortunes that are commonly regarded as evil and the source of suffering. They, too, are a kind of loss or nonbeing, and are evil only in this privative sense. Apart from this, nothing, insofar as it exists, can in any way be called evil or ugly. If afflictions did not entail sickness and death—the loss and destruction of certain creatures and the limitation of their potential development—they would not be bad. It is the loss and ruin arising from misfortunes that is inherently bad. Whatever exists in the world is good; evil pertains to nonbeing, it has not been created and does not exist.

The Qur'an, then, regards the world—that which exists—as being equivalent to good. Everything is inherently good; if it is evil, it is so only in a relative, privative sense. The mosquito that causes malaria is not evil in itself. It is evil because it is harmful to humans and causes disease. In other words, that which is created is a thing in and of itself, and hence a true existence; contingent existence has no place in the order of being and is not real. That which is real must derive its being from the Creator. Only those things and attributes are real that exist outside the mind. Relative attributes are created by the mind and have no existence outside it.[9]

Accordingly, it is not the act in itself that is evil. In fact, it is almost neutral. It receives its classification only through divine command, which in its turn correlates to the objective nature of good. However, this objective good is good because God has created it as such. It is subject neither to rational thinking nor questioning. It is God's will alone that determines its value. There are no criteria that can in any way limit or determine God's absolute will. So evil in the Qur'an is not defined by any reference to an objective criterion in itself but is reduced to that which, if performed, transgresses the limits set by God's command. This is, then, a religious ethics of obedience to divine command.

However, in describing good as the nonexistence of evil, the Qur'an seems to be treating evil in ontological terms. From the vantage point of God's wisdom, either the world must exist according to the pattern that is particular to it, or it cannot exist at all. A world without order or lacking the principle of causality, a world where good and evil were not separate from each other, would be an impossibility. It is for this reason that the Qur'an contains relatively few references to suffering, and in those cases it is treated as the mere concomitant of the real entities that give rise to it. Here evil is reduced to the privation of being, and being in itself is always good. How, then, can suffering or the infliction of pain become good? The question is no longer about suffering as a form of objective evil; it is about the relationship between God's omnipotence and human freedom.

The Qur'an assures human beings that the righteous will suffer no pain. They deserve all the goods God can bestow on them, because "God loves the good-doers" (Q. 3:142). By the same token, the wicked ought to suffer through something imposed by God in the form of punishment, because "God loves not the evildoers" (Q. 3:134). The Qur'an expresses outrage at the sight of others' wrongdoing. Even though God is absolute in his control of the entire universe, the Qur'an reminds human beings that God does not wrong people but that they wrong themselves by committing evil acts of destruction and detriment to themselves and others. Hence, it is human beings who are the authors of their evil actions; they alone bear responsibility for their failure to uphold the ideal of virtuous life and work in this and the world to come. This failure is the source of human suffering. However, the Qur'an treats suffering as a divinely ordained contingency, not as an ethical problem that casts doubt on the idea of a just and compassionate God.

The Qur'an clearly imputes the cause of suffering to humans who have been visited by "an affliction for what their own hands have forwarded" (Q. 4:63). The afflicted human is expected to reflect on the positive role suffering plays in sharpening awareness of God's infinite presence. In addition, there are passages that suggest that God has foreknowledge of suffering because "no affliction befalls in the earth or in you, but it is in a book, before we create it" (Q. 57:22). "It is in a book" suggests that the relation of human beings to affliction is eternally fixed. Any evils humans cause or suffer are fixed within it. This leads to a mysterious view that the development of evil is fundamentally immutable. However, most of the commentators on this verse regard the affliction in general to be neutral in value, that is, neither good nor evil. However, they distinguish natural catastrophe from the harm that reaches human beings through injury, illness, death, and so on. The latter occur in order to impel humans to heed to the call of faith, which requires them to spend their wealth in the path of God and to strive physically to make God's purposes on earth succeed. The theological problem about that suffering that is preordained in a Book, apart from free human action, remains unresolved. The fact that such suffering is written in a Book seems to suggest a reference to God's omniscience. Does this omniscience of God require Muslims to believe that God has foreknowledge concerning good and evil acts before they existed, from eternity?

The adverse ramifications of belief in God's foreknowledge cannot be overstated, if God's foreknowledge is understood in terms of all suffering being written on the finite preserved tablet (*al-lawḥ al-maḥfūẓ*).[10] Is God's foreknowledge, then, the real cause of suffering? Or, does it mean that God, in his omnipotence, can remove the cause(s) that impede the realization of his salutary plan for humanity? Suffering, as the Qur'an asserts time and again, is in some sense purposeful.

Yet divine foreknowledge of affliction raises serious ethical problems about a God who wills an affliction to occur despite his presumed ability to prevent it. In this case, God's omniscience seems to contradict his omnipotence. Foreknowledge would not be a cause of suffering arising from human-caused, moral evil; foreknowledge only becomes a theodicy problem if God is also omnipotent. If he creates affliction before it is inflicted, then divine authorship of evil contradicts God's justice and boundless benevolence. God's omniscience certainly led to the creedal statement in the majority of Sunni works on theology that God has indeed decreed and ordained everything, including suffering as a form of evil, such that nothing could happen either in this world or in the next except through his will, knowledge, decision, decree and writing on the "preserved tablet." However, this divine absoluteness was tempered with a declaration that God's writing in the "preserved tablet" is "of a descriptive, not of a decisive nature."[11] In other words, God's foreknowledge of suffering does not determine the occurrence of an evil human act and is not responsible for the consequent suffering; it simply "describes" the situation in which human suffering occurs and in which humans are held accountable for their evil acts.

In another passage the Qur'an admonishes human beings to endure adversity patiently because "no affliction befalls, except it be by the leave of God." (64:11) "By the leave of God *(bi idhni-llāh)*," on the one hand, seems to further confidence in the wisdom of God, who allows affliction as a necessary part of a greater plan; such a view seems to reinforce Muslim passivity in the face of afflictions. Muslim theologians have debated the adverse ramifications of the phrase "by the leave of." Some have interpreted it to mean that all suffering is written on the finite "preserved tablet" in eternity. This reading runs counter to Qur'an teachings that emphasize human agency.

Nonetheless, theodicy in the Qur'an remains marginal. It is not a major concern of the Qur'an to show that a good God does not commit evil; rather, the concern is to generate faith in God's wisdom and power over all of his creation. Further, the Qur'an does not impute evil to God. Evil is clearly ascribed to human arrogance, disbelief and disobedience. This view engenders an optimism based on the belief in an omniscient and omnipotent God whose perfect moral essence leaves no room for wrongdoing. Even if human beings are limited in their knowledge or power, they are not helpless before fate. With proper faith and constant struggle to advance their understanding of God's "tradition" (*sunnat allāh*), the details of which are not obvious to humans at all times, people can transform the world in which they live. Discovering and understanding natural laws—another name for God's "tradition"—can remove temporal suffering by fostering action that accords with divinely created human nature (*fiṭra*). The possibility of morality and the capacity to do good and avoid evil are implanted in the human nature that seeks to be perfected through suffering. Suffering, in this sense, is not evil in itself; rather, it is an essential station on the path of spiritual and moral maturity.

In view of the Qur'anic text which declares good and evil to be from God (Q. 57:22), it seems that the Qur'an is dealing with two very different claims about evil and suffering: that (a) some suffering is not evil and is from God, being a station on the path of spiritual and moral maturity; (b) some suffering is evil and is from God, perhaps as punishment for sin; (c) some suffering is evil and not from God (deriving from human arrogance); (d) some suffering is not evil and not from God (e.g., a doctor-administered inoculation). Essentially, there are two variables: whether or not the suffering is evil, and whether or not it is from God. The Qur'an focuses on (a), (b), and (c), without resolving the tension that is caused by the good God permitting some form of evil.

Theology of Suffering in the Prophetic Tradition

The subject of suffering appears in various contexts in the Tradition, sometimes in the form of further theological elaboration of the Qur'anic references, and at other times in the form of independent opinions on the subject. Just as the Qur'an treats evil and human afflictions as the part of an overall plan for human spiritual and moral growth, so the traditions ascribed to the Prophet elaborate on the ramifications of the belief in God's omnipotence and omniscience and its impact on human well-being. In the Tradition, suffering caused by illness and death is a divinely ordained tool for testing and perfecting human beings.

Suffering caused by illness or loss of good health appears to have been interpreted in the light of certain theological positions concerning divine will and human will. Hence, there are traditions that speak of illness as a form of divinely ordained suffering based on the belief that God is the author of all that befalls human beings.[12] In fact, such traditions have been the major source of a quietism and resignation that still impede the seeking of medical treatment in some quarters of Muslim society; God is regarded as the only healer, who, if he willed, could cure the illness and eliminate suffering. A true believer in these traditions should put her trust in God and depend on him and none other for deliverance from pain and suffering. Some of these traditions speak about the temporary nature of all forms of suffering, including illness; they persist only for a "fixed period" in God's decree, after which relief is guaranteed either through complete cure or death. Furthermore, in some traditions illness is evaluated as a form of divine mercy to expiate a believer's sins. According to a well-known tradition, the Prophet is reported to have said: "No fatigue, nor disease, nor sorrow, nor sadness, nor hurt, nor distress befalls a Muslim, even if it were the prick he received from a thorn, but that God expiates some of his sins for that."[13]

In contrast, there are traditions that contradict this passivity in the face of suffering. These traditions hold that because God is just, he cannot cause gratuitous pain to his creatures. In fact, there is a strong emphasis on God's goodness, a belief that he wills only beneficence. Reconciling God's benevolence and absolute goodness with the suffering of the innocent, as discussed earlier, has not been easy in any religious tradition. Even when the general trend in Muslim piety is to hold human beings accountable for their own suffering and to recommend righteous acts to rid the world of suffering, the suffering of infants and animals has presented an interpretive challenge. Some Muslim scholars have tried to explain the suffering of an infant as admonition for adults; children's suffering is viewed as a response to the parents' sins.[14] Rarely have these scholars paid attention to the suffering of animals. But when they have, they have explained away the suffering of animals in terms of a hierarchy of existence in which the creatures of lower rank, like animals, serve the purposes of the higher, like human beings. They argue that because all God's acts are purposeful, nothing can be in vain, including the suffering of children and other beings. In most theological discussions, suffering was construed only in reference to human beings. Since moral evil referred merely to human actions perpetrated upon or afflicting human beings, other instances of being were not included. In that sense, the suffering of children, and not that of animals, served as a divine sign and warning.

This view raises a serious question: is human suffering the only form of evil worth considering in the light of divine justice and benevolence? If only human suffering is regarded as evil, then other earthly creatures are relegated to a lower status. This relegation seems to conceive a unique moral status for human suffering in light of humans' capacity for willing and executing evil acts. If moral evil is the main source of human suffering, then the suffering experienced by lower forms of life are devoid of moral implications. According to this view, the desecration or destruction of the natural environment or cruelty to animals would constitute a lower order of evil than the destruction of human life. Such a doctrine has serious implications for the use of animals in medical research. In the literature examined for the present work, there are rarely rulings prohibiting the use of animals for human ends, although one can find numerous traditions that treat cruelty toward animals as a sin against God, punishable by him in the hereafter.[15]

The problem of infant suffering has also proved difficult to resolve. In Islamic jurisprudence children are minors. As minors they are not regarded as legally competent to assume the religious or moral responsibility presupposed in the idea of divine infliction of suffering as retribution for sin. It is even more difficult, then, to legally justify the suffering of animals, lesser beings, as an admonition for humans, higher beings. Although some Muslims believe that animals will be rewarded lavishly in paradise and even in this world in ways we humans cannot understand, the intricacies of divine justice in the case of the sufferings of innocents has resisted coherent or consistent interpretive resolution and may, according to some, present a mystery that is beyond human comprehension.[16]

Illness as a Form of Expiation

Good works negate suffering. No doubt illness is regarded as an affliction that needs to be cured by every possible legitimate means. The development of a vibrant medical profession in Islamic civilization in the ninth and tenth centuries is a living testimony that medicine developed as an important subject of study and research. In fact, in these traditions, the search for cures is founded upon unusual confidence generated by the divine promise reported in one of the early traditions: "There is no disease that God has created, except that he has also created its treatment."[17] Hence, the purpose of medicine is to search for cures and provide necessary care to those afflicted with diseases.

In Muslim culture, this confidence in being cured by human efforts renders a physician's role as a healer spiritually and morally commendable. Muslim physicians must regard illness not merely as a physical phenomenon, but also as one with psychological and spiritual implications; in Islam, medicine, hygiene, and communal health practices have religious implications as guidelines for good living according to God's will. In practice, Muslims have taken the responsibility very seriously. They were among the first in the world to build hospitals for more effective care of the sick. Medical doctors are exhorted to work sincerely under the guidelines of the Sharī'a, to avoid all temptations to personal arrogance or greed, and to resist various social pressures that might conflict with their calling. Medical caring and curing should therefore be practiced in a climate of piety and awareness of the presence of God.[18]

There are numerous traditions that provide religious incentives for the care and curing of the sick. Some function as prophetic directives about the proper etiquette for dealing with illness or visiting the sick and bereaved. One tradition cites a paradigm case for the community to emulate. According to this tradition, it was the Prophet's custom, when he visited the sick, to say, "Don't worry. It is a purification." On one occasion the Prophet entered into the home of an ailing desert Arab and said to him, "Don't worry. It is a purification, if God wills." The man replied, "Never! Rather it is a fever boiling on an old man, which will send him on a visit to the grave!" The Prophet replied, "Very well, then be it so."[19] In another tradition it is related that when a person fell ill, the Prophet used to rub him with his right hand and then pray to God, saying, "O Lord of the people, grant him health, heal him, for thou art a great healer."[20]

Other traditions recognize a religious purpose for illness, as for other forms of suffering, as a cleansing challenge and trial decreed by God. Hence, in one tradition, the Prophet says that the patient evolves spiritually because of these trials and can attain the rank of a true believer. "When God intends to do good to somebody, he afflicts him with trials."[21] *Aṣābahu bi maraḍin* ("He (i.e., God) afflicted him with disease or rendered him diseased"), like its converse, *aṣābahu bi ṣiḥatin* ("He rendered him healthy"), is a common expression of God's activity in everyday human situations in Muslim cultures. In a Muslim thanksgiving prayer, besides praising and thanking God for all the blessings, a believer affirms: "To you [O God] belongs praise for all the good affliction (*balā*'*in* *ḥasanin*) with which you have inured me."[22]

The characterization of affliction as "good" in the above prayer indicates that suffering as such does not create a theoretical problem in Islam. Rather, it is treated as part of the divine plan for humanity. When it occurs, it is identified, and its impact is reversed by education and discipline in a true affirmation and submission to the will of God (*islām*). The Qur'an and the Tradition provide an uncommon interpretation of suffering as a concrete human experience, an unavoidable condition of human existence. They do not always regard suffering from natural evil as an evil and hence a problem that needs to be explained or vindicated because its author is the good God.

Theological Debates about Suffering (*al-ālām*)

Ālām is the plural form of *alam*, meaning "pain, affliction, suffering, agony."[23] A theological evaluation of suffering poses the problem of theodicy in Islam.[24] In view of its preoccupation with the polytheism of the Meccans of seventh-century Arabia, it is reasonable to maintain that the Qur'an was more concerned with the question of belief and disbelief than with the question of suffering in human society. For the Qur'an, abandoning faith in God is both sinful and evil. Such evil is nothing but the withdrawal of good, just as darkness is the withdrawal of light. In this sense, evil is treated as sin which in itself has no essence. It is a state of moral inadequacy. If this explanation is applied to a specific evil like illness, it cannot be regarded as truly evil. Rather, illness as a trial imposed by God, although a form of tribulation and suffering, it fulfills a positive role in the life of a faithful, revealing God's compassion and his power to cure. The question whether God can inflict gratuitous pain on his creatures is central to any theodicy, even in the contemporary world, with its surfeit of rational explanations for the problems of human life. The conflict between the concept of a just God and the reality of human suffering constitutes one of the most crucial and perplexing problems in human history.[25] Muslims of all sects bitterly complain about the various forms of evil that prevail in their society. Can one explain the suffering of the righteous or the prosperity of the wicked without losing faith in God's omnipotence, as emphasized by Sunni Muslims? Can one harmonize the unmerited suffering of the innocent with the concept of divine justice, as maintained by Shī'ite Muslims? These questions are not merely academic concerns of Muslim theologians trying to explain the inscrutable ways of God. They are real everyday issues among the majority of Muslim peoples around the world.

Muslims, like their Abrahamic cousins, the Jews and Christians, affirm God's goodness and omnipotence. At the same time, in the face of human suffering, they are required to defend God's justice. To be sure, Islamic theodicy, as pointed out earlier, is very much a feature of its ethical monotheism, which affirms God's goodness and almightiness while accepting suffering as part of the divine plan for humanity's betterment. Moreover, religiously inspired ideals about a good society in Islam logically create an existential need to explain suffering and evil despite God's promises to the contrary. Like other religions, Islam was faced with explaining the discrepancy between the ideal and the real, the God who is all-merciful and all-powerful and the existence of injustices in human societies. A theodicy, as shown by a number of scholars of comparative religions, is necessary in any religion where any god is regarded as invariably benevolent and omnipotent.[26] However, Islam's insistence on "submission" (one of the essential meanings of the term *islām*) to the divine will would remove untenable contradictions inherent in Muslim belief about the benevolent and omnipotent God and would reduce the centrality of theodicy found in the Hebrew Bible and New Testament. Islamic theodicy was downplayed by the glorification of suffering in the path of God by the "friends of God" (*awliyā' allāh*), whose nobility and high station with God were determined by their ability to withstand affliction in any form. Yet Islam's emphasis on God's transcendence of human moral judgment led Kenneth Cragg to observe that Islam "ignores or neglects or does not hear these questions [about the wrongs in life]. . . . It does not find a theodicy necessary either for its theology or its worship."[27] This is a long-standing oversight in Islam that stems from its rational theology, which is founded on human free will. Even today, Muslim theologians undertake to make human suffering intelligible by showing why things that appear to be so painful and unjust in the world are not so in reality. More than Sunni scholars, it is the Shī'ite theologians who have ventured to show suffering as a means to greater ends, a short-lived experience that yields a higher good. In fact, in Shī'ite history a number of tragic events affirmed the role of suffering in achieving a higher spiritual and moral station.[28]

Nonetheless, Cragg's comment about the lack of interest in theodicy in Islam does have some bearing on the Sunni triumphal theology in which the absence of any interest in human suffering reflects the Sunni history of political success and power. This worldly feature of Sunni Islam has informed its theology of divine determination, which views the idea of human responsibility for the world as a relic of slave morality that depends on the master to command good and forbid evil.

In Muslim theology, as we shall see below, free-will theodicy was constructed on a foundation of Qur'anic references to human free agency and an all-powerful divine will. The notion of evil as a necessary concomitant of good was an important theme of Islam's theological, mystical, and philosophical literature. Muslims, like the followers of other traditions, have sought to reconcile specific evils, such as suffering, with God's infinite wisdom, power, and compassion. In view of God's regenerative mercy (*raḥma*) for all His creatures, regardless of whether they believe in God or not, can one explain illness as a specific evil simply by contending that it is nothing more than the lack of the good state of being that is health?

The problem of disharmony between the concept of a God of justice and the evils present in the world is encapsulated in the tradition in which God is made the sole agent of infectious disease. The Prophet is reported to have said, "There is neither contagion nor augury nor jaundice nor bird of evil omen." A Bedouin asked, "O Prophet of God, how is it then that my camels were in the sand [as healthy as] gazelles, and then a mangy camel mingled with them and made them mangy?" The Prophet replied, "Who infected the first (camel)?"[29] In other words, God has himself implanted the disease that causes suffering. As we discussed above, there are verses in the Qur'an that could be cited as supporting the predestination theology of the later period that viewed God as the source of evil.[30] There are, however, opposing verses in which God plainly delegates responsibility for suffering to free creatures' abuse of their freedom.[31] These latter verses speak a free-will theodicy in which suffering can be traced back to human agency. The Qur'an reminds human beings that "God will not wrong so much as the weight of an ant" (Q. 4:40). Moreover, the Qur'an, as previously discussed, also views suffering as a test of righteousness. "Do the people reckon that they will be left to say, 'We believe,' and will not be tried?" (Q. 29:1)[32]

In the first half of the eighth century, the debates about earthly injustice and the proper means of combating it formed the rudiments of the earliest systematic theology of the group called the Mu'tazilites.[33] Before them, some Muslim thinkers had developed theological arguments, including a doctrine of God and human responsibility, in defense of the Islamic revelation and the prophethood of Muḥammad when these were challenged by other monotheists. The Mu'tazilites, however, undertook to show that there was nothing inimical to reason in the Islamic revelation. In defining God's creation and governance of the world, they sought to demonstrate the primacy of revelation. At the same time, their recognition of a substantial role for human reason in explaining the ways of God reflected Hellenic influences. From the ninth century on, translations of the Greek philosophic and scientific heritage became available in Arabic. The result was the development of a technical vocabulary and a pattern of syntax that was substantially similar to some familiar positions in Judeo-Christian theodicy.[34]

The Mu'tazilites were the champions of human free agency and hence became known as the school that formulated the free-will theodicy. They insisted on an inseparable link between free will and divine justice. The principle of divine justice was central to their theology and ethics, which views the human intellect as capable of recognizing good and evil without any aid from revelation. In other words, human intuitive reasoning is capable of discovering the rational core of every circumstance and event. Accordingly, God must have the best interests of his creatures at heart when he permits suffering. Because all God's actions aim to produce the well-being of individual creatures, it is necessary for human beings to discover and defend God's purposeful actions in apparently unjust or irrational events.[35]

A reaction against the Mu'tazilite emphasis on free-will theodicy was bound to appear with the realization that it is not within human power to explain how God's wisdom is manifested in cases of apparently unmerited suffering of the just and the prosperity of the wicked. Even a vivid Qur'anic eschatology, with the concept of the life to come, the hereafter—where all inequities will be corrected, the wicked punished, and the righteous rewarded—could not explain the tribulations suffered by the innocent. "Whatever God does, He does for the best" was a believer's way of accepting the hardships of this world, and it was this maxim that formed the predestiny theodicy of the Ash'arites.

The Ash'arites, reacting to Mu'tazilite free-will theodicy, limited speculative theology to a defense of the doctrines given in the *ḥadīth*, reports attributed to the Prophet. These were regarded as more reliable than abstract reason in understanding individual doctrines. The Ash'arites emphasized the absolute will and power of God and denied any decisive role to nature and humankind. What humans perceive as causation, they believed, is actually God's habitual behavior. In their response to the Mu'tazilite view about the objective nature of good and evil, and in their effort to maintain the effectiveness of a God at once omnipotent and omnibenevolent, who could and did intervene in human affairs, they maintained that good and evil are what God decrees them to be. Accordingly, God's decrees cannot be known from nature but must be discovered in the sources of revelation, like the Qur'an and the Prophet's paradigmatic conduct, the Sunna. There are no inherently unchanging essences and natural laws that self-subsistent reason can discern.[36] God transcends the order of nature. Hence, the notion of free will is incompatible with divine transcendence, which determines all actions directly. Ash'arite theological views remained dominant throughout Islamic history, well into modern times, and had a profound effect upon scientific and medical theory and practice among the Sunni Muslims. The attitude of resignation, a byproduct of belief in predestination, is summed up in the Sunni creedal confession, "What reaches you could not possibly have missed you; and what misses you could not possibly have reached you."[37]

To elaborate on this creedal declaration, the Ash'arites maintained that in some actions, God adds a special quality of voluntary acquisition which by God's will makes the individual a voluntary, responsible agent. But this limited human autonomy still leaves all responsibility to divine agency, which extends to all facets of human existence, such as sustenance, span of life, pleasure, and pain. It is God who allots to human beings all that he has.

The Ash'arite theodicy of determinism does not deny the evil aspects of pain, incapacity, illness, or poverty. Nor does it ignore the painful realities of existence. They are evils, but they are not the result of social inequity or accident or human wickedness. God intends poverty or pain or disbelief for certain individuals, just as he intends wealth, well-being, and belief for others. In fact, based on the doctrine of trust in God's will, a form of optimism underlies the belief that disease, destitution, social inequity, and the like are right and just.[38]

This belief in overpowering destiny was bound to raise important questions in some sectors of Muslim society when it encountered those adversities caused by illness and other forms of suffering. The Shīʿite theological and ethical doctrines were, on the other hand, based on the Sunni-Muʿtazilite thesis about the justice of God and the objective nature of moral values. Hence, there emerged the religious evaluation of illness and suffering as being caused by human excesses in the exercise of freedom of will. However, as a minority within a Muslim community, whose leaders had suffered martyrdom in their cause, Shīʿites saw tribulations as steps toward an eternal and blissful end. Their pious literature celebrating the martyrdoms of the Shīʿite Imams, especially the grandson of the Prophet Muḥammad, al-Ḥusayn, and his family, describes the suffering of innocent women and children in a very positive way as a divine blessing meant to become a source of self-purification and preparation for the arduous spiritual journey toward God.

The Shīʿites share this positive outlook about human suffering in any form with the Muslim mystics, the Sufis. Muslim mystics, who, in general, shared the Sunni-Ashʿarite optimism about divine wisdom in their understandings of human suffering, regarded it as a necessary part of their ascetic way of life. The inward life of the soul depends upon affliction to detach itself from the world and love God only. The goal is to gain control over one's passions, which cause pain and suffering at the loss of anything to which one was attached or one has most desired. To reach a level of consciousness where one could let one's entire life be guided by the immediate will of God meant giving up anything that did not bear the marks of divine blessing, however dire the earthly consequences might be. This was their idea of trust in God. Hence, trials, afflictions, and pains are part of the journey toward the everlasting happiness that culminates in being blessed with the love of God.[39]

Ibn al-ʿArabī (d. 1240), the great mystic of Islam, sees human affliction as an expression of divine mercy as the heart of the mystic goes through the inner purification in the hands of God: "But the heart is between two fingers of its Creator, who is the All-merciful. . . . Hence He does not cause the heart to fluctuate except from one mercy to another mercy, even though there is affliction (*balāʾ*) in the various kinds of fluctuation. But there lies in affliction's midst a mercy hidden from man and known to the Real, for the two fingers belong to the All-merciful."[40]

In another place he regards affliction as an instrument used by God to measure a person's ability to reflect on the divine purposes in creation:

> God afflicted man with an affliction with which no other of His creatures was afflicted. Through it He takes him to felicity or wretchedness, depending upon how He allows him to make use of it. This

> affliction with which God afflicted him is that He created within him a faculty named "reflection." He made this faculty the assistant of another faculty called "reason." Moreover, He compelled reason, in spite of its being reflection's chief, to take from reflection what it gives. God gave reflection no place to roam except the faculty of imagination. God made the faculty of imagination the locus which brings together everything given by the sensory faculties.[41]

Concluding Remarks

Two distinct explanations for the purpose of suffering emerge from theological discussions in Islam: First, suffering is part of natural evil within God's plan for the betterment of humanity; all forms of suffering, including illness, serve two purposes: (a) they are a form of punishment that expiates a sin; and (b) they are a test or trial to confirm or reinforce a believer's spiritual status. Second, suffering is part of moral evil caused by human free will in choosing to disbelieve and face the consequences of this choice. Disbelief then is treated as the source of human misconduct that results in suffering. Suffering in this situation serves an educational function, helping to reveal the consequences of disbelief and its attendant afflictions. However, when the righteous suffer affliction, it is seen as an agent of purification and attainment of higher spiritual station.

Should one take it upon oneself to alleviate suffering when possible and endure it when it is not? Two responses follow from two above-mentioned positions, which have negative and positive implications, respectively, for medical treatment:

1. The passive response is based on the belief that God is testing human faith, so that one must endure suffering. A corollary of this belief is that, as reported in the words of Abraham in the Qur'an, God is the only healer on whom a believer should depend: ". . . Lord of all Being who created me, and Himself gives me to eat and drink, and, whenever I am sick, heals me, who makes me die, then gives me life . . ." (Q. 26:80). The statement, "whenever I am sick, heals me," becomes a source for a skeptical attitude toward medical treatment. This skepticism is not limited to any particular school of thought in Islam. Rather, it is commonly held in Muslim cultures, often without any reference to a belief in God's sole power of healing.
2. An active response is based on the belief that because a human being is the cause of his/her own suffering, he/she should undertake to do righteous acts to rid the world of suffering. Good works negate suffering. This belief generates a positive attitude to medical treatment, and it derives its strength from the oft-quoted advice of Prophet

> Muḥammad to his followers: "O servants of God, seek the cure, because God did not create a disease without creating its cure, except for one disease . . . senility."[42]

Theological-ethical debates about these two responses are based on the two forms of Islamic theodicy: determinist and free-will. In contemporary Muslim biomedical ethics, gradually, the free-will theodicy—founded upon divine justice and human moral agency—has become the dominant approach in dealing with human suffering through illness. The result is evident in the startling human and financial investment in developing first-rate healthcare institutions in the Muslim world. God's abstract justice has found concrete expression in the health care provided to the destitute and downtrodden in society. Fair distribution of limited resources remains a distant goal in the corrupt political systems where socioeconomic imbalances create a cynical attitude toward government-managed health care. It is remarkable, however, that religiously run Islamic hospitals and clinics, mostly staffed by volunteer or underpaid medical professionals, have more than adequately responded to the medical needs of largely impoverished populations. A religious revival among pious professionals, both men and women, has found expression in serving the children of God—the destitute of the Muslim world—by dedicating their services to those who are most vulnerable: women and children. It is to them that I will turn my attention when exploring the beginning of life and the nurturance of and care for that early life.

4

The Beginning of Life

We created man of an extraction of clay, then we set him, a coagulated drop, in a safe lodging, then we created of the coagulated drop a leech-like clot, then we created of the clot a morsel of tissue, then We created of the tissue bones, then We covered the bones in flesh; thereafter We produced him as another creature. So blessed be God, the best of creators!

—Qur'an 23:11–14

There are two narratives in the Qur'an that speak about the two modes of human creation: the creation of first human couple, Adam and Eve, from clay,[1] by God; and the miraculous creation of Jesus, the son of Mary,[2] which defied the natural mode of reproduction through divine intervention. Although the first mode, the *ex nihilo* creation of Adam and Eve, is clearly hailed as God's work, which requires upholding faith in God's power over creation to appreciate it, the second mode requires accepting asexual birth through one parent as a possible mode of divine creation. The Qur'an takes the extra precaution of clearing Mary of any wrongdoing in having conceived Jesus when "no mortal had touched" her. According to the Qur'an, when God sent "Our Spirit that presented himself to her a man without fault" to give her the glad tidings of the birth of "a boy most pure," Mary protested, saying, "How shall I have a son, given that I am untouched by human hand, neither have I been unchaste?" (Q. 19:15).

Both these instances of God's direct intervention establish God's absolute power over creation. Yet it is the second mode that raises moral questions connected with human sexuality and the necessity of conducting sexual relations within the bounds of legitimately conceived man-woman intimacy. According to the Qur'an, God can defy normal sexual reproduction and can intervene in natural processes to bring about the creation of another human being. But the virgin birth of Jesus is out of the ordinary. In the world of nature, as Mary asserts correctly, the presence of male and female is required for sexual reproduction. Consequently, when a woman conceives without having been touched by another human being, the situation raises serious moral questions that affect the woman's reputation and the child's lineage, on the one hand, and the parent's responsibility in assuring that the lineage remains unblemished, on the other.

These two modes of creation stories are related more than once in the Qur'an as God's special promptings for human reflection. They juxtapose God and nature to underscore God as the sole creator of all beings, who empowers natural causation to work as it does. And, although human embryonic development is mentioned with much scientific clarity, as the above-cited verse reveals, it is God's command that ultimately causes another creature to be born. The other reason for relating human creation in more than one place in the Qur'an is to remind human beings about their humble origins, tempered with God's spirit: "And He originated the creation of human being out of clay, then He fashioned his progeny of an extraction of mean water, then He shaped him, and breathed his spirit in him. And he appointed for you hearing, and sight, and hearts; little gratitude you show" (Q. 32:7–9). Ensoulment, according to this passage, occurs later when the fetus has been shaped, and not at conception, as some contemporary Shī'ite theologians would argue. With the frequent mention of creation, the Qur'an also instills a sense of finitude—a kind of urgency attached to a limited lifespan—by reminding human beings of the impending death and resurrection, when they will be brought back to life to account for their performance while on earth:

> O human beings, if you have any doubts about the Resurrection (*ba'th*), [consider how you yourselves were created in the first place]. Surely we created you of dust, then of a sperm-drop (*nuṭfa*), then of a blood clot (*'alaqa*), then of a morsel of tissue (*muḍgha*), formed and unformed, so that we may make clear to you [the creation and development of the child in the womb]. We establish in the wombs what we will, till a stated term, then we deliver you as infants, then that you may come of age; and some of you die, and some of you are kept back unto vilest state of life, that after knowing somewhat, they may know nothing. (Q. 22:5)

The beginning of life, then, leads us to probe in greater detail the ethics of sexual and asexual procreation in the light of certain reproductive technologies that transgress the boundaries of normal sexual reproduction. Today scientists speak about the possibility of noncoital production of human embryos through somatic-cell nuclear transfer (SCNT or the "Dolly technique") or using the cells from in vitro human embryos that have lost their capacity to form a new individual. The advent of new reproductive technologies made possible what is impossible in nature—except through some kind of divine intervention, such as the case of Jesus. These new technologies also challenge respect for life and human dignity in radical ways, raising difficult ethical issues for all societies. Some of these ethical concerns are conveyed in questions like, "What is the moral status of the embryo?" and "What kind of respect for its life does that require from society?"

These questions await a responsible treatment from Muslim scholars. If the Qur'an resolved the question of identity for Jesus by ascribing his birth to his mother only (the Qur'an does not regard God as more than the Creator who breathed his own spirit in him), what could happen to the child that was created from three or more genetic parents? The preservation of proper lineage (*nasab*) in order for the child to be related to his/her biological parents is one of the main purposes of the sacred law of Islam, the Sharī'a. Accordingly, a child's untainted identity through a legitimate conjugal relationship between a man and a woman in marriage is so essential in Islam and Muslim culture that it is regarded as a child's inalienable right. Proper lineage in Muslim culture—as we learn from various rulings prohibiting or questioning different forms of technically assisted reproduction outside marriage—is critical in forging an appropriate relationship between the parents and the child, and in claiming rights that accrue to the child in the Sharī'a.[3]

Nasab, meaning "lineage" or "genealogy," signifies a reputed relationship with respect to father and mother, or with respect to fathers only. The term also conveys consanguinity based on a blood relationship.[4] In the juridical tradition, *nasab* is understood as a genealogical relationship that emerges through biological reproduction relating to the union of male and female gametes in a sexual act between a man and a woman in a marriage, thereby giving rise to the parent-child and brother-sister relationships.[5] In the context of the present study, the term lineage is restricted to this latter meaning, without considering its legal ramifications. It is important to underscore the distinction that is being made between natural and assisted reproduction in Muslim societies. As long as technologically assisted reproduction occurs within a marriage, the lineage of the child remains secure by relating the infant to his/her biological parents. However, if the gametes that are fertilized in IVF clinics cannot be related to a married couple, then the Sharī'a denies the lineage to the child, unless the identity of the donors is known. In that case, the child is related to the donor of the sperm. We will come to this issue below.

Since lineage is conceived in terms of a natural process that occurs through the union of a man and a woman, the prevailing custom (*'urf*) is the major source of legitimacy that relates a child to his/her biological parents. Under one circumstance, however, Islamic law has refused to grant genealogical recognition to an offspring: when the child is conceived through an act of adultery, an illicit sexual relationship under Sharī'a law. In more recent rulings, an exception is made when the act of penetration is regarded by the man and the woman as inadvertent. In such a case, the lineage of the child is acknowledged as unblemished and he/she is related to the couple. In that way, the law has protected the child's lineage by relating him/her to biological parents even when the conception had occurred outside the legitimate sexual relation.[6]

The only way to protect the lineage of a child in the Sharī'a, then, is through marriage, and legitimate lineage is established only through married biological parents. However, in practice, Muslim societies grant lineage to the child's biological parents even if there is no certainty about such an ascription, placing the onus on adult behavior and sparing the child from any future social handicap that might result from the stigma of illegitimacy.

In view of the traditional Muslim concerns about the right of the child to have an immaculate lineage, one can begin to assess the unprecedented challenges that show the inadequacies of juridical formulations in dealing with the possibility of producing a child by technically assisted reproduction (TAR) outside the normal conjugal relationship. The issues in TAR are so novel that contemporary Muslim jurists do not have instant solutions for the challenges it poses to Islamic traditions. Although a large number of Sunni and Shī'ite scholars have endorsed TAR with the requisite intellectual caution, a number of prominent jurists have questioned the wisdom of accepting TAR in light of the genealogical considerations posed by the procedure.

Besides the emphasis on unblemished lineage, there is another aspect of the debate among Muslims that has theological roots. The prevalent doctrine about God's determination of the natural processes of birth and the creation of life raises serious questions about the nature of reproduction. If God's will determines sexual or asexual creation and the sex of a child, does God's will also dictate an end to early embryonic life? This inquiry opens a debate about the beginning of life: does it begin with conception, or does it begin when the ensoulment takes place? Although I will deal more extensively with the question in the next chapter, "Terminating Early Life," commentators of the Qur'an have carefully studied the verses that describe stages of embryonic development to determine exactly when life begins. The reason for this intensive scrutiny is not so much philosophical as legal. Clinically induced abortions carry penalties whose amount is graded in accordance with the age of the fetus and the determination of the period when the spirit (*rūḥ*) enters the body. As we shall discuss in our chapter on abortion, preimplantation genetic diagnosis (PGD), in which IVF embryos are screened for genetic diseases or abnormalities, and prenatal genetic screening (PGS) have changed the way in which Muslims view and formulate their juridical decisions about clinically induced abortions. In the context of reproduction technologies, parents' decisions to abort a "defective" fetus in order to avoid having a child with an unwanted medical condition seriously alter the nature of our relationship to our offspring. Parental love for their offspring in the pre-PGD or PGS era was never conditional, and selective implantation based on desirability of a healthy baby was never an issue. The ability to detect defective embryos by PGD or defective fetuses by PGS has posed fresh quandaries: Will such procedures lead to eugenics? Will the parental choices determine not only the sex but also the quality of a child?

I will discuss below the ways in which new reproductive genetics have affected modern medicine's potential to control the birth of defective embryos through prenatal genetic screening. The unprecedented advancements in technically assisted reproduction pose new challenges to respect for human life and human dignity and call for a renewed appreciation of the important humanitarian values taught by scriptural sources. Ignoring these values could lead to the abuse of the weakest and most vulnerable members of human society, our children.

Sexuality and Procreation

According to the creation narrative in the Qur'an, in the natural order the beginning of new life in any species requires the existence of a male and a female, whose conjugal relationship can lead to procreation. This male-female intimacy for the purpose of procreation is also the beginning of moral consciousness about the rules that govern sexuality. The relationship between the sexes raises the question of what constitutes socially and morally acceptable standards of behavior. The creation narrative in the Qur'an raises question about shame and the ensuing need to cover the private parts while still in the environment of innocence in the Garden of Eden. The consequence of eating from the forbidden "tree" (the "tree" of moral knowledge) appears to be moral awareness about one's private parts. Adam and Eve, as the Qur'an relates, discover their nakedness upon eating the forbidden fruit and feel the need to cover their parts: "They [both][7] tasted the [fruit of the] tree, their shameful parts revealed to them, so they took to stitching upon themselves leaves of the Garden" (Q. 7:20). Apparently the passage seems to be connecting nakedness with sexuality and the natural attraction between men and women. Otherwise why would the couple feel embarrassment at their nakedness? Moreover, "stitching upon themselves leaves" also suggests the existence of a naturally endowed ability to know the right course of action when faced with the sense of guilt that arises from wrong doing. This moral cognition becomes apparent precisely from the beginning of the man-woman relationship. The timing of this necessary ethical knowledge is significant, underscoring the importance given to sexuality in the preservation of the integrity of future generations through morally aware man-woman conjugal relations.

The parable of Eden can fruitfully be viewed in the context of the ethos of Semitic culture. The relativity of ethical systems in different cultures suggests an important caveat when searching for universally applicable sexual mores in

Islam. Various Muslim societies take into consideration the variability of cultural and historical experiences to formulate norms of sexuality. And although there are certain practices that claim scriptural endorsement and universal application, there can arise a tension between a particular scriptural directive, with its culture-specific ethos, and a demand for universal ethics that regulates this spousal relationship across different cultures. Evidently there are points of convergence between the relative cultural values and the universal norms that are extrapolated from the Qur'an and the Tradition. Nevertheless, there are relative aspects of man-woman relationships based on local customs and conventions that have found their way into the legal formulations that claim normative status and hence universal application.

The male-female relationship is strictly regulated in the Islamic ethics of spousal relationships. Procreation is deemed essential, but it does not seem to be the sole purpose of a spousal relationship. Rather, according to the Qur'an, the principal reason for the creation of mutual attraction (*mawadda*) between man and woman is the companionship and the repose it bestows: "And of his signs is that he created for you, of yourselves, spouses, so that you might repose in them, and he has set between you love (*mawadda*) and mercy (*raḥma*)" (Q. 30:20). The Qur'an encourages marriage and regards the sexual relationship between spouses as natural and satisfying, fulfilling both one's natural drive and the religious exhortation to procreate. Some traditions consider marriage and the ensuing sexual relationship as a prerequisite for attaining spiritual-moral perfection and purity. Consequently, the Tradition encourages intimacy and lays down detailed rules about the manner in which conjugal relations must be conducted.[8]

Procreation is a meritorious act as long as it conforms to the ethics of sexuality. One of the major concerns in regulating sexual life in Islam, as pointed out earlier, is the preservation of the lineage of future generations. The Qur'an imposes restrictions in this regard and requires that men and women guard their private parts from one another, except for their spouses: "Prosperous are the believers who . . . guard their private parts (*furūj*)[9] [by abstaining from sexual relations] except with their marriage partners . . ." (Q. 23:1). In other words, the performance of sexual acts, whether performed for pleasure or for procreation, must be guarded from adultery and from seeking offspring outside of marriage. In several other places, by praising those believers who guard their private parts (Q. 24:30; 80:29; 4:22–23), the Qur'an encourages and directs human beings to seek progeny only through licit conjugal relations; it requires both men and women to guard their private parts from becoming contaminated by illicit sexual relationships because, as the means of procreation, these private parts must remain unblemished. The issue of tainting the sanctity of the child's lineage through adultery has prompted Muslim scholars to scrutinize assisted reproduction—implanting a Petri-dish embryo in a woman's uterus—to ensure that the technology in no way compromises the legitimate lineage of the child.

The grievous nature of the act of adultery is underscored by a tradition in which the Shī'ite Imam Ja'far al-Ṣādiq was asked why adultery merited a more severe punishment than the equally sinful act of drinking wine—one hundred lashes for the former, eighty for the latter. The response was that adultery results in the depositing of semen in a place reserved by divine law for the husband.[10] In another tradition it is related that the most severe punishment awaits a person who deposits his semen in a vagina that is forbidden to him—that is, he engages in intercourse with a woman who is not married to him.[11]

At the core of the preservation of the child's unblemished lineage is the Prophet's instruction to the parents to provide a good upbringing so that the child grows up to become a virtuous and healthy member of the family and society. In Muslim culture, children born out of wedlock suffer stigmatization and loss of respect. In addition, because of a widely reported Prophetic tradition encouraging Muslims to get married, the institution of marriage in Muslim culture is the sole guarantor of a child's proper lineage and his/her right to inherit property from the biological father. Consequently, a child of uncertain lineage lacks not only dignity but also a share of the father's estate. This denigration of illegitimate children may lead to abuse and serious violation of their human rights. It is for this reason that Islam forbids any method of procreation that might cause children to grow up in questionable conditions that might cause lasting damage to their self-esteem.

Infertility and Reproductive Technologies

In the Qur'an, the story of Zachariah captures the importance of procreation and the human need to have an heir to carry on one's name and career: "He (Zachariah) called upon his Lord secretly saying: 'O my Lord, behold the bones within me are feeble and my head is all aflame with hoariness. And in calling you, my Lord, I have never been turned away unanswered. But now I fear my kinsfolk after I am gone; and my wife is barren. So give me from you, a son who shall be my inheritor and the inheritor of the House of Jacob; and make him, my Lord, well-pleasing'" (Q. 19:1–3). The possibility of treating a woman's barrenness was remote without God's intervention, as Zachariah makes clear: "O my Lord, how shall I have a son, given that my wife is barren, and I have attained to the declining of old age?" He (God) said, "So it shall be; your Lord says, 'Easy is that for me. When I created you the first time you were as nothing'" (Q. 19:5–6).

In Muslim belief, the degree of fertility was divinely ordained and accepted as part of God's will. Despite this sense of resignation about infertility, in the Semitic cultural milieu, in which the siring of children, especially sons, was a source of prestige and a sign of God's blessing and prosperity, barren women were ostracized. Whether the problem originated with the man or the woman, it was woman who suffered the disgrace. In fact, Islamic law gives the husband a unilateral right to revoke the marriage contract and remarry if the woman is infertile. For the woman to have a similar right, she needs to state that condition clearly in her marriage contract. Fortunately, with education and growing awareness about their rights, women and their representatives in many parts of the Muslim world have negotiated favorable terms in their marriage contracts to protect their rights in such contingencies.[12] Moreover, in their patriarchal setting, the Semites valued their sons above their daughters, because it was the sons who carried the name of the family and were expected to perform challenging and demanding tasks in society. In the Zachariah's petition to God, the distinction between a son and a daughter is implicit: "When the wife of Imran said: 'O Lord! I have promised to dedicate the child I carry in my womb [to the temple]. Accept my vow from me, for you hear [all promises] and know [all secrets].' When she gave birth to a daughter she said, 'O Lord! I have given birth to a daughter!' And God knew very well what she had given birth to; male is not as the female" (Q. 3:32–33).

In pre-Islamic Arab tribal culture, as reported in the Qur'an, daughters were regarded as a source of humiliation and were often buried alive on their birth. In fact, the Qur'an criticizes their mean attitude when news of the birth of a baby girl was announced: "And when any of them is given the good tidings of a girl, his face is darkened and he chokes inwardly, as he hides himself from the people because of the evil of the good tidings that have been given to him, whether he shall preserve it (the baby-girl) in humiliation, or trample it into the dust. Ah, evil is that they judge!" (Q. 16:57–58). This disgraceful attitude prevails not only in some parts of the Muslim world, but also in other cultures where having sons is a source of special honor and pride. The introduction of prenatal genetic screening as a routine medical practice in some countries has made prenatal sex selection a possibility. Some parents, with good motives, engage in sex selection as a form of gender family planning. It is critical to acknowledge that as a matter of principle, sex selection is a morally questionable, socially prejudicial, and discriminatory practice. Because of the preference for boys in some cultures, there has been systematic destruction of female embryos as "unwanted" beings. This is clearly a breach of the fundamental scriptural assessment of human beings that grants the embryo, regardless of its gender, the moral status and respect due a human being. There is no justification in the Islamic tradition for discarding an embryo through selective abortion.

Nevertheless, infertility in Muslim societies has been a problem and has had to be treated, both for social and psychological reasons. In traditional Islamic pharmaceutical literature, a number of herbal prescriptions are mentioned as a cure, and these were popular among women who could not bear children. Additionally, there is a long tradition in folk Muslim culture for the treatment of infertility through miraculous prayer and pious acts of charity. One of the prominent features of Muslim shrine culture is its popularity with women seeking a saint's intercession for fertility. In almost all shrines connected with holy women from the Family of the Prophet (*ahl al-bayt*)—whether in Cairo, Egypt; Damascus, Syria; Qumm, Iran; or Samarra, Iraq—one can observe replicas of cradles in valuable metals like silver and gold placed on the tombs of these women-saints in commemoration of miraculously treated infertility.

The introduction of reproductive technologies in the Muslim world has introduced unprecedented possibilities for treating infertility and a host of other issues. Technologies such as in vitro fertilization, gamete intra-fallopian transfer (GIFT) and zygote intra-fallopian transfer (ZIFT) have provided women with the liberty to control reproduction and find solutions to infertility and unwanted pregnancies. Birth-control technology raised ethical issues for a number of Muslim scholars, who, on the basis of the principle of rejection of harm, ruled that the use of such technology is forbidden. The option of terminating a pregnancy evoked debates about the rights of the fetus and responsibility of parents and medical practitioners in making such decisions.

In the 1970s in vitro fertilization (IVF) to treat human infertility marked the beginning of the revolution in making possible what is impossible in nature. In vitro (lit. "in glass") refers to the Petri dish in which the sperm and eggs are mixed. This technique was originally developed to get around the woman's damaged or absent fallopian tubes, which connect the ovaries to the uterus. In 1978 the technique was successfully used to fertilize the eggs and implant the resultant product as a way to treat infertility.

A typical IVF procedure involves a woman receiving hormones to stimulate the ovaries to produce more than just one egg. Shortly before ovulation would normally occur, a physician uses ultrasound to guide a needle through the cervix to the ovaries to retrieve developed ova. After inspecting the ova for any defect, the ova are combined with the prepared sperm. The resulting embryos are allowed to develop in the Petri dish for a few days, reaching the stage of two to eight cells. On the third or fourth day one or more embryos are transferred to the woman's uterus by means of a catheter inserted through the cervix. Usually more than one embryo is produced through this process because the successful implantation may not occur in the first attempt, and more embryos might be needed for further attempts. In gamete intra-fallopian transfer (GIFT), which uses a similar technique, ova and sperm are mixed and transferred directly into the fallopian tube to allow the natural process to take over the process of fertilization, thereby increasing the chances for a successful gestation leading to a birth. In zygote intra-fallopian transfer (ZIFT), the in vitro–produced embryo is transferred to the fallopian tube rather than the uterus to allow the embryo to go through natural process of fertilization for successful implantation. Both of these techniques involve a more invasive procedure than the ones used in IVF. They are also more expensive than IVF and have a poorer track record, so IVF remains the main reproductive technology to treat infertility.

The other major ethical concern with IVF is about a woman's egg being fertilized outside the body and then being injected in the fallopian tubes of the mother or surrogate mother. The lineage of the child in Islamic law has always been traced to the sexual union of a man and woman. In one case, however, the jurists had to rule on the legitimacy of a child who was conceived asexually by a woman who manually introduced into her uterus the sperm that she considered to be her husband's. An asexual pregnancy without penetration created the problem of attribution of the child to the man. When the man refused to recognize this child who was conceived asexually, the jurists ascribed it to the mother as the Qur'an did in this verse: "Their mothers are only those who gave them birth" (Q. 58:2), because they did not regard the pregnancy as adulterous.[13] By analogy, then, although assisted reproductive technology has no precedent in the classical juridical formulations, its legitimization within a marriage is not difficult to infer.

Similarly, surrogate motherhood was not known to the classical jurists. With the provision of polygamy, the immediate solution to infertility was always a second wife, sometimes with the encouragement and approval of the first wife, and at other times with the disapproval or even divorce of the first wife. But the new possibility that the second wife could now gestate an embryo that carried the gametes of the husband and the first wife (who, because of medical conditions, could not carry it to its full term) through IVF required a precise determination about whether the procreation had occurred within the same family unit. The legal doctrine provided an important rule that required the jurists to avert probable harm (*daf' al-ḍarar al-muḥtamal*) before any consideration of benefit that accrued to the agent through such a medical intervention.

The ethical debates among Muslim scholars have been prompted by the potential of a charge of illicitness for the artificial insemination with donor sperm (AID). While artificial insemination with husband's sperm (AIH) has been mostly endorsed as permissible by most Sunni and Shī'ite scholars, the traditions that prohibited depositing a stranger's sperm in a woman's vagina, in addition to the Qur'anic concern with the "guarding of the private parts" by abstaining from sexual relations outside a marriage, raised serious concerns about the morality of asexual in vitro reproductive procedures.

The misgivings about the procedures in IVF clinics were raised by some senior scholars when they accurately declared that, although there was nothing in Qur'an or the Tradition about artificial insemination, the procedure was incompatible with the values enshrined in the Sharī'a. These values included procreation within a marriage and through natural means of conception. The following assessment of the entire project of assisted reproduction, more particularly artificial insemination with a donor egg (AIH), captures the essential elements of Islamic ideals of procreation:

> The acceptance of this [reproductive] technology goes against the goals of the Islamic revelation and other important benefits (*maṣāliḥ muhimma*) that were underscored by it in legislating marriage and

> regulating the spousal relationship. The main goal of the revelation-based law is to provide stability in the family in Islamic societies. Surely, the revelation had all these societal and familial goals in mind when it provided prescriptive laws of marriage and stabilized [the] man-woman relationship within its legitimate boundaries. Those who support the technology, including AID, that is, artificial insemination with donor sperm, have not considered its legal-moral implications, for surely, this means that it is possible to inseminate the sperm of a father with the egg of a daughter, or a sperm of a brother with the egg of a sister, asexually, and regard it permissible on basis of the inference that donor sperm insemination is permissible. Given that no act of penetration has occurred to render it adulterous, its acceptance as a permissible procedure of procreation is morally reprehensible.[14]

This negative evaluation of assisted reproduction places the burden on health-care policy makers to ensure that new technology is under ethical governmental regulation. Some senior Muslim religious leaders saw artificial insemination as an encroachment upon God's act of creation and a threat to a child's right to have a clear lineage from his/her biological parents. The newly emerging Muslim scholars, however, have been inclined to take more seriously the cultural implications of infertility for a woman and have been willing to approve of artificial insemination with donor sperm by viewing the Qur'anic injunction to "guard one's private parts from other than one's spouse" as a prohibition of a sexual relationship with a man outside of marriage. Men and women are required to abstain from having sex outside of marriage, but this injunction never included a prohibition against implanting a sperm in the fallopian tube or a fertilized embryo in the uterus by means of a catheter inserted through the cervix. Hence, these scholars argue, regardless of how a husband's sperm reaches his wife's egg, the resulting child is legitimately ascribed to the couple.[15]

In grappling with ethical dilemmas presented by the new reproductive technology, jurists have taken diverse hermeneutic approaches to the Qur'anic verses and the traditions that correlated the trustworthiness of the lineage of the child with sexual modesty. The Qur'anic injunction that men and women "guard their private parts" from any illegitimate sexual relationship can be interpreted to include or exclude assisted reproduction, whether AIH or AID, assuming a logical connection between sexual modesty and legitimate lineage of the offspring. The ruling to preserve the child's lineage could not be guaranteed without restricting access to the private parts of the legitimate partners in a marriage. Hence, Fakhr al-Dīn al-Rāzī (d. 1209), the Sunni-Ash'arite commentator, declares in no uncertain terms that all the references in the Qur'an to "guarding one's private parts" refer to abstaining from adultery—except one, in which both men and women are required to refrain from looking at the private parts of each other (Q. 24:31–32).[16]

Notwithstanding the unknowns of traditional law, the benefits of IVF in treating infertility are obvious, as long as such fertilization is achieved within the legitimate boundaries of marriage. However, as is typical of Islamic juridical deliberations, little attention has been paid to the moral and social implications of the child's identity and relationship to the family, on the one hand, and, on the other, the status of the multiple human embryos that were produced in the Petri dish and then implanted to increase the likelihood of pregnancy. In the case of multiple pregnancies, the procedure requires the abortion of additional embryos to avoid endangering the mother's health and improve the chances of survival for the viable one. Aside from the two to three embryos that are injected for gestation, there are surplus embryos that are frozen for use in possible future attempts. What is the status of these inseminated and frozen embryos? Could they be used later in further attempts at having a first child or additional children? Who owns them if the couple later divorces or if one of them dies? Could they be simply discarded as "unwanted" embryos? Could they be used to derive stem cells for research or therapeutic applications?[17]

IVF has the limited goal of correcting a natural condition, allowing a would-be mother to carry a fertilized embryo to its full term of gestation. Keeping in mind the diversity of Muslim legal opinions on new bioethical issues, most have come to endorse the IVF technology with the stipulation that the procedure should not lead to any sinful act contrary to Sharī'a rulings about the man-woman relationship nor should it lead to any harm to the couple or the child. Hence, even when some scholars have had reservations about the production of gametes asexually, including the morally questionable act of masturbation to derive the sperm, IVF became a routine medical practice in the Muslim world to enhance the possibilities of conception for women who can afford these expensive reproductive procedures. In addition, doctors can now be guided by ultrasound to the ovaries to retrieve eggs vaginally, a somewhat invasive procedure that raises questions about a third-party male physician (other than the woman's father, husband, or brother) having access to the private parts of the woman. There has been no immediate solution to this problem because there are not enough female physicians to perform IVF procedures and thus pose no threat to the Islamic code of modesty.

In most cases of infertility, if the family is well-to-do, the treatment is sought abroad, where such Islamic sensibilities about male-female relationships are absent. Nevertheless, the issue, however academic in nature, is general enough to require a sensible and immediate solution in view of the shortage of female specialists in all areas of medicine. Before the spread of modern mass education, infertility was a serious problem in Islamic societies. Married couples who could not have a child spared no effort, including financial hardship, to become parents. Consequently, the legal hair-splitting that is part of the seminary culture and is meant for the consumption of the traditional scholars of Islamic law has rarely filtered down to the ordinary folks looking for practical solutions—except in the form of rulings that either permitted or forbade a procedure.

As pointed out earlier, IVF clinics were faced with serious questions about the frozen surplus embryos that were produced for the future implantation if the pregnancy did not occur the first time around. Juridical solutions were not hard to deduce when legal principles—like the principles of public good (*maṣlaḥa*) that promotes what is beneficial and necessity (*ḍarūra*) that overrules prohibition—could provide moral-legal justification for the use of surplus embryos as the source of stem cells for research. After all, as some prominent Sunni jurists have pointed out, the principle of the sanctity of life does not apply to the embryos that are outside the womb. Consequently, because stem-cell research has enhanced the possibility of curing diseases, the principle of public good provided the justification for using frozen embryos to isolate stem cells. I will return to the ethics of stem cell research in chapter 8, where I discuss recent developments in biotechnology. Nevertheless, it is important to point out that in many of these recent rulings endorsing stem cell research the inviolability of frozen embryos is ill-conceived.

The future use of frozen embryos for posthumous transfer of an intrafallopian gamete to a widow is another problem demanding a meticulous evaluation of the status of the frozen embryo to make sure it could be treated as the property of the legally married couple. If the frozen embryo is considered to be property, then it is subject to the laws governing ownership and transfer of property belonging to the biological father and mother. However, is it really property? There is no doubt that if the couple is alive, both have a right to determine the use of their embryos. What if one of them dies, however? Jurists began to question the widow's right to use the frozen embryo because the death of her husband is presumed to void the contract that wedded her to him. If she is no longer his wife, on this view, the newborn could not use the father's name as part of her/his identity.[18]

Reproductive Genetics

Muslim scholars have as yet to assess the moral and genetic implications of the asexual production of embryos through somatic-cell nuclear transfer (SCNT), which involves the introduction of nuclear material of somatic cell into an enucleated oocyte. The possibility of experiments dealing with the creation of embryos from three or more genetic parents poses new challenges for ethical-religious evaluation. It is ironic that Muslims who correlate legitimate lineage with a traditionally approved sexual relationship between biological parents have utterly failed to come to grips with the consequences of artificial insemination with donor sperm. If clarification of lineage is a prerequisite for allowing assisted reproduction within a marriage, it is necessary to carefully examine the religo-ethical implications of donor-sperm insemination. In retrospect, those scholars who opposed AID seem to have averted greater harm by insisting upon AIH. In other words, to protect the lineage of the child as conceived in Muslim cultures, the use of donor's sperm or even donor's egg had to be disapproved and even forbidden in the context of IVF clinics. According to traditional Islamic law, even when the asexually conceived child could be spared from carrying the stigma of being the fruit of an adulterous relationship and attributed to the mother only, it is difficult, perhaps even impossible, to establish the child's legitimate lineage with certainty without certain knowledge of the identity of the biological father. No Muslim scholar could endorse and justify the morality of a procedure based on the principle "Necessity overrides prohibition," even if it provided the only solution to treat infertility in a way that would spare the child social ostracism. The oft-repeated religious guidance in the matter of infertility was to trust in God's wisdom and submit to God's decree in the matter of infertility.[19]

Islamic normative sources have offered meager guidance in forging an ethics of genetics. Although the Tradition has preserved an account of a form of eugenics that was practiced in the pre-Islamic tribal culture, because the practice did not resonate with Islamic morality, it was forbidden. Although I will deal with the ethics of genetic engineering and genetic screening in chapter 8, in the context of the beginning of life some observations about genetics are in place. In modern medicine, preselection eugenics has returned as a medical procedure of preimplantation genetic diagnosis (PGD), making it possible for the parents to choose an embryo on the basis of desired and undesired physical traits and mental capacities. With its enormous therapeutic potential, the human embryo is gradually evolving into a commodity that can be ordered like any other product, with "options" chosen in advance in eerie emulation of the automobile showroom. The idea of the parent's unconditional love for their offspring seems increasingly a relic of earlier times.

As noted in the introductory chapter, there are hardly any public debates on the critical issues in biomedical ethics in Muslim countries because of the absence of democratic governance. The Muslim public is kept in the dark when decisions are filtered down from the top in the absence of public debates or hearings to determine whether any of these new reproductive technologies are beneficial or harmful to the family and the child. Because most of the autocratic governments and their representatives in the public sector are not accountable to the public when major health-care blunders are committed, the public is left with no one to turn to except medical practitioners.

To be sure, medical practice remains authoritarian in the Muslim world, where the patient has no right to question and hold a physician responsible for any detrimental procedure. On the other hand, because the religious seminaries know little about what is happening in the world of medical research and practice, ethical-legal deliberations generally lack any sophisticated analysis of genetics and the complex procedures involved in reproductive technologies. For instance, in earlier rulings allowing the use of donor's sperm or egg in IVF, the serious harm this procedure could cause to the dignity of the child was overlooked. As detailed information about IVF became available to the jurists, the rulings that once allowed the use of a donor's gamete for implantation were now reversed in favor of a ban on any tampering with the strict traditional edicts governing the use of a married couple's gamete and preserving the child's lineage.[20] Even when the jurists knew that the juridical method for deducing fresh decisions from the revealed texts had to depend upon the conventional wisdom of reasonable people (and not the other way round, as some had insisted) in the matter of reproductive technology, they sought to provide solutions solely through nonethical interpretations of the texts that made reference to sexual procreation or sexual modesty, whichever served their ultimate rulings about IVF procedures. Social interaction, as the Sharī'a visualized it, was time-bound and dependent upon realistic assessment of each case as it affected the moral fabric of society. With the huge social implications of reproductive technology, just issuing a judicial decision about one or another form of assisted reproduction was insufficient in assessing the potential damage that could be done to the social standing of a Muslim woman or child, especially as regards issues such as the traditional prohibition on the depositing of a sperm other than the husband's in the woman's vagina. But what about depositing an egg of a woman in the woman's vagina? Was it permissible? What about the implications of artificial insemination with a donor egg? Would the child be related to the donor of the egg or to the gestational surrogate mother?

In the classical formulations, a possibility of depositing one woman's egg into another woman's fallopian tube or uterus was inconceivable. There was no understanding of the genetic makeup of a gamete, and so no possibility of pronouncing on such questions. Nevertheless, the silence over depositing of egg in a "stranger's" (in this case, another probably unrelated woman) womb and its implication for the child's lineage opened up hermeneutical opportunities, for some at least, to support it as a case of "substitute" or "surrogate motherhood."[21] Based on the extrapolations from the verses that call upon Muslim women to "guard their private parts," it would be difficult to countenance gestational surrogacy, whether commercial or altruistic. According to this interpretation, implanting the zygote of a married couple in the womb of surrogate mother for gestation would flout the command to guard the private parts (*ḥifẓ furūj*). Gestational surrogacy then became another controversy weighing on the possibilities that assisted reproduction offered to infertile Muslim women.

Surrogate Motherhood (*ijārat al-raḥim*)

The issue of surrogate motherhood—acting as the fetus's incubator during the nine months of gestation—has given rise to questions about the inviolability of a woman's womb.[22] In the virgin birth of Jesus, as related by the Qur'an, the existence of Mary, as the carrier of the "Spirit of God" (*rūḥ allāh*, the title used for Jesus in Islam), was vital. In other words, part of God's miracle was dependent upon a mother's womb to carry the child. In nature there is no substitute for a mother's womb for the gestation of a child. It is for this reason Islam regards as sacred motherhood in general and the mother's womb in particular. Significantly, in the chapter entitled "Women," the Qur'an presents woman's womb[23] as the source of human relationships, and reciprocity and mutuality is negotiated through wombs—the starting place of what "you demand one of another" (Q. 4:1) in kinship. In another place, God acknowledges the critical role a mother plays in procreation and honors her by enjoining human beings to show kindness to both the parents, but more particularly to the mother. As the Qur'an puts it, "his mother bore him painfully, and painfully she gave birth to him; his bearing and his weaning are thirty months" (Q. 46:12–13). In Prophetic practice, there are numerous traditions in praise of the woman's status as a mother, enjoining Muslims to show deference to her all the time. Her role in conceiving and delivering a child are so important that if a woman dies while giving birth to a child, God forgives her by wiping her slate clean, and she enters paradise without any reckoning.[24]

All cultures accord a high degree of honor and respect to motherhood. In pre-Islamic Arabia, the Qur'an and the Tradition challenged the scandalous mistreatment of women by using the metaphor of the womb (*raḥim*) to make the point that human relationships are impossible without the generative and bonding powers of the mother's womb. Hence, preservation of natural kinship depended on safeguarding the connection to the maternal womb. In contrast, the role of the father was simply to protect the womb from the moral contamination of impregnation by another man's semen.

When artificial insemination became a treatment option for infertility, the man had the responsibility of making sure that his own semen was artificially implanted in his wife's uterus and that he was the semen donor (AIH). This would ensure the legitimacy of the child and would relate all other children born from the same biological parents. As discussed above, the Islamic norms preserved in the overall goals of the Sharī'a tend to rule against the possibility of the pregnancy of a woman using donated sperm (AID) that carries the genetic materials of a man other than her husband. In a similar vein, most jurists believe that a donated ovum also cannot be used in the case when the wife lacks either healthy ovaries or the ability to produce ova for retrieval. In other words, the Sharī'a rules out any attempt to procreate by using donor's sperm or donor's egg.[25]

Nonetheless, in a polygamous marital system, gestational surrogacy remains possible by letting a second wife carry the gametes of the first wife and the husband. For varying reasons, while most scholars have ruled out the permissibility of a woman not married to the man carrying the couple's gametes to a full term, some recent opinions have permitted that procedure.[26] In view of the Islamic tradition's emphasis on unblemished lineage, there are also opinions that allow the use of a donor's egg as long as it is combined with the husband's semen and implanted to the wife's uterus, because the prohibition explicitly deals with the depositing of the semen of a stranger in the wife's vagina. There is no ban on a donor's egg replacing the wife's defective egg. Because the semen belongs to the husband, the lineage is intact, and he is the father of the child, as declared by this well-established rule: "A child belongs to the husband."[27] But that situation leaves the identity of the mother unresolved because of the involvement of two women in the process: the woman who donated her ovum and the wife who carried the fetus for gestation. Some have maintained that the former is the mother, because the child carries some of her genetic materials; whereas the womb of the latter is nothing more than the earth that feeds the seed and helps it grow. Others have argued that mother is the owner of the womb, in accordance with the Qur'anic dictum, "Their mothers are only those who gave them birth" (Q. 58:2).[28] By this they contend that birth means "to come out of the womb." Still others have argued that both women are the mothers, since both of them have contributed in bringing about the birth of the child.[29]

The analogy based on the similarity of the role played by earth and surrogate womb in nurturing the seed in the above-cited opinion neglects to account for the influence surrogate mothers have on the development of the budding human life. The surrogate mother certainly contributes more comprehensively than the earth that nurtures the seed. The seed receives much more than simply growth from the earth. In fact, the growth of the tree reveals the effect of the nutritious minerals and the water that the seed receives from the earth. Likewise, surrogate motherhood is far more than a clinical nine-month incubation. The closest Islamic analogy to surrogate motherhood in the Sharīʿa is that of a wet nurse who suckles the child for two years and is known as "suckling mother" (*al-umm al-riḍāʿīya*). Her milk contributes to the growth of the infant's bones and flesh just as the womb nurtures the embryo with its nutritious blood supply. In this way, both the surrogate womb and the donor of the ovum that enriched the genetic make up of the infant through fertilization with the sperm have a right to be acknowledged as mothers of the infant.[30]

The "suckling mother" in the Sharīʿa is afforded a status of a "virtual mother" (*al-umm al-nisbīya*) without any right to inheritance, and is consanguineously connected to the child in such a way that a marital relationship between her and the child, if he happens to be a boy, would be considered incestuous. Moreover, marriage of the suckled boy to the daughter of suckling mother is also forbidden. Furthermore, the rule of consanguinity is extended to include the surrogate mother's relation to her uterine son. But this is disputed by the medical science, which regards only the donor of the egg to be the mother because of her participation in creating the genetic makeup of the child. In fact, some Sunni scholars believe that the owner of the egg is the mother, even when the owner of the womb has acted as the incubator of the fetus. Accordingly, they regard the surrogate mother as equal in status to the suckling mother because of the special relationship through birth that has emerged during the nine months of gestation and the possible role that the sustenance of the womb might have in giving form and substance to the child, despite the repudiation of any such possibility by modern medical science.

To recapitulate, for those who maintain that the mother is the owner of the womb, there is no reason to prohibit artificial insemination through ovum surrogacy as long as the husband's semen is involved in the fertilization. As for those who maintain that the mother is the owner of the egg, or that both are entitled to be the mother, they too have no reason to maintain the ban on either ovum implantation or the gestational surrogacy, aside from the protection of the child's lineage in cases where the identity of either parent might be in question. This is the implication of the commandment that rules out legal adoption by requiring Muslims to seek progeny only through one's marriage: "He has not made your adopted sons your sons in fact. Call them after their true fathers. That is more equitable in the sight of God" (Q. 33:4–5). Hence, the Sharī'a forbids the seeking of progeny through someone other than one's own spouse because of the ambiguity it creates in the child's lineage. Following this line of argument in the matter of adoption, effecting a relationship through surrogacy cannot be treated as an exception from the general rule against legal adoption, with its imperative of protecting the proper lineage of the child by relating him/her to the biological father rather than the social father and authorizing inheritance only from the former. Islam limits legitimate fatherhood and motherhood strictly to marriage, and the mixing of the husband's sperm with the wife's egg.

In the light of the foregoing discussion, the obvious concern among Muslims remains whether IVF procedures sully the source of kinship. The hesitation in endorsing IVF is based on a very important ethical rule: *al-'usr wa al-ḥaraj*—"protection from distress and impairment," a subsidiary rule derived from the principle of "No harm, no harassment": Did the technology cause distress and impair sanctified family relationships formed by the legitimate union of man and woman in marriage and through the honor of the womb in birth?

These issues are at the center of reproductive technology and genetics today. The critical questions are not confined to the moral and legal status of the fetus, which are important in themselves for different reasons (for instance, the right to inherit); rather, the thrust of the debate is about the woman-man relationship and its impact on the child's right to have a decent life based on clearly conceived genealogy that relates the newborn to legitimate parents and others in the extended family. The rulings examined in this connection explicitly rule out the possibility of anyone beside the married couple as the guarantor of the child's untainted genealogy. It is also in this light that artificial insemination with the sperm of a man other than the husband is construed by some as a form of adultery (*zinā*) (although the act did not involve penetration), such that the child born through such a process is illegitimate (*walad al-ḥarām* or *ibn al-zinā*).[31] As mentioned earlier, the Prophet's traditions explicitly declare that placing the seed of another man (*ajnabī*) in the womb of a married woman is a grievous sin that destroys the inviolability of a family.[32] However, most of the rulings also view as adulterous artificial insemination by means of a donated egg and the husband's sperm implanted by noncoital procedures and carried through gestational surrogacy by the wife.[33]

In addition to the textual sources that are usually marshaled as evidence against artificial insemination with donor sperm (AID), there is widespread cultural indifference to the problem of sterility connected with husband's sperm. It is inconceivable for any Muslim man to accept donor sperm to treat his wife's infertility because of the social stigma that such a procedure might attach to his offspring. The identity of the father is important not only for cultural reasons; it is also critical for medical history of the child. More importantly, although the child's upbringing contributes to the overall development of the child's personality, the natural father's DNA has an undeniable impact upon the child's intelligence, general physical appearance, susceptibility to specific medical conditions, and overall psychological tendencies. The genetic heritage makes it imperative that the identity of the child's natural father be known by the child.

The other reason for unambiguously identifying the natural father is the possibility of consanguineous marriage occurring between a half-brother and half-sister. In recent years some Muslim physicians have sought a ruling on the possibility of using an anonymous donor's sperm to avoid the adverse impact of this kind of assisted reproduction. But even the anonymity connected with the donor of the sperm could not absolve any party to the process of the responsibility of fostering the possibility, however unlikely, of incest that could result from the mating of half brothers and half sisters with a common biological father. Regardless, whether such a marriage happens intentionally or unintentionally, with or without prior knowledge of this biological relationship, the Sharī'a considers such a marriage incestuous and a clear violation of the divinely instituted laws that govern legitimate conjugal relations.

In summary, then, the use of another woman's womb as the fetus's incubator has been deemed culturally unacceptable because of the religious status of a mother's womb and traditional taboos concerning the involvement of a third party in the marital functions of sex and procreation, as evidenced in the use of the derogatory term "rental womb."[34] It is not surprising, then, to find a consensus among Muslim scholars about the need to keep the maternal womb untainted by any procedure that might cast doubt on the child's lineage.

Adoption

In Arab tribal culture it was common to adopt a son when a couple could not have children. The verse "He has not made your adopted sons your sons in fact" (Q. 33:4–5) provides an unmistakable evidence that the adoption of sons was widely practiced in pre-Islamic Arabia. Moreover, the admonition to "call them (the adopted sons) after their true (biological) fathers" in the same verse evidently criticizes the prevalent practice of confusing the genealogical truth by giving the adopted sons the adoptive father's name. The occasion that prompted the revelation of this injunction in the Qur'an has much to do with the rulings in the Sharīʿa that carefully safeguard against incestuous relationships. Because the adopted son was not a biological offspring, there was legally nothing to bar him from marrying a daughter of his adoptive father; nor could there be any prohibition against the adoptive father marrying his adopted son's biological mother, sister, or divorced wife.

The Sharīʿa, therefore, does not define adoption as an institution; rather, the care of orphans and children in need of parental care is provided through another institution, namely, guardianship (*wilāya*). Muslims are encouraged to function as guardians of children in need and assume the same responsibilities as biological parents. They must take care to provide for the child's upbringing, education, and other needs, and they must administer the child's property, making sure that the estate is used for the child's benefit, even after the guardian dies. However, in the Sharīʿa, the adoptive parents strictly function as guardians and do not become the legal parents. In this way, biological parents remain the legal parents, and the guardian fulfils the obligations to the child in substitution for the biological parents.

The Qur'an in general regards caring for orphans as a meritorious act and encourages Muslims to undertake the role of adoptive parents, as long as the child's legal status is clear so as not to confuse the child's biological lineage. Muḥammad himself was an orphan and was, in accordance with Arab tribal customs, under the guardianship of his paternal grandfather as long as the latter was alive, and then his uncle took over the responsibility. Hence, the Sharīʿa endorses a custodial role for an adoptive father. But it does not allow the adopted child to inherit from the adoptive father; he is entitled to inherit only from his biological father. The adoptive father can make a bequest for his adopted child only while he is still alive, because after his death the distribution of the inheritance strictly follows the rules that exclude all but natural children.

In sum, although Muslim culture recognizes the significant role that adoptive parents have in their children's upbringing, the Sharī'a does not accord adopted children equal status with natural children.

Eugenics (*najābat al-walad*) as an Enhancement of Biological Inheritance

Today an intense individualism has gripped global communities, with people asserting the right to determine future reproduction. Even in the Muslim world, where individualism is far less entrenched than it is in the advanced industrial countries of the West, there is an increasing emphasis on the inalienable human rights of each individual, regardless of familial or other forms of connectedness. In the context of reproductive technologies, the use of preimplantation genetic diagnosis (PGD) has allowed people freedom to eliminate a child with an unwanted medical condition.

At the same time, these technologies have also made it possible to prevent a number of hereditary, incurable diseases. Still, they impinge upon the human germ-cell line, potentially affecting the course of future generations. In the case of positive eugenics—which aims to increase the number of favorable genes in human society through biological improvement (as opposed to negative eugenics, which aims at decreasing the number of undesirable or harmful genes in order to winnow out the genetically unworthy)—the most important Islamic bioethical principle of public good states that one must avoid any technological manipulation of humans that might adversely affect their physical and cultural environments. Although there is a strong inclination to uphold genetic determinism in human hereditary traits, belief in God's absolute power allows for a divine intervention that can change anything in the DNA.

According to Islamic teachings about human development, nature and nurture interact to determine hereditary traits in a healthy social environment. Governments are obliged to pay attention to factors like nutrition, medical care, education, and a clean environment to improve human life at all levels. Hence, the ethical verdict on any reproductive genetic intervention, including positive eugenics, has to be made on the basis of predominance of comprehensive benefit (*istiṣlāḥ*). As I shall discuss in more detail in chapter 8, in emerging ethical dilemmas connected with controversial genetic engineering like eugenics, it is not unusual to find contrary views about gamete reproduction and microbiological techniques, which are still not fully understood by the practitioners of Islamic jurisprudence.

Molecular genetics, which concerns itself with the study of living systems and the transmission of hereditary characters encoded in the macromolecular structure of DNA, has become the most controversial research area in biology.

The information the DNA reveals about a person is open to potential abuse. The time has come to evaluate the social and psychological consequences of such physical-chemical encoding of the genes of humankind.

In Semitic cultures, where charisma was believed to have been inherited in a particular tribe from generation to generation, there was a belief in some measure of predetermination of the qualities of religious leaders. It was usually believed that God chose his prophets from a particular tribe whose progeny inherited the "mantle of prophethood" (*mansab al-nubuwwa*) through an act of divine grace (*luṭf min allāh*). One of the important intellectual activities in Muslim culture in Arabia was to trace genealogies of renowned individuals to show how the "blessed seed" was transmitted through a marital union of a man and a woman from famous tribes. A well-known book in classical Arabic literature is entitled *Ansāb al-ashrāf* (Lineages of the Noble Ones).[35]

Such a thesis about the "blessed seed" is contrary to the overall teachings of the Qur'an, which do not show much overt concern with eugenics. Nevertheless, Islam's abolition of one of the four types of marriages among Arabs seems to smack of eugenics. The tradition is related on the authority of 'Ā'isha, the Prophet's wife, who describes the types of conjugal relations that existed in Arabia prior to the Prophet's reform of the institution for Muslims. One of the types is mentioned as follows:

> The second type [of marriage] was that a man would say to his wife after she had become clean from her period, "Send for so-and-so [whose nobility is well-established] and have sexual relations with him." Her husband would then keep away from her and would not touch her at all till her pregnancy became evident from that man with whom she was sleeping. After the pregnancy was established, her husband would sleep with her if he wished. However, he allowed his wife to sleep with that person being desirous of the nobility of the child (*najābat al-walad*). Such marriage was called "marriage seeking exchange" (*nikāḥ al-istibdā'*).[36]

The Qur'an, which insisted that spiritual and moral awareness (*taqwā*) was the main source of all human nobility, did not support this Arab tribal practice for the improvement of human race through the control of hereditary factors, especially because it prescribed an illicit practice of sexual exchange in order to produce noble offspring. However, in some traditions the believers are counseled to choose a partner for breeding (*al-nuṭaf*) bravery among the people of Khurāsān in Iran, for increasing sexual potency among the Berber in North Africa, and for inculcating generosity and envy among Arabs.[37] These traditions do reflect an explicit awareness of eugenics in choosing marriage partners. The source of these eugenic considerations seems to have been Irano-Semitic culture, in which such concerns were commonplace. Although these traditions were never used as authoritative precedents for legislation in the Sharī'a or social policies in Muslim societies, they express popular beliefs about the choice of one's marriage partner.

Aside from the interest in genealogies and their impact upon future generations, in a number of theological and philosophical works inspired by Islamic scriptural resources, one can find references to the "innate nature" or "disposition" (*fiṭra*) with which humans have been created. There is something "given," divinely endowed, about human nature that functions as a reservoir of potentialities that can spur an evolution toward the attainment of levels of perfection. At the root of these postulates about divinely ordained disposition in human beings one can detect a constant tension in between the notions of determinism and freedom.

Each person, on this view, is endowed with a basic set of predispositions. Some may reject this idea as an unscientific, arbitrary construct, empirically unverifiable. Religion assesses human perfection in terms of the migratory growth of the self, sometimes known as the "struggle of the self," the *jihād bi al-nafs*—jihād against one's ego, as Muslim mystics maintained. This self represents enormous potential for engendering good and combating harm through self-discipline and critical self-assessment. This is self viewed as the domain of extramaterial, symbolic perceptions and interactions—the domain that defies reduction to the leveling statistical categories of social science. Any findings about the self that arise from presumed biological influences like genomes may or may not have spiritual relevance. But people of faith see the implications of such formulations in terms of immutable, inherited traits that cause generation after generation to suffer from some untold miseries such as inherited diseases.

Intellectual caution needs to be applied before labeling as absurd any great body of work that intelligent and sensitive human beings have deemed supremely important. Such is the religious doctrine about God's creation and determination of humanity's destiny. No religion can afford to neglect a long-term spiritual and moral improvement of humankind. In this connection, it is relevant to evaluate the religious dimension of genetic intervention in human affairs in the light of a belief in the divine will and its implications for human self-understanding. As a complex web of new realities and new relationships emerge between certain genes and particular human conditions that can be partly or wholly eliminated through genetic intervention, is it farfetched to speculate that molecular genetics may arrogate the right to determine both the form and the content of meaningful life?

When considering issues pertaining to medical treatment, Islamic scholars typically employ the language of obligations, duties, and interpersonal justice rather than the language of private and autonomous individual rights. The absolute obligation to save human life is accompanied by the principle of public good (*maṣlaḥa*), which demands that a doctor take into account not only the well-being of the patient but also that of family members, especially if active medical intervention leads to further suffering of the patient and his/her relatives. Such cases often carry social/political/ethical subtexts involving issues of justice, access, distribution of resources, the rising cost of preventive medicine, and so on. The availability of affordable resources, both human and technological, to sustain a patient's life must be assessed in terms of collective social needs founded upon the principle of distributive justice. In other words, the benefits of medical intervention must be open to all. Moral problems connected with the allocation of scarce resources in the majority of Muslim societies remain mostly unanswered because of authoritarian politics and paternalistic nature of health care in these countries.

Modern science and technology have uncovered a set of natural conditions that can be explored, explained, and even changed for the betterment of human life. The recently completed Human Genome Project initiative aims to make a detailed map of human DNA, the hereditary information in which one's genetic makeup is stored. This knowledge promises more advanced and effective treatments for a wide range of maladies that are thought to be genetically transmitted. It is possible that such detailed knowledge of the constituents of the human organism will lead to invidious comparisons between individuals—will some be deemed to be "superior" to others? The gains to be made in preventive medicine and research for cures to genetic diseases such as SCID (Severe Combined Immune Deficiency) and cancer need to be weighed in relation to the rise of new kinds of genetically derived discrimination (both in health care and employment) and a resurgence in eugenics.

The fear prompted by the clinical use of genetic interventions has led to set limits on research and testing that deal with human DNA. The technology itself is in the early, experimental stages, so many of these potential problems remain in the realm of conjecture. The intervention into human DNA seems to some to tamper with what are regarded as basic building blocks of human life. Moreover, much of the proposed research on human molecular biology depends upon the uses of gametes or early embryonic tissue, which in turn triggers controversies over abortion and the reality of the personhood of the human fetus.

Much of the concern among Muslim scholars in this area has focused on the fetus and the point at which it attains human personhood with full moral and legal status. The problem occurs when prenatal genetic testing determines that a fetus will develop into a child with a disability. In a case where it is possible to do harm by giving birth to a child whose life will be one of constant suffering, the question arises whether the parents, in consultation with the medical team, can decide to abort the fetus. Termination of early life in Islam requires assessing the exact moment when personhood or ensoulment occurs, and with it the developing human's possession of the full array of rights. The next chapter will explore the Islamic quest to pinpoint an answer to this vexing.

5

Terminating Early Life

Slay not your children for fear of poverty; we will provide for you and them. Surely the slaying of them is a grievous sin.

—Qur'an 17:31

The previous chapter previewed the issue of embryonic sanctity, especially in regard to the ethical quandaries presented by advanced reproductive technologies. The new reproductive genetics, especially preimplantation genetic diagnosis (PGD), in which IVF embryos are screened for genetic diseases or abnormalities, poses problems for the principle of embryonic sanctity if couples choose to abort fetuses that are doomed to suffer a debilitating disease. Such a decision raises both religious and moral problems because, in the Islamic tradition, there is no blanket permission to abort a defective fetus. The possibility of discarding a fetus because of physical defects seems to dispense with any notion of even minimal dignity for the zygote, even when there is only a remote potential of life for a preimplanted fertilized ovum. Any deliberate suppression of the life of an embryo poses problems for Muslims, even given the likelihood that a mother will give birth to a diseased or disabled child.

The question connected with the moral standing of embryonic and fetal life remains unresolved in Islamic jurisprudence because of the lack of a precise definition of life and of the beginning of life. In fact, there is no distinction made between embryo and fetus in the literature. The Qur'anic embryology, as I shall discuss below, does not fully accord with biological distinctions of the stages of development. Hence, my own usage in Islamic context in this chapter is an approximation of the fetal development in the womb. Although the jurists do not dispute the biological fact of life and the sanctity of the fetus, they differ about which stage of fetal development marks the advent of absolute inviolability (*dhimma ṣāliḥa*) and the possession of full human rights.[1] Hence, there are disagreements about the moment of conception and the onset of ensoulment, and whether "viability" pertains only to newborns capable of living outside the womb. By definition, since the fetus (*janīn*) is "concealed" (*istajann*) in the mother's womb until it is born,[2] it has no independent claim to life. In juridical terminology, the fetus is defined as an entity that in one sense does not directly acquire the personhood (*nafs*) that can benefit from rights.[3] Furthermore, in Islamic jurisprudence, abortion rulings are not framed in terms of a resolution to a conflict of rights between the pregnant woman and her fetus. According to the Ḥanafī scholars, for instance, as long as the fetus remains *in utero* it does not have independent and absolute inviolability because it is regarded as a part of the mother's body. However, as soon as it becomes separated from the uterus with the capability of surviving outside the womb, then it is regarded as a person (*nafs*) possessing inviolability and rights like liberty, inheritance, proper lineage, and so on.[4]

As such, the fetus in the womb has a relative claim to life and for rights because it is a potential human being. The closer to birth the fetus is, the closer it is to personhood and the attendant array of human rights.[5] Such an estimation of the personhood of the fetus is behind the contemporary liberal juridical opinions among Ḥanafī Sunni scholars, who do not regard abortion as forbidden if the mother's life is in danger at any stage of gestation, including the last days before the child is born.[6] This linkage to the health of the mother is often overlooked when clinical abortions are readily performed in the Muslim world with no impunity. There have also been rulings that permit abortions for reasons of poverty,[7] a practice that has led to the abuse of abortion as a method of population control. Certainly, no school of Islamic jurisprudence intends to allow abortion as a method of population control.[8]

The problem is that it was not until recently that abortion began to be treated independently under its own rubric in Islamic juridical formulations. Like a number of topics that involve some kind of criminality in medical jurisprudence, abortion as an unlawful act found its place in Islamic criminology (*jināyāt*). Yet the juridical tradition has produced scant discussion of the ethical dimensions of embryonic personhood. The fundamental assessment of an embryo in the Sharī'a is based upon a Qur'anic passage—and its elaboration in the Tradition—that speaks of a progressive acquisition of a human status without any concern for moral issues connected with the independent status of a fetus as a moral entity. Although there are a number of studies devoted to fresh rulings that deal with legality of abortion occasioned by adultery (*zinā*) and rape (*ightiṣāb*), there is hardly any serious debate among Muslims about the ethical issues connected with preimplantation embryos and/or the fetus as a person with its own rights and needs for protection.[9]

There are two issues related to terminating potential life: one is the temporary prevention of conception, and the other is the permanent control of fertility to avoid future pregnancies. Both these procedures have long been common in the Muslim world. Whether viewed as forms of family planning (*tanẓīm nasl*) or abortion, the issues have dense moral and legal implications. Muslim legal scholars have treated the subject of birth control in great detail, and a consensus has emerged regarding its permissibility as a means of population control, especially insofar as it can improve the living standards of predominantly poor Muslim societies.[10] However, the ethical dimension of preventing conception or terminating pregnancy within marriage remains unexplored. What is clear is that the moral dimensions of the issue are closely tied to cultural attitudes about the need to have children as part of one's entry into manhood and womanhood. Procreation is taken as a divinely ordained obligation provided it is not harmful to one of the spouses. Sexual pleasure is to be confined to marriage. It is the balancing of these two factors that seems to underlie the juridical rulings on preventing conception.

Who Decides?

Because the Qur'an gives men the power to regulate and manage the affairs of women (Q. 4:24), it is commonly assumed that even in critical matters pertaining to procreation, the man's preference would prevail. Most jurists, however, have not stipulated the need for the husband's permission in a decision to prevent conception. In other words, there is no objection if the woman decides to use any method of birth control to avoid becoming pregnant without her husband's approval as long as that method does not cause any harm to her health. However, some Ḥanafī and Ḥanbalī scholars have required that permission. According to Ibn Nujaym, (d. 970/1562) among the Ḥanafīs "it is forbidden for a woman to clog her uterus, as is customary for them to do in order to prevent becoming pregnant, without the husband's permission, just as it is forbidden for a man to practice coitus interruptus (*'azl*) without her permission."[11] By requiring each spouse to seek the other's permission about an act that prevents pregnancy, the judicial decision seems to insinuate a preference for procreation. This encouragement to procreate is implied in the ruling given by the Mālikī jurist al-Ḥaṭṭāb al-Andalūsī (d. 954/1547). He maintains that a woman cannot require her husband to practice coitus interruptus in order to avoid becoming pregnant.[12] The Shāfi'ī jurist 'Abū Isḥāq al-Shirāzī (d. 476/1083) believes that coitus interruptus is reprehensible (*makrūh*) even if the woman participant is legally free (not a slave) who has the right to dictate her terms to her spouse; her decision must be taken in concert with her husband.[13] The Ḥanbalī jurist Ibn Mufliḥ has no problem with a woman taking a medicine to induce menstruation.[14] However, he cites an opinion of a well-known Ḥanbalī judge, Abū

Ya'lā, who stipulates that the husband's permission to induce menstruation is necessary, just as wife's permission is required to practice coitus interruptus. Nevertheless, on the basis of an opinion ascribed to Aḥmad b. Ḥanbal himself, Abū Ya'lā requires the wife to seek the permission of her husband.[15] The latter opinion seems to have been preferred in traditional circles because another Ḥanbalī jurist, Mardāwī, endorses Abū Ya'lā's citation, "It is appropriate [for her to do so]."[16]

From the above opinions it is possible to conclude that seeking a husband's permission is required for a woman to prevent conception temporarily because it is the right of a man to have offspring. Hence, it is not permissible to deprive him of his right without his consent. This condition is also stipulated in the resolution passed by the Islamic Juridical Council (*majma' al-fiqhī al-islāmī*) under the auspices of the Organization of Islamic Conference (OIC) in their Fifth Session in Kuwait in December 1988: "It is permissible to decide temporarily to postpone having children for the sake of putting distance between pregnancies or preventing conception for a short period if there is a valid reason recognized in the revealed texts of Islam (*shar'an*), as long as there is an agreement between the spouses on the matter following consultation, and provided there is no harm in doing so. In addition, the means of preventing pregnancy should be legitimate, and there should be nothing in it that can be construed as aggression toward an existent pregnancy. Indeed God, the glorified and exalted, knows best."[17] All Muslim jurists agree that it is not permissible to prevent conception permanently, even if the husband approves of such a decision. According to the Mālikī jurist al-Qairawānī al-Birzilī (d. 844/1440), any attempt to prevent the semen or to obstruct the uterus in order to avert conception is impermissible.[18] This view is supported by one of the major figures of the fourteenth century, 'Abd al-Raḥmān al-Jazūlī (d. 741/1340), who ruled that it is forbidden for any person to take medication that would lead to a decrease in his progeny.[19] The Shāfi'ī jurist, Zarkashī, who cites the opinions of several leading jurists, maintains that it is illicit for a man or a woman to take any medication to avoid having children. In the case of a woman, according to some, it is forbidden outright, even if the husband does not object.[20] According to Ibn Ḥajar al-Haythamī, it is forbidden to obstruct the source of conception.[21]

Accordingly, preventing conception permanently is actually violation of one of the five ends of the Sharī'a for the people: to protect their lineage (*nasl*).[22] The Sharī'a urges the preservation of the lineage and multiplication of the progeny. There are a number of traditions ascribed to the Prophet in which he is reported to have encouraged large families.[23] On the basis of such traditions, jurists regard permanent prevention of conception as undesirable for both men and women. Some argue that, after having some children, if the couple were to decide to implement permanent fertility control, there was no guarantee that the children would not die or get killed. In such a situation, because of the permanent obstruction of fertility, the couple would be deprived of having more children. Based on the principle of "No harm, no harassment" the Islamic Juridical Council has issued a number of resolutions reaffirming the impermissibility of irreversible methods of birth-control without a religiously valid reason, regardless of the husband's permission or lack of it.[24]

Abortion (*al-ijhāḍ*) in Early Usage

The Arabic word *al-ijhāḍ* denotes a "miscarried fetus discharged from the womb before completing the nine-month period of gestation."[25] In line with this lexical meaning, Muslim jurists define abortion as an induced ejection of a fetus prematurely with or without a proper justification. The other common juristic terminology like *al-isqāṭ* (literally, "elimination"), *al-ṭarḥ* ("expulsion"), *al-ilqā'* ("caused to throw out"), and *al-imlāṣ* ("caused to slip") suggests the intentional aspect of the miscarriage and not simply the fact of a discharged fetus with no signs of life. Such an understanding of abortion as a deliberate act of terminating pregnancy has consequences for its estimation as a criminal act.

The issue of intentional abortion does not come up in the Qur'an. All the standard juridical references to the Qur'anic passages actually deal with homicide (*qatl al-nafs*) rather than abortion of the fetus through a miscarriage before it completes nine-month gestation. In fact, there is no definition anywhere in the Tradition of the embryo as a living entity right from the zygotic stage. In their assessment of the tort committed against the fetus, jurists have regarded implantation of the drop in the uterus (*istiqrār al-nuṭfa fī al-raḥim*) as the determining stage of fetal life beyond which any infliction of harm to it requires compensation. This ruling is extrapolated from the interpretation of the following verse in the Qur'an, which reads, "It is he who produced you from one living soul (*nafs wāḥida*), and then a lodging-place (*mustaqarr*) and then a repository (*mustawda'*)" (Q. 6:98).

The uterus is "a lodging place," whereas the loins are "a repository" in which specific characteristics are preserved for future generations.[26] Yet the assessment of the criminality of abortion is dependent upon forced ejection of the fetus. Most of the Ḥanbalī jurists treat abortion as a culpable action only when the ejected fetus is dead or when its partial ejection is caused by blows to the stomach of a pregnant woman or by her having induced abortion through taking a medicine. A majority of the Ḥanafī, Mālikī jurists, and a group of Shāfi'ī jurists have followed the Ḥanbalīs in this opinion. However, the rest of the Shāfi'īs are of the opinion that abortion is a culpable action if it is proved that the fetus died during the procedure, even if it was not ejected from a woman's womb. Obviously, these rulings in no way suggest an endeavor to define the beginning of fetal life in the womb. Apparently, lack of scientific information on *in utero* fetal development did not allow for an evaluation of life until the moment of emergence, dead or alive, from the womb. It was for this reason that some jurists did not maintain that the criminality of abortion could be established simply on the grounds of the expulsion of blood or tissue in which there is a sign of growth without any indication of a human shape (*takhlīq*). However, if there was evidence of a human shape (*ṣūrat al-ādamī*), then the abortion would be regarded as killing the fetus and hence homicide.

The verses quoted for the assessment of the compensation due to the fetus or any other party who participated in this wrong act treat the developing fetus as a growing entity that resembles another organ of the body. The verses do cover gestation stages from fertilization to personhood. But they do not in any way define or explain the nature of the zygotic stage—whether it holds life or carries totipotent cells to biologically make up a human being. According to some recent rulings on allowing abortion in pregnancies that result from rape, like those that took place in the Balkans, it appears that the embryo is treated as an entity that does not have all the biological factors needed to evolve into a human being.[27] In fact, an interesting discussion providing guidelines to determine whether intentional abortion inflicted at the stage of coagulated drop (*al-dam al-malqā*) constitutes a tort underscores a completely different understanding of the crime against the embryo. According to the majority of the jurists, if the aborted material dissolves in hot water, then it cannot be regarded as aggression toward the embryo.[28] In other words, it is only when the embryo has coagulated and lodged itself in the uterus and has grown into a clot and tissue that there is any imputation of criminality.

Most of the verses quoted against abortion actually deal with life's sanctity. For instance, one of these oft-quoted verses in this section declares, "If anyone slays a human being unless it be [in punishment] for murder or for spreading corruption on earth—it shall be as if he had slain the whole of humankind" (Q. 5:32). Another verse forbids killing of children: "Slay not your children for fear of poverty; we will provide for you and them. Surely the slaying of them is a grievous sin" (Q. 17:31). Still another verse forbids the pre-Islamic practice of *wa'd*—a practice of burying live female infants for fear of poverty or disgrace: "And when the female infant, buried alive, is questioned for what crime was she killed . . ." (Q. 81:8). None of these verses deal with abortion per se; nor do they define or deal directly with the ontological or legal-moral status of the fetus or the religious-legal consequences of expelling it before complete gestation. Their only connection to the subject of abortion appears to be the sanctity of socially protected life, which must be accorded to the fetus when it takes the shape (*takhalluq*[29]) of a human being—beyond which point its destruction or harm is deemed to be a crime. Nevertheless, these passages do provide incontrovertible documentation for prohibitive abortion rulings to the extent that they convey a general interdiction about killing (*qatl al-nafs*) and recommend a suitable punishment for those who commit intentional homicide: "And slay not the soul God has forbidden, except by right. Whosoever is slain unjustly, we have appointed to his next-of-kin authority; but let him not exceed in slaying; he shall be helped" (Q. 17:33; also 5:32).

Verses 12–14 of chapter 23 describe the stages of biological development of the embryo: "We created man of an extraction of clay, then we set him, a drop (*nuṭfa*) in a safe lodging, then we created of the drop a clot (*'alaqa*), then we created of the clot a tissue (*muḍgha*), then we created of the tissue bones, then we covered the bones in flesh; thereafter we produced it as another creature. So blessed be God, the best of creators." Some important conclusions have been drawn from the biological development of the embryo into a human being: First, perceivable human life is possible at a later stage in the biological development of the embryo when God says, "Thereafter we produced him as another creature."[30] Second, because all the factors that make up a human being are not present, it is possible to make a distinction between biological animation and moral-legal personhood, and, as indicated by the consensus among Sunni jurists over the interpretation of the above verses, to place the latter stage after the first trimester in pregnancy. This consensus is based on the traditions that provide further elaboration of the Qur'anic notions of embryology.

The tradition that has provided the most significant religious grounds for the legal estimation of fetus inviolability has been reported in both the Sunni and Shī'ite compilations. In the version preserved in Bukhārī's compilation, which in the Sunni estimation is the most authentic collection, the Prophet is reported to have said as following: "Each one of you in creation amasses in his mother's womb [in the form of a drop (*nuṭfa*)] for forty days; then he becomes a blood clot (*'alaqa*) for the same period; then he becomes a lump of flesh (*muḍgha*) for the same period; then the angel is sent with a mandate [to write down] four things [for the child]: his sustenance, his term of life, his deeds, and whether he will be miserable (*shaqī*) or happy (*sa'īd*)."[31] There is no mention of the breathing of the spirit (*rūḥ*) in this version. However, another equally authoritative version related in the last part of the tradition includes an additional sentence: "Then the angel is sent to breathe into him the spirit (*al-rūḥ*)."[32] In another variant reported in the same compilation, the angel is present from the time of implantation, some forty-five days after conception, when the embryo lodges itself in the uterus. This report also mentions the determination of the sex of the child.[33]

These traditions provide the ontological interpretation of biological data in forming judgments about when the embryo attains human status. Different versions of this tradition speak about the stage of recording human destiny by an angel who is sent by God to breathe the spirit; depending on the source, this occurs either on the fortieth, forty-second, or forty-fifth night or after one hundred and twenty days. The jurists have identified this stage as the moment of ensoulment, when the fetus attains the ontological unity and identity of personhood. The moral-legal implication of this ensoulment is not the subject of these traditions.

With their limited knowledge of human embryology, ancient Muslim jurists did not emphasize the distinction between two periods of pregnancy to arrive at decisions about the criminality of induced abortion. In fact, the inference regarding the first trimester is particularly absent in Bukhārī's above-cited version. Others, like Ibn al-Qayyim al-Jawzīya, have argued that the tradition suggests that all the three early stages, from drop to clot to lump of flesh, are covered in the first forty days because the tradition clearly states, "Each one of you in creation amasses (*yajma'u*) in his mother's womb for forty days."[34] Moreover, none of the authenticated traditions refer to the sperm drop (*nuṭfa*) stage as a separate gestational stage. According to some jurists, even the phrase that literally means "like that" does not suggest that the reference is to "the same period," that is, forty days. The tradition simply suggests that before the angel is sent to write the child's destiny there is no spirit in the fetus whether in drop, clot, or lump form. For these jurists the ensoulment occurs at the end of the first forty days and not after that as asserted by others.[35]

However, it is possible to infer the beginning of life from the time of conception in some Shī'ite traditions. Consider, for instance, the following tradition, in which a disciple of the seventh Shī'ite Imam Mūsā al-Kāẓim (d. 800) asks for a solution to a case involving an induced abortion: "[Isḥāq b. 'Ammār reports:] I asked Abū al-Ḥasan [al-Kāẓim]: [What is your opinion about] a woman who, fearing pregnancy, takes a medicine and aborts what she has conceived? He responded: No, [it is not right.] At that I said: But it is a drop (*nuṭfa*). He said: The beginning of human creation is a drop."[36] This tradition explicitly mentions the beginning of human creation and rules abortion at that stage to be illicit. The same view is implied by another tradition, ascribed to 'Ali b. Abī Ṭālib; he specifies the five stages of fetal development in order to clarify the amount of compensation that must be paid when the abortion is induced: "He specified five stages for man's semen [in order to fix the compensation]: when it is fetus before the ensoulment 100 dinars, this is because God created a human being from an extraction of clay. This is the drop (*nuṭfa*). Hence, this is a part [of human creation]. Then it is a blood clot. This is another part. . . ."[37] In both these traditions, and in the light of this verse, it is possible to argue that the zygotic stage is regarded as the beginning of life and that abortion at that stage therefore carries the prescribed penalty. However, there is another tradition that expressly takes up the issue related to the timing of ensoulment. Sa'īd b. al-Musayyab is reported to have asked the fourth Shī'ite Imam 'Alī b. al-Ḥusayn (d. 713) about this issue in the following case:

> I asked [the Imam]: [In your opinion] do the changes from one state to another that take place [in the fetus] during the gestation occur with or without the spirit (*rūḥ*)? He said: The changes occur through the spirit, with the exception of the preexistent life that is transferred in the loins of men and the wombs of women. If the fetus had no

> [independent] spirit other than the life that was there [because of the parent's existence], it could not have changed from one state to another in the womb. [The existence of the spirit and ensoulment are proven by the fact that had it not been for the presence of the spirit] the killer would not have been required to pay the blood money (*dīya*) at that [early] stage [of fetal development].[38]

This last case provides a clearer understanding about what constitutes the beginning of life and ensoulment in the Shī'ite tradition. Based on these accounts, a number of Shī'ite jurists have argued that embryonic inviolability begins much earlier than the 120-day cutoff period.

In any event, Sunni jurists agree that abortion is impermissible after ensoulment. Al-Qurṭubī has stated this most clearly in his juridical exegesis of the Qur'an: "There is no disagreement among the scholars that the ensoulment occurs after 120 days. This is after completing four months of gestation and having entered the fifth."[39] More importantly, the jurists regarded the deliberate termination of pregnancy at any stage of embryonic development to be sinful. For most jurists, abortion is absolutely prohibited (except to save the life of the mother) after the fetus obtains the ontological status of an individual at the end of the first trimester.[40] Variant readings and interpretations notwithstanding, Sunni jurists mostly agree that, based on the above-quoted traditions from the two highly respected compilations of Imam Bukhārī and Imam Muslim, the fetus attains personhood after 120 days.[41] Nevertheless, the differences of opinion about the absolute inviolability of the fetus had to wait for the biomedical advancements of modern times, when the biological data on the embryonic journey to full personhood at times contradicted the traditional account.

Culpability and Penalty for Willful Termination of Pregnancy

There has been no dispute among scholars about fetal inviolability. However, the determination of culpability hinged on two key issues: the timing of ensoulment and whether the husband was a party to the decision. Given these variables, the jurists have had to pay close attention to the early exegetical materials of the revealed texts. This was the context of much of the interest in the early interpretations of the Qur'anic passages and the relevant traditions that helped to lay the groundwork for juristic practice. But the opinions about the initial stages of life, extracted from the Tradition, have varied from the time of conception to the end of the first trimester.

Analyses of the question of spousal culpability were organized on the basis of two periods of abortion: (a) abortion following ensoulment, usually the first trimester; and (b) abortion prior to ensoulment. There was overall agreement among the jurists that abortion after ensoulment is unlawful unless the mother's life is in danger.[42] As for abortion prior to ensoulment, opinions of the early Muslim jurists can be divided in accordance with the first three stages of forty days each—that is, roughly the first trimester of embryonic development as reported in the traditions:

1. The drop stage: The majority of the Ḥanafī, Shāfiʿī, and Ḥanbalī, and some of the Mālikī and Shīʿite jurists allow it. The majority of the Mālikī and Shīʿite, some Ḥanafī, al-Ghazālī among the Shāfiʿī, and Ibn al-Jawzī among the Ḥanbalī jurists prohibit it.[43]
2. The clot stage: The majority of the Ḥanafī, Shāfiʿī, and Ibn ʿAqīl among the Ḥanbalī jurists permit it. All the Mālikī, the majority of the Ḥanbalī and Shīʿite, some Ḥanafī jurists and al-Ghazālī prohibit it.[44]
3. The tissue stage: The majority of the Ḥanafī and Shāfiʿī, and Ibn ʿAqīl among the Ḥanbalī jurists permit it. All the Mālikī, the majority of the Ḥanbalī and Shīʿite, and some Ḥanafī jurists and al-Ghazālī prohibit it because this is the ensoulment stage.[45]

While mostly in agreement about abortion before the first trimester, the jurists have disagreed about what legal rights are due the fetus. The rulings about the legal status of the fetus are inferred more from the approximate estimation of the biological stages than from an ontological assessment of the nature of the human person. Accordingly, there is no discussion about the dignity of the person as the foundation of human rights. In jurisprudence, there is an assumption that the term *nafs* self-evidently stands for the personhood (*ādamī*) of a human whose life must be protected through a detailed penal code rather than a theory of the inherent dignity of the fetus. Any attempt to assert fetal inviolability at all stages of the biological journey toward human status would have required the jurists to seriously engage the Qur'an in deriving an ethical framework for a definition of human personhood that would affirm the inherent dignity of the pre-ensoulment fetus. The juridical trend is simply to deny personhood to the pre-ensoulment fetus and, as a consequence, to permit abortion at that stage. The Ḥanafī jurists have even relaxed the requirement of the husband's permission for pre-ensoulment abortion.[46] This ruling implicitly treats fetal inviolability in that phase as less of an issue.

The other reason for this relaxed attitude toward early fetal personhood is the religious tradition that holds that no pre-ensoulment fetus will be resurrected on the Day of Judgment (*al-qiyāma*). In other words, anyone who has not been infused with a soul is not to be resurrected. Hence, it is not forbidden to abort the fetus at this stage because it is not a being as yet.[47] The problem with this argument is that, from the point of view of the doctrine that speaks about God's omnipotence, how can human beings know in advance that the fetus will not be ensouled and will not reach personhood? Certainly, to abort the fetus at this stage is an act of aggression toward it, and unless there is a valid reason to do so, it is forbidden. Moreover, according to another tradition, the fetus will intercede on behalf of its parents on the Day of Judgment. The tradition does not specify the phase of fetal development. It simply states, "Indeed the fetus will haul his mother with the umbilical cord to Paradise when he will anticipate [God to reward] him [by allowing his mother to enter the Paradise]." If this is the spiritual status of the fetus, then how can one say that it has not attained personhood and that its life is not inviolable? It appears that the traditions uphold the inviolability of the pre-ensouled fetus, whether it can be resurrected or not; if so, it cannot be aborted even at that early stage, absent danger to the mother's life.[48]

With the growth of IVF reproductive technology and the so-called "surplus" embryos readily available for experimentation, the Muslim conception of the integrity and the life of the early human embryo is in serious danger. Stem-cell research is promising critical therapeutic benefits, and it is hard to imagine that Muslim scientists are not interested in harvesting stem cells from human embryos and fetuses in the hope of treating hitherto incurable diseases. I will discuss the ethical dilemma posed by stem-cell research on embryos created either by in vitro fertilization or nuclear transfer cloning in chapter 8 on recent developments in biotechnology. Here it is important to emphasize that the problem is a serious one. Whether created for reproductive purposes or research, there is no legal or moral basis to deny the dignity of the so-called spare embryos. The loosely applied principle of public good (*maṣlaḥa*) seems to have provided an easy justification for any procedure that actually requires more scrupulous ethical analysis because it is a potential life that is involved. A more relevant principle in this case states, "Averting corruption has preponderance over advancing public good." Nevertheless, in the juridical tradition, on the basis of the penalties prescribed for feticide, there is an agreement that the fetus before ensoulment cannot be accorded the status of a full person. Also no funeral rites are to be performed for a fetus before the first trimester.[49]

Overall the law stipulates the fetus's right to life, even in the absence of a universally recognized definition of an embryo that pinpoints the onset of personhood. Accordingly, in cases of capital punishment, the law requires postponement of a pregnant woman's execution until after she has delivered her baby and made provisions for its care after her death. Most Ḥanafī, Shāfi'ī, and Ḥanbalī scholars and some Shī'ite scholars rule that abortion may take place during the first trimester if the woman's pregnancy threatens the well-being of an already existing infant. In the case of a pregnancy that threatens a woman's life, a majority of the jurists have given priority to saving the life of the fetus when ensoulment has already occurred.[50]

Advancements in biomedical technology have led to a reconsideration of some classical formulations about abortion. A number of juristic principles, including the "Contrariety between two harms" (*ta'āruḍ al-ḍararayn*) and "Protection against distress and constriction" (*al-'usr wa al-ḥaraj*), have been invoked to rule in favor of the priority of saving the mother's life on whose well-being the life of the fetus depends. Also, in the case of a rape or incest, the psychological damage suffered by a woman has been duly recognized as a justification for abortion (*ijhaḍ janīn al-ightiṣāb*).

Different legal schools hold conflicting opinions about the appropriate penalty for the act of feticide; but none of the schools punish the crime as homicide. If a man causes a woman to miscarry (or aborts her) and the fetus is unformed, his crime carries the penalty of *al-ghurra* (monetary compensation); but if the expelled fetus is formed, then the penalty is *diya kāmila*, which is full blood money. An additional penalty of *al-kaffāra* may be levied, requiring the aggressor to fast for two consecutive months.[51]

Under Islamic criminal law the penalty for self-induced abortion or abortion inflicted by others, intentional or not, is treated in some detail.[52] There the abortion of the fetus at any time is regarded as a crime because it prematurely removes the fetus from the womb where it was created in order to complete its gestation toward independent life outside the uterus. According to the Ḥanafi jurist, Ibn ʿĀbidīn, contrary to the modern liberal rulings, the allowability of abortion to save the mother's life is not unconditional, because the assessment of the situation is based on probabilities rather than certainties: "If the fetus is alive, and [even] if there is fear for the life of the mother, as long as the fetus remains alive, it is not permissible to dismember it. The reason is that the mother's death on account of the fetus is conjectural. As such, it is not permissible to kill a human being (*ādamī*) on the basis of a conjecture."[53] So abortion is permissible only if it is *certain* that the mother's life is in danger and that abortion is the sole recourse for saving the mother, as dictated by the requirement to choose the lesser of the two harms. There is a precedent for this ruling: the case where the law permits removal of a living fetus from a pregnant woman who has died in the childbirth, even when such a procedure requires the dissection of her womb in order to save the life of the unborn. This medical procedure has been permitted by Ḥanafī, Shāfiʿī, some Mālikī, and Shīʿite jurists. However, the Ḥanbalī and some well-known Mālikī jurists have forbidden cutting open the womb because it poses, again, a probability rather than a certainty: the unborn child may or may not survive, so these jurists deem it unlawful to cut open the womb to remove the baby.[54] But even these scholars approve of salvaging the living fetus in the dead mother's womb if it is certain or even likely that the fetus will survive the procedure. It is important to keep the context of the rulings in mind. Current advancements in medical technology and knowledge were not available to these medieval jurists, who based their rulings on the conjectural information they received from attending physicians.

The penal law of Muslim jurisprudence contains some references to the total absence of fetal liability or rights as long as it is in the uterus since it is still regarded as part of the mother's body. However, as soon as it emerges of the womb, it attains a status of being treated as a full person with all the rights and obligations under the Sharī'a. But Ḥanafī scholars, in their assessment of the crime of abortion, treat the fetus as less than a person; therefore, anyone involved in aborting it has to pay monetary compensation (*ghurra*) rather than the full blood money (*diya kāmila*), which is instituted specifically for homicide.[55] They base their opinion on a tradition attributed to the Prophet, which says, "In the case of a fetus, it is monetary compensation in the amount of 500 [dirham], regardless whether it is male or female."[56] As for the Mālikī, Ḥanbalī, and the majority of the Shāfi'ī jurists, they treat abortion as a crime against the fetus and prescribe progressive monetary compensation in accordance with the developmental stage of the fetus: gamete, zygote, blastocyst, organogenesis, and visible physical development.[57] Most of these rulings requiring payment of compensation at different stages of fetal development are based on traditions that treat abortion at any stage as an aggression and sin against the fetus as long as it is *in utero*.

The question of fetal rights assumes importance in relation to determining the fetus's personhood. The penal system imposes monetary fines pegged to the age of the fetus on anyone involved in inducing the abortion, including the physician, father, or mother. However, if the wife decides to abort with the permission of her husband, then, according to some Ḥanafīs, there is no need to pay monetary compensation to anyone.[58] In these cases, the fully formed fetus is treated as an independent human being with the right to inherit property and to be compensated for any damage done to it. This is so even when the law regards the fetus as the integral part of the mother's body, identical to an organ. It is for this reason that the law permits donating fetal tissue for medical research (e.g., for the derivation of stem cells), since it is treated like other bodily organs. However, in the context of IVF reproductive technology, the jurists seem to maintain a moral distinction between the embryo that has already been implanted and is developing in the uterus, and "surplus" or "spare" embryos. Whereas the implanted embryo enjoys fetal rights, including the right to life, the surplus embryos are not treated as aborted since these existed outside the body of a woman and never reached the stage of ensoulment. Hence, there is no prescribed penalty for discarding these pre-implanted embryos. In fact, using them to derive stem cells is permissible.

Such a devaluation of pre-implanted human embryos in the IVF clinics can lead to their exploitation for therapeutic purposes or even commercial undertakings that seek to profit from their research potential. As we shall discuss in chapter 8, Muslim jurists have not considered all the negative facets of their ill-conceived countenancing of both unregulated in vitro fertilization and the discarding of the unused embryos, as if potential human life could be treated like a commodity. The problem, as discussed in the introductory chapter, is rooted in Islamic jurisprudence, which ignores any ethical analysis of such cases and simply bases its rulings on legal principles that imply but do not expressly articulate an ethical code. If Muslim jurists had paid due attention to Islamic theological ethics wherein the objective nature of human action is analyzed in terms of good and evil, and which inform much of the legal doctrines and methodology of Islamic jurisprudence, then they would have considered the moral status of the embryo meticulously, a task rendered all the more urgent by advancements in medical technology.

The human embryo is a potential human life. In my opinion, it has moral-legal status and deserves respect from the time it is conceived. If that were not the case, why would the Islamic penal code impose fines for induced abortion from the earliest stage of progressive fetal development? Viewed in this light, the fetus cannot be simply used as a product or as a means to an end. Hence, any ruling that permits the creation of human embryos expressly as material for medical research, to be destroyed pell-mell in the process, is an affront to the divine edicts of the Sharī'a. Those who support such permission regard the destruction of pre-implanted, unensouled embryos that existed outside the uterus as a kind of "collateral damage" incurred in fostering a greater good—the potential cure of grave illnesses—for the entire society.

The major problem, as I see it, pertains to the denial of the moral status of a fetus outside the mother's womb. There is little doubt that the progressive development and viability of the embryo indicate and express a moral and legal progression of rights and dignity. Even if full personhood and ensuing complete rights are achieved only after birth, the Sharī'a takes into account the various stages of biological development to assess the level of damage done to the fetus, thus reaffirming a progressively growing respect for the dignity and rights of the fetus. At no point does the tradition differentiate between pre-implanted embryos and those that are already implanted in the uterine wall. All the laws in the criminology speak only of the *in utero* embryo.

Nonetheless, the reference in Qur'anic embryology about God breathing divine "spirit in him" (Q. 23:5) raises the question: When does this happen? From a purely scientific viewpoint, debates about the "ensoulment" of the fetus are irrelevant, a matter of arid theological and metaphysical conjecture rather than fruitful logico-empirical inquiry. But in Islamic jurisprudence, the matter of ensoulment is of critical importance because the need to demarcate the beginning of a legally recognized personhood that would render abortion a crime unless the mother's life were at stake. This view of abortion is also supported by modern Arabic usage, in which the word *ijhāḍ* denotes a fetus that is aborted from the womb before the first trimester, that is, before the ensoulment; whereas the word *isqāṭ* denotes a fetus that is miscarried between the fourth and the seventh months. However, in popular understanding, only this later stage of fetal development gives rise to personhood, in which case the abortion of pre-ensouled fetuses would be permissible.

Ensoulment and Legal-Moral Status of Embryo

The legal-moral status of an entity is described in terms of the obligations and relationships that it shares with other moral agents. If fetal tissue is treated as an organic nonhuman life form, then it might be permissible to treat it as an organ in a woman's uterus, and, when aborted, lawful material for research, especially the socially redeeming medical quest to foster human health and longevity. On the other hand, if human embryonic cells are considered human entities, then our moral relationships and obligations toward them shift sharply. In Islam, as pointed out earlier, the fetus is guaranteed legal rights by the Sharīʻa, and the evidence for this view is abundant in many works of Islamic jurisprudence. If the moral status of the fetus is conceded from the moment of conception, then this acceptance of the moral-legal stauts puts constraints on medical research that wishes to use the "spare" IVF embryos to derive stem cells, because of our obligations to another entity that is not capable of protecting itself, much less consenting to being used for research. The Shīʻite moral tradition echoes Catholicism in deeming the eradication of a fetus is a sin. But not all Shīʻite jurists share the Catholic view that ensoulment coincides with the moment of conception. Some Shīʻite jurists maintain that ensoulment occurs at the time of the implantation of the fertilized egg in the uterine wall (that is, after eleven to fourteen days), when the embryo turns into a fetus; whereas others, taking the hint from the Prophetic tradition, rule that it occurs at the end of first trimester (one hundred and twenty days).

That the fetus has a moral-legal status in the legal corpus is abundantly clear. As regards inheritance, the Sunni and the Shīʻite jurists have ruled the following:

1. If a man dies and a pregnant wife survives him, the right of the fetus is secure, and the inheritance cannot be disposed of before the share of the fetus is set aside. If the wife delivers more than one baby, the legatees have to pay back the share of the others.
2. If a woman aborts a fetus at any stage of its life, and it betrays any sign of life, such as a cough, sneeze, or finger movement, etc., the fetus is entitled to the inheritance of any legitimate legator who dies after its conception. If the fetus does not survive, its legal legatees inherit its share.

The jurists have ruled that because the Sharīʻa guarantees the sanctity of fetal life, it protects a fetus against deliberate abortion without an overriding excuse. As we noted earlier, if a pregnant woman is sentenced to death, the execution is postponed until after delivery, and according to some jurists, until the mother completes nursing the child. The paradigm case is provided by the Prophet Muḥammad, who postponed the stoning of a pregnant adulteress until her child was born. An illicit conception does not justify an abortion either. To be sure, the embryo is not simply a dormant mass in the Islamic penal system. The treatment of both induced or accidental abortions at any stage, in the form of interdiction, admonition, or penalties indicate that the Sharīʿa recognizes human dignity at conception. It safeguards the life of a fetus, as well as its rights, while it is still in the womb. These clearly defined permissions and prohibitions have been blurred by interpretations of modern scientific conceptions of the stages of fetal growth. The question in Islamic law is: When does the union of a sperm and an ovum entail sanctity and rights? When does fetal sanctity begin? To formulate their response to this question the jurists have turned their attention to the Qur'anic embryology. As detailed above, the Qur'an describes the life of a fetus inside the womb in a detailed and precise manner.

In the Tradition, however, the stages of fetal development were the source of differences of opinion in dealing with establishing the moral status of fetus. The time before and the period after the appearance of form provided a line of division in the embryonic development to personhood. According to the question raised by Ibn Qayyim al-Jawzīya (d. 1350), a leading medieval authority in Islamic traditions, ensoulment takes place at a later stage with voluntary movement in a fetus: "Does a fetus move voluntarily or have sensation before the ensoulment? It is said that it grows and feeds like a plant. It does not have voluntary movement or alimentation. When ensoulment takes place voluntary movement and alimentation is added to it." Another traditionist, Ibn Ḥajar al-ʿAsqalānī (d. 1449), maintains: "The first organ that develops in a fetus is the stomach because it needs to feed itself by means of it. Alimentation has precedence over all other functions for in the order of nature growth depends on nutrition. It does not need sensory perception or voluntary movement at this stage because it is like a plant. However, it is given sensation and volition when the soul (*nafs*) attaches itself to it." When the Prophet was asked about the timing of ensoulment in an embryo, he described stages of embryonic development until he reached the description at the end of the fourth month, when bodily organs begin to become distinct. It is also at this stage, as a tradition reports, that the fetus takes a proper human form. The fetus now hears and moves voluntarily, and expresses pain and happiness on its face. All this suggests that the ensoulment takes place at the end of the fourth month, which is both supported by the tradition that speaks about the three forty day stages of embryonic development and the verse of the Qur'an (24:12–14).

The grand Mufti of Jordan, Shaykh ʿAbd Allāh al-Qalqīlī, regards it permissible to take medicine to cause an abortion as long as the embryo is still unformed in the human shape. The period of this unformed state is given by him as 120 days. Muslim jurists concur that during this period the embryo or the fetus is not yet close to independent viability. A tradition reports that the second caliph, ʻUmar b. al-Khattāb (d. 644), did not regard abortion as infanticide unless the fetus were already past the limit.

According to Ibn Ḥazm (d. 1064), another medieval legal scholar, the penalty for killing a fetus after ensoulment, if it is possible to determine the age of fetus with certainty, is equal to killing it after it is born. Hence this is a crime deserving punishment, not merely compensation.

Recent Rulings on Abortion

Abortion is permitted in some circumstances and is required in others, especially when the mother's life is in grave danger. Islamic sources have recognized a threat to mother's life as grounds for abortion; but they have not given the same consideration to the condition of the fetus because until recently it was not possible to know anything about the genetic or medical makeup of the fetus before birth. Any consideration regarding the fetus's health raises serious questions as to what constitutes a sufficient defect to warrant abortion. It certainly represents a novelty in Islamic jurisprudence, which requires the jurists to be extremely cautious in providing rulings that might be abused in inferring a general permission to abort a defective fetus. In fact, the Islamic Juridical Council that meets regularly to deliberate and decide on such matters has already approved clinical abortion of embryos that have been genetically screened as suffering from Down's syndrome. Now it is true that the principle of "No harm, no harassment" has provided some jurists with a justification for abortion in severe cases like those in which the fetus has minimal brain tissue or a degenerative disease like Tay-Sachs that will lead to the infant's death within a few years of birth at most. But overall there are too many unknowns as far as the rulings' impact on the future of human society goes. Are we moving toward a negative eugenics, which tends to define qualifications for a genetically superior race that leads to depreciation of disabled people?

Islamic jurisprudence requires unequivocal evidence to support any ruling that might have adverse impact upon the future of human society. The advances of modern genetics have given rise to fundamental ethical problems in dealing with what constitutes a defect in justifying abortion. Some Muslim jurists have strictly forbidden abortion under any circumstances before or after the ensoulment has occurred. Actually, contrary to some contemporary opinions held by some Muslim physicians-cum-interpreters of Islamic medical ethics who seem to maintain the unquestioned legitimacy of abortion during the first trimester, at the end of which, according to the majority of the jurists, ensoulment occurs, the Sharīʻa views the process of gestation developmentally from the time the embryo attaches itself to the uterus. This occurs around the tenth or eleventh day after the conception. However, after the trimester, that is 120 days, the Sharīʻa equates clinically induced abortion to murder and imposes a penalty in proportion with the age of the fetus. The reason is that the Sharīʻa accords the fetus the same sanctity that the mother as a person enjoys. Both deserve the same respect and as such neither has preponderance over the other.

As pointed out earlier, the abortion rulings that deal with the danger to a pregnant woman's life are clearly formulated without any reference to the fetus's life, since such information was not available until recently. In the case of a life-threatening situation for the mother, the Sharīʻa requires extreme care in determining the gravity of the situation for saving the mother or the fetus. The mother has no guaranteed preponderance over the fetus. In fact, in the case of disagreement (*al-tazāḥum*) between the two demanding the same consideration, the rule states that no preference can be given to one over the other simply because it would inevitably lead to destruction of life. At the same time, it is obvious that only one of the two lives will survive. Hence, saving that one life becomes imperative. The rule that allows the mother to choose between her life and the life of the fetus, even when it requires treating both lives with necessary reverence, is the "Necessity to choose" (*al-takhyīr*). Under this rule it is permissible for her to prefer herself over the child. However, this choice must be exercised before the ensoulment, after careful assessment of the level of harm the pregnancy has caused. It is only after such an assessment of the situation and the certainty that emerges that abortion is considered legitimate. An additional reason is that the mother possesses an external existence, that is, she is already there; whereas the fetus, more particularly the fetus before the ensoulment, is regarded as potential life, being still protected internally in her womb like any other part of her body. Moreover, the rule "No distress, no intimidation" when applied to the mother's condition makes the child a cause for the impairment of her life and consequently allows her to choose to have the abortion. In other words, in order to save her life it is permissible for her to decide to kill the child.

Here it is important to cite an example of fresh extrapolations in affording the fetus consideration, however less than a full person, separate from the mother. The questions were put to the Egyptian popular preacher, Shaykh al-Shaʻrāwī, whose opinions do not carry the same authority as those of the establishment scholars at the Azhar University of Cairo. Nevertheless, the opinions reflect popular concern with abortion rulings:

> Q: Isn't abortion before 120 days regarded as an assault on the fetus?
>
> A: The fetus, who is being assaulted, is he potentially (*bi'l-quwwa*) or actually (*bi'l-fiʻl*) human? Potentially human means if allowed it will develop into a full person; whereas actually human means he has already become one. This latter stage cannot take place without completing 120 days. Before that the fetus is simply potentially capable of becoming human.

Here the Shaykh cites the example of a date pit, which he calls potentially a date palm, that is, if it is put in the ground and receives the necessary nutrition then it will become a fully grown palm tree. However, is that date pit actually a palm? No.

> Q: Isn't termination of life in itself forbidden?
> A: If one breaks a date pit is it an assault on the palm?
> Q: In that case, there is no relationship between the soul and the motion [of a fetus].
> A: The meaning of human soul [and the ensoulment of the fetus] is that when it infuses all parts and organs of a human being the human becomes like a living being, and without which he is no more a living being. A hare when dissected is found to be close in its physiology to a human being but is not a human because the angel does not come to it and tell it to become a human. In contrast, the human fetus becomes human [after the ensoulment], capable of learning and subject to something more than possessing the basic instincts. All plants and animals act according to their instincts without using their mind to understand why they act in that way. Human beings use their reason to choose between several options. Such is not the case of other beings.

In his final analysis, the Shaykh's ruling about abortion is as follows: Induced abortion is not permissible except when it is performed to save a mother's life. I will once again treat the matter of embryonic sanctity when I discuss the ethics of stem cell research in chapter 8.

As the above opinions indicate, Muslim scholarly estimation continues to treat the pre-ensouled fetus as a biological entity and not a legal-moral one. Although the classical rulings regard the ensouled fetus as capable of possessing inheritance rights, the lack of moral estimation has led to desecration of fetal inviolability, with widespread misinformation current among Muslim scientists and physicians that the pre-ensouled fetus can be used to derive highly valued embryonic stem cells. In several articles written by Muslim healthcare professionals and submitted to international bioethics journals and UNESCO publications about cloning, stem-cell research, and genetic engineering, these authors have totally ignored the ethical and theological dimensions of embryonic sanctity, thereby lending their enthusiastic support for research on "surplus" embryos in the name of the public good (*maṣlaḥa*) endorsed by Islamic juristic practice. As long as these articles remain confined to collating and commenting on judicial decisions (*fatāwā*) pronounced by prominent jurisprudents of different Sunni and Shī'ite legal schools without correlating them to Islamic ethics, opinions on embryonic sanctity as well as other related issues like genetic engineering and human cloning will lack the ethical analysis that is essential for understanding the beginning and end of human life. What I am proposing here is an educated partnership between the medical professions and religious sciences in the Muslim world to solve the pressing problems in modern biotechnology with global dimensions. Without this internal dialogue among Muslim healthcare professionals and Muslim theologian-jurists and ethicists, Islamic biomedical ethics will continue to be plagued by a superficial treatment of ethical issues connected with patient care and human rights.

6

Death and Dying

> Blessed be he in whose hand is the kingdom—he is powerful over everything—who created death and life, that he might try you which of you is fairest in works; and he is the All-mighty, the All-forgiving—who created seven heavens one upon another.
>
> —Qur'an 57:1–2

The advent of new medical technologies has rendered the task of defining death the most pressing issue in the field of biomedical ethics. Just as technically assisted reproduction has given rise to ethical problems in defining embryonic life and terminating it, so the new modes of treatment raise serious questions about medical decisions to terminate artificial life-support systems when incurable patients face prolonged suffering. The answer to the question about the timing involves an attempt to understand the moment of imminent death. Any error of judgment in this regard could lead to a morally and legally questionable decision to end an individual's life by either actively acquiescing in the patient's death or actively causing it. The formulation of a proper definition of death requires an understanding of the religious estimation of human life and an endeavor to unravel the secret of the soul (*nafs*) or the spirit (*rūḥ*) which, according to Muslim belief, is infused in the body and departs at the time of death.[1]

For Muslims the definition of death cannot be derived from medical facts or scientific investigation alone. Physicians can only provide an account of empirically observed physiological states but cannot, on those terms alone, address religious-ethical and legal questions about the onset of death. Hence, the most critical issues in the determination of the time of death are essentially religious and ethical, not medical or scientific. In the community of the faithful, it is God, the giver of life and death, who has the knowledge of the time of death; and death occurs upon the separation of the soul from the body. Of course, this separation is not open to direct empirical observation, and this is the major source of ambiguity in determining the exact moment of death. Today the traditional view of death, which focused upon the cessation of circulatory and respiratory functions as the criteria of departed spirit, has been overshadowed by the ability of the new medical technologies to intervene by artificially sustaining a patient's normal heartbeat, blood pressure, respiration, and liver and kidney functions. Contemporary medical science has developed highly sophisticated techniques for determining the presence or absence of vital bodily functions. This possibility of restoring cardiovascular functioning even in the case of massive brain damage, when there is little likelihood of an individual recovering consciousness, has given rise to the problem of defining cerebral death.

Whether or not Muslim jurists accept the validity of irreversible coma as a new criterion of death, it is important to explore a host of Islamic and medical problems connected with defining death and understanding the religious and cultural dimensions of accepting death as yet another chapter in human saga toward ultimate repatriation to humanity's origin in God. The Qur'an states this beautifully, emphasizing the need to prepare for this final leg of the journey in the presence of God: "Give thou good tidings unto the patient who, when he is visited by an affliction, says 'Surely we belong to God, and to him we return'" (Q. 2:156).

Death in the Revealed Texts of Islam

Although the Qur'an contains various death themes that add significantly to our insight into the purpose of death, the concept is left undefined and is always intimately juxtaposed with creation and resurrection. God is omnipotent and controls everything that has to do with life and death. The ultimate proof of God's existence is the fact of death and the promise of resurrection, which is viewed as a new creation (*khalq jadīd*) (Q. 17:49). Yet the purpose of creation or resurrection would remain incomprehensible if death did not constitute an integral part of life and the ultimate proof that God controls it by assigning it a final destiny.

The Qur'an, however, seems to be more concerned with countering disbelief about life after death and the final day of reckoning. A number of passages emphasize the limited nature of the human sojourn on earth and remind humanity that life in this world is the preparation for the return to the creator. Even more significant is the emphasis the Qur'an lays on death as simply a stage before the final judgment, when all the dead will be resurrected to render their account of their time on earth. In this sense, death is not extinction. It is, rather, an altered state of being. The Prophet's contemporaries had a hard time believing that God could bring back to life the decomposed bodies of the dead for the final judgment: "Has not man regarded how we created him of a sperm-drop? Then lo, he is a manifest adversary. And he has struck for us a similitude and forgotten his creation; he says: 'Who shall quicken the bones when they are decayed?' Say: 'He shall quicken them, who originated them the first time; he knows all creation" (Q. 36:77–79). The references to death are reminders to take one's performance in life seriously because there is an afterlife in which humans face a reckoning for their earthly deeds. This accountability to God was unpleasant to the ears of Meccan Arabs, who ridiculed the concept of the afterlife because it morally challenged them to rise above the present moment and take responsibility for sharing their wealth with the less fortunate in society.

Consequently, the Qur'an connected the creation to the themes of the ephemerality and fragility of life. All that has been created will perish (Q. 55:27). Nature is the scene of constant birth, death, rebirth, and death as a divinely ordained destiny. But human beings, out of self-cultivated ignorance and an arrogance born of partial technical mastery of nature, deny the finality of death and the impermanence of the physical world. The Qur'an, therefore, reminds humanity: "Wherever you may be, death will overtake you, though you should be in raised-up towers" (Q. 4:78).

Accordingly, life in the Qur'an is linear in development. It has a beginning and an end. Death is one of the critical stations in this linear journey, the point at which the external physical life comes to an end; it is an intermediate period before the final day of resurrection (*yawm al-qiyāma*), the day of final restoration, when God will raise the dead as a new act of life-giving creation. In the Qur'an the themes of resurrection and death form the decisive argument for belief in God's omnipotence and omniscience. Resurrection in particular marks the closing stages of the individual life-history that began with the ensoulment of the fetus in its mother's womb.

The Qur'an does not define life in terms of body-soul fusion. It simply affirms the existence of the source of human life which must be separated from the body at the time of death. Thus, in speaking about the agonies of death suffered by the wicked (Q. 6:93), it uses the crucial term *nafs*, which means "the entity that infuses human body with life"; when this entity departs, the body dies. In addition, in three places the Qur'an uses both the word *nafs* and death (*mawt*) to declare that death is bound to occur for "every *nafs*": Qur'an: "Every *nafs* shall taste of death; and we try you with evil and good for a testing, then unto us you shall be returned" (Q. 21:35–6; 29:57; 3:185). In other words, the Qur'an says that it is an ensouled individual who tastes death, not just a physical existence separate from the person. Here death is equated with the complete loss of the body's integrating capacities. When the *nafs* departs, the human body ceases to exist as a part of an integrated person. Death occurs, then, when an individual ceases to be a person. It is the termination of features that are essential to being a person capable of reasoning, remembering, feeling emotion, possessing the will to believe and disbelieve; it is not simply the dissolution of a biological organism. In other words, the Qur'an by introducing the notion of "giving up one's person," provides a set of criteria to determine death that has more to do with the quality of life than the activity of the central nervous system and the brain.

The complex use of the reflexive pronoun *nafs* in the Qur'an requires further clarification. Although in some verses it is possible to extract the meaning "soul" or "spirit" (*rūḥ*) from *nafs,* which leaves the body upon death (Q. 39:42), its translation as "soul" is not contextually adequate in all its manifestations in the Qur'an, especially when it refers to the fundamental characteristic of personhood (*al-dhāt al-insānīya*).[2] Among the several possibilities of rendering the term in the sense of the "personhood" that departs at the time of death, one can cite the verse that employs the term *nafs* in the meaning of "human life" when it sets the law of retribution: "And therein we prescribed for them (the Children of Israel): 'A life for a life (*nafs*), an eye for an eye, a nose for a nose . . ." (Q. 6:45). In another place it uses *nafs* for "human being" when it declares that "God does not charge any individual (*nafs*) beyond his/her capacity" (Q. 2:286). In still in another instance it commands, "Do not kill one another (*anfus*)" (Q. 4:29). Hence, by using the complex term *nafs* and its plural form *anfus* (which are usually reflexive pronouns in the Qur'anic usage) to connote this element in creation (*asl al-khilqa*)—the integrating capacity in human existence—it signifies personhood and not simply soul. In the context of this chapter, then, it is accurate to interpret "every *nafs* shall taste of death" as "every person shall face death." Later Muslim theologians' conceptualizations about the soul-body dualism notwithstanding, the Qur'an, by introducing the term *nafs* in the context of imminent death, is speaking about some complex entity that provides an essential feature of personhood. Accordingly, when death occurs, the *nafs* leaves the body, depriving it of its vital functions.

The Qur'an emphasizes death as an inescapable human condition that can be conquered only by God. It is only God who can deliver humanity from death for the sake of new creation: the resurrection. Humans must wish to live long and pray to God for a healthy life to serve God's purposes; in the words of the following prayer of the Imam 'Alī b. al-Ḥusayn, "[Oh God,] let me live as long as my life is freely given in obedience to Thee, but if my life becomes a pasture for Satan, pull me to Thee before Thy abhorrence overtakes me, or Thy wrath against me becomes entrenched."[3] It is forbidden to wish for death even though the tradition encourages believers to remember and prepare for death.[4] The following guidance of the Prophet teaches Muslims the value of life even when faced with affliction and calamity: "None of you should long for death because of a calamity that had befallen him, and if he cannot but long for death, then he should say: 'O my God, let me live as long as life is good for me, and take my life if death is good for me.' "[5]

In this sense, life and death convey two metaphysical rather than physical states. A famous tradition from the Prophet, usually reported by great mystical teachers, commands, "Die before the death comes." The tradition is quoted in the context of the spiritual journey undertaken by a novice who must begin by detaching himself from the world so that he can enter the state of pure intentions and progress toward perfection on the spiritual path (*ṭarīqa*). In this sense, metaphorical death before the real death at the end of one's life is freedom from attachments. By the same token, metaphorical life is an involvement with the world and concentration on real life as a temporary period of preparation for eternal life in the hereafter. According to the Qur'an, those who believe are ever ready to meet their Lord because they are not controlled by their material possessions and bodily gratifications. By detaching themselves from the blandishments of this life, they are prepared to be taken by God.

This conceptual clarification of death is important to understand the way Muslim jurists formulated an Islamic definition of death. The rulings of Muslim jurists were deduced not solely on the basis of normative sources like the Qur'an and the Tradition; they also incorporated social and community values and standards. Before modern medical science drew a distinction between cessation of cerebral and cardiovascular/pulmonary functions, the pronouncement of death in Muslim societies was based upon an evaluation of the vitality of mutually dependent organic systems of human body. The terms "cerebral death" and "brain death" are neologisms in Islamic jurisprudence. The jurists continue to regard death as the cessation of vital functions in an integrated body rather than in a part of the organ. The difficulty in deriving the main criteria for determining death in jurisprudence is underscored by the fact that a definition of death was based on the physiological state described by such signs that indicate both the symptoms of death and the state of death itself. The distinction between the symptoms and the state of death requires further explanation about what exactly constitutes the state of death. The cessation of respiration as the definition of death is insufficient because it simply indicates a prior cessation of cardiac activity.

Life and Death in the Juridical Sciences

Given the lack of clear definition of death in the Qur'an, there has been much speculation about the exact identification of the indicators of death in the Tradition. To be sure, the task of defining death cannot be relegated to the literary sources that describe death in imprecise terms. Moreover, as pointed out earlier, the definition of death is not merely a matter of collecting relevant data from medical facts or scientific investigation alone. The exercise involves understanding of the very essence of human life, which is marked by an interaction between an ephemeral physical substance and an eternal spiritual entity that departs it at the time of death.

The elusive component that transforms the human body into a living being is the spirit (*rūḥ*) or the soul (*nafs*). This is the substance that enters the fetus and ensouls it in the beginning of its embryonic journey to personhood, thereby effecting a change in the moral and legal status of the developing fetus. At the end of life, this substance leaves the body to return to its original source in the world of the spirits (*'ālam al-arwāḥ*). Of course, both the existence of the spirit and its infusion or separation from the human organism are not subject to direct empirical observation.

In the section dealing with funeral rituals (*al-janā'iz*) and last will and testament (*waṣīya*), the Islamic juridical literature recommends that there be no funeral preparations or estate distribution to the heirs without making sure that death has indeed occurred. These sources do not provide any list of tests (for instance, placing a feather or a straw under the nose of a dying person to detect respiration) that should be performed before declaring an individual to be dead. However, in sections dealing with hunting and the ritual slaughter (*tadhkiya*) of animals for food, Muslim jurists have equated death with decapitation, the implications of which I shall discuss below.

The Severance of the Linkage between the Spirit and the Body

The exact nature of the relationship between body and spirit is a pivotal issue in the debate about the criteria of death. There are essentially two theories concerning the relationship between the physical body and the spirit. According to one, the kernel of human existence is its spiritual substance or the divine element, and human body is simply an instrument that serves this spiritual substance. In this sense, the spirit is not something that resides in matter; rather, it is created by God as a source of life and is linked to the body. This spirit manages the body—it is, in effect, the body's master.[6] According to Abū Ḥāmid al-Ghazālī and other Sunni scholars, the spirit (*rūḥ*) is the subtle divine essence (*al-laṭīfa al-rabbānīya*)—knowing, thinking, and percipient, abiding in human beings. The concept of the spirit, as Ghazālī teaches, is synonymous with the heart (*al-qalb*), the soul (*al-nafs*), and the intellect (*al-'aql*). The bodily parts are the tools of the spirit, which, infusing the body, enables the organs to perform different tasks and allows the heart to know the true nature of things. The "heart," as Ghazālī explains, is merely another expression for the "spirit," which is able to learn and independently feel emotions without any link to bodily parts. When the body dies, the spirit is separated and the body's ability to function comes to a halt.[7] A tradition ascribed to the sixth Shī'ite Imam, Ja'far al-Ṣādiq (d. 765), likens the relationship between the spirit and the body to the jewelry and the box safeguarding it, such that the box would be rendered useless if the jewelry were removed from it.[8]

Another theory regards the spirit to be an attribute of life infused by God at the time of fetal ensoulment. In this sense, the spirit and body become one, and from their union personhood emerges.[9] The spirit as an attribute enables humans to learn and to feel emotions. With death, as the spirit separates from the body, the latter falls into disuse. In the words of Ghazālī, "Just as the onset of an incapacitating disease may mean that the hand is no longer a tool of which use is made, so death is an incapacitating disease spread throughout all members."[10]

Whatever the precise nature of this relationship between spirit and body, the spirit is the source of an individual's humanness, of the personhood that begins when the spirit is fused with the body. From some Shī'ite traditions it is possible to construe that human being has two spirits or two lives: one, the "ancient transmitted spirit" (*al-rūḥ al-qadīma al-manqūla*) that has come down generation to generation from the father's loins (*aṣlāb al-rijāl*) and the mother's womb (*arḥām al-nisā'*); and the spirit that is known as the "spirit of life and survival" (*rūḥ al-ḥayāt wa al-baqā*).[11] According to this tradition, the major criterion of human life is the linkage between the spirit and the body. In this sense, death is viewed as the permanent severance of this linkage between the spirit and the body,[12] whether that severance results from a liberation achieved through spiritual asceticism[13] or the incapacitation of the body.[14]

In chapter 5, I have related a number of traditions, both from Sunni and Shī'ite sources, and discussed those that attempt to describe the stage of ensoulment and thus the beginning of human life.[15] In some versions, ensoulment vaguely ensues upon the creation of the body.[16] In other traditions, the exact moment of the ensoulment is specified. Some traditions mention the ensoulment after the completion of four months; some others after five months; and still other report a gradual ensoulment of forty-day periods until after one hundred twenty days, and so on.[17] Furthermore, some traditions regard the physical form of a fetus—its movement, its crying, and the opening of eyes and ears—as evidence of ensoulment.[18] From a number of traditions in both the Sunni and the Shī'ite sources it can be surmised that the spirit is breathed into the body after the fetus has grown flesh, at which point the physical development of the fetus is complete. The appearance of human form completes the fetal development. It is for this reason that some jurists judge ensoulment to coincide with the clear appearance of human features. Furthermore, according to Ibn Qayyim al-Jawzīya, as cited in the previous chapter, it is then that the fetus is able to feel sensation and its movement becomes willful.[19]

However, this infusion does not necessarily occur at the end of the fourth month; rather, as some traditions suggest, it takes places in the course of a month following that period, that is, beginning at the end of the fourth month of pregnancy and continuing until the end of the fifth month, the exact time of which is known only to God. [20]

It is not difficult to ascertain the beginning of life, especially with highly sophisticated techniques for determining the presence or absence of vital signs; it is not so easy to pinpoint the end of life. From the religious point of view, despite the fact that it is not known when exactly the spirit departs from the body, a number of criteria have been cited in the revealed texts that speak about the separation of the spirit from the body when death occurs. Among these signs, which are also accepted in medicine, are the deterioration and ultimate decomposition of the body, the whitening of the skin, the sweating of the forehead, discharge of fluids from the eyes, discharge of sperms, slackening of the muscles, the contortion of the eyes, and wrinkling of the lips.[21] In medicine death has been classified in two ways: physical and cellular death. The symptoms cited for the occurrence of each type correspond to those mentioned in the Islamic traditions.[22]

The existential aspect of death that serves a critical purpose in relieving an individual from a lengthy period of physical suffering can be discerned from the following verse of the Qur'an, which glorifies God for having created both life and death:

> Blessed be he in whose hand is the kingdom—
> He is powerful over everything—
> who created death and life, so that he may try you
> which of you is fairest in works. (Q. 67:1–2)

In this passage, the act of creation is portrayed as an external phenomenon for which God is exalted. The act includes the creation of death as God's blessed activity, even though some commentators argue that, because death suggests opposite of life, there is seemingly a contradiction in their correlation in creation.[23] Even on this view, however, life and death are linked as logical correlates, each of which limits and defines the other.

"Stable" and "Unstable" Life in Jurisprudence

As stated earlier, Muslim jurists deal with the cessation of cardiac and respiratory functions in the section of the law that deals with hunting and the ritual killing of an animal for food. The law states that the sacrificial animal should be slaughtered completely to ensure that it is clean for consumption. Hunted animals must be alive before the religiously prescribed slaughter is performed; if the animal dies prior to the ritual, it is to be treated as an unclean carcass unfit for consumption. Juridical deliberations that sought to clarify the moment of death of a hunted or decapitated animal provide some criteria that conform to brain-death criteria in contemporary medicine. In the Sharī'a, the irreversible cessation of spontaneous respiration is both a necessary and sufficient condition of death. This is not compatible with the brain death criteria, which include lack of response to external stimuli or internal need; absence of movement or breathing as observed by physicians for at least one hour; and the absence of elicitable reflexes.

In determining the last moments of life—for instance, following an accident or decapitation—Muslim juridical sources identified two forms of life that provided clues for determining physical-neurological indicators of death. These two forms were described as the "stable" (*mustaqarr*) and "unstable" (*ghayr mustaqarr*) states of life.[24] The juridical category of a "stable" state presupposed some continuation of blood circulation or respiration because there was both movement and a discernible pulse. The category of an "unstable" state revealed not only a decreased rate of blood flow, significantly below the level necessary to maintain viability, but also the lack of consistent cardiac function. In the unstable state, a person could not be pronounced dead without the irreversible cessation of both cardiac and respiratory activity. The presence of a heartbeat in unstable state was thus conclusive indication of life even in the absence of brain function or spontaneous respiration.

The Criteria to Establish Stable and Unstable Life

Establishing the lawfulness of consuming the hunted or decapitated animal was of critical importance in this analysis. Because eating a dead animal that had not been ritually slaughtered was forbidden, Muslim jurists scrupulously worked on identifying the criteria to avoid pronouncing the cattle dead before it could be ritually slaughtered for consumption. The following four criteria emerged as the key factors in validating stable or unstable conditions:

1. **Duration of Cardiac Activity:** The presence of cardiac activity was regarded a sign of life, but there were differences of opinion about its duration. For instance, according to some Shī'ite jurists, life was stable if a dying person could continue to breathe. Respiration was the crucial factor indicating the existence of life and a stable state. In contrast, if regular respiratory activity was undetectable, then the condition was unstable and death was imminent.[25] The Ḥanafī jurists did not regard the residual movement of a decapitated animal or person that did not last for a day or more as indicative of life and hence of a stable condition.[26] The Shāfi'ī jurists, while recognizing the stable condition of a hunted animal, did not consider the duration of the condition. Their concern was to assure that the animal was slaughtered before it died.[27]

2. **Physical Conditions:** Some jurists spoke about certain physical features to distinguish between stable and unstable life. The features of a stable condition included cognition and voluntary movement; convulsive movement; circulation and discharge of blood. All these factors indicated cardiac activity and thus lingering life.[28] In speaking about a butted or fatally hit or fallen animal who had to be slaughtered while still alive for lawful consumption, the Shīʿite jurists pointed out that it was the movement of the animal and the flow of blood that could serve as the vital signs of life in the animal. If no pulse was discernible and respiration had ceased, then the animal was dead and it could not be consumed.[29] Most of the Sunni jurists agreed that death was contingent on the examination of physical conditions, including the nostrils, to determine the extent of respiration and cardiac activity.[30]
3. **Duration and Physical Symptoms:** Sometimes respiratory activity in itself was insufficient to establish stable life; a waiting period was considered necessary to avoid possible error in hastening to declare stability. Accordingly, some jurists argued that both physical symptoms and duration should be taken into consideration. For some, however, one of the two factors appeared to be sufficient for such an evaluation. Some Shīʿite jurists maintained that both elicitable reflexes and duration had to be considered in evaluating stability; others, however, maintained that either voluntary movement or duration sufficed to establish stable life.[31] Such a differentiation between two types of movement—one indicative of life and the other of residual movement—was absent among the Sunni jurists. Sunni jurisprudence treats the subject of slaughter with relative leniency, making it lawful to consume the hunted animal even before it was ritual slaughtered.[32]
4. **Ordinary Language:** Ordinarily people observe and comment on their understanding of stable and unstable life. Their commonsense identification of a stable or unstable state includes clinical symptoms accepted as valid criteria of lingering life. According to Shīʿite jurists, it was possible to determine stable life by referring to what was customarily regarded as an absolute criterion of life (e.g., beating of the heart as in indication of spontaneous cardiac activity), even for a brief interval.[33]

Critical Analysis of the Criteria for Stable Life

From a Muslim theological perspective the duration of cardiac activity is beyond human prediction. It cannot serve as a factor for determining stable life, since its duration is known only to God. How, then, can one claim that a certain human or animal will die in a certain number of days or in less than an hour?

The most advanced medical technology is not capable of making such predictions. For this reason some jurists rejected the duration of cardiac activity as a criterion for determining a stable state. According to some Shīʿite jurists, stable life signified life that was known to be free from any resemblance to the convulsive movement of a decapitated animal. In such cases, it did not matter whether the duration was long or short, nor did it matter if it was known that the animal would die soon. The problem, according to these jurists, was lack of certainty about the duration.[34]

Furthermore, there was a problem in relying on the extent of physical movement as a criterion of life. Movement could be caused by physical or chemical factors in the body. For instance, a dead body might make slight movement even when the reflexes could not be elicited. Shīʿite jurists noted this in their opinion regarding the blood money that was due to be paid when a person was killed. According to them, even if there was a possibility of movement due to wind or twitching, one could not rule that the person was alive. The reason, as they contended, was that when a corpse was compressed hard, it twitched, just as a slaughtered animal twitched spasmodically or moved convulsively before it died.[35] In some recent cases of brain death it has been observed that an individual in a coma remains alive without any movement for years. It is for this reason that some contemporary Shīʿite jurists have ruled that, although voluntary movement can be taken as a sign of life, its absence does not necessarily mean death.

Some jurists have correctly observed that there was a problem with the dependence on customary understanding of symptoms of death among common people to determine its occurrence. By resorting to the common understanding about what constitutes life, one could not ascertain a stable state of life. How could then the common knowledge and scant attention of common people to the details of the situation be used as a criterion for determining a stable or unstable condition? If such customary understanding were employed, anyone who had fallen into a coma or who had suffered a nonfatal stroke or heart attack could be pronounced dead.

Understanding the State of Unstable Life

The existence of an intermediate state between life and death, which is identified as an unstable life in Islamic jurisprudence, has given rise to problems that have engaged Muslim jurists for many centuries. This is the state that shows the presence of certain conditions indicating lingering life but not consistent cardiac and respiratory functions. The onset of death, which is the separation of the spirit from the body in Islamic tradition, is a gradual process accompanied by a variety of symptoms. The absence of life is indicated by the body's inability to link itself with the spirit and continue with consistent cardiac activity;

whereas its presence is indicated by the lack of complete and absolute severance of the spirit from the body, as manifested by residual vital forces. Muslim jurists have customarily identified this state as "unstable" life. According to this view, if a hen is decapitated and let loose, it can still run around for a little while. Such observations have prompted some Shī'ite jurists to doubt the presence of movement and discharge of blood as signs of stable life. While expressing doubt that movement and the continuation of circulatory function could by themselves be construed as signs of stable life, they asserted that it was equally problematic to rule that the spirit completely left upon severance of the parts of the body. As such, a person could not be regarded as dead until after the spirit had left completely, that is, until the irreversible cessation of cardiac and respiratory functions. Furthermore, as they argued, it was problematic to base one's validation of death on lack of movement or of pulse, because both these were insufficient to establish the separation of the spirit from the body.[36]

However, other Shī'ite jurists questioned this conclusion. According to them, it was true that one could not declare that death had occurred in the state of unstable life, for in that state the spirit had not completely departed from the body and that people in an unstable state had continued to live for an hour or even more.[37] Nonetheless, these jurists could not, of course, have defined life on the basis of modern criteria such as brain activity.

While the former jurists were inclined to accept the body's ability to hold on to the spirit by reasoning that cutting off parts of the body deprived the body of its ability to link with the spirit, the latter group maintained that from the time the spirit began to separate itself from the body until it completely left it, it retained a weak linkage to the body. This linkage produced certain symptoms such as bodily movement and continued respiratory and circulatory activities that in themselves did not convey the sense that the body was able to continue living.[38]

Although modern neurological criteria do not satisfy the Sharīa definition of death, partial cellular destruction of the brain with cessation of blood circulation to the brain is comparable to the religious description of the partial severance of the linkage between the spirit and the body. Some traditions reported in the Shī'ite sources actually describe the ruling about the right of the dying individual to his/her property. Some of these traditions state that the dying person has a right to his estate as long as "some of the spirit" (*shay' min rūḥ*) is still linked to the body. In the following two traditions, reference is made to existence of "some of the spirit" while the person is in the throes of death: "It is related on the authority of Ja'far al-Ṣādiq who said: 'The dying person has overriding right over his property as long as the spirit is in him'; "In another tradition he says: 'The owner has more right over his estate as long as there is some of the spirit [in him]. He can dispose it as he wishes.'"[39] Such traditions, on the one hand, indicate that a person has a right over his property as long as he has the spirit—that is, the presence of vital signs like breathing and pulsation;

on the other hand, they suggest that it is possible to regard such a condition as a continuation of an unstable state wherein a person is in the throes of death even though the spirit has not left him completely. This is the purport of the phrase "some of the spirit," which indicates that the spirit does not leave the body all at once, leaving the person to continue to have the minimum linkage with the spirit.

The following tradition, related on the authority of the Imam Ja'far al-Ṣādiq, explains the temporary departure of the spirit when a person is asleep: "Indeed when a believer is asleep his spirit leaves him and ascends vertically toward the heaven. [The narrator asked the Imam:] 'Does the spirit of a believer ascend to the heaven?' [The Imam replied:] 'Yes!' [The narrator asked:] 'Does it leave him completely so that nothing is left behind?' [The Imam said:] 'No. If [the spirit] left him completely so that nothing was left, then the person would surely die.'"[40] In other words, the person in the state of sleep is both alive and dead because of the temporary departure of "some of the spirit." However, in the unstable state following an accident or severe brain damage, the person is both alive and dead with this caveat: she is alive inasmuch as she has some linkage with the spirit as manifested by a discernible heart beat and respiration; whereas she is dead because the part of the spirit that has separated from her is irreversible, manifested in the cessation of the circulation of blood to the brain. This is close to the modern neurological criterion of brain or cerebral death.

The stable and unstable states toward the end of life act in opposition to each other, affecting the vital signs as death approaches. However, death does not occur except through a gradual, total disconnection and separation between the spirit and the body. In this context, just as one can apply the term "dead" to anyone whose spirit has completely severed its link to the body, so also can one apply the term "dead" to the one whose spirit has partially severed its link to the body and whose body has begun to lose its vitality because of this irreversible severance. To be sure, in Islamic juridical sciences, applying the term "dead" to a person whose spirit has not been completely severed is not precise; in legal rulings one cannot employ loose or figurative terminology.

Some jurists paid close attention to blood flow test as a reliable indication of stable life. Hence, a forceful flow of blood from the body was taken as a sign of stable life.[41] The reason was that cutting the veins of a living creature caused its blood to gush forth as long as its respiratory and circulatory functions were intact. In contrast, if a person was dead and if his veins were cut, the flow of the blood would be weak and slow. The evidence for such an opinion was provided by another Shī'ite jurist, Ibn Fahd al- Ḥillī (d. 1437), who wrote, "If you can ascertain that the animal was alive after it was decapitated [for food] then it is lawful for you to consume it. However, if you are certain that the animal was dead before it was slaughtered, then it is forbidden to eat it. If there is confusion caused by convulsive bodily movement and moderate but not heavy flow of blood and if you are unable to determine, then regard it to be forbidden [because of the weak flow of blood]."[42] In modern forensic medicine, the absence of bleeding from a severed vein is one of the established ways of determining death after heartbeat and breathing have stopped. In the light of the foregoing, it is possible to discern the reason why some jurists compared unstable life with the decapitation of an animal. According to these jurists, there was a valid indication that death occurred when a creature's throat was cut, the blood continued to flow without being perfused, and breathing stopped.

Brain Death in Contemporary Medicine

Defining death has become difficult because the traditional Muslim view—that death occurs upon the separation of the spirit from the body—is not susceptible of empirical verification. Accordingly, traditional definitions of death are coming under renewed scrutiny. With advances in medical technologies, the failure of the cardiac and respiratory functions is no longer a valid indicator of death. Even the absence of respiratory activity is insufficient.

The definition of death is complicated by the advent of modern medical life-support interventions, which can maintain heartbeat, blood pressure, respiration, and liver and kidney functions within a normal range. Even a patient with irreversible brain damage can breathe mechanically by means of a respirator that pumps air through a tube in the patient's mouth. The proponents of the idea of brain death define expiration as the complete loss of the body's integrating capacities as signified by the activity of the central nervous system, a state indicated by the absence of brain waves as recorded by an electroencephalogram. This definition, set forth by the Ad Hoc Committee of the Harvard Medical School, takes into consideration irreversible coma or a chronic vegetative state suffered because of disease or accident in which higher cortical functioning of the brain is permanently damaged.

The notion of brain death has been challenged by Muslim jurists, most especially on the point of equating death with irreversible loss of consciousness. This state is also identified as the death of the higher brain, even though the brain stem continues to regulate breathing and heartbeat. If such a definition were to gain acceptance, a patient would be considered dead if the cortex is nonfunctional even though lower brain functions persist. In contrast, there are others who maintain that death occurs only when there is no electrical activity in the brain at all. This issue becomes even more pressing when a comatose individual is a potential source of transplant organs. If the individual remains alive by any reasonable definition, then harvesting the organs would amount to killing the patient.

The criteria for applying brain death need to be evaluated in light of the following four concepts of death that have emerged during the last two decades.

It is worth keeping in mind the difference between specifying the concept of death and determining the specific circumstances that conform to it.

1. **Damage to the higher brain:** In this case death is considered to involve the permanent loss of consciousness. Hence, someone in an irreversible coma would be considered dead, even though the brain stem continues to regulate cardiac and respiratory functions. Clinical, electroencephalographic, and imaging data are important in arriving at such a determination. The inadequacy of this definition is evident from a number of instances in which patients have either made partial or complete recoveries despite electroencephalogram readings that registered no brain activity over an extended period of time.
2. **Damage to the lower brain:** In this case, there is a total stoppage of the circulation of the blood and a consequent cessation of the animal and vital functions, a state that gradually leads to the cessation of the higher-brain functions. However, improvements in resuscitative and support measures now at times make it possible to restore life. This can be the case even when there is little likelihood of an individual recovering consciousness following massive brain damage. Therefore, death of the brain stem is not a sufficient indicator of the death of the patient.
3. **Damage to the whole brain:** In this case death is almost certain because of irreversible cessation of all brain functions. Essentially, there is no electrical activity in the brain, and even the brain stem is not functioning. Of course, the validity of a declaration of death depends on the results of electroencephalographic and imaging data. The whole-brain concept of death has the advantage of being relatively clear-cut in application. But it, too, presents its difficulties and controversies. Some view the concept as too restrictive, failing to resolve some of the difficulties that prompted the need for a new concept. For example, both Karen Quinlan and Nancy Cruzan would have been considered alive by whole-brain criteria.[43] Those who favor concepts of death based on the loss of higher-brain function or the loss of personhood might argue that in these cases the affected individuals were dead in the applicable technical sense of the term. Furthermore, the whole-brain concept is not really as straightforward in its application as it might seem. Even when there appears to be complete lack of cognitive functioning, and even when basic brain-stem functions seem to have disappeared, a brain may remain electrically active to some degree. Isolated cells or group of cells might remain alive, and in which case test data would be subject to conflicting interpretations.
4. **Damage to personhood:** In this case, death occurs when an individual ceases to be a person. This may mean loss of features that are essential

> to personal identity or (in some statements) the loss of what is essential to being a person. Criteria for personal identity or for being a person typically include activities such as reasoning, remembering, feeling emotion, possessing a sense of the future, interacting with others, and so on. The criteria for applying this concept have more to do with the way an individual functions than with the data about his or her brain.

This concept of damage to personhood comes closest to ideas in the Islamic tradition. As discussed earlier in this chapter, the Qur'an regards death as an end to the personhood. This is suggested in the several possibilities of rendering the term *nafs*, the "personhood" that departs at the time of death. However, the criteria of personhood must be formulated in such a way that they are accepted as nonarbitrary and as sufficient grounds for deciding that an individual's "personhood" is not present when death occurs. But securing agreement on even universal criteria for determining when an entity either becomes or ceases to be a person is a conceptual difficulty that remains a challenge to theologians or philosophers.

A Comparison between Brain Death and Unstable Life

The problem of establishing the connection between what Muslim jurists identify as "unstable life" and neurological criteria of death is difficult. Even with highly sophisticated scanning technology, it is impossible to determine whether total destruction of brain tissue has occurred. It is remarkable that some of the earlier discussed juridical opinions referred to the flow of blood as an important indication of the presence or absence of life. Modern radioisotope technologies are used to determine whether the perfusion of the brain has totally ceased.[44] However, these technologies indicate cessation of circulation to the cerebrum, which is the seat of higher brain functions, thus identifying cerebral death rather than brain death. Moreover, radioisotope techniques do not demonstrate total cessation of circulation to the cerebrum but only that effective circulation has decreased below the level necessary to maintain its integrity. Even if current scanning methods are accurate, they do not indicate that all circulation to even a part of the brain, that is, the cerebrum, has been interrupted, but only that the rate of flow is below that necessary to maintain viability. On the basis of some of the juridical opinions discussed above that described the weak flow of blood as a sign of unstable life, it is possible to extrapolate the feasibility of maintaining the validity of some form of brain death from Islamic juridical perspective.

Some historical rulings suggest that death may be deemed to have occurred only upon cessation of cardiac activity. The absence of a perceivable heartbeat is not, in itself, evidence of death, not because heartbeat is irrelevant, but because the nonperception of a heartbeat is, in itself, inconclusive. Respiration is more readily perceivable than a heartbeat, and hence the negative finding of an examination for respiration is a more reliable indicator. It is quite understandable that a faint heartbeat may not be detected (particularly without the aid of a stethoscope) because of the intervening rib cage, muscle tissue, and fat, whereas even faint respiration can be perceived by placing a feather or straw to the nose of a patient. On the other hand, in the absence of mechanical assistance, there can be no heartbeat after respiration has ceased. Thus, the absence of perceived respiration is an indicator not only of the cessation of respiratory activity but also of the cessation of cardiac activity. It then follows that the patient cannot be pronounced dead without the irreversible cessation of both cardiac and respiratory activity. The presence of a heartbeat is thus a conclusive indication of life, even in the absence of brain function or spontaneous respiration.

From the Islamic juridical perspective the consideration of factors such as brain waves as criteria of life can be entertained only because the absence of respiration does not, in itself, always establish conclusively that death has occurred. The juridical category of "unstable life" seems to be close to some criteria used to determine brain death. But it cannot conclusively be equated with it, because unstable life occurs in the case of an individual who shows some signs of life despite the fact that his body is incapable of sustaining minimal normal functionality. However, in the case of brain death, the body is capable of life, because there is blood circulation and exchange of oxygen, whether self- or artificially sustained. What human vital signs depend on are the circulation of blood and the supply of oxygen to body organs, and this process can be carried out not only by the heart and lungs but also by artificial organs or instruments such as a ventilator.

The Traditional and Brain Death Criteria

In the usual course of events, determination of death in Muslim cultures is not enigmatic at all. In general, the responsibility of determining clinical symptoms of death like pulse beat and respiration has fallen on medical professionals, who have wedded scientific criteria with sensitivity to the widely accepted traditional Islamic views. The function of Muslim religious authorities has been to ensure that there has been no deviation from the traditional criteria before an official pronouncement of death is issued. Problems began to arise when modern medical technology acquired the ability to sustain signs of life through respiratory support in a brainstem-dead patient. With the invention and refinement of life-saving apparatus, the life of terminally ill or brain-damaged patients may, in some instances, be prolonged for a significant period of time. As a result, a redefinition of the traditional understanding of death becomes critical. As long as the patient reveals the presence of any vital signs, no medical hastening of death can be introduced.

There are two interrelated reasons that have prompted countries like Iran and Saudi Arabia to reconsider their stance on brain-death criteria in the case of patients with irreversible brain damage but technologically sustained cardiovascular functioning:

1. Can recognition of brain death lead to the unethical and illegal retrieval of organs for transplantation in patients whose cardio-respiratory physiology can be kept functional for successful retrieval? In many poor countries in the developing world, there is an irresistible temptation to profit from the sale of these organs.

2. Can a government policy authorize health-care providers to withdraw treatment when organ viability can be maintained by active medical intervention? Until recently, health policies in the Muslim countries generally reflected insensitivity to the public's moral and cultural sensitivities connected with death. The authoritarianism of the medical profession in Muslim societies is abundantly clear in the following decision, which was imposed as a government policy in Saudi Arabia under the rubric "Religious Aspect of Organ Transplant":

> The Purport of the Senior Religious Scholars Commission's Decision No: 99 dated 6 Dhū al-Qa'da,1402 AH/25 August 1982:
>
> The board unanimously resolved the permissibility to remove an organ, or a part thereof from a Muslim or a non-Muslim (*dhimmī*) living person and graft it onto him, should the need arise, should there be no risk in the removal and should the transplantation seem likely successful.

According to a leading physician, 'Alī Muḥammad al-Bārr, who is also trained in Islamic juridical sciences, the above policy statement requires the following elaboration: "Should the diagnosis of brain death be established unequivocally, the physician in charge may keep the corpse ventilated for the purpose of prearranged organ donation until receiving the consent of the heirs, or an order from the magistrate (*qāḍī*), in the case of an unknown corpse. The ventilated corpse is considered dead from the time of declaration of brain death and not from the time of turning off the mechanical respirator." This elaboration is contradicted by the Council of Islamic Jurisprudence, which includes jurists from all schools of thought in Islam and which meets regularly to review some of these new rulings. Their ruling reads as follows: "It is permissible to switch off the life support system with total and irreversible loss of function of the whole brain in a patient if three attending specialist physicians render their opinion unequivocally that irreversible cessation of brain functions has occurred. This is so even when the essential functions of the heart and the lungs are externally supported by life support system. However, legal death cannot be pronounced except when the vital functions have ceased after the external support system has been switched off."[45] In none of the rulings examined for this study have any Muslim jurists tried to define or determine the criteria for accepting the validity of brain death from an Islamic legal perspective. They have depended on consulting physicians to provide expert opinions, some of whom, however, seem motivated by an interest in harvesting organs for transplantation. Hence, the debate in North America concerning the acceptance of "higher brain formulations of death" and the controversial aspects of providing medical care of patients with advanced forms of dementia and PVS is absent in the Muslim juridical literature dealing with the definition of death.

The Ministry of Health in Tehran asked one of their leading jurists, Ayatollah Tabrīzī, whether death is defined by the cessation of brain function or heart function. His response is quite revealing of the early stages of debate on brain death in Shīʿite jurisprudence. He says that for that distinction, one must refer to a physician: "It is necessary to refer to the medical specialist in order to decide whether the first or the second conforms to the definition of death. Some experts are of the opinion that if the brain waves show the cessation for more than two and a half minutes, then death is definite and there is no way that life could return." He then proceeds to define death as it is accepted in the tradition: "Death is the passing away of the spirit from the body, as some commentators have indicated in their explanation of the verse from the Qur'an: 'Muhammad is not but a messenger; before him also there were messengers.'" In other words, this jurist hesitates to regard irreversible cessation of brain function as a valid form of death. However, the government-appointed council of Islamic Jurisprudence in Qumm, Iran, under the section regarding "Rulings Concerning Organ Transplantation," writes: "The criterion for death is that normal pulse and the heart by means of which a person continues to live has come to a complete halt. When a person reaches this stage he is regarded as dead. Reviving the pulse in his heart through an electronic device does not constitute life for him. However, if by means of a ventilator or other mechanical device the heart begins to function or by means of an artificial heart a person's life is restored, then the person is regarded as being alive." Hence,

1. As long as he is not dead, if he himself gives the permission to remove an organ, with the conditions stated in number two above (i.e., damage to the lower brain), then it is permissible to remove that organ for transplantation.
2. After he dies, even when the heart is kept alive by some electronic device, it is permissible to remove his organs for transplant, provided

> he has made a will to that effect. Or, there is no problem in removing his organs under the two above-mentioned circumstances.

The redefinition or expansion of the traditional criteria of death is dominated by two factors: retrieval of organs and termination of medical treatment. There is little conceptual or philosophical discussion regarding the confusion over conceptions of higher-brain functions and their implications for continuation of treatment. In other words, under the present paternalistic system of medical care, there is little room for intellectual interaction between religious thinkers, doctors, jurists, and policy makers to forge a precise understanding of the implications of developments in medical technology for traditional Islamic beliefs about life and death. In fact, there is abundant evidence that the neologism connected with brain death among Muslims, adopted from Western languages, is fraught with persistent ignorance of the facts about brain death. The true state of patients with irreversible brain damage whose other organ systems continue to function remains non-comprehensible among various sectors of Muslim society. And, in the absence of any public debate geared toward educating the society that has accepted the brain-death criterion for practical reasons without questioning its validity in certain controversial cases, it seems unlikely that any well-considered criteria for or definitions of brain death will emerge among Muslim jurists.

The exception is Iran, where the interaction between policy makers and the religious establishment has been vibrant, a model for the Muslim world. The Iranian parliament in 1995 rejected the acceptance of the present brain-death criteria as sufficient to initiate a state-supported policy of organ retrieval for transplantation. The debates have centered on the inevitable connection between the notion of brain death and the permissibility of organ retrieval. Is the society unwittingly endorsing killing one patient in order to save the life of another? After all, success in the transplant surgery requires that organs be removed from still-breathing patients. In the eyes of the public, still attuned to the traditional criteria of death in Islam, the surgeons seemed to be terminating the lives of these helpless patients.

However, the juridical rejection of the brain-death criterion as a valid basis for pronouncing death raises the critical ethical issue of allocation of meager resources for the health care of other patients. What is the responsibility of health-care providers to keep the brain-dead person alive with expensive intensive-care technology? Here the Muslim jurists have resorted to practical principles like rejection of harm and proportionality to provide sanctions for turning off the life-sustaining equipment. In the end, pragmatic considerations, rather than philosophical or theological precepts, have determined actual decisions. And, in view of the ever-evolving state of medical technologies, jurisprudential edicts must remain provisional, subject to further clarification and dialogue among physicians, jurists, theologians, and politicians, and not as absolutely binding as they are portrayed in the public.

Deciding When to End Life

In Muslim communities, decisions about when to end life have not yet become a politically charged topic. The emphasis laid on the temporariness of human sojourn on earth is partly responsible for the acceptance of death as part of the divine plan for humanity. Closely related to this acceptance or even anticipation of death is the belief in the hereafter, the permanent abode for which humanity needs to prepare itself while living, remaining ready to leave this earth when visited by the angel of death (*malak al-mawt*). Death occurs only through God's will, as the Qur'an reminds humanity. Human beings who are endowed with intuitive reason need to understand the importance of inner peace that is generated by faith in God's justice and mercy in creating death as a bridge that must be crossed to reach the next world.

The onslaught of modernity and the phenomenal advancements in science and technology have spurred a longing to prolong the human lifespan for as long as possible. Understandably, death appears as an obstacle to the enjoyment of the expanding material pleasures of the world. The unquenchable desire to live has weakened or even ignored belief in the world to come. More and more people in the affluent regions of the earth view death as an evil to be subjugated through biomedical research and technology. At the same time, there is an inevitable recognition of the reality that diseases or trauma cause death. In Islam, health-care providers have an obligation to do all that is possible to prevent premature death. The question that is often asked is: Is the goal of health-care professionals to maintain life at any cost or merely to provide comfort so that death may come as quickly and comfortably as possible? The question has wider implications because it evokes different and often competing ethical values in deciding the course of action dictated by various medical interventions. On the one hand, there is the obligation to save and prolong life; on the other, there is a call to exercise restraint in life-sustaining treatments, as required by the principle of distributive justice in resource allocations. Nevertheless, the real question is about the authority that can make such decisions. Who should draw the line between personal values and beliefs of the people and a more objective medical analysis made by health-care providers? Should the financial burden of life-sustaining treatment ever dictate its termination?

Medical judgments about death are usually based on probability. It is only very close to the time of death that physicians can predict the end with certainty. Hence, the Qur'an reminds us that there are times when humans need to recognize their own limits and entrust nature to take its own course

(Q. 39:42).[46] Refusal to recognize the inevitability and naturalness of death leads to ever more aggressive life-saving interventions. At the same time, to withhold specific interventions at the most critical time leads to deliberate avoidance of the responsibility to save the patient's life.[47]

Religious and psychological factors play a major role in any decision that leads to termination of life. With the scientific information on the function of brain the problem for Muslim jurists centers on a determination of the exact location of the human spirit that departs at the time of death. Classical legal definitions, as discussed earlier, connected death with traditional signs, including complete cessation of the heartbeat; whereas biological data about the function of heart and other major activities connect life with the functions of human brain.[48] This discrepancy between the religious and scientific definitions of death has posed novel challenges for family members and the health-care professionals who must grapple with life-or-death decisions, such as whether to withhold life-saving medical intervention in the treatment of cardiopulmonary arrest. Cardiopulmonary arrest is regarded as the final common physiopathological event in the dying process. In that situation, failure to undertake CPR means certain death.

The other related question for jurists is to determine the level of financial investment that society should make in providing aggressive treatment of long-term care patients. In the oil-rich countries, where financial corruption is rampant and resources, even if plentiful, are mismanaged, the issue of the proper allocation of a nation's resources takes center stage. In view of a physician's scientific knowledge and clinical experience that enable him to recognize when a life-sustaining treatment is futile; and, when the society has an interest in limiting futile interventions to divert limited resources to more productive use within, or even outside, the health-care system, the juridical assessment needs to expand its ethical analysis to derive judicial decisions in this regard.

As we have demonstrated throughout this study, in Islamic ethics, the individual's welfare is intimately linked with that of his/her family and community. Accordingly, it is not the principle of autonomy (which emphasizes individual liberty and the capacity to make a decision without coercion or other conditions that restrict one's options) that is evoked to determine a course of action in matters related to the end of life decisions. Whether a physician can prolong life by introducing aggressive invasive treatments without causing further harm is decided by all parties connected with the patient. There are, however, instances when the matter is referred to religious leaders, who are asked to provide guidance to the families of terminally ill patients. In the following section I will examine some of the approaches that are in place among Muslims to help health-care providers to deal with this critical period in the lives of those for whom death is imminent.

Right to Die?

"How fortunate you are that you died while you were not afflicted with illness." Thus said the Prophet, addressing the person whose funeral rites he was performing. Such an assessment of death without illness, coming from the founder of Islam, indicates the value attached to a healthy life in Muslim culture. To be sure, good health is God's blessing. Whenever a Muslim is asked, "How are you (literally, "How is your health?")?" he or she responds, "All praise is due to God!" This positive appraisal of good health might seem to suggest that illness is an evil that must be eliminated at any cost. No doubt illness is regarded as an affliction that needs to be cured by every possible legitimate means. In fact, the search for a cure is founded upon the unusual confidence generated by the divine promise that God has not created a disease without creating its cure.[49] Because the tradition mentions God as the author of diseases and their cures, it is still a divine promise, regardless of whether we find a cure for certain diseases or not. Hence, the purpose of medicine is to search for a cure through scientific research and knowledge, and to provide the necessary care to those afflicted with diseases. Decisions about ending the life of a terminally ill patient, however, are beyond the moral or legal purview of the Muslim physician. The Qur'an states quite clearly that "it is not given to any soul to die, save by the leave of God, at an appointed time" (Q. 3:145). "By the leave of God" here means the destiny that is fixed by God for each individual. Moreover, "God gives life, and he makes to die" (Q. 3:156). And hence, "A person dies when it is written" (Q. 3:185, 29:57, 39:42).

Death, then, comes at the appointed time, by God's permission. In the meantime, humans are faced with the suffering caused by illness. How is suffering viewed in Islam? Is it, too, part of God's plan? If so, to what end? Such questions inevitably arise when families and doctors face the agonizing dilemmas associated with patients on artificial life support or those who suffer grievously with no hope of relief or cure. Does such an existence, which borders on nonexistence, warrant continuation? Beneath these concerns remains a deeper question about the quality of life that individuals and society regard as worth preserving.

Question about the Quality of Existence

The importance attached to the issue of the quality of life has sometimes led Muslim scholars to evaluate suicide (in Arabic expressed as *intihār,* and *halākat al-nafs*) in very ambiguous ways. On the one hand, there is unanimity in declaring the act as irrational and impermissible; on the other hand, some interpretations in classical sources intimate a degree of extenuation, especially when coping with circumstances.

Most of these circumstances that lead to commit a suicide appear to be culture-specific and informed by relational expectations. In a typical Muslim cultural setting, when a person's reduced circumstances result in extreme poverty and social ostracism, the decision to take one's life might be viewed with as much understanding as condemnation. Some might even praise it as a splendid act that indicates a staunchness of spirit in defying such cruel and unbearable suffering. However, it is impossible to justify the decision from a religious point of view. From a strict theological viewpoint, suicide trades a transient, unbearable life in this world for an even more horrible, eternal one beyond. In Sharī'a such actions are forbidden, along with less drastic measures of self-harm, because suicide might occur when the person's state of mind is unbalanced. Later on, in the hereafter, the person who committed suicide under such circumstances would realize the baseness of his action and the great mistake he made; at that point he cannot repair, correct, or retract his decision.[50]

Human Stewardship of the Human Body and Suffering

The discussion about the quality of life points to the cultural and religious attitudes regarding human existence and the control over life and death decisions when an individual is overcome by suffering. Furthermore, it underscores the view that the human being has only the stewardship, not the ownership, of his or her body, and thus is not free to do with it whatever he or she pleases. He is merely the caretaker, the real owner being God, the creator. As a caretaker, it is a human's duty to take all the necessary steps to preserve himself in a manner that would assist him in seeking the good of both this world and the next. To seek the good of this world requires Muslims to pay attention to their health by maintaining a balanced diet and exercise. They have an obligation to maintain their own health.[51] If, despite such precautions, a person falls prey to pain or illness, the Tradition instructs the believer to understand that suffering as a form of a test or trial to confirm a believer's spiritual station (Q. 2:153–57). As discussed in chapter 3 in greater detail, suffering in this situation is a divinely ordained trial, a way of revealing that humanity belongs to and will return to God. Accordingly, suffering cannot be regarded as evil at all. In a well-known tradition, the Prophet is reported to have said: "No fatigue, nor disease, nor sorrow, nor sadness, nor hurt, nor distress befalls a Muslim, even if it were the prick he received from a thorn, but that God expiates some of his sins for that."[52]

In other words, human travail and suffering should not lead to despair and a lack of faith divine mercy. Other traditions recognize this view of illness and suffering as a test of human faith, as God's way of inculcating humility and compassion through suffering. In a tradition the Prophet says that the patient earns merits under these trials and can attain the rank of a true believer: "When God intends to do good to somebody, he afflicts him with trials."[53]

This religious and spiritual valuation of suffering does not answer the critical question: Should one take upon oneself to alleviate suffering where possible and endure it otherwise? This question is critical to the present day discussion, namely, the patient's "right to die." In Islam this question cannot be negotiated because, in the first place, life is a divine trust and cannot be terminated by any form of active human intervention; and, in the second, its term has been fixed by the unalterable divine decree.

End of Life Decisions in Islam

The belief in God's immutable decree is also revealed in the Muslim ethics where not only the right to die is not recognized; the right to be assisted in dying, whether through "passive" or "active" means is also ruled out. It is important to clarify here that since the end of life decision is through divine decree, the Sharīʿa refuses to recognize an individual's right in that matter. However, with its emphasis on the principle of promoting or seeking what is in the best interest of all concerned (*istiṣlāḥ*), Muslim jurists have recognized the possibility of arriving at a collective decision through consultation (*shūra*) by those involved in providing the health care, including the attending physician and the family. Besides the principle of *istiṣlāḥ*, it is the ethical principle affirmed in the most unequivocal terms by the Prophet that has been evoked when matters concerning critical care have been under consideration. This is the principle of "No harm, no harassment."[54] It lays down the justificatory force of the ruling to avoid causing harm or harassment to the patient. It also allows for important distinctions and rules about life-sustaining treatments in terminally ill patients. The distinctions upon which ethical decisions are made include the distinction between "mercy killing" (active euthanasia) and "letting die" (passive euthanasia). The killing-letting die distinction often underlies distinctions between suicide and forgoing treatment or between homicide and natural death. The rule of "No harm" in some ways functions like the principle of nonmaleficence. But it goes beyond preventing harm. It raises a critical moral question about the intention of the healthcare providers in forgoing life-sustaining treatment: whether such a decision can be regarded as a form of killing, and if so, whether it is assisted suicide or a homicide. There is no immunity in Islamic law for the physician who unilaterally and actively decides to assist a patient to die.

Pain Relief Treatment and Withdrawal of Life-Sustaining Treatments

There are, however, two situations in the treatment that could be interpreted as "passive" assistance in allowing a terminally ill patient to die. Pain-relief treatment that could shorten life, but which is administered to relieve physical pain and psychological distress and not to kill, is permitted in Islamic law simply because the motive is regarded as a sufficient justification, protecting the physician against criminal or other liability in such circumstances. As long as the situation does not involve an intention to cause death, a medical intervention to provide necessary treatment for the relief of pain or other symptoms of serious physical distress is not regarded as criminal.

Similarly, in relation to withdrawing treatment, whether pursuant to a refusal of a death-delaying treatment or through a mutual and informed decision-making by patient, physician, and other parties involved in providing care for the patient, although there is an intention to allow the person to die when it is certain that death will result from its omission, Islamic law regards it a nonculpable act. The reason is that delaying the inevitable death of the patient through life-sustaining treatment is regarded as being against the benefit of the patient. Moreover, the principle of juristic preference protects the physician by authorizing departure from the already established ruling about the prohibition of allowing death to occur in order to avoid any rigidity and unfairness in recognizing the incurable preexisting conditions of the patient. Furthermore, by authorizing the removal of life-sustaining treatment in cases where it results merely in a death-delaying procedure, the juristic preference serves the ideals of justice and public interest in a better way. Notwithstanding a fine line between having and not having an intention to cause the death in such omissions, Islamic law does not forbid withdrawal of futile and disproportional treatment on the basis of the consent of immediate family members who act upon the professional advice of the physician in charge of the case. Some Muslim jurists have recognized the validity of a competent patient's informed refusal of treatment or "a living will" which allow the person to die under circumstances when there is no medical reason to continue treatment. However, even in such rare recognition of the patient's autonomy in Muslim culture, the law actually takes into consideration the patient's long-term treatment relationship with a physician whose opinion, in the final analysis, serves as the grounds for turning off the respirator, for example. In this case, the death is regarded to have been caused by the person's underlying disease rather than the intentional act of turning off the respirator.

The moral principle that is operative in this ruling is that intention alone does not make an act culpable. The person's death is actually caused by the preexisting disease when the withdrawal of the treatment becomes justified through the expert medical opinion. In other words, the Sharī'a would not consider withdrawal of the treatment as the cause of the person's death. This can be contrasted to the death that occurs by giving a person a lethal injection. The injection is the sole cause of the person's death and is clearly regarded as the cause of this in fact and in law by Muslim jurists, and hence, forbidden.

To recapitulate Islamic ethical-legal perspective on the "right to die" of a terminally ill patient without any hope of getting better, it is important to restate that the justificatory force of the rulings on "allowing to die" by withdrawal of life-sustaining treatments is contingent upon a well-informed consultation with the physician and other parties involved in the patient's treatment. More importantly, since Islamic legal deliberations contain and ground morality as part of its spiritual response to God in interhuman relationships, the patient's own determination and the physician assisting him to terminate life, are both held accountable for acts of disobedience against God. Pain relief treatment or withholding or withdrawing of life-support treatment, in which there is an intention of allowing the person to die when it is certain that the disease is causing untreatable suffering, are permissible as long as the structures of consultation between all the parties concerned about the well being of the patient are in place. In final analysis, besides the exceptions noted in the two situations, there are no grounds for the justifiable ending a terminally ill person's life, whether through voluntary active-euthanasia or physician assisted suicide in Islam.

7

Organ Donation and Cosmetic Enhancement

Whoso slays a person not to retaliate for a person slain, nor for corruption done in the land, shall be as if he had slain humankind altogether; and whoso gives life to a person, shall be as if he had given life to humankind altogether.

—Qur'an 5:35

In the last chapter the focus of our investigation was an individual in the throes of death. There was hardly an occasion to deliberate on the suffering of those who were closely related to the patient. Serious illness overwhelms everyone in the family. It is undoubtedly that moment in family life that demands a collective response to handle the pain and suffering of the patient, on the one hand, and the loss and separation that would come to pass following the imminent demise of the patient, on the other. The social-psychological dimension of death includes the way in which the family undertakes to preserve the dignity of the dead and the honor of those left behind. The preservation of the dignity of the dead includes avoiding all the decisions that would lead to desecration or mutilation of the human body and safeguard respect for human personhood.

In this situation, brain-dead people are the most vulnerable. Any surgical procedure that involves making an incision on the newly dead patients for organ retrieval or medical research and other humanitarian and educational purposes evokes reprehension. More critically, any suggestion to retrieve their organs before their hearts stop beating, even though they may not be brain dead, evokes repugnance because there is no way to secure the patient's consent.

Critics of the practice have correctly pointed out that using the cessation of heartbeat as a proper criterion for death may make it too easy for the parents or other representatives of the comatose patients on life support to decide to withdraw support and end the person's life. Given the currently limited supply of organs, serious questions about the proper criterion of death have been prompted by cases concerning those patients who have suffered brain damage and whose families have consented to organ removal. For example, the patient on a respirator wanting to be weaned off the machine may ask that his organs be used for transplant, should the withdrawal result in his death. The respirator is removed in an operating room, and at least three minutes after the patient's heart has stopped beating, the organs are removed. The question arises: Is three minutes a long enough interval to determine death? Such doubts have led relatives of such patients to deny permission for organ removal in the interests of preserving the dignity of the dead.[1]

In the Islamic juridical tradition on death and dying, a large number of the rulings deal with the social and psychological implications of death for those who are left behind: parents, spouse, children, and other relatives. As a matter of fact, Muslim funeral traditions appear to enable the bereaved relatives to cope with the loss of the loved one, even if it is a child whose departure has become a major source of disruption in the normal familial life. Accordingly, the tradition deals with death on two levels: (1) at the formal level of rituals that must be performed for the dead by the family and the community; and (2) at the legal level of rulings that outline the rights and duties of the immediate family members toward the dead and the survivors.

At the ritual level the Sharīʿa lays down the rules about the number of days the mourning should be held; the religious personages (the Prophet, his Companions, his Family) who should be remembered in these ceremonies; those who should bring food to the family of the dead; visitations of the graves in the cemetery; recitation of the Qur'an on the grave; and so on. Ghazālī has aptly captured the spirit and purpose of these funeral rituals to encourage people to visit and console the bereaved family members for their loss: "The properties of attending funerals include meditation, heedfulness, preparedness, and walking before the pall in humility. The man of insight looks to the graves of others and sees his own place amongst them and then readies himself to join them. In general, the visitation of graves is a desirable thing, for it instills the remembrance of death and acts as an admonition."[2]

The additional facet of these detailed rulings in the sections on the ritual side of death and funerals reveal the preoccupation of the jurists to purge the tradition from pre-Islamic mourning practices that were prevalent in Arab tribal culture and were now regarded as reprehensible or forbidden. The following ruling under the rubric of *Discourse on Mourning over the Dead, and the Related Matters that Arise* captures the corrective discourse forbidding the pre-Islamic practices:

> According to the Mālikī and Ḥanafī jurists, it is forbidden to mourn over the dead loudly and to let out a cry. The Shāfi'ī and Ḥanbalī jurists regard this [as] permissible. However, they all agree that mourning [in silence] while letting the tears flow without a loud cry, is permissible. Similarly, lamentation (*al-nadb*) recounting the merits of the dead is not permissible (*lā yajūz*); nor is it proper what the hired mourner does [to make the family cry]. It is equally improper to disfigure or to slap the face, and to tear the front of the garment [as a sign of mourning]. The Prophet has this to say about [these practices]: 'The one who slaps the face and tears the garment, and calls people to follow the Jāhiliyya (pre-Islamic age), is not among my followers.' The tradition has been reported by al-Bukhārī and Muslim.[3]

Note the absence of any attention to the ownership of the cadaver, and whether it is within the right of the deceased or his family to donate any organ needed by the living. Muslim jurists of that era could hardly have anticipated modern invasive postmortem procedures and their implications for the dignity of the deceased. The Sharī'a formulations dealing with the last will and testament (*waṣīya*) did not go beyond the external assets of the deceased and their distribution to the heirs. One does not come across a single ruling, for instance, dealing with permissibility or prohibition to leave advance directive regarding the donation of one's cadaver for research. Although the sanctity of life and the dignity of human beings were at the center of the classical rulings regarding life and death in Islam, there is conspicuous absence of any treatment of the status of human body (*al-jasad*), per se.[4] In the absence of surgical techniques and organ preservation, it was inconceivable to think about donating, harvesting, and banking of a variety of tissues and organs for future transplants. To save a life through medical intervention was and remains the goal of medicine. But the use of organs of the newly dead to save the living, although known in some rudimentary forms in the early days of Islam,[5] was repulsive because of the aggression against the human body that it suggested.

The Inviolability (*ḥurma*) of Human Body

As noted in the previous chapter, there is no separation between body and spirit or body and soul in Islam. Body and spirit are regarded as an integrated, unitary entity.[6] Since bodies and spirits are regarded as God's gift, human beings do not possess absolute ownership of their body or spirit. They are like stewards charged with preserving and dignifying their life by following the guidance provided in the revealed texts. Stewardship in the Qur'an suggests freedom of action while recognizing that this freedom is not unlimited. To be a steward is to acknowledge responsibility and accountability to the ultimate source of life and sustenance, God, the Almighty. Accordingly, as pointed out in chapter 6, suicide is a criminal act and strictly forbidden in the Sharī'a. A person who commits suicide is not accorded full burial rites. No rites of mourning, which are regarded as an honor for the dead, are to be performed for a suicide victim. In general suicide is treated as an affront to God's authority as the giver of life and death. Moreover, it constitutes denial of God's creation and desecration of human personhood made up of integrated body and spirit.

One source of controversy in Islam is the modern medical practice of making an incision into the body of deceased.[7] A living individual who donates a kidney must undergo surgery that requires a twelve-inch incision. Performing the same procedure on a cadaver, however, poses a host of theological and ethical problems for Muslim jurists. In the Sharī'a there was never any objection to performing an autopsy for the purpose of understanding the cause of death in specific cases or to advance medical knowledge in general. Autopsy is a well-established procedure of modern medicine. It is performed to correlate clinical aspects of disease for diagnostic and therapeutic evaluations to determine the cause of death as well as to serve an educational function. With the spread of modern medicine all over the world, Muslim countries have more or less allowed postmortem biopsies under certain conditions. In comparison to the traditional complete or limited chest or abdomen only autopsy, contemporary postmortem tissue sampling through a non-mutilating procedure performed immediately after death seems to have overcome religious and cultural opposition to postmortem in many Muslim societies.

Modern advancement in tissue sampling through needles and other non-mutilating procedures notwithstanding, public perceptions about postmortem dissection and postmortem examinations continue to regard these acts as carrying the stigma of mutilation, which affects public opinion in many societies. Current medical diagnostic techniques that tamper with the corpse or delay its burial are often viewed by the public as mutilation of the dead. The Prophet emphatically advised his followers to bury their dead promptly, "not waiting for morning to bury if the person died at night; and not waiting for nightfall if the person died in the morning. Make haste in taking them to their resting place."[8] Muslim regard for the dignity of the dead entails both prompt burial and respect for the dignity of the corpse. Nevertheless, the rule of arranging objectives in an ethical hierarchy—*qā'ida bāb al-tazāḥum*[9]—provides the needed justification to make an incision in the corpse when such a procedure may help resolve any dispute about the cause of death or the settlement of a bequest or when it might help to save a life by providing a vital organ like a heart, lung, or cornea for transplantation.[10]

Classical Paradigm Cases for Postmortem Dissection

It is worth reminding ourselves that the search for paradigm cases in this connection was prompted in modern times by the use of cadavers in the training of medical students. The increasing use of this practice early in the twentieth century prompted a number of articles written in response to questions posed to the religious authorities in Cairo, Egypt, or in Najaf, Iraq, about the possibility of desecration of the dead. The search for paradigm cases supporting such use of cadavers led to the identification of two sections of jurisprudence where such cases involving limited desecration of the dead had been resolved. The two sections that provided the rulings dealt with the burial of the dead (*al-janā'iz*) and the distribution of the heritage (*al-irth*) left by the dead.

The earliest ruling about postmortem dissection in the Sharī'a was based on the precedent of a living fetus in the womb of a dead woman.[11] A number of early juridical sources used the case to grant permission for dissection to remove the fetus before burial of the woman if there was any chance of saving the fetus; another precedent was provided by the dead having swallowed a valuable object that belonged to another person. The latter precedent also provided the justification for excavating a grave (which was forbidden) to remove the object or even to search for evidence of a suspicious case of murder.[12]

The Ḥanafī jurists saw no problem in removing a fetus under such circumstances. The incision, they ruled, had to be made on the side from where it was easier to remove the child, even if it meant overriding the rule against desecration of the dead. If the child was dead in the mother's womb while she was living, and if there was a fear that she might die if the fetus was not removed immediately, then the dead fetus had to be promptly removed by making an incision to save the mother's life. The principle that was applied in this situation was the sanctity of life and the priority that was given to saving the threatened existence. The Shāfi'ī jurists also maintained that if the woman was dead with a living fetus in her womb, then it was permissible to perform postmortem incision to remove the fetus, and for similar reasons. If there was no hope for survival of the fetus outside the womb then, according to one Shāfi'ī opinion, the postmortem incision was not allowed to be performed, and the burial had to be postponed until the fetus died.[13]

As for the retrieval of a valuable object, the Ḥanafī jurists ruled that if it belonged to the deceased, then it was not permissible to dissect him because the inviolability (*ḥurma*) and dignity (*karāma*) of the dead are far more important than the swallowed object. The rule was that one could not sacrifice the dignity of a superior being over that of an inferior object. Even if the swallowed object belonged to someone else but did not affect the worth of the heritage significantly and did not land in the stomach of the deceased through his own action, then the body could not be incised. If, however, the object was intentionally swallowed to deprive someone of it, then his stomach had to be slit open and the object retrieved because the violated right of the owner in this case took precedence over the right of the deceased to have his corpse treated with respect. Moreover, the deceased had, in that case, committed an act of transgression. By committing this sin, he had compromised his own dignity.[14]

The Mālikī jurists permitted the postmortem incision of the dead to remove a valuable object, whether it belonged to him or to some other person. However, they did not permit incision to remove the fetus even if it stood a chance to survive outside the womb.[15] The Ḥanbalī jurists ruled that if the woman died and she had a child that is moving, then instead of making an incision to remove it, the midwife had to remove the child from its normal birth route. In the case of a valuable object that had been swallowed by the dead while he was alive, if it belonged to him, then no postmortem incision was to be made because he had squandered his own wealth. However, if the procedure was feasible and if the object was precious, then it was permissible to open his stomach and remove the object for the benefit of his heirs who might otherwise suffer hardship. On the other hand, if the object belonged to someone else and if the deceased swallowed it with his permission, then it could not be retrieved, because the object was squandered with the permission of its owner.

As for the Shī'ite jurists, they discussed the paradigm case of the pregnant woman in great detail to extrapolate the ruling that stated that if a child died in the womb before birth, then the midwife or anyone who was in charge of the delivery at that point had to insert her hand in the opening of the vulva and remove the child from it, and then perform the burial rites of washing and shrouding in order to bury it.[16] If the mother died before giving birth, then it was permissible to make an incision (*shaqq*) on the side where it was possible, in order to remove the child.[17] As for the swallowed valuable item, since there was no specific revealed text that addressed the problem, the decision was based on juridical principles and rules. There were a number of possible solutions based on the ownership and value of the object: whether the swallowed item belonged to the deceased or to someone other than him; whether it was swallowed with the owner's permission or with the intention of depriving him of his goods; and, lastly, whether the value of the object was substantial or paltry. The overriding concern in these rulings was to avoid granting easy permission to slit open the dead body to retrieve a swallowed item, unless the deceased was proven to be a usurper, because the inviolability of the human body proportionally weighed heavier than the value of the swallowed item. Consequently, it was only to protect or redress the legitimate claim on the swallowed item that the incision on the dead body was tolerated. Regardless of the value of the item, no incision was permitted to retrieve it based on the rule about the continuation of the injunction about the inviolability of human body at all times. If the heirs claimed the item as part of their heritage, the rule stated that such claim was applicable only on the estate that was left as a legacy. It did not include the swallowed item. Hence, the heirs had no right to desecrate the body to claim the item as their heritage.

If the item was wasted with the full knowledge of its original owner, then it was treated as squandered goods. In this particular instance, neither the actual owner nor the heirs had any right to demand the retrieval of the wasted item. However, if the item was swallowed without the owner's permission, then the deceased was regarded as usurper and squanderer and was held responsible for its return. If possible, then the owner had to be compensated with the equivalent value of the item from the deceased estate. At any rate, desecration of the body had to be avoided except as a last resort to satisfy a legitimate property claim in cases of a swallowed stolen object that was deemed to be unique or irreplaceable.[18]

Nevertheless, even under these highly restrictive circumstances, when an autopsy was permitted in Shīʿite law, there was an acknowledgement of the overriding rights of the living over the dead. In the Sharīʿa tradition, saving the living fetus takes priority over the dignity of the corpse of the dead mother, and saving the living mother has a priority over the dignity of the dead fetus. Similarly, incurring an incision to retrieve a valuable object belonging to someone other than the deceased or being part of the heritage revealed the significance of the rights of ownership in the Sharīʿa. Hence, among Muslim jurists in general, incision of a corpse is permissible—with varying degrees of flexibility in different traditions—to save the life of the mother or the fetus, when one of them is dead; to retrieve a valuable object that belongs to other than the deceased; to determine the cause of death when a person has died under suspicious circumstances. However, this permission is granted only to slit open or make an incision (*shaqq*), and still debars anything like mutilation (*qaṭʿ*). As pointed out by the Shīʿite jurists, even in the case of saving a living child in the dead mother's womb or vice versa, the procedure should avoid unnecessarily aggressive procedures and should avoid cutting the body if possible. Instead, the child should be removed by a midwife from its birth route.

Modern Situations Demanding Autopsies

Today anatomical dissection and postmortem examinations are a routine part of medical education and diagnostic techniques that stress the need for such procedures in understanding illnesses and evaluating incompletely known disorders or discovering new diseases. Accordingly, the scope of clinical diagnosis requiring autopsy has expanded beyond the three traditional justifications mentioned in the classical juridical formulations in Islam.[19] One of the major decisions facing a dying person and his family is the possibility of donating organs for transplant. This means allowing surgical procedures that constitute a desecration of the dead in the Sharīʿa in order to retrieve an organ. A visible incision into the body or the removal of externally visible or internal organs represent true desecrations. Muslim jurists have had to search for a principle or a rule that could permit an incision or mutilating procedure for the immediate saving of the life of a patient who is dying of organ failure. Such permission depends upon establishing that the donor is dead at the time the organ is removed for transplantation. It is important to reiterate that the brain-death criteria discussed in the previous chapter are still being contested by some prominent Sunni and Shīʿite jurists. And although the Islamic Juridical Council has permitted the turning off of extraordinary life-support equipment in the case of brain-dead patients, there is no agreement among the scholars that organs can be removed while the patient is on artificial life support.

The possibility of organ transplantation for saving a critically ill patient did not exist in the past. Only in the recent past have surgical techniques and immunosuppressive drugs made this an option and thus an issue for Muslim jurists. The relatively high rate of success in organ transplantation has encouraged Muslim jurists to search for legal-ethical justifications to formulate their rulings to keep pace with the demand for such medical procedures, which are already a de facto practice in many hospitals in Muslim countries. In their rulings in this area, some jurists have relied on the principle of public good, which allows postmortem dissection following a stillbirth and for the purpose of retrieving swallowed valuable object belonging to someone other than the deceased. Yet the Prophet's well-known tradition states, "Breaking a bone of a dead is like breaking a bone of a living person."[20] This tradition has served to remind Muslims to show deference to honor the dead and forbid the desecration of the body unless required to promote the larger good. All the jurists agree that the saving of life, as the Qur'an requires, makes it possible to approve the lesser evil of desecration for the larger good that such an act promises. More pertinently, desecration carried out in aggression is certainly different than clinical incision made with the deceased's permission left in the advance directive to retrieve an organ. This latter procedure is still within the accepted treatment of the dead, as discussed above.

If one grants limited permission to slit open the corpse under exceptional circumstances, then it does not matter whether it is a Muslim or non-Muslim cadaver. The human body, whether it belongs to a Muslim or non-Muslim, has the same inviolability and dignity that is afforded to all humans in the Qur'an. Hence, all those rulings that treat Muslim and non-Muslim bodies differently need to be revised in the light of the Qur'anic verse that states, "We have honored the Children of Adam and carried them on land and sea, and provided them with good things, and preferred them over many of those we created" (Q. 17:71). Some of the recent rulings have done away with this distinction in death and have reinstated the equality of all humans in death.[21]

The Role of Advance Directives

Who has the authority to determine the legality of deriving benefit from the human body, whether living or dead? Does a person have unlimited rights over the disposition of his/her body? Can one derive monetary gain from selling part of one's body? Like so many issues in Islamic bioethics, the ownership of the body has been discussed only recently in the context of organ donation. Until now often decisions about whether a patient has a right to donate parts of his body are made by physicians and families acting as surrogates on their own authority. Such decisions do not represent so much the intention of the patient as an acknowledgement of the physician's obligation and the family's concern to do what is best for the patient. Religious counsel, if sought at all, functions as an endorsement of the *fait accompli*, and it is quite possible that the physician's decision to retrieve organs for transplant or other medical use may not reflect the wishes of the patient or his/her family.

In the case of brain death, when the patient's competent consent is impossible to obtain, the problem of authoritarian medical practice in the Muslim world becomes acute. Compared to the Muslim world, where patient autonomy in medical treatment is almost nonexistent and where physicians' decisions on behalf of the patient usually prevail, Western medical practice has reinforced the notion that patients should have some say in what happens to them should they fall victim to hopeless injury or illness. Ironically, such an autonomy is acknowledged in the revealed texts of Islam as part of the individual's obligation to leave advance directives not only about the disposition of one's material estate, but also about how one wishes to be treated during serious illness and after death. It is through such a document that the autonomy of the individual is acknowledged. In fact, generally, leaving a last will and testament is reckoned as an individual's right in the Sharī'a. According to a tradition in Shī'ite sources, "Leaving a last will is a right. Since the Prophet left a last will, so should the Muslims take the matter of leaving a will seriously."[22] In a Sunni tradition the Prophet is reported to have said, "It is not appropriate for a Muslim who has something to will to spend two nights without leaving advance instructions in writing ready with him."[23] There is no doubt that such traditions simply establish the legality of leaving a proper will for the distribution of one's estate to legitimate heirs. Evidently, this is the sense in which ordinary people understand the purpose of this critical document in Muslim culture. But can a person will the use of his or her body after death?

A theological doctrine that assumes importance in this regard is the concept of right in the meaning of discretionary authority to make decisions independent of any pressure. Muslim jurists make a fine distinction between God's right (*ḥaqq allāh*) and the right of a human being (*ḥaqq al-'abd*) as it pertains to one's personhood (*nafs*). In jurisprudence God's right is defined as that in which a human being has no option but submission, whether that right makes sense or not; whereas the right of a human being is defined as that which reverts to promoting human interests (*maṣāliḥ*) while in this world. Excluded in this latter right are his interests in the hereafter, which are part of God's right.[24] As for the human body, God's rights include the human obligation to preserve it with dignity and not to cause any harm to it in any form, including suicide.[25] An individual's right on his/her body includes the right to retribution (*qiṣāṣ*) if any part of the body is injured in an attack; or the right to seek compensation (*diya*) for such a physical harm intentionally caused by others. The Sharī'a makes an exception and justifies the sidestepping of God's right under special circumstances like endangering one's life in defending one's family and honor. But at no time can an individual assume total discretion in matters of life and death and claim the right to terminate his/her life.

Actually, if an individual can establish his or her absolute discretion over his/her body then the matter of donating parts of his/her body through a living will becomes resolved. The problematic of such a decision in light of less than absolute discretion over one's claim to ownership of one's body can be located in the analogy that applies to one's material possessions. What belongs to a person while alive continues to be so after one dies. It is only with such a presumption about the ownership that one can leave advance directives about the estate. This claim to ownership is acknowledged by the Sharī'a when it endorses a person's right to make a will about one's possessions, and it requires the heirs to strictly abide by its terms. This right is non-transferable to anyone in the family. However, when it comes to one's person (*nafs*), which constitutes a total existence that includes the human body, since there is an explicit charge not to cause any harm to it or to put it in situations that could endanger its well-being, the question about the permissibility to will removal of an organ for donation arises. Since mutilation of body is not allowed in life, it is also forbidden after death. A number of juridical rulings that forbid postmortem dissection underscore the Islamic belief that a Muslim's body is inviolable both in life and in death. Consequently, what is forbidden in life is also forbidden after death.[26]

Accordingly, some jurists have explicitly ruled against the inclusion of one's body in one's last will and testament (*waṣīya*) in the Sharī'a. According to these jurists, the last will and testament in the technical usage is the conveyance of ownership beyond the death. In this sense, then, *waṣīya* in the Sharī'a is applicable to goods, benefits, and debts. It is the right of disposal of the estate left by the deceased as per his/her advance directives. However, the body of the deceased does not meet the criteria for inclusion in the will in its technical sense in the Sharī'a, because the human body is not among those things that are "left behind" as a dead person's property. Yet if a person were to leave such a will, then the document is valid as a "living will" in its lexical sense only. In the latter signification, *waṣīya* is used in the meaning of commissioning, delegating, or entrusting the other to undertake to fulfill something during or after the death of the person leaving the directives.

In Islam, the ultimate authority over this body lies outside human personhood. According to the Qur'an, the human being is created with a nature (*fiṭra*) that acknowledges both divine sovereignty and stewardship, but the ultimate responsibility is God's. Thus by denying the validity of the last will in this specific situation, the Sharī'a negates the modern cultural attitude that humans have complete control over their own bodies, to the extent of dictating postmortem procedures without accountability to a sacred authority outside of themselves. It is for this reason that the Sharīʿa denies an individual the right to issue an advance request to be cremated. Such a will is legally null and void on the grounds that it breaches a divine trust. The will is also morally objectionable because it fails to consider the psychological needs of the bereaved family members, who, in the Muslim cultural context, might not approve such a drastic handling of their loved one. In other words, the invalidity of the last will regarding what happens to one's body after one dies is established by the mere fact that such matters are judged to be beyond human jurisdiction.[27]

Nevertheless, the invalidity of the living will does not necessarily translate into a total ban on donating, say, a kidney or other parts of the body. The law acknowledges the person's autonomy in such matters, as long as no decision detrimental to one's health and well-being is made. Thus, according to most jurists, it is permissible to donate an organ or a part of one's body if the attending physician is absolutely certain that, by removing that organ from the living donor, the latter will not be harmed and the patient dying of organ failure will be saved. But these jurists do not permit the donor to receive monetary advantage in return for the organ because any transaction involving the sale of a free person or any part of his body is illegal.[28]

The Problem of Monetary Advantage

Deriving monetary advantage from the dead has been, more or less, a universal problem in all cultures. The problem is accentuated in modern times because only recently advances in biological and medical sciences and technology have invited profiteering from harvested organs used for transplantation. The public reaction to the marketing of organs has been strongly negative. Any form of market approach to the human body is as an affront to human dignity. While practical decisions in the application of the religious values like sacrifice and altruism have been more or less recognized by leading Muslim jurists in endorsing organ donation through advance directives, the problem of individual autonomy to lead his/her own life as he/she pleases, even at the risk of harm to the common good, has inevitably led to opposing the communitarian ethics of Islam. More and more Muslims conduct their lives as a matter of an individual's right of self-determination, treating their personal interests and decisions in isolation from a mutual and social decision that affects others in the family or in the community.

Muslim jurists have endeavored to underscore the need to put limits on the individual right to self-determination when it comes to decisions that are potentially harmful to the overall good of others in the family and in the community. In fact, as the Mālikī jurist Shāṭibī explains, the assertion of one's autonomy in order to do things that are forbidden by God (like endangering one's life or removing or destroying a part of one's body even at the risk of harm to the common good) is to defeat God's purpose in providing various means to perfect an individual's life, his body, and his intellect. Any lack of concern for one's well-being in the context of divinely ordained interpersonal relationships is a violation of God's right.[29] There is no illusion in the revealed texts of Islam that an extreme form of individualism based on the right of self-determination about one's life and person without moral anchorage in human relationships would lead to disregard the importance of human perfection as a member of society. The legitimacy of God's rights as regards the human body requires the human being to do what promotes the interests of the entire community.[30] It is in the context of God's right over the human body that the question about organ retrieval and its donation for transplantation requires important consideration whether such an act can be regarded as a violation of God's right and the right of an individual to donate. From what has been said above it is not difficult to extrapolate that legally it is improper for an individual to assume his/her right of disposal over God's right, except when besides the individual's consent in such transference there is also a justification in the revealed texts permitting to sign over God's right to the human right over the body. Nevertheless, that justification can be valid only when such a discretionary handling of the body by an individual can be shown to constitute an exclusive means for the regeneration of God's greater right. In other words, organ donation cannot be justified unless it averts some greater evil than the evil of desecrating the body by removing an organ from it.

Evidently there are two blameworthy acts involved in donating an organ: a greater blameworthy act pertains to violation of God's right over human body, which needs to be tolerated for the sake of a lesser blameworthy act of desecrating the body by removing an organ. Now, if the permission of the donor to relinquish his right is added to the situation, then the right of disposal is shared commonly between God and the human being due to the donor's consent and the revelation-based justification regarding God's right.

Some jurists have raised the problem of conflicting rights and interests in assessing the extent to which God's rights over the body can be superseded by those of the individual. Admission of some documentation found in the revealed texts does not solve the problem of how exactly a particular interpretation can support transportation of parts of dead body to a living person for transplant is clearly seen as a violation of God's right. At the root of the problem is the Sunni view about the right that accrues to an individual: since that right is an act of divine grace, it can be established only by the revealed text.[31] It is God who legislates rights and requires human beings to claim and exercise them in a particular way. Hence, if exercising a specific right (e.g., organ donation) leads to contradicting this program, then it is forbidden. The most prominent principle of this outlook is to avoid causing harm to oneself or others in exercising one's rights: "No harm, no harassment."

The principle of "No harm" is the most widely cited principle in resolving the ethics of organ donation. Both Sunni and the Shīʿite jurists have resorted to the rule of exceptional circumstances that might require the sidestepping of a prohibition (*ḍarūra*) to argue the case for organ donation.[32] But the validity of this argument depends on a meticulous assessment of the situational context (*mawḍūʿ*) of each case, a clear examination of the harm and benefit—whether physical or emotional—that accrue to donor, recipient, and their families. It is worth bearing in mind that the assessment of the harm was not limited to the physical harm that could be suffered by the donor and the recipient; it also extended to the psychological and social harm that could be experienced by the close family.[33] While the permission to consume carrion when faced with a life-threatening situation has served as a paradigm case for deducing examples of the rule of necessity, the principle of "No harm" has provided the rationale for allowing or prohibiting organ transplants.

It would appear, then, that if a person were to donate an organ that would cause his death, then organ donation would be forbidden, however much such an act would benefit the recipient. In this case the act of altruism is actually the cause of an equal or greater harm, even if it leads to saving the recipient's life. However, if a person were to donate an organ without causing harm or death to himself, and if that act could save the life of a patient dying of organ failure, then the Sharīʿa would regard the violation of God's rights over the human body as permissible. Furthermore, the act of donating an organ would be permissible if it benefits both the donor and the recipient, and if such an act would not affect their health adversely.[34]

Framed in this balance of benefit and harm, it would appear that the new rulings on organ donation have a single objective: to preserve the health and well-being of the two parties involved in an organ transplant, without any reference to other aspects of the issue. Hence, any considerations regarding other social and religious distinctions have no place in the rulings. In more recent discussions the unintended harm done to the donor's immediate family (spouse and children) has figured prominently. Evidently, acts of altruism (*īthār*) are under closer scrutiny in terms of their adverse impact upon the family.[35] Some jurists have asked whether donating one's organs to save a life of a non-Muslim is permissible or not. In my opinion, the spirit of Islamic revelation does not permit any distinction when it comes to saving a life of another human being.[36] If these jurists regard it permissible to receive organs from non-Muslims, such as the Peoples of the Book (*ahl al-kitāb* = Jews, Christians, and Zoroastrians), then the principle of reciprocity makes it obligatory to do the same for others in return. The discriminatory attitudes that proscribe organ donations to non-Muslims are based on classical juridical decisions that need reevaluation in light of basic moral principles.[37]

The issue of receiving monetary benefit from the newly dead raises questions that are related to the sanctity of human body. Legally speaking, it would seem that the sale of human organs, as long as there was no harm to the person who does so, would appear to present no problem if it were not for two aspects of such a transaction: the unsoundness of any transaction involving human corpse (*mayta*) and the problem of establishing discretionary ownership (*milkīya*) over one's body.

There is a debate among the jurists about whether a removed organ can be regarded as part of the corpse, which by definition constitutes of the whole body that has severed its linkage to the spirit.[38] Evidently, such a distinction between whole and part of the body is missing in the common usage of the term *corpse*. For the most part, people treat a severed limb, for instance, as a dead body (*mayta*). Accordingly, all the rules that apply to the corpse also apply to the detached limb. Nevertheless, most people equate the notion of the corpse with the entire body, not just with detached pieces of it. On this view, the sale of an organ would not be equated with the sale of a cadaver. Some jurists have extrapolated the verses that prohibit the consumption of carrion to include prohibition against its sale.[39] Others have resorted to the rules about the prohibition of the sale of impure objects (*al-a'yān al-najisa*) to include bodily organs of a deceased as ritually unclean and, therefore, unfit for sale. Whatever the reasons for the injunction against the sale of carrion or organs derived from it, these rulings reflected the limited ways in which human bodies were open to illegal exploitation for purely monetary advantage. There was as yet no conception of medical treatment based on the use of organs for transplantation.

As regards the second aspect, there is a difference of opinion among Muslim jurists. Undoubtedly, one cannot engage in a transaction for sale without first establishing one's ownership on it. As pointed out earlier, there are a number of prominent jurists who maintain that human beings have no legitimate ownership over their body. Consequently, they cannot derive monetary advantage from its sale. In fact, if such an advantage occurs, then it is tantamount to illicit consumption. At the same time, some scholars acknowledge that an individual has discretion over one's person (*mālik li-nafsih*); but this discretion does not translate into ownership because it is elemental—that is, it establishes one's essential identity as a person. In order to establish the right of disposal, one needs to prove legal and institutional discretion.[40] However, based on this notion of limited ownership, some jurists have supported monetary advantage, arguing that because the Sharī'a requires monetary compensation (*diya*) when a part of body is injured or destroyed through criminal aggression, then it should be legitimate to receive money for an organ that is removed for the benefit of the recipient. Yet it is forbidden to cut off a part of one's body in order to sell it.

There is no argument among the jurists that human body is not a commodity (*māl*) that can be turned to commercial or other advantage. It is not an object whose use can be negotiated in other than exceptional and unavoidable conditions. Consequently, Muslim jurists have ruled that a human being, whether alive or dead, cannot be an object of a commercial transaction. Since human beings cannot be treated as a commodity, the Sharī'a has forbidden handling of a human person, who is endowed with dignity and honor, as merchandise in a commercial dealing. Nevertheless, the question arises about selling parts of human body: are they similar in status to the human person?

Classification of Human Organs

In the classical juridical corpus, there was no attempt at categorizing bodily organs into vital and inconsequential or renewable and nonrenewable, even though the sections dealing with compensation for injury or destruction of bodily parts recognized a functional hierarchy and the attendant value attached to, for instance, eyes or limbs. Hence, some jurists had classified human parts into three types: those that were unique; those that were in pairs; and those of which there were four of a kind. The first kind included nose, tongue, penis, loins, bladder, and rectum. When any of these were destroyed they were irreplaceable; therefore, full blood money was due because not only had the destruction of the organ deprived the person of its vital functions, but there was also some likelihood of external deformity. The second kind included eyes, ears, lips, eyebrows when no hair could grow, breasts and nipples, and limbs (hands, legs). If one or both of these pairs was destroyed, then the compensation was full blood money. The third kind included the edge of eyelid where eyelashes grow, which when destroyed deprived a person of the multiple functions of the eye and beauty; the eyelashes; a bodily part which remained in form (like a head injury) while losing its functions such as reasoning, sight, smell, taste, sexuality, and procreation. The destruction or injury to this multifunctional organ was the basis for fourfold compensation when, for instance, only the head was injured, because the victim lost the functions of the brain, the eye, the ears, and so on, which depended on the fully developed brain.[41]

In more recent discussions, based on the questions submitted for religious responses, jurists have identified the need to at least distinguish between vital and inconsequential organs. However, the definition of *vital,* besides being consequential to the very survival of human person (e.g., heart, liver, and so on), is extended to include aesthetic considerations like maintaining one's appearance. The assumption in such deliberations is that the donor is a living person motivated either by altruism or profit. As a rule, the Sharī'a regards the inflicting of any physical deformation as tampering with nature's gifts. Since both eyes are vital for maintaining healthy vision and overall appearance, a person cannot decide to donate his/her eye even when he/she can continue to live with the other. In contrast, donating a kidney is not a problem as long as no harm is done to the donor or the recipient. While it is admitted that both eyes and kidneys are vital organs, donating an eye would constitute a deformation of one's appearance, whereas donating a kidney would not. In general, the principle of "No harm" encompasses a notion of physical well-being that includes cosmetic wholeness. Consequently, Muslim jurists have ruled that it is impermissible to cut any part of the body in order to consume it for survival, except under dire conditions.[42]

All renewable parts of the body, such as fluid and soft parts (*a'ḍā' sā'ila*) like hair, skin, nails, bone marrow, blood and so on form the second major category in the juridical opinions on organ donation. The term *inconsequential* simply conveys the meaning of being renewable (*mutjaddid*) body elements that could be donated without endangering one's well-being.

Donation of Human Blood and Milk

Blood and milk deserve separate treatment because both these fluid parts have symbolic as well as religious significance in Muslim cultures. While donating soft and fluid parts by a living person in general does not give rise to any serious ethical problem, blood and human milk create serious concerns when any monetary compensation is involved. Since both these parts, like other parts of human body, cannot be treated as commodity, their sale is banned.[43] Because some jurists have forbidden the sale of blood[44] and the need for blood has risen sharply in the context of medical treatment, others have ruled it as a collective duty (*farḍ kifāya*) for the entire Muslim community to make sure that supplies of blood are kept in blood banks for use in emergency situations like accidents and wars. The most commonly cited reason for the prohibition to sell blood is the general rule in juristic practice that when God forbids an item he also forbids its exchange as a commodity for money. The Qur'an in this connection states its commandment as follows: "These things only has he forbidden you [for food]: carrion, blood, the flesh of swine, what has been hallowed to other than God" (Q. 2:173).

Out of the four forbidden items, the first three things are harmful to human health, whereas the fourth item (that is, the meat that is not slaughtered ritually) is harmful to one's faith, because it is an act of disobedience against the divine commandment.[45] In one tradition the Prophet is reported to have declared that when God forbids people to consume something, then it is also forbidden for them to engage in selling it.[46] Another tradition makes it explicit that it is forbidden to obtain monetary advantage by selling blood.[47]

The ban on sale notwithstanding, there is a consensus among scholars that permission to donate blood in Islam is self-evident because cupping (*al-ḥijjama*) in traditional Arabic medicine was practiced even by the Prophet for reasons of health.[48] Although the process of cupping involves withdrawal of blood for overall health, the withdrawn blood is not contaminated; hence its use for transfusion, provided all other medical conditions are fulfilled, is permissible. These conditions include careful monitoring of the donor's ability to donate without causing harm to his own health and his being free from any contagious disease that could be transmitted to others through transfusion. Since blood is among the renewable, fluid parts of the body, a healthy person can donate it to help a patient in need of it. It is important to reiterate that Muslim jurists, as a rule, do not accept human ownership of one's own body. Hence, the permission to donate blood is extrapolated on the basis of the well-known Arab practice of regular withdrawal of blood through cupping rather than on a person's claim to its ownership.

As for milk, which is also regarded as part of the body, most Sunni jurists permit its sale because, according to Qur'an (Q. 65:6), it is appropriate to pay the wife or wet-nurse if she is willing to suckle the child.[49] In other words, the Qur'an treats suckling as a service for which the wife/wet-nurse should be paid something in return. This latter permission to pay for suckling has been interpreted as allowing the sale of human milk. However, unlike blood, milk is regarded as a source of consanguinity and, therefore, its donation/sale is stringently regulated to avoid any irregularity in preservation of a child's lineage and future conjugal relationship. The Qur'an lays down this rule: "You are forbidden to marry . . . your foster-mothers and foster-sisters (*min al-riḍā'a*)" (Q. 4:24). The tradition of the Prophet expounds this prohibition by making it clear that marriages that become forbidden because of the close lineage also become forbidden because of the suckling.[50] According to the Sharī'a, suckling (*riḍā'*), regardless of whether it takes the form of sucking or drinking the donated milk—in other words, whether it involves breast or bottle-feeding—contributes to the growth of bone and flesh of the infant and establishes an intimate consanguinity with the foster-mother. Consequently, as reported in the Tradition, if an infant is suckled to its full five times, then legally speaking, the infant shares the womb with other offspring of the foster mother,[51] whose other children become the infant's consanguine siblings, rendering any future marriage between them incestuous.[52] It is for this reason that, although blood and organ banks are gradually getting acceptance, milk banks are problematic in Muslim societies unless the donor mother's identity is known for future reference in order to avoid a potentially incestuous relationship. The principle that is operative in the case of donating human milk with social implications for future conjugal relationship of the child is: "Aversion of corruption has a priority over promoting the good."[53] When promotion of good (donating human milk for an infant's nourishment) is offset by the uncertainties of future corruption (the possibility of a mixed identity of the donor and resulting incestuous marriage), then the jurists prefer to suspend the donation of human milk in the absence of a certain identification of the donor.

Cosmetic Surgery and Sex Change

Classical sources reveal a number of occasions in which the Prophet performed a sort of organ transplant and repaired a detached limb or a broken nose. Bone and teeth transplants were also common, and the jurists regarded such transplantations as permissible in the Sharīʿa.[54] Even the use of parts of animals forbidden for food—like swine bone grafts—were permissible when there was no other alternative. In most of these examples in the early sources, the goal was very clear: the procedure was permissible mainly for corrective purposes. Since the Qur'anic injunction was to preserve one's person, it also provided the grounds for extrapolating permission and even the obligation to seek a remedy for any injury that led to dysfunctional or deformed organs. Implicit in such rulings was the duty to maintain one's health and appearance; accordingly, the Prophet emphasized natural instincts to perform cosmetic and hygienic tasks such as the regular cutting of nails, trimming of the beard, and dental care. Dental hygiene assumed great importance in the rules of cleanliness and was emphasized on different occasions by requiring the regular use of a toothbrush at different times in a day and by discouraging the eating of sweets, which the Prophet regarded as harmful to teeth.[55]

This traditional Islamic emphasis on healthy appearance and adornment supports cosmetic surgery, as long as the procedure causes no harm.[56] An additional condition mentioned in some sources suggests that cosmetic surgery should not lead to deception regarding one's true identity. Hence, while permitting women to get rid of excessive facial hair (*ilnimāṣ*), the ruling required them to seek their husband's permission to avoid deception (*tadlīs*).[57] The Ḥanbalī jurists have forbidden women to undergo any cosmetic enhancement (e.g., making one's eyebrows stand out) that made them resemble a prostitute (*fājira*).[58] A more prohibitive case is given in Bukhārī's compilation, in which a woman, having lost her hair during an illness, sought the Prophet's permission to use false hair.[59] The Prophet denied her the permission, saying that God curses the one who engages in such an act of cosmetic enhancement.[60] In other words, according to a number of traditions in authoritative Sunni sources, corrective cosmetic procedures to enhance one's beauty are impermissible if they lead to deception about one's true identity and if they cause corrupt social behavior.

Among reasons cited for the prohibition of enhancement surgery is the presumed inviolability of various parts of the human body. However, the Shāfiʿī jurists, on the basis of the principle of necessity (which also permits the consumption of a cadaver under dire conditions), approved of the use of bodily parts to perform such surgical procedures, whether involving skin, bone, or muscle tissue, and whether derived from the body of the patient or a fresh cadaver.[61] In addition, these jurists required that the attending physician should verify, however speculatively, that such a cosmetic surgery would be beneficial.

As seen above, cosmetic surgery to enhance one's appearance that would also lead to a change of one's features so that it would change the identifying imprint of an individual is regarded as suspicious in the Sharī'a, and hence illicit. The Qur'anic passage that has been commonly cited as documentation for this ruling is the one in which the rebellious Satan promises God, "I will assuredly . . . lead them (human beings) astray, and fill them with fancies . . . and I will command them and they will alter God's creation.' (Q. 4:119) The last part of verse ("they will alter God's creation") is interpreted to mean that Satan will lead human beings to change their nature and the way they look physically so that they will not be identifiable with their original identity as given at birth.[62] In other words, introducing changes in and tampering with God's original creation is regarded as satanic.

This brings us to the issues of sex-change surgery. Is it permissible? A real change of sex by means of a surgical procedure is not regarded as objectionable by some jurists. However, there is no exception to the ban on looking at and touching of the private parts by a person who is legally forbidden to do so. The surgery should be done in such a way that it would not lead to this or any other forbidden act. However, other jurists regard any tampering with male and female identity as immoral and an affront to God, the creator, especially when it involves the changing of an organ or destroying one to replace it with another. In addition, these latter jurists rule out any corrective surgery to create male or female reproductive organs for a man or woman who emotionally feels like he/she is existentially a member of the opposite sex.[63]

The jurists who oppose sex-change operations cite the potential harm that such a procedure can cause in mutilating the original organs in order to create the desired sexual identity. Moreover, as these jurists argue, when someone is essentially created as a man or a woman, then a true change of sexuality is impossible and is beyond the reach of scientific technique. The reason is each sex has basic characteristics that are implanted in the womb and that are so essential to one's being that no earthly power can alter them.

In sum, according to the jurists opposed to sex change, medical intervention through surgery and administration of special medicine which causes man's facial hair to disappear or woman's breasts to grow in size, or a vagina to replace male and a penis to replace female reproductive organs, does not actually make a man a woman or vice versa. Anyone who undertakes this unlawful procedure has disobeyed God's command. Moreover, according to these scholars, as far as the Sharī'a goes, the legal status of this individual remains what it was prior to the sex change. In other words, by mere elimination of some parts of the body the situational aspect of a person's manhood or womanhood does not change in such a way that one can assert that the legal status should also change. This impossibility of a real change in a person's sex, according to these scholars, can be construed from some of the verses of the Qur'an. Thus, for instance, God says: "He creates what he will; he gives to whom he will females, and he gives to whom he will males or he couples them, both males and females; and he makes whom he will barren" (Q. 42:49–50).

The Case of the Hermaphrodite (*al-khunthā*)

Gender classification according to dimorphic categories is not a new phenomenon in science or in religion. In medical science the category of hermaphrodites, whose bodies did not conform to arbitrarily quantified criteria for the male or female body, are treated with corrective surgeries to define uncommon or ambiguous sexual anatomies. The hermaphrodite possesses physical traits of both sexes; such a person might have ambiguous genitalia or an otherwise amorphous sexual makeup. The common medical justification for such corrective surgery for hermaphroditism was to provide a strict social boundary between two sexes so that those patients whose bodies were not immediately recognizable as male or female could overcome the fears of abnormal sexual behavior.[64] In the Islamic juridical tradition one observes dimorphic gender classification in only one of the two varieties: male or female, for different reasons. There was an acknowledgement of the category known as *al-khunthā*—literally, neutral in gender; such an individual's gender was not so clearcut.[65] The individual bore some aspects of one gender and some aspects of the other. Although Muslim physicians were fully informed about aberrant bodies, there were as yet no medical techniques to surgically correct and establish norms of male and female bodies. However, Muslim jurists were concerned with rehabilitating the individuals with sexual ambiguities within the acceptable social norms of the Muslim culture that also included sexual segregation. More importantly, although the jurists acknowledged that anatomically it was difficult to determine the sexual identity of the hermaphrodites, it was legally and ritually essential to ascertain the predominant biological, psychological, and social traits to identify them in one or the other gender category for the distribution of inheritance and carrying out of religious and social obligations.

Muslim societies, like many other groups, regard gender differentiations as part of a whole system of social relationships that are underpinned by issues of gender, on the idea that men and women do and should look different, act differently, and contribute differently to society. Although gender roles are probably more relaxed now than at any time in Western history, in Muslim societies cultural gender expectations sometimes lead to repression and even deadly acts of violence against men or women whose sexual identity is ambiguous. How one dresses, speaks, walks, and with whom one has sex are all determined by ethical norms that regulate gender relations in the Sharī'a. To be sure, in the case of the hermaphrodite, it is the culture rather than physiology that defines the male or female identity and the attendant role. The culture treats an ambiguous social gender as defective male or defective female. Modern surgeons have developed surgical procedures to provide clearcut norms for male and female bodies. But stereotypical roles for men and women have also colored traditional understanding of the evolution of sexual characteristics. And yet, the problem is far from resolved because, as it turns out, some females actually are born without ovaries—and indeed without any other internal female equipment (vagina, womb, fallopian tubes)—and develop into essentially genderless individuals. Some males are born with bodies completely unable to respond to their own testosterone, and they develop womanly traits.[66]

In Islamic jurisprudence the purpose of sections dealing with hermaphrodites had been to provide criteria to transform anyone whose gender was socially and psychologically ambiguous into one who would legally pass as either male or female. In this connection, especially in light of medical advancements, anyone whose sexual identity was unclear could undergo surgical procedures to establish a clear gender. However, the jurists acknowledged that there was no doubt that any type of sex-reassignment surgery was not without risk of mutilation, disfigurement, and/or rejection of foreign implants. In Islamic jurisprudence a permanent legal remedy to rectify gender identification was deemed not only worthy but essential. Sex designation (*al-'unwān*) as male or female, however difficult in the case of hermaphrodite, was regarded as critical for an individual's interaction and relationships with others in society. Hence, if an outwardly female individual's anatomy developed clearly along nonfemale lines (no breasts, no milk glands, no child-bearing hips, no menses, sterility), then it was ruled appropriate to live in the male social gender role; however, if the anatomy developed along nonmale lines (no early beard growth, no male vocal chords, no male skeletal structure, no male musculature, no male libido, no male genetic patterning) then the person was justified in choosing the female social gender role. However, there was also the recognition that sometimes corrective genital operations become necessary to enable proper social sex classification consistent with inherent gender identification and sexual proclivity. The increased efforts to surgically establish norms for gender identification were treated as corrective surgery and hence accepted as part of the solution to help an individual whose male or female identity was anatomically aberrant. In general, the jurists endorsed corrective surgical procedures to treat both types of hermaphrodites: the nonproblematic hermaphrodites that had an additional or defective private part of the opposite sex, or the problematic hermaphrodites that could not be categorized as a man or a woman.[67]

Religious-Ethical Implications of Sex Change

The Sharī'a, in keeping with its strict rules about sexual segregation, prescribed different religious practices for men and women: From the ordinances that were covered in those sections of the Sharī'a that deal with human-divine relationship (*'ibādāt*) to the detailed rulings provided in the sections that govern human-human relationships (*mu'āmalāt*), gender determination assumes a central part of regulating legitimate interaction between sexes. The most sensitive area of this interaction was the intimacy that was shared between a married man and woman. Medical attempts at defining male and female through surgeries were not always regarded as sufficient in assessing what was normal sexual behavior when it was unclear who was male and who was female. More than physicians, it was Muslim jurists who were concerned about normal sexual behavior. Accordingly, when dealing with the implications of the changes that would arise from sex-change surgery, whether for cosmetic or medical reasons, it is important to assess four areas of an individual's life with others:

1. Individual duties, which were performed personally and regardless of one's relationships to others. These included one's duties to God such as daily prayers and other acts of piety performed as religiously required. The validity of these rituals depended upon preserving one's individuality as a male or female member of the community, both in the privacy of the home or in the mosque.
2. Relational ethics, which were informed by reciprocity and responsibilities one had toward others in the family and in the society. These duties were defined in terms of gender roles, especially roles that included specific duties toward family members, such as parents, siblings, offspring, in terms of assumption of guardianship, providing sustenance, housing, custody of children, and so on.
3. Rights concerning inheritance, amount of shares that one claims in terms of one's relationship and gender; the level of seclusion (*ḥajb*) one observes in terms one's relationship to male or female members of the family, and so on.
4. Specific ordinances that touch a person in terms of penal code; retributive and restorative justice.

To be sure, sex change is a change of identity as well as change of legal personhood. Whereas the process of identification is gradual and full of challenges that take shape in due course, the altered legal personhood takes effect immediately. The rules and the restriction apply as soon as one's outward persona is established. Hence, for instance, the mode of ritual performance requiring proper covering of the head and body along with other rules of sexual segregation apply as soon as maleness or femaleness is validated. Moreover, spousal and all other interpersonal relationships require revisiting and adjustment of negotiated rights and responsibilities prior to sex change. Here the rulings that govern sex change surgery are in many instances similar to those that are applied to a hermaphrodite's social sex classification, with this caveat: although the surgical correction of hermaphroditism is encouraged, optional sex-change surgery is often discouraged and even regarded by some scholars as forbidden.[68]

8

Islamic Bioethics—Recent Developments

It is God who brought you out of the wombs of your mothers. He gave you hearing and sight, and hearts, so that you give thanks to God.

—Qur'an 16:78

Recent advancements in medicine and biotechnology have entailed forms of experimentation in which humans—especially the most vulnerable humans (infants, pregnant women, the retarded, the dying, the sick, and condemned prisoners)—are treated as research specimens rather than as inviolable creations of God. The inviolability (*ḥurma*) of life, as we often stressed, has been the most important religious value in Islam and other Abrahamic and non-Abrahamic traditions—hence their prohibitions of abortion, suicide, euthanasia, and other forms of aggression toward human life. Unforeseen applications of biotechnology in various areas—technically assisted reproduction, human cloning, and genetic engineering—have posed unexpected ethical challenges to traditional views of humans and their role in the natural and divine order. According to the Qur'an: "We shall show them [human beings] our signs in the horizons and in themselves, so that it will become clear that it is the truth. Is it not enough that your Lord is witness over all things?" (Q. 41:54).

The "signs in the horizons" are, collectively, nature, which moves in an orderly fashion that suggests the purposiveness of creation; the "signs" in human beings suggest the human capacity to understand right from wrong and to promote the good of the larger community of which they are a part.[1] Biotechnology's claim that it can genetically produce healthier babies or clone more desirable persons threatens the meaning of an individual's relation to society and nature, promising progress through genetic manipulation rather than the organic connectedness of morally and spiritually aware members of a community that consciously wills justice and compassion for its members in accordance with a divine order or plan.

The principle of interpersonal relations in Muslim social ethics—"No harm, no harassment"—has served as an important check on potentially harmful or dehumanizing implications of advanced medical technology or the life sciences. Muslim jurists have approached many modern medical treatments with caution. On the basis of the probability of causing even greater harm Muslim jurists have ruled out any medical treatment of doubtful efficacy. At the same time, in a number of cases involving incurable diseases for which a cure depends on further scientific experimentation, which might expose the patient to a significant degree of risk or inconvenience, the scholars have raised the issue of averting probable harm and protecting patients' right to reject the harm in accord with the principle, "Averting harm has preponderance over promoting benefit." This principle applies with special force to using humans as subjects of medical experimentation in which they are given an as-yet unproven treatment in order to test its effectiveness.[2]

The problem is serious in the competing world of recognition and financial advantage. Medical professionals and scientists are no exception to this human trend. Today young physicians/scientists in the Muslim world, like their counterparts in other countries, have been known to yield to competitive pressures by promoting ethically questionable modes of research and experimentation upon human subjects. The impact of human experimentation on medical practice awaits full investigation in Muslim countries. Although the international standards for biomedical research involving human subjects are gradually being adopted in Muslim countries through the ministries of health under the guidance of World Health Organization (WHO), the local research ethics committees (REC), usually made up of medical professionals and researchers in the life sciences, lack the training and sophistication needed to deal with major ethical and theological quandaries. In the Muslim world, where there is a widespread lack of accountability of the researchers in life sciences in general, the RECs have had little impact. The RECs in a number of Muslim countries have proved unable to impose effective regulations on research involving human beings, in large measure because of the lack of enforcement by well-informed government agencies.

Frequent misrepresentations about free consent have led to violations of the human rights of patients and other disadvantaged groups who were not fully informed about the risks and benefits of the experimental protocols to which they were subjected. In fact, the whole concept of the subject's free and informed consent is in need of critical reevaluation in the light of ethical and moral values that are outside the purview of medical science. There is a clear need for guidance by knowledgeable religious and ethical specialists who could provide moral analysis and not simply juridical rulings (*fatāwā*) about what is permissible or impermissible when human life and dignity are at stake.

The peculiar feature of human experimentation is that its ends are determined by human subjects themselves, since their understanding of the issues involved can provide a sound basis for consenting to or rejecting their participation in experimentation. There is no way to separate the subject and the object of experimentation when the investigation deals with human beings. No amount of medical erudition or expertise can by itself provide the ethical criteria necessary for rulings that may involve life-and-death decisions. Although it is essential to have competent medical information about an experimental protocol, the subject's consent must ultimately rest not on technical data but on a moral sense of what is right or wrong for his or her own life. To find solutions to the medical problems facing humanity today the subject must interactively convey the information about his/her personal moral convictions and ability to consider the merit of necessary sacrifice for altruistic or other reasons.

At the center of ethical issues involving human experimentation is the scientific concern that any drug or medical procedure should not be widely prescribed for humans without extensive trials and experiments to verify its effectiveness. This aspect of experimentation was anticipated by the Muslim philosopher and physician Avicenna (Ibn Sīnā, d. 1037) when he wrote that "the experimentation must be done with [the] human body, for testing a drug on a lion or a horse might not prove anything about its effect on man."[3]

Nevertheless, it is important to bear in mind that any and all experimentation dealing with human beings carries with it a moral responsibility—a responsibility to the subject, who has a right to know, to comment, and to seek guidance before agreeing to any experimental procedure. As required by Article 1.2 of the Helsinki Declaration (1989), research involving human subjects "should be clearly formulated, in an experimental protocol which should be transmitted for consideration, comment and guidance to a specially appointed committee independent of the investigator and sponsor. . . ." This is the basis for ethical deliberations that must determine the boundaries and goals of experiment and the attendant obligations to any human subjects. The role of the REC, then, is not only to assess and regulate all human experimentation, but also to seek public participation and opinion to avert future undesirable consequences for all concerned parties.

In Muslim biomedical research the principle of public good is often invoked to justify medical experimentation that seeks to promote public health. The Prophetic tradition that encourages the search for remedies for all diseases generates enormous confidence that the physician, in his/her role as God's agent for healing, furthers the noble ends of medical sciences.[4] In the same vein, the researcher also serves the highly cherished values of promoting public health by undertaking scientific experiments to further the critical knowledge needed to advance treatments and cures. The social dimension of such experimentation often supersedes a concern with the good of the individual subject, which is thereby sacrificed in the name of public good in the community-oriented ethics of Muslim cultures. Rationalizations based on notions of the public good can never overshadow the concerns of a pitifully uninformed individual who might be recruited for a study and experimental trial for the greater good of others in a manner that runs roughshod over his basic, God-given human dignity.

At the same time, the revealed texts do remind Muslims that no society can afford to ignore the harm and destruction that can descend on the entire population if an epidemic sweeps a region unchecked. The very fact that the Tradition provides various guidelines in personal and public hygiene when an epidemic breaks out shows the seriousness with which every person was made aware of a duty not only to protect his own health but also that of society as a whole.[5]

In the Muslim world poor standards of general health weigh heavily in such judgments. In certain parts of Africa endemic malaria and other sicknesses claim the lives of thousands of people. Under such conditions, there is a collective obligation in the Islamic legal-ethical system that qualified members of the society search for remedies, even at the risk of infringing on the good of individuals. However, in the effort to take control of disease of any kind, whether a threat to a large number or not, any such encroachment on the dignity of the individual runs counter to the moral teachings of Islam.

The most crucial question in such controlled experimentation is whether the proposed treatment is relatively safe or is likely to do harm to the patient. It can be safely assumed that the subjects of experimentation will not be recruited from the healthy members of society. If the goal of the experimentation is to further knowledge about a particular disease, then in most cases, the recruitment will target those who suffer from the disease and are under treatment and observation. This quest for trial subjects puts to the test the most cherished value of the medical profession—placing the well-being of the patient above all other considerations. The sole responsibility of the physician is to the patient. In no way does he/she represent any one else's interests, including the interests of the future sufferers from the same disease. Accordingly, he/she cannot decide to compromise his/her care for the patient by taking into consideration the long-term benefit such experimentation on his/her patient might confer on others.[6]

One of the major issues in human experimentation is the requirement that the treatment be available to any patient under the physician's care, without any discrimination. But the selection process has suffered from an endemic problem related to the patient's informed consent. The question of informed consent depends on the patient's ability to understand all the pros and cons of the new therapeutic measure that is being introduced by the doctor. In the

Muslim cultural context, where literacy levels are not always high enough to understand the doctor's explanation, the competent medical expert's opinion alone counts because he/she is required to take all measures necessary for curing, alleviating suffering, and saving life. This requirement puts an enormous moral burden on the medical expert, who is both professionally and culturally invested with absolute authority to make all decisions pertaining to the patient's care. Most Muslim jurists have favored authoritarian medical practices that have ethical ramifications for both experimentation, the standard treatment of patients, and the selection of subjects. Such rulings have stifled public debate in the Muslim world, where the absence of democratic governance has restricted decision-making about public health to a narrow elite. In Muslim societies, individuals have lacked the power to assert their own interests in the face of this institutional juggernaut of experimentation. In addition, the health care needs of women in many Muslim countries have been sidestepped to make room for men as the sole provider of the family.

In general, there is little debate on ethical issues in Muslim countries. The religious discourse on any new research is dominated by the language of licit and illicit action. There is scant interest in exploring the rightness or the wrongness of specific research. The paucity of such ethical sensibilities in the Muslim world has become so serious that when, on February 23, 1997, the news broke that Dolly the sheep was cloned, there was little public interest in or discussion of this technique and what might portend for human identity and genealogy. Cloning is actually just one technique in a class of techniques developed over the past four decades. More astonishing is the moral indifference to the techniques related to human genetic engineering that can be defined "as the intentional transformation of genes in the body (somatic engineering) or the descendants of a person (germline engineering) through chemical manipulation."[7] Numerous judicial decisions have appeared justifying or rejecting these techniques, but there is hardly any ethical debate based on the moral teachings of Islamic revealed texts. From the viewpoint of someone who has worked with many Muslim societies in the last four decades in several religious and non-religious capacities, it is not an overstatement to say that the Muslim world has in general neglected to pay close attention to the moral aspects of human cloning or genetic engineering with the purpose of careful examination of human life and welfare and the human future that lie behind the growing biomedical research enterprise. This deference to the authority of science and technology has its roots in three aspects of Muslim cultures: (1) authoritarian political institutions; (2) paternalistic, authoritarian medical practices; and (3) a tendency toward religious discourse that emphasizes legal rather than ethical issues. As we shall see in the following discussions, the emphasis hardly shifts from doing the correct in accordance with the ruling based on far-fetched reading of the scripture than rationally understanding the morally right from the incorrect and the wrong.

The Paradigm Case of Human Cloning

Since the cloning of Dolly the sheep in 1997, a number of Muslim scholars have deliberated on the legality of human cloning and on the relationship between religion and science and culture. Although human cloning is not yet possible, the urgency of the cloning debate among some Muslim scholars has led to an unprecedented interfaith cooperation in formulating a proper response to such a possibility and the adverse ways in which this scientific advancement will affect human relationships, both interpersonal and social. Most of the Muslim jurists' decisions studied for this chapter show that these concerns are, as we saw in in chapter 4's discussion of IVF, centered on the cloned person's hereditary relationship to the owner of the cell and the egg, and the relational ramifications of that person to other individuals in the child's immediate families. It is not difficult to see that religious-ethical questions are spurred by cultural sensitivities about an individual's identity within familial and extended social relationships. In addition, there are questions about the ways in which human cloning will affect the culture of intense concern with a person's religious and social distinctiveness. It is precisely at this juncture that cross-cultural communication between Muslim and Christian scholars becomes critical in highlighting variations among their communities. Whereas the individuality of a cloned human being is central to much discussion in Western-Christian cultures, it is the concern with a child's lineage, his familial and social relationships, that dominates Muslim cultural sensitivities.

One of the most important studies dealing with the subject in Arabic is *al-Istinsākh bayna al-islām wa al-masīḥīya* (Cloning in Islam and Christianity).[8] The study aims to demonstrate plurality as well as mutuality among the cultures of the peoples in the Middle East. Leading Christian, Sunni, and Shī'ite scholars, representing shared cultural concerns while holding different opinions, have contributed to the debate on the way in which human cloning will affect the future of marriage and parent-child relations. The interfaith discourse is based on a common concern in these communities: the potentially negative impact of human cloning (and related technologies such as nuclear transplants) on human interaction. Cloning is just one of the several methods of technically assisted reproduction. Nuclear transplant technology makes possible birth from one parent without conception, leaving the offspring genealogically in a precarious state, and socially unrelated to a family in the traditional sense.

The guiding principle of any scientific advancement in Islam is the precautionary note in the Sharī'a, the idea that there is seldom any benefit to humans that does not carry some inherent disadvantage in people's religion, life, lineage, reason, and property.[9] Islam's concern to combine noble ends with noble means rules out the idea of a good end justifying a corrupt means. In the case of human cloning, the most important rule is avoidance of anything that might adversely affect human nature and human relationships. Islam forbids any tampering with human nature in any way other than legitimate methods of correction. Anything that is done for prevention or treatment of medical condition is legitimate. Ethical judgments on medical procedures are made on the basis of the predominance of benefit (*istiṣlāḥ*) over probable harm (*daf' al-ḍarar al-muḥtamal*).

Scholarly Opinions in Their Cultural-Religious Context

The success in animal cloning in 1997 prompted a number of prominent Muslim scholars representing both Sunni and Shī'ite centers of religious learning in the Middle East—mainly Cairo, Beirut, and Qumm—to express their opinions on human cloning. A common feature of these opinions is the lack of even minimal moral analysis of the technique that has found acceptance in the context of IVF clinics by some Muslim jurists.[10] The Arabic term used for this process in the legal as well as journalistic literature is indicative of the widespread speculation and popular perception regarding the goal of this technology, namely, *istinsākh*, meaning "clone, copy of the original." This interpretive meaning is not very different from the fictional cloning portrayed in *In His Image: The Cloning of Man* by David Rorvik or the horrifying ramifications of cloning projected in *The People Shapers* by Vance Packard in the 1970s, when cloning by nuclear transplantation was the topic of the day in North America. It is also because of the popular misperception about human "copies that can be produced at will through cloning" that the leading Mufti of Egypt, Dr. Naṣr Farīd Wāṣil, declared human cloning as a satanic act of disbelief and corruption that would change the nature with which God created human beings, thereby impacting negatively upon social order and practice. Accordingly, his juridical decision was that the technology had to be regulated and controlled by the government to protect Muslim society from such an inevitable harm.[11]

However, a leading Egyptian scholar, Yūsuf al-Qarāḍāwī who, when asked if cloning was interference in the creation of God or an affront to God's will, asserted, "Oh no, no one can challenge or oppose God's will. Hence, if the matter is accomplished then it is certainly under the will of God. Nothing can be created without God's will facilitating its creation. As long as humans continue to do so, it is the will of God. Actually, we do not raise the question whether it is in accord with the will of God. Our question is whether the matter is licit or not."[12] Although in these early rulings on cellular nuclear transfer there was little discussion of cloning,[13] there has since been much concern with the possible biological and social effects of cloning, as discussed by al-Qarāḍāwī. In brief, al-Qarāḍāwī raises a fundamental question about the impact of this technology on human life: "Would such a process create disorder in human life when human beings with their subjective opinions and caprices interfere in God's created nature on which God has created people and has founded their life on it? It is only then that we can assess the gravity of the situation created by the possibility of cloning a human being, that is, to copy numerous faces of a person as if they were carbon copies of each other."[14] The fundamental question, based on the laws of nature, as al-Qarāḍāwī states, centers on the possibility that this procedure might interfere with the process of organic coming of age in a family that is founded upon fatherhood and motherhood. It is in a family that the child is nurtured toward fully developed personhood. In addition, al-Qarāḍāwī says, because God has placed in each man and woman an instinct to procreate, why would there be a need for marriage if an individual could be created by cloning? Such a procedure may pose the prospect of males not needing females for companionship but only for their capacity to carry the embryo to gestation. Such an imbalance in nature could fatally undermine the most fundamental ties of human society, "leading to the illicit relationship between man and man and woman and woman, as has happened in some Western countries." This reference to "Western" culture needs to be understood as the central issue in the traditional evaluation of Islamic values of family life that would be affected by an invasive biotechnology.

Most Muslim jurists in the seminaries have regarded Western culture as having a kind of cultural imperialism that is extending its grasp over the non-Western world. Traditional scholars have resisted this dominance in all areas of modern culture in Muslim societies. This view has been felt even in the area of international law, which is regarded by many as the product of Western cultural consensus without regard to the multicultural reality of the international community. Consequently, major moral problems confronting the world today are seen as the byproduct of a modern materialist reason that ignores revelation, the only reliable source for the spiritual and moral well-being of people.

Cultural dislocations have evidently gripped modern Muslim societies. As a consequence of imported modernization programs without local cultural legitimacy, Muslims have suffered "cultural homelessness" in their own societies since the early part of the twentieth century. The emerging oppositional discourse against Western encroachment on Muslim social values has led militant Muslims to look askance at anything emanating from the West, including scientific advancements like human cloning, genetic engineering, harvesting the organs of brain-dead patients, and so on, regarding them all as portents of a godless assault on all the spiritual values that Muslims hold dear. With the growing presence of Western armies and grim reminders of the colonial age, religious-minded Muslim sense a further deterioration of social and familial values that are already under siege by modern secular education and pervasive mass media. To be sure, science is not viewed amorally in the Muslim world. Any human action involves cognition and volition, the two processes that determine the moral course of an action. Hence, cloning of human beings was viewed with much suspicion by Muslim religious leaders in the beginning, and it was only gradually that more knowledgeable analyses took place among the jurists.

The other argument by al-Qarāḍāwī against cloning is based on the Qur'anic notion of variations and cultural diversity among peoples as a sign from God who created human beings in different forms and colors, just as God created them distinct from other animals. This plurality reflects the richness of life. However, cloning might erase this diversity. A semblance through "copying" might even undermine marital relationships, with spouses unable to recognize their true partners. From the point of health also, al-Qarāḍāwī argues, one could assume that cloned persons, sharing the same DNA, will be afflicted by the same virus. However, he maintains that it is permissible to use the technology to cure certain hereditary diseases, such as infertility, as long as it does not lead to aggression in other areas.[15] Among Muslim scholars there is almost no reference to eugenics in any of the opinions studied for this chapter. In contrast, drawing from modern European history, in which eugenics culminated in the genocidal policies of Nazi Germany, several Arab Christian scholars have opposed cloning technology, making reference to the danger of the abuse of the technology if used with the intention of exterminating "undesirable" peoples.[16]

Postscript on Responses to Inquiries about Cloning

In the last four years more meaningful discussions and legal rulings on the subject of cloning have emerged among Muslim jurists.[17] In fact, most of these rulings have introductions dealing with the scientific information needed by the religious scholars to understand the exact nature of the problem. For example, careful analysis of embryo splitting is part of the responsa literature. It is not uncommon to read the following introduction to human cloning:

> There are two ways of acquiring a human or animal embryo:
>
> **Natural**: This procedure enables the male sperm drop to reach the female ovum through sexual intercourse. In the uterus the drop encounters ova, and enables one of them to fertilize, thereby becomes coagulated drop and implants itself in the uterus. It then goes through the stages of leech-like clot and a lump of flesh, until it develops into a complete being.
> **Artificial**: this is a new method developed some years ago to cure infertility. The method takes the sperm and ovum and fertilizes it outside the womb in a test tube in a special type of cytoplasm. After it fertilizes the embryo is returned to the womb in order to complete the biological process of becoming a complete being.

Prefacing new rulings with relevant scientific information is certainly a fresh approach in dealing with biotechnical progression in culturally sensitive areas of human sexuality and reproduction. The sophistication with which

Muslim jurists are differentiating and collating information on biotechnology to formulate appropriate responses is unprecedented in the history of Islamic jurisprudence. Although the trend is to keep citations from the scriptural sources to a minimum, the relevant Qur'anic passages, interpreted in the light of evolutionary biology, occupy a central position as the main source of justification for fresh legal deductions. The following summary of scientific information serves as a detailed exposition of cloning technology appended to the fresh juridical decisions: "After much experimentation, scientists have now discovered a new technique to produce a living being. With the success of this technology in cloning animals and plants, Muslim scholars have declared that this technique can be regarded as a legitimate method for cloning humans. The technique is known as: embryo cloning (*al-istinsākh al-jinī*)." This is followed by a standard explanation of reproductive cloning used to generate an animal that has the same nuclear DNA as another currently or previously existing animal. Dolly was created by reproductive cloning technology. In a process called "somatic cell nuclear transfer" (SCNT), scientists transfer genetic material from the nucleus of an adult cell to an egg whose nucleus, and thus its genetic material, has been removed. The reconstructed egg containing the DNA from a cell is treated with chemicals or electric current in order to stimulate cell division. Once the cloned embryo reaches a suitable stage, it is transferred to the uterus of a female host, where it continues to develop until birth. The implications of this technology are taken up next:

> Among the features of this new being is its being completely a clone of the person to whom the nucleus belongs. Moreover, the reproduction has occurred without the natural procedure that requires a male and a female to engage in a sexual intercourse for the sperm and ovum to meet and fertilize. This new procedure, which has occurred through cellular nuclear transfer, needs the female only to carry it to its complete term. In fact, this creation of an individual in this manner takes place outside the framework of a family. This technique is known as cloning because it is not possible to distinguish the new creature from the original at all. It is said that this procedure will engender [a] lot of ethical problems, especially when the experiments will use condemned criminals. In these situations the two persons will look alike and it will be impossible to ascribe the crime to the right person.

The main objection to cloning, according to this citation, appears to be the noncoital creation of an embryo. In this light, the rulings that reject this technology have become decisive precedents in resolving the problems that arise out of a concern for the lineage and inheritance of the fetus. The concern for regulating social relations that are affected by births occurring outside the conventional marital relationship does not appear to be pivotal in these new rulings. Despite the fact that this technique does not now apply to human beings,

Muslims, anticipating this possibility, have turned to religious scholars to seek authoritative opinions about the religious and legal basis for technologically assisted reproduction in general. They are also concerned to understand how religious law views the relation of the child to the owner of the original nucleus used in cloning.

The Problems Raised in the Context of Islamic Values

In Muslim cultures reproductive cloning has given rise to a variety of questions concerning familial and social relationships. These questions reveal both communitarian and universal ethical/legal concerns about the status and social placement of the cloned human being. Moreover, they reflect specifically Muslim values that would be undermined if that biotechnology were to succeed. The concern with relationship and religious identity of the cloned individual are the major causes for fear of the technology in the following questions:

- It remains to be established whether there is permission to actually conduct such experiments [in the area of reproductive cloning] in the manner described above. If it is permissible, what are the conditions that must be met?
- Is the child legally an offspring in the conventional sense in the light of the fact that he/she was created through an extracted cell instead of a natural coital process?
- Is the child to be regarded illegitimate? How should he/she be related to the biological owner of the cell or to the DNA-carrying nucleus? In other words, how should he/she be related to the living person to whom he/she genetically resembles?
- How should the child be classified in terms of his/her religious affiliation? Is he/she to be regarded as Muslim or non-Muslim? Or should he/she be connected to the religion of the donor of the cell?
- What is his/her lineage?
- What is the ruling about his religious affiliation while still young: Is he to be considered a Muslim or a non-Muslim? Or, should his religious affiliation be the same as the donor of the cell? [Keep in mind that a Muslim child's religious identity is connected with the father.]
- What is the ruling about the responsibility of the blood relationship and full compensation that must be paid in case of homicide, and the responsibility for the crime? [This is related to the Islamic penal code, where an unintentional homicide has to be compensated by the blood relatives.]
- Are there any rights and responsibilities between the cloned offspring and the owner of the cell?

- What is the ruling about marriage with other naturally born children of the owner of the cell, if the cloned child is regarded as an outsider? Can he marry, for instance, the donor's daughter?
- There is a possibility of cloning human organs in the laboratory and preserving them for that person or for someone else for transplant? Is this permissible? Does this permission include cloning organs of reproduction, since these belong to a person whose privacy must be guarded, according to the rules of modesty in the Sharī'a? Also, does this permission include cloning of the brain?

The complexity of the issues related to the emerging relationship between the cloned child and the donor of the cell and the egg is self-evident in the foregoing questions. They also reveal the cultural sensitivities of Muslim societies. However, they also underscore universal legal problems that might arise across nations in settling disputes about ownership and assuming responsibilities for the child's welfare.

The following responses show the way in which some jurists understand the technology and its ramifications for society. It is important to keep in mind that there is no unanimity among these scholars. Moreover, I have not ascribed specific opinions to one or another jurist. The responses have been selected to provide rulings that would be commonly accepted as representing Islamic values:

- As for the permissibility of undertaking to create another being by means of reproductive cloning, there is permission to produce another living being by means of this technique or any other means, by discovering and applying the laws of nature that God has placed at human disposal. Hence, this procedure is not forbidden unless it involves morally objectionable acts. Moreover, a precautionary measure is necessary to avoid fertilization of the sperm of a stranger with the egg of anyone other than a legal spouse. This way the offspring can be legitimately ascribed to the two parents who are legally married. In principle, then, experimentation with cloning is not forbidden except when it leads to other forbidden acts that might adversely affect the man-woman relationship.

  However, there are some issues that require caution and may well lead to the prohibition of this mode of reproduction:

  The argument that cloning is reproduction of a child outside the framework of a family:

  There are no grounds for prohibiting cloning when there is no evidence in the Sharī'a to restrict human scientific activity and the human ability to create by following his potential to discover the laws of nature. Rather, this development is tied to the scientist's ability to break new paths and employ the laws of nature entrusted to humanity by God through investigation and intuitive reasoning, within the framework of a family.

- The argument that this technique will cause major ethical problems because of the possibility that criminals might abuse it:

  As mentioned in the context of an earlier response, such a possibility does not necessitate its prohibition. Just because a criminal might abuse an otherwise beneficial procedure, there is no need to ban the procedure. It is possible that cloning technology for cosmetic enhancement might provide great benefit to criminals. Yet, has anyone prohibited cosmetic use of technology because of this abuse?
- The success of this technique is preceded by a number of failed experiments in which embryos, before they can develop into a full pregnancy, have been destroyed:

  That which is prohibited in any such experiment is destroying a living being whose blood cannot be shed. Also, it is prohibited to kill a fertilized ovum that is on its way to life. This is similar to abortion. It is not forbidden to conduct an experiment on a person in which a living being might die before the conditions for life are completed, without his having intentionally desired so. Hence, it is permitted for a man to approach his wife for sex when she is ready for pregnancy, even though the pregnancy might risk miscarriage because of other factors, such as a weakness in the sperm or the lack of other necessary conditions for the embryo to develop and grow into a child. At any rate, we do not see any objection for the technique, as long as it does not lead to any other forbidden act, like looking at the private parts and touching them.
- The relationship of a cloned child to a man or a woman from whom the cell was extracted for nuclear transfer:

  If the child was created in the manner described above, then he/she does not have a father in the conventional sense. The reason is that ascription of fatherhood is connected with the fertilization of the sperm and the egg to create a living being, as pointed out by God in the Qur'an: "Then He fashioned his progeny of an extraction of mean water" (Q. 32:4). In this experiment there is no role for the sperm; rather it is the enucleated cell from the body. More particularly, when the cell is extracted from a woman it is inappropriate to attribute to her fatherhood for the cloned child. It has been narrated in several traditions that God created Eve from the rib of Adam. Regardless of the reliability of these traditions, do these parables tell us that we must regard Eve as Adam's daughter? This clearly reveals that the standard used to determine the child-father relationship does not include that the idea that offspring should be created from a part of his body; it simply states that he should be created from his sperm, as mentioned earlier. As for the child-mother relationship, this follows the creation of a new life from her egg. It is clear that not all of her eggs can be the source of creation. Rather, only some fertilize. It is only then that the ascription of relationship to her materializes.

- Nevertheless, it is difficult to rule out any relationship between the clone and the donors of cell and egg, just as it is not possible to rule out that the child is the cell or egg donor's brother, especially when it is the brother who shares with his brother one of the two parents. More importantly, the criterion for this ascription cannot be derived from the fact that the clone is the carrier of specific hereditary traits, because conventionally these factors are not critical for the ascription of relationship between the child and the parent:

  It is important to keep in mind that, in the final analysis, it is the custom and convention that determines the criterion for ascription of a relationship. The sacred lawgiver has depended on the custom to promulgate the ordinances related to social relationships. It cannot be assumed that the relationship between the clone and the donor is automatic, regardless of the normal, agreed-upon social conventions regarding such relationship.
- The ruling about the child's religious affiliation while still young:

  As long as the child remains unable to distinguish his own religious affiliation, the rule that applies to the child who is under the custody of another person applies to this child. Consider the case of a child prisoner in the care of his captor. When he attains maturity and hence the ability to distinguish the good from bad, then he is a member of the religion to which he converts. Assuming that he adopts a religion other than Islam, he cannot be regarded as an apostate, even if the cell donor happens to be a Muslim. The reason is that the cell donor is not his father in the conventional sense.
- The ruling regarding the child's lineage: (a) In terms of his responsibility to pay full compensation in case of a murder committed by his family member or his liability in the case of a crime:

  Because the family connection depends on relationship to the father, the clone lacks that connection to the donor of the cell; in terms of being a son and the donor's being his father, as discussed earlier, there is a requirement negating any relation to the family of the donor. Accordingly, he is not required to have his family pay his full compensation. In fact, his full compensation is restricted to the one who is liable for the crime.

  However, inasmuch as there is doubt in his relationship to the owner of the egg, there is also hesitation in connecting him to those related to the donor. In this situation his status appears to akin to that of a grandchild to his parents and his sisters are his aunts. In any case, there is no evidence to prove or disprove the relationship. Additionally, there is no proof to establish his vestiges or to deny them. Hence, the case requires caution in specifying definite legal rulings.

- As for the rights specified by the Sharī'a between the cloned individual and the donor of the cell, since the conventionally acknowledged norms to establish a relationship are absent, there are no rights.
- The rulings regarding permission for him to marry children related to the donor:

  Since the determinant of a close blood relationship between the donor and the clone does not exist, it is not possible to regard the donor's children as the clone's siblings. Nevertheless, some traditions suggest that in the beginning of the creation there was a proscription against marriage between Adam and Eve's children. This text, even when it cannot serve as an incontrovertible evidence to deduce a prohibition, confirms the legal precedent for prohibiting marriage between the clone and other children of the donors. Hence, it is necessary to apply a caution in permitting the marriage because it is possible to assert that motherhood to the donor of the egg. Actually, this caution extends between the clone and all those who are connected to him through the donor of the egg, such as her sister, her son, her daughter, and so on.
- Permissibility of using the cloned parts of the body in the laboratory and preserving them for the future use for that person or for others when needed:

  It is permissible to clone the body organs, including the sex organs. It is also permissible to look at them because of the lack of its attribution to a specific person, which is the criterion for prohibition. Because attribution with specificity is the criterion of the prohibition, it is forbidden to transplant a male organ to a woman and vice versa. As for separating them from the body, it is problematic to regard it as prohibited.

The conclusion that can be inferred from the above responses points to the need to be cautious in overly utilizing these advancements of modern biotechnology without putting in place proper restrictions to forestall harm and calamity to humanity. Indeed, as these scholars remind their followers, God created this universe to serve humanity and to advance it toward its own betterment, just as God says in the Qur'an: "It is God who has created everything on earth for you [human beings]" (Q. 2:29). In another place, God says, "Haven't you seen that God has made serviceable to you all that is in the heavens and the earth, and has showered on you his external as well as internal blessings" (Q. 22:63–65). Hence, one should not depart from God's purposes, otherwise human beings will deserve God's abandonment and punishment; as God reminds people time and again, "Haven't you seen those who exchanged God's bounty with ingratitude, and caused their people to dwell in the abode of ruin?" (Q. 14:28).

The contemporary rulings by Muslim scholars around the world confirm my findings in the legal-ethical sources of Islamic tradition. Following the cloning of Dolly the sheep, in my testimony to the National Bioethics Advisory Commisison (NBAC) I had pointed out the ethical issues associated with cloning: namely, that in providing religious guidance in matters connected with the future of humanity, it is advisable to take into account people's religious beliefs in the social and cultural contexts. Consensus has now emerged among prominent scholars of the Sunni and the Shīʿite juridical tradition that, although the Sharīʿa has no problem in justifying and legitimizing DNA cloning (the transfer of a DNA fragment of interest from one organism to a self-replicating genetic element such as a bacterial plasmid) or therapeutic cloning, reproductive cloning outside marriage and the idea of human cloning are regarded with suspicion or forbidden outright.

Research with Human Embryonic Stem Cells

On August 7, 2005, Christian groups in the United States announced the "Snow Flake Embryo" adoption program as part of their campaign to oppose stem-cell research that uses IVF clinics' surplus embryos to derive stem cells.[18] The groups believe that the only natural way to give moral weight to the lives of frozen embryos is to adopt and implant them, and carry the fetus through a full pregnancy. They are not opposed to assisted-reproduction technology, which uses these frozen embryos to help couples to have their first or second child. They have problems with modern science reducing potential human lives to "surplus" unwanted embryos that can be destroyed for research. From a strictly religious point of view, they contend, there cannot be anything like "surplus" or "unwanted" embryos, since such a description of an embryo is an affront to God's claim on life. In the context of religiously informed bioethics, as long as the embryo is defined ontologically as possessing the potential to become a human being, there will be moral qualms and religious opposition to embryonic cloning that expressly aims to retrieve stem cells for biomedical research. Further, ethical questions are bound to arise about the destruction of preimplantation frozen embryos for research purposes. The litmus test for according full moral status to the blastocyst centers on the presence or absence of a nervous system and differentiated organs at that very early stage (five to eight days after fertilization when it is totipotent with the potential to generate all the cells necessary for development *in utero*).

Embryonic stem cells are undifferentiated cells produced after a fertilized egg has divided several times and developed into a blastocyst. The blastocyst contains the inner cell mass consisting of fifteen to twenty embryonic stem cells. As development proceeds, embryonic stem cells differentiate and become specialized. They turn into adult stem cells that form tissues and organs such as the blood, brain, bone, and liver. Adult stem cells have been found in the bone marrow and the brain, but scientists believe that adult stem cells are associated with every organ. Before embryonic stem cells begin to differentiate, they can become any of the specialized cells. Hence, they are defined by their potential for differentiation as totipotent, pluripotent, and unipotent, and by their source as embryonic or adult. Although all types of embryonic stem cells are being studied for their potential to yield medical advances that will help treat diseases, improve the quality of life of patients, and save lives, most scientist agree that embryonic stem cells from the inner cell layer of the blastocyst offer the greatest prospect for the study and treatment of many chronic, debilitating, and life-threatening diseases. The recent report that appeared on November 22, 2007, in the *New York Times* about a new way to turn ordinary human skin cells into what appear to be embryonic stem cells without ever using a human embryo does not in any significant way diminish the importance of using embryonic stem cells for their potential therapeutic benefits. And, although this new source has certainly eased the ethical concerns over the destruction of human embryos, it has not totally eliminated the controversy between religion and technology over the use of human embryos in other fields of medical research. There is little controversy over the morality of using adult stem cells, because they can be derived from living donors of bone marrow and other tissues. However, according to the American Academy of Neurology, adult stem cells, which are undifferentiated and unipotent cells, have limited potential to reproduce themselves in a culture and differentiate into cell types besides those tissues and organs from which they were isolated.[19] Consequently, the scientific community has concentrated its research on embryonic stem cells.

Embryonic stem cells are usually harvested from donated frozen embryos that were produced for the purpose of assisted reproduction. The religious-legal acceptance of the IVF technology in the Muslim world is corroborated by the fact of mushrooming of fertilization clinics in all major Muslim cities. In spite of this endorsement of IVF technology, the problem is the total lack of ethical discussion in Muslim sources regarding the beginning of life and the morally questionable attitude toward clinical abortion. As discussed in chapters 4 and 5, the revelation-based principle of the sanctity of life would appear to rule out termination of fetal life through clinically induced abortions in the early stages. And yet, both in the liberal opinions on abortion and legal permission to use "surplus" frozen embryos there is total disregard for the embryo's inviolability. By concentrating on the legal implications of feticide and totally neglecting the moral philosophical dimensions of human embryology, Muslim jurists have limited the extension of the principle of the sanctity of life to the embryo that is in the womb. That sanctity principle is not extended to the embryos that are not implanted and that are frozen.[20]

One of the intriguing questions connected with embryonic sanctity in the Islamic revealed texts deals with the beginning of life. The Qur'an and the

Tradition, which provide textual evidence in support of gradual biological development and ensoulment of the fetus, are open to all sorts of symbolic and legal interpretations. Until now, as we saw in chapter 5 on early termination of life, the moral standing of embryonic and fetal life remains unresolved in Islamic jurisprudence because of the lack of precise definition of life and the beginning of life, which involves religious, ethical, legal and social considerations. Islamic jurisprudence does not provide an ontological interpretation of biological data that would yield certainty about when the embryo attains human status. In different versions of this tradition, it is possible to speak about the stage of recording human destiny by an angel who is sent by God to breathe the spirit as occurring either on the fortieth, forty-second, or forty-fifth night or after 120 days. The jurists have identified this stage as the moment of ensoulment when the fetus attains ontological unity and identity in human person.

Nevertheless, the differences of opinion about the exact time of ensoulment—the infusion of the spirit into the body of fetus, thus conferring moral status on the fetus—had to wait for the modern biomedical data on the embryonic journey, which at times contradicted the traditional description of the phenomenon of life. But, even then, the jurists remained oblivious of the moral and metaphysical dimensions of embryonic inviolability in their challenge to the assumptions of technological powers over human creation and the concomitant demotion of the human being from God's envoy on earth to a commodity that can be produced as desired by genetic manipulation.

The Problem of Endorsing Stem-Cell Research

Although some forms of assisted reproductive technology have been endorsed by the Muslim jurists, one of the controversial issues in this technology, as pointed out earlier, is the noncoital production of embryos through somatic cell nuclear transfer (SCNT)—that is, therapeutic or embryonic cloning. The nuclear-transplant procedure enucleates or denculeates an egg (one's own or another's); the original nucleus with its genetic code is removed and replaced with the nucleus of either a donated unfertilized egg or the nucleus from a body cell (either a man's or a woman's), which is then implanted and brought to term in one's own or a host's womb. It is the birth from only one parent, noncoitally.

The use of a donor egg or sperm is out of the question in the Islamic tradition, since the preservation of the child's lineage to its biological parents through his/her descent from a legally married couple is obligatory. The ethical issues in assisted reproduction are associated with the SCNT technique through which the embryo is created. While the moral status of the embryo remains at the center of the controversy connected with the permission to use the frozen embryos, the problem of producing embryos with the SCNT technique raises questions about the commodification of early forms of human life. Since the retrieval of stem cells necessitates the embryo's destruction, its production just for that reason gives rise to incompatible notions of embryonic sanctity and the respect and rights owed to preimplantation embryos at the blastocyst stage. SCNT-derived stem cells may lead to the acceleration of research in reproductive genetics with direct impact on interhuman relationships that occur from a naturally occurring pregnancy, uninterrupted by science, through its natural course of development within a marriage. As discussed earlier in the context of embryonic sanctity, there is enough evidence in the revealed texts of Islam to argue for the moral status and rights of the embryo at the zygotic stage. Hence, its destruction for the derivation of stem cell cannot be ethically justifiable. And, although there is an absolute and collective moral duty in Islam for the physicians and scientists to undertake biomedical research that may result in beneficial treatments for a number of incurable diseases that afflict humanity today, there is an equally valid concern about whether the potential benefits of the research involving embryos can translate into therapy. This requirement puts the burden of proof on public and private agencies in the Muslim world to provide evidence that the stem cell research adheres to the standards of religious-ethical and scientific oversight.

Accordingly, Muslim scholars and their governments need to assess the risks and the benefits of stem cell research in the light of Islamic values related to the dignity of embryonic beings. Thus far the ethical-religious assessment of research uses of pluripotent stem cells derived from human embryos in Islam has been inferentially deduced from the rulings that deal with fetal viability and embryo sanctity in the classical and modern juristic decisions. The jurists treat a second source of cells derived from fetal tissue following abortion analogically similar to cadaver donation for organ transplantation to save other lives, and hence, permissible. As discussed above, the moral consideration and concern in Islam have been connected with the fetus and its development to a particular point when it attains human personhood with full moral and legal status. Based on theological and ethical considerations derived from the Qur'anic passages that describe the embryonic journey to personhood developmentally, and the rulings that treat ensoulment and personhood almost synonymously, as occurring over time rather than at the time of conception, it is correct to suggest that majority of the Sunni and Shī'ite jurists will have little problem in endorsing regulated research on the embryonic stem cells that promises potential therapeutic value, provided therapeutic benefits are not simply speculative.

The inception of embryo life is an important moral and social question in the Muslim community. Anyone who has followed Muslim debates over this question notices that the answer to it has differed with different ages and in proportion to the scientific information available to the jurists. Accordingly, each period of Islamic jurisprudence has come up with its ruling consistent with the findings of science and technology available at that time. The search for a satisfactory answer as to when an embryo attains legal rights that must be protected has continued to this day.

Accordingly, the question of fetal rights assumes importance in relation to determining fetus's personhood. As detailed in chapter 5, the penal system imposes monetary fines progressively in relation to the age of the fetus on anyone involved in inducing an abortion with the intention of terminating the pregnancy, including the physician, father, or mother. However, if the wife decides to abort with the permission of her husband then, according to some Sunni jurists, mainly Ḥanafī, there is no need to pay the monetary compensation to anyone.[21] The fully formed fetus is treated like an independent human being with full rights of inheritance and compensation for any damage done to it. This is so even when, in another situation, the law regards the fetus as the integral part of the mother's body, identical to an organ. It is for this reason that it permits donating fetal tissue (treating it like other bodily organs pegged for medical research) including derived stem cells. However, in the context of IVF reproductive technology, the jurists seem to maintain a moral distinction between an embryo that is already implanted and developing in the uterus and "surplus" or "spare" embryos. Whereas the implanted embryo enjoys fetal rights, including the right to life, the surplus embryos are not treated as aborted since these existed outside the body of a woman and never reached the stage of ensoulment. Hence, there is no prescribed penalty for discarding these preimplanted embryos. In fact, most jurists allow their use to derive stem cells.

Such a devaluation of preimplanted human embryos in IVF clinics gives rise to their exploitation because of their potential therapeutic and hence commercial value. It might even lead to the commercialization of human embryos expressly fertilized to serve as the source of therapeutic products. Muslim jurists have not considered all the negative aspects of their ruling allowing both unregulated in vitro fertilization and the discarding of unused embryos, as if potential human life could be ethically treated like a commodity. The advancement of medical technology makes it imperative to reconsider the moral status of the fetus in the light of fresh interpretations of religious, cultural, and social beliefs.

It is not difficult to find revealed texts in the Tradition to deduce a judicial decision that a human embryo is a potential human life. It has moral-legal status and deserves respect from the time it is conceived. If that were not the case, why would the Islamic penal code impose fines for induced abortion from the early stage of progressive fetal development? It certainly cannot be simply used as a product or as a means to an end. Hence, any ruling that permits creation of human embryos for purely therapeutic purposes that ends up destroying them in the process, is an affront to the divine purposes of the Sharī'a. The Qur'anic description of the human embryonic journey toward human status underscores God's special purpose to endow humans with meaning in life. At no point does the Qur'an or the Tradition suggest that using human embryos to benefit human society is permissible. Those who support such permission base their opinion on the argument that regards destruction of pre-implanted, unensouled frozen embryos that existed outside the uterus for the greater good of the entire society.

As for experimentation on human embryos in the Muslim world, at this time there is very little hardcore evidence available even to regional government agencies. But with the growth of IVF reproductive technology and the so-called surplus embryos readily available for experimentation in the field of biomedical research and biotechnology, it is not farfetched to assert that in Muslim societies the moral aspects connected with the integrity and the life of early human embryos are not articulated for public education and, hence, only the licit or illictness of the experimentation on embryonic cells are filtered in the media and discussed in the scientific journals. The loosely applied principle of public good seems to have provided unproblematic justification for any procedure that actually requires more scrupulous ethical analysis because it is a potential life that is involved. A more relevant principle in this case states in no uncertain terms that "averting corruption has preponderance over advancing public good."

With all the social changes and scientific findings today, we find ourselves before an open window, with hands almost reaching in to tamper with the lives of fetuses. Permission and prohibition seem to be obscured by the interpretations of modern science concerning fetal growth, stages, and movement, as well as the inception of embryonic life. Modern methods of fetal diagnosis, such as fetoscopy, ultrasound, and other means of examining a fetus and monitoring its growth inside the uterus were not available to ancient scholars. These scientific methods allow us now to see the embryo inside the mother's womb from the earliest moments and to follow its growth hour after hour and day after day, until it fully grows into a human being.

On the basis of the textual evidence examined, it is possible to maintain the following conclusions about stem cell research in Muslim societies: (1) The silence of the Qur'an over a criterion for moral status of the fetus allows the jurists to make a distinction between a biological and moral person, placing the latter stage after, at least, the first trimester in pregnancy, and extrapolating a number of rulings that deny dignity to pre-implanted "surplus" embryos in IVF clinics and allow the use of cyropreserved embryos for stem-cell research. (2) Since the Tradition regards perceivable human life possible at the *later* stage in biological development of the embryo, and since there is hardly any discussion of the early stages of fetal development on the basis of which to assess moral culpability if the embryo were destroyed, Muslim jurists tend to ignore the ethical dilemmas concerning their use to derive stem cells. (3) All Sunni and some Shī'ite jurists maintain that embryonic inviolability extends only to the embryos that are implanted in the uterus. Hence, they do not see any moral problem in using frozen embryos for biomedical research.

Genetic Engineering and Genetic Screening

In Islamic bioethics, when framing questions regarding medical treatment, the language of obligations, duties, and interpersonal justice takes precedence over the language of private and autonomous individual rights. Unlike secular bioethics and its emphasis on the autonomy that empowers individuals to act in their own interest, sometimes at the expense of those related to them, the communitarian ethics of Islam requires that an individual's well-being must be weighed in the scale of general good of those who are related to the patient and society in general. Allocation of affordable biotechnological resources to sustain a patient's threatened life must be assessed in terms of collective obligations, which dictate that the benefits of medical intervention must be shared fairly among rightful recipients.

Principles of justice (one of the many interpretations of this principle is the goal of providing all legitimate claimants with a decent minimal level of health care) and utility ("usefulness" of an action, with a focus on consequences of actions, rather than upon some feature of the actions themselves) as expounded and applied in secular bioethics would be hard to implement in the case of the inclusiveness and community-oriented nature of the Islamic ethics of medical treatment. Ethical problems connected with the allocation of scarce resources in a majority of Muslim societies in the developing countries remain unaddressed because of political and economic corruption as well as the authoritarian and the paternalistic nature of health care in these countries. However, the principle of equal worth of all human lives suggests that no human life should be treated lightly when it comes to the distribution of limited medical resources.

Modern science and technology have uncovered a more flexible set of natural conditions that can be explored, explained, and even changed for the betterment of human life. Genetics has produced unparalleled technological innovations that challenge the way we understand what it means to be human. One of the outstanding accomplishments in medicine is the development of an understanding of the molecular structures and processes involved in genetic inheritance. At the same time, knowledge of genetic inheritance gives rise to moral and social issues connected with the problems its application generates for individuals, their families, and society at large. Healthcare providers today have access to a large body of information about the ways in which genetically inherited diseases are transmitted within families. In the last four decades the technology has advanced to such an extent that it can detect some genetic disorders before birth. A variety of new technological developments in prenatal genetic diagnosis (PGD) now make it possible to secure accurate information about the developing fetus while it is still *in utero*. Ultrasound, radiography, and fiber optics allow examination of soft tissue and skeletal development. Anatomical abnormalities can be detected early enough to provide medical interventions to correct them. Muslim jurists have discussed the issues related to hereditary diseases and have recommended prenatal genetic screening (PGS), providing a number of rules to guide the parents' decisions about their offspring. The clear object of the religious counseling is to see that the couple is educated in ways relevant to their religious and social life.[22] The jurists have also endorsed preimplantation genetic diagnosis (PGD) and have left open the option of abortion to the parents based on the genetic information if the fetus is under forty days of age and if the parents' consent is available.[23] PGD is encouraged in many Muslim countries and declared as "mandatory" (*ijbārī*) in religiously defined obligations so as to bring the spread of hereditary diseases under control and to educate the parents in adopting a right course of action in connection with the harm that an unborn child and the mother could suffer. Hence, one can surmise that, among both religious scholars and their governments, there is general support for the Genome Project initiative, which aims to make a detailed map of human DNA, the hereditary information in which one's genetic makeup is stored. With this knowledge will come major social benefits, for people will begin to understand the etiology and pathophysiology of several genetically transmitted diseases.

Yet, on a more basic level, attempts to change genetic makeup by using the therapeutic cloning technique have raised serious concern about genetic engineering research. The potential advantages of recombinant DNA technology, which can transfer hereditary material from almost any plant or animal cell to totally unrelated hosts, are several. Insulin, antibiotics, antiviral agents, and numerous other drugs, chemicals, and vaccines are synthesized in large quantities by the technology of genetic engineering. Patients suffering from genetic disorders as hemophilia, sickle-cell anemia, and the like can now be given a replacement gene. This technology has the capacity to rearrange the genetic heritage of many generations. On the other hand, some scientists have raised serious concerns about potential hazards of human genetics research if it is not regulated by government agencies. One such potential hazard is suggested by a much more ambitious plan of human genetics, namely, deliberate enhancement or improvement of the entire species. Although Muslim jurists do not rule out positive eugenics and do not consider it wrong to seek beauty in addition to good character and spirit, there is a justifiable concern among some that such enhancement may lead to discrimination and injustice in society.[24] In other words, through recombinant DNA techniques one can control human evolution by formulating practices designed to alter the genetic composition of the human population—a more efficient form of eugenics.

The other danger of this research lies in the possibility of an accidental or hostile release into the environment of organisms carrying the infections hazardous to plant or animal life. Moreover, cloning in humans raises horrifying potential scenarios and grim reminders of the eugenic abuse of these technologies. Since the technology of genetic engineering is so potent that even a slight deviation from the intended path may cause devastating consequences to society, its adoption without necessary legal and ethical restraints could prove disastrous.

The fear prompted by the clinical use of genetic interventions has led to a quest to set limits on research and testing that deal with human DNA. The technology, being in its experimental stages, has not been able to clearly foresee potential harm connected with highly risky procedures. The mere intervention into human DNA seems to tamper with what are regarded as basic building blocks of human life. Moreover, much of the proposed research on human molecular biology depends upon the uses of gametes or early embryonic tissue, and since such use involves questions of abortion and fetal sanctity, these areas of investigation potentially violate fundamental moral principles that require protection of early embryonic life.

But the enormous potential of such genetic intervention is a powerful incentive to pursue knowledge of the genetic etiology of many complex human disorders. As the practical technical skills of genetic scientists have improved, private corporations have continued to fund university researchers, and the work on the human genome and embryonic cellular manipulation has continued. In fact, the research in human embryonic stem cells and the possibility of successful germ-line intervention have proceeded swiftly, and recent breakthroughs in this technology have raised questions about the ethical implications of such interventions, especially in the IVF industry. Artificial insemination, as I have argued in chapter 4, if not conducted within a legitimated marital relationship, is considered by most Muslim jurists to be an abomination and strictly forbidden for a variety of reasons, including the possibility of incest, ambiguous genealogy, and the problem of inheritance.[25]

The Ethical Dimensions of Genetic Intervention (*al-faḥṣ al-ṭibbī*)

With a large number of human diseases being identified as involving genetic factors there is a growing concern over genetically transmitted diseases, especially in Arab countries, where first-cousin marriages are common. To bring this under some control, Muslim religious and governmental authorities have sanctioned premarital genetic screening, and in some countries like Iran, a marriage license cannot be issued without genetic screening.[26] Even prenatal and preimplantation genetic screening and diagnosis, as pointed out above, have been accepted and religiously endorsed as valid medical procedures to arrest the probable harm that might be suffered by the fetus and the parents. However, serious questions have been raised about research associated with life-threatening conditions arising from degenerative and acquired structural damage in neurological conditions such as Parkinson's disease, Huntington's disease, spinal-cord injury, and stroke; much of this research involves embryonic cloning, use of the blastocyst and its subsequent use for stem cell-techniques. The research into genetic components of diseases may lead to the acceleration of research into reproductive genetics, with adverse effects on the parent-child relationship within a marriage.

Since the first duplication of genetically defective human embryos by blastomere separation in 1993, Muslims have raised questions about the manipulation of human embryos beyond IVF implantation, especially as regards their impact on the fundamental relationship between men and women and the life-giving aspects of spousal relations that culminate in unconditional parental love and concern for their offspring. The Qur'an declares sex-pairing to be a universal law in all things (Q. 51:49). As debates rage about the ethics of genetic replication, some Muslims are concerned about the use of embryonic stem cells that have been derived from blastocysts and removed from their ordinary reproductive context. Whether for basic research, cell or tissue transplantation, pharmaceutical development, or some other as yet undefined purpose, the more intricate issues associated with embryo preservation and experimentation have received less attention in Islamic biomedical deliberations.

Besides the relationship issue, in the world dominated by multinational corporations, Muslims, like other peoples around the globe, do not treat technology as amoral. No human action is possible without intention and will. In light of the manipulation of genetic engineering for eugenics in the recent history, it is reasonable for Muslims, like Christians and Jews, to fear possible commodification of the products of stem-cell research.

9

Epilogue

Every scientific novelty in the area of medical treatments and cures has sparked global interest and, in some cases, has fueled unending controversy. Scientists everywhere are enthusiastic about research that might provide potential cures for a number of incurable and genetically transmitted diseases. But religious communities are not always convinced about the moral rightness of the proposed medical procedures that involve questionable use of, for example, human organs or embryonic stem cells. However, Muslim religious leadership has not always taken a critical stance on such issues, partly because the governments in the Muslim countries have not considered it necessary to consult the jurists except in some controversial issues like organ retrieval from brain-dead patients, and partly because the jurists have concentrated on formulating prescriptive rulings rather than providing moral guidance on problematic issues connected with biomedicine. The idea that pluripotency in stem cells could come from a five-day-old human embryo from in vitro fertilization went unnoticed in the Muslim world because the classical tradition had already assigned fetal inviolability after the infusion of the spirit in the fetus—the so-called state of ensoulment—at the end of first trimester. In general, morally and religiously questionable derivation of embryonic stem cells from a zygote or genetic engineering affecting future generations, to take only few examples, remains in the limited confines of the ad hoc licit-illicit pronouncements of the seminarian culture. In Muslim societies the intellectual exchange between religious communities and medical researchers has not been satisfactory for the development of biomedical ethics. The problem-solving method adopted by the prestigious *Majma' al-fiqhī al-islāmī* (the Islamic Juridical Council) of the World Muslim League in Mecca, Saudi Arabia, is founded upon searching for normative responsa based on revealed sources only. The Council, represented by Sunni and Shīʿite jurists, has deemphasized the human dimension of medical enterprise by ignoring an evaluation of human moral action and its ramifications for Islamic biomedical ethics. The Council has, more or less, functioned as a formal body that provides legal rulings justifying a number of modern advancements in biomedicine without fully investigating related ethical issues in the Islamic juridical methodology or Islamic ethical theories.

The classical juridical heritage, as I have demonstrated in this study, instead of functioning as a template for further moral reflection about critical human conditions and vulnerability in the context of modern healthcare institutions, has simply been retrieved to advance or obstruct legitimate advancements in biomedicine. Normative essentialism attached to evolving interhuman relationships has reduced Islamic jurisprudence to the search in the revealed texts rather than in theological ethics to estimate human nature and its ability to take the responsibility of actions performed cognitively and volitionally under variable circumstances. Religious and moral empowerment of the average human person appears to be out of question for the Islamic religious establishment across the Muslim world. It is this lack of empowerment of an individual capable of discerning right from wrong that makes Islamic juridical rulings in biomedicine inconsonant with international standards of human dignity and autonomous moral agency. In this connection, this study is a step in the direction of acknowledging and emphasizing the epistemic value of divinely endowed individual intuitive reasoning, capable of engaging in an internal moral dialogue with one's conscience to arrive at a reasonable decision about critical issues related to life and death.

The complexity of formulating ethical-legal response to the issues covered in this volume has required me to search for appropriate Islamic legal-ethical methodology and its application in deriving ethical resolutions to contemporary biomedical problems. The Islamic juridical corpus includes paradigm cases in many areas of interhuman relations that deal with conflicting claims, interests, and obligations. I concentrated my research on these paradigm cases so that I could inferentially detect generalizable moral principles like "No harm, no harassment," or "Necessity overrides prohibition" that I regard as critical to my emphasis on the moral underpinnings of the cases for bioethics. For every issue in biomedicine I examined juridical opinions of both the Sunni and Shīʿite jurists that I suspected would yield biomedical information on the human body, beginning of life, status of the fetus, definition of death, and so on. I investigated minutely modern *fatwā*-literature on biomedical issues, collating them with appropriate chapters in historical juridical literature where I could locate, for instance, the concepts like "stable" and "unstable life" to ascertain whether any further extrapolation was justifiable to relate that information to brain-death criteria in modern medicine. Meticulous deciphering of the ethical foundations of the judicial decisions was crucial for this book because published works on Islamic biomedical issues until now were devoid of any theological-ethical analysis. Issues like the end-of-life decisions, for example, which demanded a detailed treatment of the subject under the classical formulations which had not, even speculatively, anticipated the ability of medical sciences to prolong the life of a terminally ill patient, required going back to those chapters of the juridical tradition that potentially held some solutions to determine the moment of death. To be sure, the judicial rulings that were issued by leading Sunni and Shīʿite jurists did not take up the challenge of providing all the possibilities that existed in the normative sources for defining the moment of death and coming to terms with medical interventions in prolonging life. Hence, my approach was to search in the historical juridical tradition and identify authoritative precedents to determine whether it was appropriate for Muslim medical professionals to look for additional criteria in determining the final moment of what Muslims know as "the moment of the departure of the spirit."

The most critical part of this research is definitely the search for specifically Islamic principles and rules for biomedical ethical deliberations and resolutions. The most important work in the Western biomedical ethics that provided me with some leads into the parameters of formulating the Islamic inquiry into bioethical methodology was *Principles of Biomedical Ethics* by Tom L. Beauchamp and James F. Childress. *PBE* served as a paradigm and I began treating Islamic bioethics as a subfield of Islamic social ethics rather than Islamic jurisprudence. Consequently, my investigation of morally problematic areas in medical practice had to fully account for rationally and scripturally derived justifications in Islamic tradition. The two major principles of Islamic social ethics, namely, "Public Good" and "No harm, no harassment" and a number of subsidiary rules that were commonly cited as justification in the numerous rulings that had been published on various biomedical and biotechnological issues in the last two decades resonated with some of the principles that *PBE* had identified in secular bioethics. Despite its communitarian aspects, what prompted me to argue for specifically Islamic and yet cross-culturally applicable principles of bioethics was the common moral language that existed between secular and Islamic ethics. Chapter 2, consequently, forms the theoretical foundation for the Islamic bioethics that, on the one hand, can engage other religious or secular bioethics in a meaningful conversation, and, on the other, can provide healthcare providers ways of assessing moral dilemmas and determining rationally and religiously acceptable solutions. In addition, this theoretical articulation of Islamic ethics and its principles prepares Muslim healthcare professionals to adequately handle morally problematic clinical situations with necessary acumen without totally depending upon juridical decision for every new medical procedure and intervention.

I am fully aware that the major thesis of this book that the function of ethical inquiry is to recommend a course of action in congruence with universal moral values that have application across cultures will not be accepted in the seminarian culture of religious authoritarianism which reserves the right to make and unmake all the decisions pertaining to Muslim religious life. The proposal to shift the paradigm in Islamic juridical studies to take ethics seriously has as its major goal to think globally about issues that must aim at reducing the widening gap between the patient's welfare and government healthcare policies in the context of burgeoning and financially lucrative healthcare institutions in Muslim societies. Healthcare policies cannot be formulated without public debate or proper assessment of moral (and not simply legal) and cultural resources and without respect of human dignity and accruing human rights in furthering public and private health. The emphasis on discovering universal moral principles that undergird Islamic bioethics in this study also meant to prompt Muslim jurists working in the area of biomedical issues to actively develop totally neglected Islamic moral discourse and participate in international deliberations about public health. Islamic moral discourse can revive the tradition of compassion and care for others in a world torn by deadly conflict and destruction of human life and environment. In the final analysis, every chapter of the book invites further investigation in the religious and moral issues that confront major decisions about human welfare. Faced with ever expanding possibilities and opportunities for advancing human health through innovative medical therapies, we are also faced with philosophical and metaphysical questions about the quality of life and about a crucial moral question: "What life is worth living?" Recognizing the structure of DNA, or understanding the miracle of life is just the beginning. Intelligent participation in debates about medical research and the future direction of biomedicine and biotechnology requires Muslim jurists and ethicists to understand the underlying risks and benefits of new technologies and the way these impact upon human relationships and future developments. Without this epistemic shift in Islamic juridical inquiry, Muslim concerns based on their cultural and religious values will always remain marginal to international organizations like WHO or UNESCO.

Glossary

Abortion: in the context of Islamic legal tradition defined as an induced ejection of a fetus prematurely with or without a proper justification. The other common juristic terminology with similar signification include: *al-isqāṭ* (lit. "elimination"), *al-ṭarḥ* ("expulsion"), *al-ilqā'* ("caused to throw out"), and *al-imlāṣ* ("caused to slip"). They all suggest the intentional aspect of the miscarriage and not simply the fact of a discharged fetus with no signs of life. See also: *ijhāḍ*.

"Averting corruption has preponderance over advancing public good": one of the major ethical principles in Islamic jurisprudence that is operative in the case of donating human milk with social implications for the future conjugal relationship of the child. When promotion of good (donating of human milk for an infant's nourishment) is offset by the uncertainties of future corruption (the possibility of a mixed identity of the donor and resulting incestuous marriage), then the jurists prefer to suspend the donation of human milk in the absence of a certain identification of the donor.

ḍarūra: In medical practice among Muslims, "necessity" is an essential rule which renders a forbidden act permissible under certain critical conditions. For example, in the case of a female patient who must be treated by a female physician, in an emergency situation the practical demand is to override the prohibition because the rule of necessity (*ḍarūra*). The rule of necessity determines the teleological solution and provides the incontestable rationale for the permission granted to a Muslim female patient to refer to a male physician not related to her.

daf' al-ḍarar al-muḥtamal: A juridical-ethical principle of "rejection of probable harm," a subsidiary rule under the principle of public good.

diya kāmila: penalty of full blood money for feticide.

fatwā (plural *fatāwā*): legal, judicial decision deduced by a well-qualified jurist (*muftī*) after researching the sources of jurisprudence—the Qur'an and the Tradition.

fiṭra: A Qur'anic doctrine that signifies "innate nature" or "disposition" with which humans have been created. There is something "given," divinely endowed, about human nature that functions as a reservoir of potentialities that can spur an evolution toward the attainment of levels of perfection. These postulates are in a constant tension with the notions of determinism and freedom.

ghurra, al-: reduced penalty of monetary compensation.

ijhāḍ, al-: denotes a "miscarried fetus discharged from the womb before completing the nine-month period of gestation." The word *isqāṭ* denotes a fetus that is miscarried between the fourth and the seventh months. See also: Abortion.

'illa (pl. *'ilal*): In juridical sciences effective cause that underlies some judicial decisions that deal with primary and fundamental moral obligations. It is *ratio legis* or the attribute common to both the new and the original case.

istiḥsān: In jurisprudence the method of prioritization of two or more equally valid judgments through juristic practice; also known as "juristic preference." This juristic rule, within the context of recognized sources of Islamic law, is evoked to justify a legal-ethical solution whose actual rationale is considerations of common welfare that is unrestricted and that reaches the largest number.

istiṣlāḥ: One of the major principles in promoting and securing benefits and preventing and removing harms in the public sphere. *Maṣlaḥa* has been linked to the term *istiṣlāḥ*, that is, "to seek to promote and secure common good." *Istiṣlāḥ* is a kind of a guiding principle, formulated on the basis of sound opinion through which its public utility is inferred. It also conveys the meaning of "seeking to maximize benefit and minimize harm." In the context of this book it is the principle of "seeking the common good (*istiṣlāḥ*)," and it serves as an important source of legislation that requires a rational investigation of all aspects of benefit and harm that are included in the goals of the Sharī'a. See also: *maṣlaḥa*.

kaffāra: Expiation, in addition to other penalties, when the sin performed carries spiritual consequences requiring the aggressor to fast for two consecutive months.

lā ḍarar wa lā ḍirār fī al-islām: In the context of this study its various meanings are taken into consideration. Among these are: "In Islam there shall be no harm inflicted or reciprocated." "There shall be no harming, injuring or hurting, of one man by another, in the first instance, nor in return, or requital."

"There shall be no [ruling that will lead to] harming of one man to another." "There shall be no [adopting of a course of action that leads to] harming of one man to another." This is the principle of "No harm, no harassment." See also: "No harm, no harassment."

maḍarra: In the context of public good, an obligation to prevent and remove evil. It comes close to the principle of "non-maleficence" in secular bioethics. See also: *nafy al-ḍarar*.

manfa'a: In the context of public good, an obligation to seek and promote good. It comes close to the principle of "beneficence" in secular bioerthics.

maṣāliḥ al-mursala, al-: The phrase signifies public good that is established by reason. Technically, *al-mursala* means "extra-revelatory," that is, not requiring scriptural proof. When used with *maṣlaḥa*, the phrase signifies seeking the good of the people without any reference to a particular text in the revelation. *Al-maṣāliḥ al-mursala*, then is the public good attained by rules that arise on the basis of intuitive reason that interacts with guidelines inspired by a cultural matrix external to the Qur'an or the Tradition.

maṣlaḥa: General principle of "public good." This principle is evoked in providing solutions to majority of novel issues in biomedical ethics. It also means "considerations that promote benefit and prevent and remove harm." *Maṣlaḥa* can refer to actions that customarily agree with what reasonable people do. It is positive obligation that requires people to act beneficently whenever possible. It emphasizes "bringing about benefit (*manfa'a*) or forestalling harm (*maḍarra*)." Its admission as an independent source for legislation has been contested by some Sunni and Shī'ite legal scholars. See also: *istiṣlāh*.

mawḍū': It literally means "subject matter." In jurisprudence it signifies meticulous assessment of the situational context of each case. In the context of bioethics it is a clear examination of the harm and benefit—whether physical or emotional—that accrue to donor, recipient, and their families.

mulāzama: the rule or the principle about the "correlation" between rules derived by revelation and those derived from reason. The principle of correlation (*mulāzama*) intuitively discovers the congruity between the judgment of reason and revelation to determine the rightness or the wrongness of an act.

nafy al-ḍarar: An obligation not to inflict harm has been closely associated in Muslim ethics to an obligation to promote good (*istiṣlāḥ*). Obligations of nonmaleficence and beneficence in Islamic bioethics are treated under a single principle of promoting good.

Negative Eugenics: Aims at decreasing the number of undesirable or harmful genes in order to winnow out the genetically unworthy. See also: Positive Eugenics.

"No harm, no harassment": functions both as a principle and a source for the rule that states "hardship necessitates relief," it connotes that there can be no legislation, promulgation, or execution of any law that leads to harm of anyone in society. For that reason, in derivation of a legal-ethical judgment the rule is given priority over all primary obligations in the Sharī'a. In fact, it functions as a check on all other ordinances to make sure that their fulfillment does not lead to harm.

"Preventing harm has a priority over promoting good": As a subsidiary rule, provides the jurists with the principle of proportionality. This principle is the main source for careful analysis of harm and benefit when, for example, a medical procedure prolongs the life of a terminally ill patient without advancing long-term cure.

Positive Eugenics: Aims to increase the number of favorable genes in human society through biological improvement, as opposed to Negative Eugenics, which aims at decreasing the number of undesirable or harmful genes in order to winnow out the genetically unworthy.

qā'ida bāb al-tazāḥum: The juristic rule of arranging objectives in an ethical hierarchy, to provide the needed justification to make an incision in the corpse when such a procedure may help resolve any dispute about the cause of death or the settlement of a bequest or when it might help to save a life by providing a vital organ like heart, lung, or cornea for transplantation.

qawā'id fiqhī: Primary Rules in juridical methodology for deducing rulings. See also: *qawā'id uṣūl*.

qawā'id uṣūl: Primary Principles in Islamic juristic ethics that are stated as obligations and their derivatives are stated as *qawā'id fiqhī*.

qiyās, al-: In legal theory methodological stratagems based on analogical reasoning. The power of the conclusions in analogical deduction depended on the ethical considerations deduced from the rules that were operative in the original cases and the agreement of the scholars about analogical deduction that sought to relate the new case to the original rationale as well as rules.

ra'y, al-: "Sound opinion" formulated by a jurist in order to promote the good of the people. Accepted, mainly by Ḥanafī jurists.

"Relief from responsibility": *barā'a al-dhimma* is the rule that "relieves a person from further responsibility" under certain unavoidable circumstances.

sadd al-dharāyi': Legal method to remove obstruction to resolving a problem.

shūrā = Juristic rule of consultation, a feature of Islamic communitarian ethics, against the dominant principle of autonomy that is based on liberal individualism.

Sunna: "Tradition." The word *sunna* strictly meant a legal precedent from which Muslim jurist could derive further laws for the growing needs of the community. The term also conveys the "Tradition" (with capital "T") to indicate the information that was handed down to posterity—a *ḥadīth*-report, collected and compiled to form the basis for legal-ethical rulings.

ta'āruḍ al-ḍararayn: The rule that requires to consider the "contrariety between two harms" in order to reach a right solution.

takhyīr, al-: The rule that allows a person to choose between two courses of action in a moral situation, like the permission for a woman to prefer herself over her child in a dire situation like a pregnancy that threatens her well-being.

taslīṭ: The rule that recognizes the absolute "right of discretion" of an owner over all his possessions.

Theodicy: A theological doctrine that attempts to justify the omnipotence of God in the face of earthly evil and suffering. Theodicy in the Qur'an remains marginal. It is not a major concern of the Qur'an to show that a good God does not commit evil; rather, the concern is to generate faith in God's wisdom and power over all of his creation. Further, the Qur'an does not impute evil to God. Evil is clearly ascribed to human arrogance and disbelief.

'urf, al-: "ordinary language"; the conventional and customary sense of terms used in social transactions. It is regarded as one of the important sources in deriving judicial rulings based on conventions and customs of the region. Since the use of public good as an important source for change of rulings at times depends on local custom and convention, Muslim jurists have also discussed *al-'urf* in the context of legal methodology.

'usr wa al-ḥaraj, al-: Most commonly cited juridical principle of "Protection against distress and constriction," applies to social relations and transactions, which must be performed in good faith but are independent of religion.

Notes

CHAPTER 1

1. The full title used by Sunni Muslims to designate themselves as the bearer of the only true and real Islam is *ahl al-sunna wa al-jamā'a*, meaning the "people of tradition and community."

2. They use *shī'at 'alī* as their proper designation, meaning "supporters" or "partisans" of 'Alī. Hence their claim to validity is connected with the acknowledgement of a rightful Imam from among the descendants of the Prophet. The last in the line of these Imams is believed to be living an invisible existence since his disappearance in 940 CE.

3. Literally, the principle translates: "There shall be no harming, injuring, or hurting, [of one person by another] in the first instance, nor in return, or requital, in Islam." See Edward William Lane, *An Arabic-English Lexicon*, offprint ed. (Beirut: Librairie du Liban, 1968), 5:1775. In this work I will refer to this principle as the principle or the rule of "No harm, no harassment."

4. Wael B. Hallaq, *Authority, Continuity and Change in Islamic Law* (Cambridge: Cambridge University Press, 2001), 131–32 lists the manner in which preponderance was determined in terms of which rule or rationale had the force of settling the dispute about the probable outcome of the quandary.

5. George Hourani, *Islamic Rationalism: The Ethics of 'Abd al-Jabbār* (Oxford: Clarendon Press, 1971). For full discussion of this and Majid Fakhry's works see chapter 2.

6. See Abdulaziz Sachedina, *The Islamic Roots of Democratic Pluralism* (New York: Oxford University Press, 2001), where I discuss the universalism founded upon "equality in creation" in the revealed texts. I have further developed this moral discourse in my forthcoming study on *Reform through Human Rights: Islamic Political Theology* (New York: Oxford University Press, 2009).

7. Abdolkarim Soroush, *Reason, Freedom, and Democracy in Essential Writings of Abdolkarim Soroush*, trans. and ed. M. Sadri and A. Sadri (New York: Oxford University Press, 2000), in several places introduces the crisis of epistemology in juridical sciences caused by traditional moralism and dogmatism.

8. See, for instance, several books authored by Khaled Abou El Fadl on these themes more particularly his work on *Islam and the Challenge of Democracy: A Boston Review Book*, ed. Joshua Cohen and Deborah Chasman (Princeton, NJ: Princeton University Press, 2004).

9. See: David Heyd, ed., *Toleration: An Elusive Virtue* (Princeton, NJ: Princeton University Press, 1996).

10. George Hourani, *Reason and Tradition in Islamic Ethics* (New York: Cambridge University Press, 1985), 17 introduces the latter distinction in deontological norms.

11. Sayyid Murtaḍā Taqavī, "Tahavvul-i mavdū'āt dar fiqh," in *Majalla-i fiqh-i ahl-i bayt* 3 (1365/1987): 207–20.

CHAPTER 2

1. Edmund Pellegrino, Patricia Mazzarella, and Pietro Corsi, eds., *Transcultural Dimensions in Medical Ethics* (Frederick, MD: University Publishing Group, Inc., 1992), 13.

2. By "scriptural" I mean not only that which is regarded by Muslims to have been revealed to Muḥammad, the Prophet, by God; but also the pattern of conduct of Muḥammad himself, usually known as the *sunna*. In other words, "scriptural" also denotes the normative in Islam. Throughout this work I have rendered *sunna* with capitalized "T" in the translation of this technical term (Tradition), which refers to all that is reported having been said, done, and silently confirmed by the Prophet. The translation of *ḥadīth* (the vehicle of the *sunna*, through which it is reported) is rendered with lower case "t" (tradition) or simply *ḥadīth*-report. The Sunna (=the Tradition) in religious sciences is composed of major compilations of the *ḥadīth*-reports, which include the six officially recognized collections of the *ṣaḥīḥ* ('sound' traditions) among the Sunni Muslims, and the four *Kutub* ("books") among the Shī'ites.

3. In the recently published essays in the volume edited by Edwin R. DuBose, Ronald P. Hamel, and Laurence J. O'Connell, *A Matter of Principles? Ferment in U.S. Bioethics* (Valley Forge: Trinity Press International, 1994), various authors have critically assessed the relevance of principle-oriented bioethics in the context of growing consciousness about the need to meet the demands of ethical pluralism in the multicultural society of North America. There is no doubt that bioethicists need both principles and rules to determine why some moral judgments lead us to classify an action as prohibited, required, or permitted.

4. Besides G. I. Serour and K. Zaki Hasan's contributions in *Principles of Health Care Ethics*, ed. Raanan Gillon and Ann Lloyd (Chichester, UK and New York: John Wiley & Sons, 1994), Hassan Hathout has also attempted to delineate the legal theory in his article, "Islamic Concepts and Bioethics," 103–17. A word of caution is appropriate here about the way the term "Islam" appears in these articles by Muslim scholars. In all these articles "Islam" conveys a normative religious system with its timeless norms that all Muslims accept as revealed in the Qur'an, the Muslim scripture, and

as provided in the traditions of the Prophet Muhammad, the Sunna. There is little, if any, acknowledgement of Islam as a cultural system or as a civilization (the other two senses in which the term appears), with its secular, intellectual resources engaged in dialectical and dialogical relation with heterogeneous elements with which it came into contact through its phenomenal territorial expansion between North Africa and Indonesia. I believe that such an acknowledgement is necessary for understanding the dominant features of the Islamic worldview that determine its specific approach to the practical dilemmas that lead to reflection.

5. By moral-theological discourse I mean an organized group of humanly conditioned statements about the everyday experience of living as a member of an organized religious group. Ostensibly, these statements also reflect practice, because they are situated within a certain set of conditions that make them possible and put them in relation to other similar statements, past, present, and future. In this sense, moral-theological statements are not devoid of the reality of the practical world. Rather, as practical acts undertaken by the believers, they always refer and feed back to that world. Hence, theological and ethical discourse in Islam, which appears as a closed system of formalized discourse, is a temporally conditioned practical knowledge positioned in an ever-changing flux of possibilities and of other ways of understanding the moral dilemma of living as a conscientious believer. In order to present critical perspectives to principles and rules that lead to general action guides in Muslim bioethics, one cannot afford to neglect moral-theological discourse dealing with the theoretical framework that allows for specific practical religious-moral decisions.

6. G. I. Serour, "Islam and the Four Principles," in *Principles of Health Care Ethics*, ed. Raanan Gillon and Ann Lloyd (New York: John Wiley & Sons, 1994), 75–91; and K. Zaki Hasan, "Islam and the Four Principles: A Pakistani View" in ibid., 92–103.

7. In her recently published work entitled *Islamic Medical Ethics in the Twentieth Century* (Leiden: E. J. Brill, 1993), Vardit Rispler-Chaim seems to be suggesting that there is no tradition of medical jurisprudence in Islam under which issues pertaining to bioethics would have been naturally discussed, and hence she differentiates medieval ethics from contemporary medical ethics. Furthermore, she complains about the dearth of written materials on the latter subject. The underlying problem in such assertions is to regard Islamic legal and ethical discourse as separate domains. Quite to the contrary, the revealed law of Islam includes various issues that we specifically categorize as issues of bioethics today. These rulings are scattered all over the juridical corpus, and, in the recent decades, especially following certain Western medical education curricula, courses in medical ethics, including medical jurisprudence, have been introduced in many parts of the Islamic world. The prominent Iranian Bahā'i physician and ethicist at University of Mashhad, Dr. Eshraghi, compiled the earliest text in Persian dealing with bioethical issues in Islam for medical students. There are now published works in Iran, Iraq, and Egypt that systematically deal with these issues under their modern rubrics. See my general article on "Islam" and the one on "Iran" coauthored with Eshraghi in the *Encyclopedia of Bioethics* (New York: Macmillan, 1995), where I provide the list of published works dealing with biomedical ethics in Iran.

8. To speak about such a possibility in the highly politicized "theology" of international relations is not without problems. Like the development language for which modern Western society provides the model that all peoples in the world must follow,

any suggestion of creating a metacultural language of bioethics runs the risk of being suspected as another hegemonic ploy from Western nations. However, there is a fundamental difference in the way development language is employed to connote Western scientific, technological, and social advancement, and a biomedical vocabulary that essentially captures universal ends of medicine as they relate to human conditions and human happiness and fulfillment across nations. It is not difficult to legitimize bioethical language cross-culturally if we keep in mind the cultural presuppositions of a given region in assessing the generalizability of moral principles and rules.

9. The method of problem resolution offered by Muslim jurists actually leads to furthering such paternalistic policies. In most practical judgments, Muslim jurists make a reference to the "experts" in the medical profession, almost surrendering to a physician's expert opinion in each case of an ethical dilemma—for instance, a terminally ill or brain-dead patient. It certainly reflects their inability to equip themselves with minimum technical information and to search for appropriate principles and rules in the legal theory to formulate more just decisions.

10. Contemporary moral discourse has been aptly described as "a minefield of incommensurable disagreements." Such disagreements are believed to be the result of secularization marked by a retreat of religion from the public arena. Privatization of religion has been regarded as a necessary condition for ethical pluralism. The essentially liberal vision of community founded on radical autonomy of the individual moral agent runs contrary to other-regarding communitarian values of shared ideas of justice and of public good. There is a sense that modern, secular, individualistic society is no longer a community founded on commonly held beliefs of social good and its relation to responsibilities and freedoms in a pluralistic society. See Heyd, ed., *Toleration.*

11. Ann Elizabeth Mayer, *Islam & Human Rights: Tradition and Politics* (Boulder, CO: Westview Press, 1991), in chapter 1 on "Comparisons of Rights Across Countries," has endeavored to analyze charges of cultural relativism against the Universal Declaration of Human Rights made by Muslim governments guilty of violating human rights of their peoples. However, in the process of arguing for the universal application of the UDHR document, she has paradoxically led to the relativization of the same by ignoring the historical context that actually produced the UDHR in the first place. See my review of her book in the *Journal of Church and State* 34, no. 3 (summer 1992): 614–16.

12. Tom L. Beauchamp and James F. Childress, *Principles of Biomedical Ethics,* 5th ed. (New York: Oxford University Press, 2001).

13. The deontological ethical norms determine the rightness (or wrongness) of actions without regard to the consequences of such actions. By contrast, the teleological norms determine the rightness (or wrongness) of actions on the basis of their consequences of these actions.

14. See above note 3 for the reference to the article. Recent publications in Urdu on the subject of new rulings in Islamic jurisprudence indicate a growing interest in the deliberations of the *Majma' al-fiqhī al-islāmī* (Islamic Juridical Council) in Saudi Arabia, with chapters in India and Pakistan, and participation of ulema in these two countries in formulating fresh juridical decisions in bioethics. *Jadīd fiqhī mabāḥith,* ed. Mawlānā Mujāhid al-Islām Qāsimī (Karachi: Idārat al-Qur'ān wa al-'Ulūm al-Islāmīya,

1409/1989), vol. 1, deals with the proceedings of the seminar in which Indian and Pakistani *ulema* presented papers on various new issues, including organ transplant and birth control.

15. The usual practice among Muslim jurists is to end their judicial opinion (*fatwā*) with a statement *allāh 'ālim*, that is "God knows best," indicating that the opinion was given on the basis of what seemed most likely to be the case (*ẓann*), rather than claiming that this was an absolute and unrebuttable (*qaṭ'*) opinion, which could be derived only from the revelatory sources like the Qur'an and the Traditions.

16. Hourani, *Islamic Rationalism*, calls the Mu'tazilite theory of ethics "rationalist objectivism" because natural human reason is capable of knowing real characteristic of the acts, without the aid of revelation. Majid Fakhry, *Ethical Theories in Islam* (Leiden: E. J. Brill, 1991), 35–43, regards this as quasi-deontological theory of right and wrong in which the intrinsic goodness or badness of actions can be established on purely rational grounds. Hourani calls the Ash'arite theory of ethics "theistic subjectivism" rather than "ethical voluntarism" because the value of action is defined by God as the judge and observer. However, since it is the divine will that is the determinant of right and wrong, it would be more meaningful to retain voluntarism in this particular type of divine command ethical theory. See Majid Fakhry, "The Mu'tazilite View of Man," in *Philosophy, Dogma and the Impact of Greek Thought in Islam* (Brookfield, VT: Variorium, 1994), 107–21, and his *Ethical Theories*, 46–55. Further refinement in specifying the Ash'arite theory on the basis of Fakhry's discussions is provided by Richard M. Frank, "Moral Obligation in Classical Muslim Theology," *The Journal of Religious Ethics*, Vol. II (1983): 207, where he regards Ash'arite ethics "a very pure kind of voluntaristic occasionalism."

17. Madkūr, Muḥammad Sallām, *Mabāḥith al-ḥukm 'inda al-uṣūliyīn* (Cairo: Dār al-Nahḍa al-'Arabīya, 1960), 1:169.

18. Ibid., 162.

19. Ghazālī, Muḥammad b. Muḥammad al-, *Kitāb al-Mustaṣfā min 'ilm al-uṣūl* (Cairo: Būlāq, 1904–7), 1: 56–57; Madkūr, *Mabāḥith*, 1:168.

20. Hourani, *Islamic Rationalism*, 56. In chapters 3 and 4 Hourani outlines the definitions of the ethical categories and contrasts them with the Sharī'a categories. The distinction between the subjectivist and objectivist ethical theories is made clear by expounding divine commands and prohibitions as they relate to the two categories of ethical/legal acts: obligatory and evil, respectively. See, in particular, chapter 4 on "Evil."

21. Ṭūsī, Muḥammad b. al-Ḥasan al-, *Tamhīd al-uṣūl dar 'ilm-i kalām-i islāmī*, being a translation of the commentary on al-Sharīf al-Murtaḍā's section on theology in *Jumal al-'ilm wa al-'amal*, trans. 'Abd al-Muḥsin Mishkāt al-Dīnī (Tehran: Anjuman-i Islamī-yi Ḥikmat va Falsafe-yi Irān, Tihrān, 1358 Sh/1980), 208 equates the ethical category of *wājib* with the Sharī'a category of *farḍ* and *maktūb*. In both cases, according to Ṭūsī, who represents the rationalist objectivism followed by the Shī'ite theologian-jurists, the categorization of the generic terms of ethics and Sharī'a are defined by some relation of desert or blame. See also a good summary of the Sunni position on the ethical-legal classification of human acts in Madkūr, *Mabāḥith*, 1:168–73.

22. There is much disagreement among theologian-jurists in the matter of the definition of *wājib*. The difficulty stems from the way an act is attributed to the agent.

Those who regard human activity to be the result of human free will define *wājib* as an act whose omission deserves punishment. The term "deserves" imputes the responsibility of the omitted act entirely to the agent. On the other hand, those who regard human activity to be the result of the Divine will define the *wājib* act as decreed by God, for the omission of which the agent is legally (*shar'an*) censured. For these and other theological views and their analysis, see Juwaynī, al-Imām al-Ḥaramayn Abū al-Ma'ālī 'Abd al-Malik b. 'Abd Allāh al-, *al-Burhān fī uṣūl al-fiqh* (Cairo: Dār al-Anār, 1400 AH/1976), 1:308–10. For the Mu'tazilī and Shī'ī views and objections see Ṭūsī, *Tamhīd al-uṣūl*, 203–4.

23. Muslims in general believe that a true understanding of any matter related to the faith in the hereafter is impossible without divine revelation. If we are to understand anything related to God, God himself must tell us. God tells people who he is by speaking through the prophets. His words are recorded in the books of the prophets, that is, the scriptures. Hence, in understanding God and his plans for humanity we must rely on the Qur'an as God's revelation to humanity. As for the impending harm in the hereafter for those who disobey God, this is known through the Qur'an.

24. Fakhry, *Ethical Theories*, 33–34.

25. Madkūr, *Mabāḥith*, 1:168–69.

26. Muẓaffar, Muḥammad Riḍā, *Uṣūl al-fiqh* (Najaf: Dār al-Nu'mān, 1966), 2:24; Ṭūsī, *Tamhīd al-uṣūl*, 205; Ghazālī, *Mustaṣfā*, 1:61. Hourani, *Islamic Rationalism*, 44–45; Fakhry, *Ethical Theories*, 32–34.

27. Juwaynī, *Burhān*, 1:309–10; Hourani, *Islamic Rationalism*, 44–47.

28. Muẓaffar, *Uṣūl*, vol. 2 discusses the objectivist ethics in Shī'ite Islam and how it is related to the juridical definition of *wājib*. See also: Ṭūsī, *Tamhīd al-uṣūl*, 205–7.

29. Juwaynī, *Burhān*, 1:310; Ghazālī, *Mustaṣfā*, 1:61.

30. Madkūr, *Mabāḥith*, 1:169.

31. Ghazālī, *Mustaṣfā*, 1:56–58.

32. Hourani, *Islamic Rationalism*, 37; Juwaynī, *Burhān*, 1:309.

33. Juwaynī, *Burhān*, 1:310 gives the Sunni definition: "[*wājib*] is an act required by the Lawgiver, whose omitter is legally (*shar'an*) blamed. Indeed, as we have mentioned, the meaning of *wājib* is that "required by the Lawgiver"; whereas Ghazālī, *Mustaṣfā*, vol. 1, 39, captures the general Ash'arī definition: "*wājib* has no meaning but what God the exalted has made necessary and commanded, with threat of punishment for omission; so if there is no revelation what is the meaning of *wājib*?"

34. Frank, "Moral Obligation in Classical Muslim Theology," 206–7.

35. Ibid., 214–15. See also Madkūr, *Mabāḥith*, 1:170.

36. Ṭūsī, *Tamhīd al-uṣūl*, 207; Muẓaffar, *Uṣūl*, 2:24–25; Hourani, *Islamic Rationalism*, 103.

37. In *Iḥya 'ulūm al-dīn* (Cairo: 1334/1916), 1:100, Ghazālī argues that good and evil are relative to the end specified: "The evil (*qabiḥ*) is what is incompatible with objective, so that something may be evil in one individual's opinion, good in another's; for it conforms to the end of one, but not the other."

38. Juwaynī, *Burhān*, 1:87–88; 'Allāma al-Ḥillī, al-Ḥasan b. Yūsuf al-Muṭahhar al-, *Kashf al-murād fī sharḥ tajrīd al-i'tiqād* (Mashhad, Kitāb-furūshī Ja'farī, n.d.), 185, summarizes the Sunni-Ash'arite view: "As for the Ash'arites, they maintain that good and

evil are made known by the revelation (*shar'*): whatever the revelation commands is good and whatever it forbids is evil. Had it not been for the revelation, there would be no good and no evil. If God had commanded what He has forbidden, the evil would be turned into the good."

39. 'Allāma al-Ḥillī, *Kashf al-murād,* 186; Hourani, *Islamic Rationalism,* 103.

40. 'Abd al-Jabbār al-Asadābādī, *al-Mughnī fī abwāb al-tawḥīd wa al-'adl,* vol. 6, pt. 1 (Cairo: 1361/1942), 9, 31.

41. Ghazālī, *Mustasfā,* 1:56–57.

42. Hourani, *Reason and Tradition,* 143.

43. Ghazālī, *Mustasfā,* 1:61–62.

44. Ibid., 1:58.

45. Hourani, *Islamic Rationalism,* 32 compares W. D. Ross's "prima facie duty" with Qāḍī 'Abd al-Jabbār, the Mu'tazilite rationalist's view about the principle that lying is wrong, so long as it does not come into conflict with a more insistent ethical consideration. The Qāḍī maintains that certain things are sometimes good and sometimes evil, depending on the presence and strength in them of a few components pertinent to value. This is a way of saying that injury is *prima facie* wrong, therefore *prima facie* evil, and that an actual injury may be made right by the presence of compensating *prima facie* aspects.

46. Also known as "deductivism," it is used in Islamic law to justify a judicial decision when theoretical reasoning based on normative precepts and rules derived from a textual ruling, together with the relevant facts of a case, support an inference to the correct or justified judgment. For further details that equally apply to Islamic ethical deductivism see James F. Childress, *Practical Reasoning in Bioethics* (Bloomington: Indiana University Press, 1997), 17–21.

47. The other two terms commonly used by Muslim theologians as synonyms for *sam'* (literally, "heard") and constrasted with *'aql* are *naql* ("transmitted") and *shar'* (related to revealed law and its sources). Understood as revelation or "transmitted" revelatory sources, the terms indicate that the referential point in this kind of knowledge is sacred, whether God or the Prophet of God, and as such beyond rationalization. See Hourani, *Islamic Rationalism,* 17–36.

48. A. J. Arberry, *Avicenna on Theology* (London: J. Murray, 1951), 64–76 is the translation of Ibn Sīnā, *Kitāb al-najāt.*

49. Frank, "Moral Obligation in Classical Muslim Theology," 204–23.

50. Hourani, *Islamic Rationalism,* especially 29–33, 62–81.

51. Mohammad Hashim Kamali, *Principles of Islamic Jurisprudence* (Cambridge: Islamic Texts Society, 1991), chapt. 12.

52. Ibn Qudāma, 'Abd Allāh b. Aḥmad, *Rawḍat al-nāẓir wa jannat al-manāẓir* (Riyāḍ: Jāmi'at al-Imām, 1399/1979), 169; Ghazālī, *Mustasfā,* 174; Ibn Badrān al-Dimashqī, *al-Madkhal ilā madhhab imām Aḥmad ibn Ḥanbal* (Beirut: Mu'assasa al-Risāla, 1401/1981), 93.

53. Ghazālī, *Mustasfā,* 174. This is also the opinion ascribed to Khwārazmī with the difference that he says *maṣlaḥa* means to preserve the aims of the law in order to ward off corruption. See Shawkānī, Muḥammad b. 'Ali b. Muḥammad al-, *Irshād al-fuḥūl ilā taḥqīq al-ḥaqq min 'ilm al-uṣūl* (Beirut: Dār al-Fikr, 1412/1992), 403.

54. Rāzī, Muḥammad b. 'Umar b. al-Ḥusayn al-, *al-Maḥṣūl fī 'ilm al-uṣūl al-fiqh* (Riyadh: Jāmi'at al-Imām, 1400/1979), 5:218–19.

55. Ibn Amīr Ḥāj, Muḥammad b. Muḥammad, *al-Taqrīr wa al-taḥbīr* (Beirut: Dār al-Fikr, 1996), 3:201.

56. Shawkānī, Muḥammad b. 'Ali b. Muḥammad al-, *al-Darārī al-muḍi'a* (Beirut: Dār al-Jīl, 1407/1987), 1:344.

57. Ghazālī, *Mustasfā*, 174. Ghazālī' "Five Purposes" (*al-maqāṣid al-khams*) has become an accepted phrase in the Sunni works on legal theory and is often quoted in discussions about the principle of *maṣlaḥa*. See: Shawkānī, *Irshād al-fuḥūl*, 216.

58. Ghazālī, *Mustasfā*, 1:286–87.

59. Shāṭibī,Ibrahīm b. Mūsā b. Muḥammad al-, *al-Muwāfiqāt fī uṣūl al-sharī'a* (Beirut: Dār al-Ma'rifa, n.d.), 2:4–5, believes that legislating laws and promulgating religions should promote the welfare of humanity. Furthermore, he maintains that even when theologians have disputed this doctrine pointing out, as the Ash'arite theologian Rāzī has done, that God's actions are not informed by any purpose, the same scholars in their discussions on legal theory have conceded to the notion, however in different terms, that divine injunctions are informed by God's purpose for humanity. Shāṭibī clearly indicates that deduction of divine injunctions provides evidence about their being founded upon the doctrine of human welfare, to which Rāzī and other Ash'arites are not opposed.

60. Subkī, Taqī al-Dīn 'Alī b. 'Abd al-Kāfī al-, *al-Ibhāj fī sharḥ al-minhāj:'alā Minhāj al-wuṣūl ilā 'ilm al-uṣūl* (Beirut: Dār al-kutub al-'Ilmiya, 1404/1984), 3:62.

61. Ḥusayn Ṣābirī, "Istiṣlāḥ va pūyāyī-yi fiqh," in *Majalla-yi Dānishkada-yi Ilāhiyāt Mashhad* 49–50 (1379 Sh/2000): 235–86, gives an overview of the principle and its acceptance or rejection among the Sunni and Shī'ite jurists.

62. Shāṭibī, *Muwāfiqāt*, 2:6–7.

63. Subkī, *Ibhāj*, 3:178; Ibn Amīr Ḥājj, *al-Taqrīr wa al-taḥbīr*, 3:201, 281 attributes the rejection of *maṣlaḥa* to Ḥanafites, most of the Shāfi'ites, and later Ḥanbalites; Ibn Taymīya, Aḥmad b. 'Abd al-Ḥalīm, *Majmū'a al-rasā'il wa al-masā'il* (n.p., 1976), 5:22–23, defines the principle as one by means of which jurists must investigate whether a particular case will cause benefit and holds that there is nothing in the revelation that would negate it. He also mentions that some jurists have disputed its validity as a source of law; others have equated it with *al-ra'y*, that is, a sound opinion; still others have regarded it being close to *istiḥsān* (choosing the better of the two or more decisions). Some others have claimed quite the opposite, holding that all legal schools among Sunnites have admitted the principle as a valid source for the derivation of fresh rulings. See, for instance, Būṭī, Muḥammad Sa'īd Ramaḍān al-, *Ḍawābit al-maṣlaḥa fī al-sharī'a al-islāmīya* (Beirut: Mu'assasa al-Risāla, 1410/1990; 1386/1966), 278, 319–25.

64. Subkī, *Ibhāj*, 3:178; Ghazālī, *al-Mankhūl min ta'liqāt al-uṣūl* (n.p., 1970), 354; Ibn Amīr Ḥājj,*Taqrīr wa al-taḥbīr*, 3:371; Būṭī, *Ḍawābit al-maṣlaḥa*, 3:319 regards Mālik as the main propounder of the principle of public good.

65. Ibn Amīr Ḥājj, *Taqrīr wa al-taḥbīr*, 3:201; Ghazālī, *Mankhūl*, 354 attributes two views to Shāfi'ī: one in which he regards only that *maṣlaḥa* is admissible where the documentation is derived from one of the well-established principle source such as the Qur'an or the Tradition; second in which he says that once admitted it can be invoked in any relevant case.

66. Muḥammadī, Abū al-Ḥasan, *Mabānī-yi istinbāṭ-i ḥuqūq-i islāmī* (Tehran: Mu'assasa-i Intishārāt-i Dānishgāh-i Tihrān, 1373/1994), 227.

67. Madkūr, Muḥammad Sallām, al-, *al-Wajīz li al-madkhal li al-fiqh al-islāmī* (Cairo: Dār al-Nahḍa al-'Arabīya, 1978), 97–98; Zanjānī, Maḥmūd b. Aḥmad, *Takhrīj al-furū' 'alā al-uṣūl* (n.p. 1962), 39.

68. Ibn Taymīya, *Majmū'a al-rasā'il*, 5:22–23; also, Subkī, *Ibhāj*, 3:186–87.

69. Subkī, *Ibhāj*, 13:187.

70. Rāzī, *Maḥṣūl*, 6:224.

71. Madkūr, *Madkhal al-fiqh al-islāmī*, 102–3.

72. Haythamī, Nūr al-Dīn 'Alī b. Abī Bakr, al-, *Majma' al-baḥrayn fī zawā'id al-mujāma'ayn* (Al-Ṭā'if, Saudi Arabia: Maktabat al-Ṣiddīq, 1992), 4:329.

73. Ibn Qayyim al-Jawzīya, Muḥammad b. Abī Bakr, *A'lām al-muwaqqa'īn* (n.p., 1969), 3:10–11.

74. *Nahj al-balāgha*, ed. al-Shaykh Muḥammad 'Abduh (Beirut: Dār al-Ma'rifa li al-Ṭibā'a wa al-Nashr, n.d.), 4:5.

75. Būṭī, *Ḍawābit al-maṣlaḥa*, 3:288.

76. Ghazālī, *Mustaṣfā*, 174.

77. Ibid., 174ff., Shāṭibī, *Muwāfiqāt*, 2:8ff.; Ibn Badrān al-Dimashqī, *Madkhal*, 295; Ibn Qudāma, *Rawḍat al-nāẓir*, 3:170.

78. Ibn Amīr Ḥāj, *Taqrīr wa al-taḥbīr*, 3:213; Shāṭibī, *Muwāfiqāt*, 2:7–8, regards performance of all duties under the category of the God-human relationship as fulfilling the need to protect one's religion; eating and drinking as fulfilling the need to protect one's life; performance of all duties under the category of interhuman relationship, such as marriage, procreation, subsistence, and other similar matters, as fulfilling the need to protect future generations; and implementation of the penal code as fulfilling the need to maintain orderly life and protect property. For the protection of reason no general principles are articulated. It is assumed that reason will be protected by the right kind of legal-moral education that was prevalent in the Muslim cultures.

79. Shāṭibī, *Muwāfiqāt*, 2:9. Other jurists have mentioned these categories in different order, with different examples in each category. See, for instance: Ghazālī, *Mustaṣfā*, 175.

80. Rāzī, *Maḥsūl*, 6:220 quotes Ghazālī regarding the lack of authoritativeness of the principle of *maṣlaḥa* in the area of the necessities. In general, Ghazālī maintains that to derive a legal decision only on the basis of the public good, without any reference to another principle based on the revelation, is not appropriate. However, he adds, such a ruling is necessary in positive law, and it is for this reason that it is possible that a jurist's final judgment may end up citing this principle without any proof from the revelation itself (*Mustaṣfā*, 175). In other words, Ghazālī does admit the possibility of independent reasoning based on public good to derive a legal-ethical ruling.

81. Shāṭibī, *Muwāfiqāt*, 2:9.

82. Ghazālī, *Mustaṣfā*, 175.

83. Shāṭibī, *Muwāfiqāt*, 2:9–10; Buṭī, *Ḍawābiṭ al-maṣlaḥa*, 219.

84. Shāṭibī, *Muwāfiqāt*, 24.

85. For instance, Shāṭibī, after explaining the good of this and the next world, opens up a new section and states very clearly: As for the public good and corruption,

if they happen to be outside customary law, then it requires further investigation [before any ruling can be given]. He provides examples of eating a dead body or other contaminated foods under certain circumstances out of necessity, cutting a limb that has been affected by irremediable disease, and so on, on the basis of disagreement between the good the potential corruption that might occur while adopting one or the other course of action. See *Muwāfiqāt*, 2:23–25.

86. Madkūr, *Madkhal al-fiqh al-islāmī*, 102.

87. Since the establishment of the Shī'ite ideological state in Iran, the question of public good has become an important source of legal thinking and problem solving, similar to that which has prevailed in the Sunni states from premodern days to the present. Under the leadership of Ayatollah Khomeini, Shī'ite jurisprudence has once again become research oriented. A number of conferences have been held since the revolution in 1978–79 to discuss the role of time and place in shaping rulings through independent reasoning. The proceedings have been published in several volumes under the title: *Ijtihād va zamān va makān: Majmū'a maqālāt* (ed. and written by a number of scholars under the supervision of Committee for Investigation of the Juridical Foundations of Imām Khumaynī), 15 vols. (Qumm: Mu'assasa Chāp va Nashr-i 'Urūj, 1384/1995–96).

88. In all major works on legal theory there is a conspicuous absence of any discussion on the principle of *maṣlaḥa*. See, for instance, Sharīf al-Murtaḍā, 'Alī b. al-Ḥusayn al-Musawī, al-, *al-Dharī'a ilā al-uṣūl al-sharī'a* (Tehran: University of Tehran Publications, 1346/1967); Ṭūsī, Muḥammad b. al-Hasan, al-, *'Uddat al-uṣūl* (Tehran: Maṭba'a Āqa Mīrzā Ḥabīb Allāh, 1317/1900); Muḥaqqiq al-Ḥillī, Abū al-Qāsim Ja'far b. al-Ḥasan al-, *Ma'¯rij al-uṣūl* (Qumm: Mu'assassa Āl al-Bayt, 1403/1983); 'Allāma al-Ḥillī, *Mabādī al-wuṣūl ilā 'ilm al-uṣūl* (Najaf: Maṭba'at al-Ādāb, 1970); and 'Āmilī, *Ma'ālim al-uṣūl*. None of these sources take up *istiṣlāḥ* as a source for the derivation of rulings. Among the modern works of legal theory, it is only Mīrzā Qummī, Abū al-Qāsim b. al-Ḥasan al-Gilānī, *Qawānīn al-uṣūl* (Lithograph edition, n.p., 1303/1886) that discusses the subject of public good.

89. Ḥakīm, Muḥammad Taqī al-, *al-Uṣūl al-'āmma li al-fiqh al-muqāran* (Beirut: Dār al-Andalūs, 1983), 386, quoting Khafīf, *Muḥādirāt fī asbāb al-ikhtilāf*, 244.

90. Ḥakīm, *Uṣūl al-'āmma*, 403–4.

91. Jannātī, Muḥammad Ibrāhīm, *Manābi' ijtihād dar dīdgāh-i madhāhib-i islāmī* (Tehran: Intishārāt-i Kayhān, 1370/1991), 336 maintains that even when *al-maṣāliḥ al-mursala* can be admitted as a source for legislation, it cannot be regarded as an independent source like the Qur'an, the Tradition, or reason. Rather, its authority is relative and dependent upon other well-established principles.

92. Mīrzā Qummī, *Qawānin al-uṣūl* , 2:85.

93. Muḥaqqiq al-Ḥillī, *Ma'ārij al-uṣūl* 202.

94. See "urf" in *The Encyclopaedia of Islam*, 2nd ed. (Leiden: Brill, 1989), 10:887–88.

95. Shahīd al-Awwal, Muḥammad b. Makkī al-, *al-Qawā'id wa al-fawā'id* (Najaf: Jam'īya Muntadā al-Nashr, 1980), 1:151.

96. Suyuṭī, Jalāl al-Dīn, *al-Ashbāh wa al-naẓā'ir fī qawā'id wa furu' fiqh al-Shāfi'īya* (Mekkah: Maktabat Nizār Muṣṭafā al-Bāz, 1990), 7, 89; Mujaddidī Barakatī, Muḥammad 'Amīm al-Iḥsān, *Qawā'id al-fiqh* (Karachi: Dār al-Ṣadaf Publishers, 1407/1986), 80, 369; Juwaynī, *Burhān*, Vol. 1, 378; Dimashqī, *al-Madkhal*, 297.

97. Muḥaqqiq al-Ḥillī, Abū al-Qāsim Ja'far b. al-Ḥasan al-, *Sharā'i'al-islām fī masā'il al-ḥalāl wa al-ḥarām* (Najaf: Maṭba'at al-Ādāb, 1969), 275.

98. Ibid., 251.

99. Ṭūsī, Muḥammad b. al-Ḥasan al-, *al-Mabsūṭ fī fiqh al-imāmīya* (Tehran: al-Maktaba al-Murtaḍawīya, 1378/1958), 6:22.

100. Khumaynī, Rūh Allāh Mūsavī, *Saḥīfa-yi nūr: majmū'a rahnamūd-hāy-i imām khumaynī* (Tehran: Ministry of Islamic Guidance, 1361/1982), 21:98.

101. 'Abd al-Jabbār Ḥamd Sharāra, *Naẓarīya nafy al-ḍarar fī al-fiqh al-islāmī al-muqārin* (Tehran: Rābiṭa al-Thiqāfa wa al-'Alāqāt al-Islāmīya, 1418/1997), is among the few contemporary Sunni scholars who has studied the principle in comparative law among Muslim legal schools.

102. Ṭūfi, Sulaymān b. 'Abd al-Qawī al- , *Risāla fi ri'āya al-maṣlaḥa*, ed. Ahmad 'Abd al-Raḥīm al-Sāyiḥ (Cairo: Dār al-Miṣrīya al-Lubnānīya, 1413/1993), 23–24.

103. Suyūṭī, *Tanwīr al-Ḥawālik: is'āf al-mubatta' bi-rijāl al-Muwaṭṭa'* (Beirut: al-Maktaba al-Thiqāfīya, 1969), 2:122, 218.

104. Suyūṭī, *Ashbāh wa al-naẓā'ir*, 92.

105. Shahīd al-Awwal, *Qawā'id*, 1:27–28.

106. Lane, *An English-Arabic Lexicon*, bk. 1, pt. 5, p. 1775.

107. For details of the discussion on the language of the Prophet's statement see: Muṣṭafā Muḥaqqiq Dāmād, *Qavā'id-i fiqh* (Tehran: Nashr-i 'Ulum-I Islāmī, 1370 Sh/1992), 133–68.

108. There is a sustained discussion among jurists about the nature of harm that this tradition conveys. Undoubtedly, *ḍarar* refers to general forms of harm that include setbacks to reputation, property, privacy, and setbacks to physical and psychological needs. See Sīstānī, 'Alī al-Ḥusaynī al-, *Qā'ida lā ḍarār wa lā ḍirār* (Qumm: Lithographie Ḥamīd, 1414/1993), 134–41.

109. Shahīd al-Awwal, *Qawa'id*, 1:123.

110. Ibid.

111. Ḍiya al-Dīn al-'Iraqī, *Qā'ida lā ḍarar wa lā ḍirār*, ed. and comm. al-Sayyid Murtaḍā al-Mūsawī al-Khalkhālī (Qumm: Intishārāt-i Daftar-i Tablīghāt-i Islāmī, 1418/1997), 135.

112. Majlisī, Muḥammad Bāqir al-, *Biḥār al-anwār* (Tehran: Dār al-Kutub al-Islāmīya, 1983–84), 2:277.

113. Majlisī, *Mir'āt al-'uqūl fī sharḥ akhbār āl al-rasūl* (Tehran: Dār al-Kutub al-Islāmīya, 1981), 19:395.

114. Ḥakīm, Sayyid Mundhir al-, "Qā'idat nafy al-ḍarar: Ta'rīkh-ha—Taṭawwur-ha ḥatta 'aṣr al-Shaykh al-Anṣārī," *al-Fikr al-Islāmī* 7 (1415/1994): 264–90.

CHAPTER 3

1. The major compilations of Prophetic traditions consist of *ḥadīth*-reports that advise Muslims on dietary laws and permissible foods and drinks. Among these traditions are those that teach the followers of the Prophet to be moderate in eating. For instance, in Ibn Māja, Muḥammad b. 'Abd Allāh al-Qazwīnī *Sunan* (Beirut: al-Maktaba al-'Ilmīya, 1972.), 2:1111, in the section on foods, one reads the subtitle: *Bāb al-iqtiṣād fī al-'akl wa kirāhat al-shib'* [Section on moderation in eating and reprehensibility

of (eating)] to satiation]. This section has traditions in which the Prophet declares explicitly that those who eat to the point of full stomachs in the world shall suffer hunger for a longer period on the Day of Judgment.

2. The tradition is reported on the authority of 'Umar, the caliph, who said: "The Prophet instructed to teach the children swimming, archery and horse riding." See:'Alī b. 'Abd al-Malik Muttaqī, *Kanz al 'ummal fi sunan al-aqwāl wa al-af'āl* (n.p. 1945) Vol 16, *ḥadīth* 45343; Bayhaqī, Ahmad b. al-Ḥusayn, al-, *al-Sunan al-kubrā, Kitāb al-sabq wa al-ramīy* (Hydrabad, India: Maṭba'a Majlis Dā'irat al-Ma'ārif al-'Uthmānīya, 1355/ 1968), vol. 10:15, *ḥadīth* 20233.

3. Peter Antes, "Medicine and the Living Tradition of Islam," in *Healing and Restoring: Health and Medicine in the World's Religious Traditions,* ed. Lawrence E. Sullivan (New York: Macmillan, 1989), 173–208, discusses the problem of assessment and diagnosis of culturally diverse individuals in Germany and underscores the importance of understanding Muslim patients' religious and cultural backgrounds for a successful diagnosis and treatment.

4. A number of traditions to this effect have been cited in George F. Hourani, "Ibn Sina's 'Essay on the Secret of Destiny,'" *Bulletin of the School of Oriental and African Studies, University of London,* Vol. 29, No.1 (1966): 25–48.

5. In recent years I have reviewed several articles written by Saudi physician-cum-Islamicists in which these authors have demonstrated a tendency to show that there is only one valid and legitimate interpretation of Islam, which, understandably, is the Saudi-Wahhabi-Sunni version. It is worth keeping in mind that even among Sunni legal-religious scholars, plurality of opinions is a rule.

6. See Marshall Hodgson, *The Venture of Islam: Conscience and History in a World Civilization* (Chicago: University of Chicago Press, 1974), 1:217–23.

7. Abiodun Raufu, "Polio Cases Rise in Nigeria as Vaccine is Shunned for Fear of AIDS," *British Medical Journal* (2002): 324, quotes Dr. Masur Kabir, commissioner for health in Kano state, where the incidence of polio was believed to be the highest in Nigeria, who said: "I blame misguided elements who preoccupy themselves with misinforming the people into believing that the polio vaccine is a mischievous creation of western countries to pass on the deadly HIV virus to them." He assured the author that steps had been taken to inform people that the vaccine was safe and effective, and free of complications and side effects. When I visited Kano in the summer of 2004 the government was still engaged in immunization against polio and there were widespread reports that the imams of the mosques continued to misinform the public about the conspiracy.

8. In this and the following section I have depended upon classical commentaries of the Qur'an, both Sunni and Shī'ite, to derive various interpretations of the verses dealing with suffering.

9. For detailed discussion on evil in relation to God's justice see Sayyid Mujtaba Musavi Lari, *God and His Attributes: Lessons on Islamic Doctrine,* trans. Hamid Algar (Potomac, MD: Islamic Education Center, 1989), 139–49.

10. For a sample of Sunni creed on this subject and its theological discussion see A. J. Wensinck, *The Muslim Creed* (London: Frank Cass, 1965), 188–90.

11. Ibid., 190.

12. Bukhārī, Muḥammad b. Ismā'īl al-, *Ṣaḥīḥ, Kitāb al-marḍā* (Beirut: 'Ālam al-Kutub, 1986), 7:209, *ḥadīth* 5 reports on the authority of the Prophet, who said: "When God wishes good for someone, He afflicts him [with suffering].'" Similar traditions are found in various other compilations of Muslim traditions.

13. Bukhārī, *Ṣaḥīḥ, Kitāb al-marḍa* , 7:208, *ḥadīth* 2.

14. Eric L. Ormsby, *Theodicy in Islamic Thought: The Dispute over Al-Ghazali's 'Best of All Possible Worlds'* (Princeton. NJ: Princeton University Press, 1984), 241–48 discusses various views held by Muslim theologians, both Ash'arite and Mu'tazilite, regarding the suffering of children and animals in the context of God's "doing the best for His creatures."

15. Muslim b. al-Ḥajjāj al-Nisābūrī, *Ṣaḥīḥ* (Beirut: Dār Iḥyā' al-Turāth al-'Arabī, 1972), 4:1760–61, *ḥadīth* 2243 and 2244 specifically require the followers to treat animals with kindness and report a case of a woman who was punished by God for neglecting to provide food and other care for her cat.

16. Ormsby, *Theodicy in Islamic Thought,* 244–45 cites Ash'arite opinion on the fate of children and animals who suffer in this world.

17. Bukhārī, *Ṣaḥīḥ, Kitāb al-ṭibb,* 7:222, *ḥadīth* 1.

18. First International Conference on Islamic Medicine, *Islamic Code of Medical Ethics,* Kuwait Document, Kuwait Rabi I, 1401 (January 1981), 16–23.

19. Bukhārī, *Ṣaḥīḥ, Bāb 'iyād al-marīḍ,* 7:216, *ḥadīth* 23.

20. Muslim, *Ṣaḥīḥ, ḥadīth* 5432–38 reported various forms of the prayer for the sick.

21. Bukhārī, *Ṣaḥīḥ, Kitāb al-marḍa,* 7:209, *ḥadīth* 5.

22. 'Abbās Qummī, *Mafātīḥ al-jinān* (Tehran: Kitābfurūshī-yi Islāmī, 1381/1962), 405.

23. In theological texts both the traditionalists and the rationalists have treated the subject under their discussion of God's justice and whether suffering can be regarded as evil or good. Ṭūsi, Muḥammad b. al-Ḥasan al-, *al-Iqtiṣād al-hādī ilā ṭarīq al-rashād* (Tehran: Maktaba Jāmi' Chihilsitūn, 1400/1979) has a sub-section in his discussion on the doctrine of divine justice, entitled "Discourse on Suffering" (*al-kalām fi al-ālām*), 83–89.

24. Ormsby, *Theodicy in Islamic Thought* provides a detailed examination of theodicy and the problem of evil in Islamic theology in the context of the scholastic debates in the classical age.

25. Ronald M. Green,"Theodicy," in the *Encyclopedia of Religion,* ed. Mircea Eliade (New York: Macmillan, 1995), 14:430–41.

26. Wendy Doniger O'Flaherty, *The Origins of Evil in Hindu Mythology* (Berkeley: University of California Press, 1976), 2 cites Gananath Obeyesekere, "Theodicy, Sin, and Salvation in a Sociology of Buddhism," in *Dialectical in Practical Religion,* ed. E. R. Leach (Cambridge, 1968), 8. Clifford Geertz, *The Interpretation of Cultures: Selected Essays* (New York: Basic Books, 1973), 103 writes: "There are few if any religious traditions, great or little, in which the proposition that life hurts is not strenuously affirmed, and in some it is virtually glorified."

27. Kenneth Cragg, *The House of Islam* (Encino, CA: Dickenson Publishing Co., 1975), 16.

28. Mahmoud Ayoub, *Redemptive Suffering in Islam: A Study of the Devotional Aspects of 'Ashura' in Twelver Shī'ism* (The Hague: Mouton, 1978).

29. There are different versions of this tradition in Muslim sources. The shorter version in Bukhārī *Saḥīh, Kitāb al-marḍa*, 7:409, *ḥadīth* 608 simply states first part of the tradition in the section on leprosy. On the other hand, Tirmidhī, Muḥammad b. 'Īsā, *Jāmi' al-Ṣaḥih* (n.p., 1970), 3:306, *ḥadīth* 2230 mentions the detailed version which ends with the declaration by the Prophet: "There is neither contagion nor jaundice. God created every person and then decreed his term, his sustenance and his afflictions (*maṣā'ib*)."

30. See Q. 6:125, which reads: "Whomsoever God desires to guide, He expands his breast to Islam; whomsoever he desires to lead astray, He makes his breast narrow, tight. . . ." Or, Q. 61:5, "When they swerved, God caused their hearts to swerve; and God guides never the people of ungodly."

31. See the Q. 2:24, "He leads none astray save the ungodly . . ." Or, Q. 4:80, "Whatever good visits thee, it is of God; whatever evil visits thee is of thyself."

32. "Theodicy," in the *Encyclopedia of Religion*, 14:438.

33. Hodgson, *Venture of Islam*, 1:384–86.

34. Ibid., 412–15 and Hourani, *Reason and Tradition in Islamic Ethics*, Introduction, 1–5.

35. Hourani, *Islamic Rationalism*, 100–2.

36. Hodgson, *Venture of Islam*, 1:440–41.

37. *Fiqh akbar*, article 3, cited by A. J. Wensinck, *The Muslim Creed*, 103. See also the *ḥadīth* reported in Tirmidhī, *Ṣaḥīḥ*, 3: 306, *ḥadīth* 2231, which actually specifies that which unavoidably reaches human beings through the divine decree, namely, "affliction."

38. Ormsby, *Theodicy in Islamic Thought*, 253–58.

39. Annemarie Schimmel, *Mystical Dimensions of Islam* (Chapel Hill: University of North Carolina Press, 1975), 136–38.

40. As cited and trans. by William Chittick, *The Sufi Path of Knowledge* (Albany, NY: SUNY, 1989), 107.

41. Ibid., 107.

42. Bukhārī, *Ṣaḥīḥ, Kitāb al-ṭibb*, 7:222, *ḥadīth* 1, does not mention the exception. The exception is recorded in the version reported by Ibn Māja, *Sunan, Kitāb al-ṭibb*, 2:1137, *ḥadīth* 3426.

CHAPTER 4

1. The Qur'an speaks about the creation of a human being (*insān*) out of clay, without mentioning the creation of man or woman directly (Q. 32:7). However, verse 4:1 speaks about creation from "a single soul, and from it its mate, and from the pair of them scattered abroad many men and women." In other words, the biblical sequence of creation of man and then from his rib a woman is absent in the Qur'an.

2. Chapter 19 is entitled "Mary" and relates the virgin birth of Jesus.

3. In October, 1986, the Islamic Juridical Council met under the auspices of the Organization of Islamic Countries (OIC) in Amman, Jordan, to consider the new reproductive technologies and their impact upon Islamic family values. With the help of

Muslim physicians seven different procedures were identified in the context of in vitro fertilization and embryo transfer (IVF-ET) in infertility practice, of which five were declared forbidden for reasons of the ambiguity that these created in ascertaining the infant's genealogy and the forbidden procedures they involved. The two procedures that were approved by the council in the IVF context were gamete intra-fallopian transfer (GIFT) and zygote intra-fallopian transfer (ZIFT) as long as it was the husband's sperm that was fertilized with the wife's ovum in the Petri dish. For the details, see Bārr, Muḥammad 'Alī al-, *Akhlāqīyāt al-talqīḥ al-iṣṭināʿī* (Jedda: Dār al-Saʿūdiyya, 1987), chapter 8.

4. The Arabic *NSB* signifies relationship (*al-qarāba*) between two individuals through marriage or kinship. See Lane, *An Arabic-English Lexicon* 8:2787.

5. Najafī, Muḥammad Ḥasan al-, *Jawāhir al-kalām fī sharḥ sharāʾiʿ al-islām* (Tehran: Kitābfurūshī Islāmīya, 1392/1972), 31:222–23. Muḥammad Jaʿfar Jaʿfari Langarūdī, *Mabsūṭ dar terminologie-yi ḥuqūq* (Tehran: Kitābkhāne Ganj-i Dānish, 1378/1999), 5:3631–32. The author makes it clear that if assisted reproduction takes place outside marriage, lineage cannot be ascribed to the child because *nasab* is not materialized in a legitimately recognized method in the Sharīʿa.

6. 'Abbās Nāyibzade, *Bārvarī maṣnūʿī* (Tehran: Intishārāt-i Majd, 1380/2001), 263 cites Mahdī Shahīdī's article: "Waḍʿiyyat-i ḥuqūqī-yi kūdak-i azmāyishgāhī," in *Majmūʿ-i maqālāt-i ḥuqūqī* (Tehran: Nashr-i Ḥuqūqdānān, 1375/1996), 164–65, which deals with the legal status of the child born through assisted reproduction in the lab.

7. The Arabic uses a dual pronoun when referring to two persons. Consequently, the blame for disobedience to God's command in the Qur'anic narrative of genesis is put on both Adam and Eve.

8. All compilations of *ḥadīth* narrate traditions about the merits of marriage and the way marriage leads to peace and tranquility in spousal relationship. For instance, Bukhārī, *Ṣaḥīḥ, Kitāb al-nikāḥ*, 7:2–3, lists several traditions on the merits and purposes of marriage.

9. Among lexicographers the term *farj* (plural *furūj*) is commonly understood in the meaning of "the opening" signifying external portions of the organs of generation of a man (penis and surrounding area) and of a woman (vulva and surrounding area). The admonition in the verse is inclusive of men and women, who must protect their private parts from performing any illicit sexual act. See Ibn Manẓūr, Muḥammad b. Mukrim, *Lisān al-ʿarab* (Beirut: Dār Ṣādir, 1991), 2:342.

10. 'Āmilī, Muḥammad b. al-Ḥasan al-Ḥurr al-, *Wasāʾil al-shīʿa ilā taḥṣīl masāʾil al-sharīʿa*. (Beirut: Dār Iḥyāʾ al-Turāth al-ʿArabī, 1391/1971), *al-nikāḥ al-muḥarram*, 14:267, *ḥadīth* 4. 'Āmilī.

11. Ibid., *ḥadīth* 1.

12. See my article entitled: "Marriage Contract: Protection of Spousal Rights in Islam," in *Our Marriage Ways: Will They Survive the Next Millennium* (Birmingham: R & K Tyrell, 1998), 1–12.

13. Sayyid Muḥammad Ṣādiq al-Rūḥānī, *Masāʾil mustaḥdatha* (Qumm: Mu'assasa Maṭbūʿa Dār al-Fikr, 1964–65), section on *Talqīḥ al-ṣanāʿī*, 1:9 endorses technically assisted reproduction on the same grounds, as long as the gametes belong to a lawfully wedded husband and wife.

14. The response given by the Ayatollah Ṣāfī Golpaygānī to the question about artificial insemination with donor sperm (AID), published in the journal *Rāhnamūn* (1371/1992): 222. See also, for similar concerns, Muḥammad Taqī Ja'farī, *Rasā'il-i fiqhī* (Qumm: Mu'assasa-yi Nashr-i Karāmat, 1377/1998), 307–8.

15. See, for instance, a written responsum from the senior jurists like Muḥammad Riḍā Gulpaygānī, dated 4 Rabī' al-Thānī, 1388/1 July 1968; Khū'ī, Abū al-Qāsim b. 'Alī Akbar, al-, *al-Masā'il al-shar'īya:istiftā'āt* (Beirut: Dār al-Zahrā', 1996), 42–43, attaches several conditions for artificial insemination between a husband's sperm and his wife's egg. Among the upcoming younger jurists one can mention Ayatollah Muḥammad Mu'min, *Kalimāt sadīda fī masā'il jadīda* (Qumm: Mu'assasa-yi Nashr-i Islāmī, 1415/1994), 57–58; and Ayatollah Muḥsin Ḥaram Panāhī, "Al-talqīḥ al-ṣanā'ī," in *Fiqh ahl al-bayt: Majalla fiqhīya takhaṣṣūṣīya faṣlīya* 9, no. 10 (1419/1998): 68–92.

16. Rāzī, Muḥammad b. 'Umar Fakhr al-Dīn al-, *al-Tafsīr al-kabīr* (Cairo: al-Maṭ ba'a al Bahīya al-Miṣrīya, 1938), 23:205.

17. As far as Muslim jurists are concerned, the sanctity of life principle applies to the embryo that is in the womb. That sanctity is not extended to the embryos that are not implanted. See, for instance, *Masā'il fī al-talqīḥ al-ṣanā'ī*, in *Masā'il wa Rudūd*, comp. Muḥammad Jawād Raḍī al-Shihābī and ed. 'Abd al-Wāḥid Muḥammad al-Najjār (Qumm: Dār al-Hādī, 1412/1992), 1:99. The opinion is ascribed to Abū al-Qāsim al-Khū'ī.

18. See, for instance, Nāyibzade, *Bārvarī maṣnū'ī*, 42–45, who points out that the marriage contract is valid for another four months and ten days following the husband's death, when the widow is, according to the Sharī'a, required to observe the waiting period (*'idda*) before she can remarry. It is after this period that the marriage contract with the deceased husband becomes null and void. In other words, she has a legal right to choose to become pregnant with the frozen gamete of her husband until that time.

19. See Nāyibzade, *Bārvarī maṣnū'ī*, 60.

20. In his earlier ruling Aytollah Sayyid 'Alī Khamenei had endorsed artificial insemination using the donor sperm or egg, which he repudiated later by actually withdrawing the collection of opinions in the area of bioethics. See his *Pizishkī dar ā'ina-yi ijtihād: Istiftā'āt-i pizishkī* (Qumm: Intishārāt-i Anṣāriyān, 1375/1996), 111, where he sees no problem in artificial insemination of donor sperm and donor egg. However, the majority of the Sunni and Shī'ite jurists do not regard the procedure permissible. See Nāyibzade, *Bārvarī maṣnū'ī*, 45–57.

21. In a detailed study by Mīr Qāsim Ja'farzade, entitled "Dar āmadī bar masā'il-i fiqhī-ḥuqūqī ART," in *Bulletin-i tavlid-i mithl va nāza'ī'*, Biological and Biotechnological Research Center of Jihād-i Dānishgāhī 7 and 8 (1378/1999), it is conceded that there is no revealed text that could be used to infer a prohibition for a woman to donate an egg to another woman, whether the donor is legally married or unmarried to the latter's husband or not. However, the rule to proceed with necessary precaution (*iḥtiyāṭ*), requires that the purposes of the Sharī'a should not be overlooked in allowing such a donation.

22. Another technical term in Arabic is *ḥaḍānat al-mar'a* that is commonly used to express "the womb that acts as the fetus's incubator." In expressing "surrogacy"

the phrase used here is employed to convey "the act of hiring the womb" of another woman during the nine months of gestation. In other words, it conveys "gestational surrogacy."

23. The Qur'an uses plural form *arḥām* (singular *raḥim*) for wombs to indicate that all relationships through marriage must be traced back to a single womb to ascertain uterine kinship. See Ṭabāṭabā'ī, Muḥammad Ḥusayn al-, *al-Mīzān fī tafsīr al-qur'ān* (Beirut: Mu'assasa al-A'lamī, 1972), 16:277 and other places for similar usage.

24. Early sources mention the delegation of women coming to the Prophet and asking him to explain why women could not participate in *jihād* and die as martyrs like men to enter the Paradise without reckoning since all their sins were forgiven by God. In response the Prophet is reported to have mentioned the *jihād* women engaged in when giving birth to a child and the reward they earned as men did when they fought and died in the path of God.

25. Zaydān, 'Abd al-Karīm, *Al-Mufaṣṣal: Aḥkām al-mar'a wa al-bayt al-muslim* (Beirut: Mu'ssasa Risāla, 1417/1997), 390–91, has discussed all the possible procedures of artificial insemination from a Sunni point of view, citing different schools of legal rite, to conclude that the only permissible procedure is the one in which it is the husband's sperm and the wife's ovum that have been fertilized in Petri dish outside the womb and implanted in the wife's uterus, or through zygote intra-fallopian (ZIFT) or gamete intra-fallopian transfer (GIFT). Sayyid Shihāb al-Dīn al-Husaynī, "Al-talqīḥ al-sanā'ī bayn al-'ilm wa al-sharī'a," *Fiqh Ahl al-Bayt* 6, no. 23 (Qumm: Mu'assasa Dā'irat al-Ma'ārif al-Fiqh al-Islāmī, 1422/2001): 187–90, has discussed all the Shī'ite and Sunni views on the subject, citing the sources and the general agreement among the majority regarding the prohibition to procreate using donor's egg or donor's sperm.

26. See, for instance, Ayatollah Muntaẓarī, *Aḥkām-i pizishkī* (Tehran: Nashr-i Sāye, 1381 Sh/2002), 92, responsum no. 198, with a condition that first the egg should be inseminated in the wife's womb and then transferred to the "rental" womb. The assumption here is that the wife's womb is not able to carry the pregnancy to its full term. However, if the egg is artificially inseminated, then it can be implanted in the surrogate womb, as long as the procedure does not lead to any act that is forbidden in the law.

27. Literally the rule reads: "The child belongs to the bed [of the husband]."

28. *Masā'il fī al-talqīḥ al-ṣanā'ī*, 99 quotes Abū al-Qāsim al-Khu'ī's opinion on the child belonging to the mother whose womb gestated it until delivery.

29. Muḥammad Sind, *Fiqh al-ṭibb wa taḍakhkhum al-naqdī*, researched and critically annotated by Muḥammad Ḥasan al-Raḍawī (Beirut: Mu'assasa 'Umm al-Qura, 1423/2002), 85–87, mentions these opinions and then proceeds to critically evaluate their validity.

30. See Raḍawī's critical discussion of al-Khū'ī's ruling about the gestational surrogate's right to the child in Sind, *Fiqh al-ṭibb*.

31. Sind, *Fiqh al-ṭibb*, 83–84 mentions a number of things that are negated for an illegitimate child: inheritance in particular from the father, the qualifications to administer justice, to lead prayers, and other such religiously ordained tasks.

32. Falak 'Urayb al-Ja'farī, "Haḍānat al-mar'a li-bayḍa mulḥaqa li-'imrat ukhra," *Ḥaḍārat al-Islām* 19, no. 5–6 (2001): 42–43, where the author warns of the impending danger in abusing a woman's womb by turning it into a "rental" incubator. She cites

several verses of the Qur'an and the traditions to support her contention that such a procedure is against God's religion.

33. Rūyā Karīmī Majd, "Ijār-i raḥm: nuqṭa-yi pāyān-i bārvarī," in *Zanān* 13, no. 87 (2002): 40–49, takes up the issue of artificial insemination as a solution to infertility in the Shī'ite religious culture of Iran as it is practiced today. It is interesting to note that as a rule a surrogate mother must be a widow, and before the implantation of the gametes the husband is required to perform a temporary marriage with the candidate in accordance with the Shī'ite tradition, without seeing her. This allows the surrogate mother to be a "temporary" wife to the husband, resolving all the problems related to the lineage. However, in her field research she found that surrogacy was given to a beautiful widow in the belief that the child would turn out to be as beautiful. And, sometimes, as she relates a real incident, if the husband finds out that the woman he has temporarily contracted to be the rental womb for his child is beautiful, there is nothing to stop him from taking her as a second wife, and abandoning the first wife as "defective."

34. Ja'farī, *Haḍānat al-mar'a*; see also ibid.

35. Balādhūrī, Aḥmad b. Yaḥyā al-, *Ansāb al-ashrāf* (Cairo: Dār al-Ma'ārif, 1987; also, Sam'ānī, 'Abd al-Karīm b. Muḥammad, *al-Ansāb* (n.p., 1962). Pierre Bonte and others have studied the Arab tribal genealogies as part of historical anthropology in *Al-Ansab: la quête des origins: anthropologie historique de la société tribale arabe* (Paris: Editions de la Maison des sciences de l'homme, 1991).

36. Bukhārī, *Ṣaḥīḥ, Kitāb al-nikāḥ*, 7:36, *ḥadīth* 60.

37. 'Āmilī, *Wasā'il al-shī'a*, 7:29.

CHAPTER 5

1. In the section on "The Crime against the Fetus," Jazarī, 'Abd al-Raḥmān al-, *Kitāb al-fiqh 'alā al-madhāhib al-arba'a, Kitāb al-ḥudūd* (Beirut: Dār al-Kutub al-'Ilmīya, 1392 AH), 5:372–375 takes up detailed comparative rulings on the status of the fetus and culpable actions leading to its abortion among four Sunni schools.

2. *Lisān al-'arab*, and other lexicons: Zāwī, al-Ṭāhir Aḥmad al-, *Mukhtār al-qāmūs: murattab 'alā ṭarīqat Mukhtār al-ṣiḥāḥ wa al-Miṣbāḥ al-munīr* (Al-Riyāḍ, Saudi Arabia: Dār 'Ālam al-Kutub, 1998); and *al-Mu'jam al-wajīz Majma' al-lugha al-'arabīya* (Cairo: al-Majma', 1980).

3. This is the Ḥanafī definition of *janīn* as mentioned by Ibn 'Ābidīn, Muḥammad Amīn, *Ḥāshiya Radd al-mukhtār li khātimat al-muḥaqqiqīn Muḥammad Amīn al-shahīr bi Ibn 'Ābidīn alā al-Durr al-mukhtār fī sharḥ Tanwīr al-abṣār fī fiqh madhhab al-Imām Abī Ḥanīfa al-Nu'mān* (Cairo: Shirka Maktaba wa Maṭba'a Muṣṭafā al-Bābī al-Ḥalabī, 1386/1966), 6:587. See also: Ibn Nujaym, Zayn al-Dīn, *al-Baḥr al-rā'iq: Sharḥ kanz al-daqā'iq* (Cairo: al-Maṭba'a al-'Ilmīya, 1983), 8:389; Kāsānī, Abū Bakr b. Mas'ūd al-, *Badā'i' al-ṣanā'i' fī tartīb al-sharā'i'* (Beirut: Dār al-Kitāb al-'Arabī, 1982), 7:325.

4. Jazarī, *Fiqh 'alā al-madhāhib al-arba'a*, 5:372.

5. Ibn 'Ābidīn, *Ḥāshiya*, 5:517; Ibn Nujaym, *Baḥr al-Rā'iq*, 8:389; Kāsānī, *Badā'i' al-sanā'i'*, 7:325.

6. *Al-Mawsū'a al-fiqh al-islāmī* (Cairo: al-Majlis al-A'lā li Shu'ūn al-Islāmīya, 1472/1953) 3:158–179.

7. Ibid.

8. See the declarations made at the UN International Conference on Population and Development (ICPD), September 5–13, 1994, Cairo, Egypt.

9. In recent years a number of articles have appeared in Arabic and Persian that discuss abortion in the context of modern medicine. Unlike articles in Western languages on the subject of abortion in the Islamic tradition, these are written by Muslim scholars of Islamic law, whose thorough grounding in juridical sources and methodology make these studies important contributions to our understanding of the issue in jurisprudence. However, there is little attention paid to the ethical issues connected with the rightness or the wrongness of abortion with due analysis of personhood and rights that accrue to a fetus. See, for instance, a number of articles on the subject in *Majalla al-sharī'a wa dirāsāt al-islāmīya*, published by the Kuwait University in the last five years.

10. Maḥmūd Shaltūt, *al-Fatāwā: Dirāsa li-mushkilāt al-muslim al-mu'āṣir fī ḥayātihi al-yawmīya al-'āmma* (Beirut: Dār al-Shurūq, 1963), 289–97, in his discussion on family planning has claimed the consensus of all the scholars in the matter of birth control for the purpose of protection of the offspring, especially when the Sharī'a has laid down the rule that states: "Harm must be rejected as much as possible." Also, see an important study on the comprehensive sense of family planning, including population control, by Abdel Rahim Omran, *Family Planning in the Legacy of Islam* (London: Routledge, 1992). Also of significance are the proceedings of the first international Muslim conference on family planning held in Rabat, Morocco in December 1971. The Arabic version entitled *al-Islām wa tanẓīm al-'usra,* in two volumes was published by International Planned Parenthood Federation, Middle East and North African Region, Beirut in 1973. The English version *Islam and Family Planning* in two volumes appeared in 1974. In the second volume the consensus of the Sunni and Shī'ite scholars appears to endorse birth control through methods that may not affect permanently the couple's ability to bear children.

11. Ibn Nujaym, *Baḥr al-rā'iq*, 3:200.

12. Ḥaṭṭāb, Muḥammad b. Muḥammad b. 'Abd al-Raḥmān al-, *Mawāhib al-jalīl sharḥ mukhtaṣar khalīl* (Tripoli, Libya: Maktaba al-Najāḥ, 1969), 3:477.

13. Abū Isḥāq al-Shīrāzī, Ibrahīm b. 'Alī b. Yūsuf al-Fīrūzābādī, *al-Muhadhdhab fī fiqh al-imām al-shāfi'ī* (Beirut: Dār al-Shāmiya, 1992–96), 2:66.

14. Abū Ya'lā Muḥammad Ibn Mufliḥ al-Maqdisī, *al-Furū'* (n.p., 1962–67), 1:281.

15. Ibid., 1:281.

16. Mardāwī, 'Alī b. Sulaymān b. Muḥammad al-, *al-Inṣāf* (Cairo: Maṭba'a al-Sunna al-Muḥammadīya, 1955), 1:383.

17. *Qarārāt wa tawṣiyāt majma' al-fiqhī al-islāmī* (Beirut: Dār al-Qalam, 1998) 89, no. 34, (11–16 October 1986).

18. Ḥaṭṭāb, *Mawāhib al-jalīl*, 3:477.

19. Ibid., 3:477.

20. Ramlī, Muḥammad b. Aḥmad, *Nihāyat al-muḥtāj ilā sharḥ al-minhāj* (Beirut: Dār Iḥyā' al-Turāth al-'Arabī, 1939), 8:416.

21. Ibn Ḥajar al-Haythamī al-Makkī, Aḥmad b. Muḥammad b. ʿAlī, *Tuḥfat al-muḥtāj bi-sharḥ al-Minhāj* (Bombay: Muḥammad ʿAbd al-ʿAzīz al-Surtī, 1970–), 8:241. See also Mardāwī, *Inṣāf*, 1:383, citing a Ḥanbalī juridical work *al-Fāʾiq* by Aḥmad b. al-Ḥasan b. ʿAbd Allāh b. Abū ʿUmar al-Maqdisī.

22. Ghazālī, *Mustasfā*, 1, p. 286–87 mentions the five ends for the people as follows: (1) their religion, (2) their lives, (3) their reason, (4) their lineage, and, (5) their property.

23. See, for instance, Bukhārī, *Ṣaḥīḥ*, *Bāb al-nikāḥ*, 6:161.

24. See a number of resolutions passed by the Islamic Juridical Council in their meetings that took place in the years 1400/1978–79 and 1409/1987.

25. Zāwī, *Mukhtār al-qāmūs*, under *JHD*.

26. Ibn Kathir, ʿImād al-Dīn Ismāʿīl, *Tafsīr al-qurʾān al-ʿaẓīm* (Beirut: Dār al-Fikr, 1970), 3:70. He also cites other opinions in which "a lodging" is interpreted as this world and "a repository" as the next after death.

27. Saʿd al-Dīn Masʿad Hilālī, "Ijhāḍ janīn al-ightiṣāb fī ḍawʾ aḥkām al-sharīʿa al-islāmīya: dirāsa fiqhīya muqārana," in *Majalla al-sharīʿa wa dirāsāt al-islāmīya* 15, no. 41 (1421/2000): 282–315 deals with the new situation that arose when the Serbs in the Balkans used rape as a weapon against Muslim women.

28. Ibn Rushd, Muḥammad b. Aḥmad (al-Ḥafīd), *Bidāyat al-mujtahid wa nihāyat al-muqtaṣid* (Beirut: Dār al-Maʿrifa, 1986), 2:416; Ibn Qudāma, Muwaffaq al-Dīn ʿAbd Allāh b. Aḥmad, *Mughnī* (Cairo: Hajr, 1992), 9:539, 556–57; Ibn Ḥazm, ʿAlī b. Aḥmad, *al-Muḥallā bi al-āthār* (Beirut: Dār al-Kutub al-ʿIlmīya, 1988), 7:30.

29. The term appears in the juridical literature and seems to be used to indicate the zygotic stage before the embryo's cell totipotency goes through chimerical aggregation to end up receiving the spirit at the end of 40 or 120 days.

30. Qurṭubī, Muḥammad b. Aḥmad al-, *al-Jāmiʿ li-aḥkām al-qurʾān* (Cairo: Dār al-Kātib al-ʿArabī, 1387/1967), 12:6; Rāzī, *Tafsīr al-kabīr*, 23:85; Ṭabarsī, Abū al-Faḍl b. al-Ḥasan al-, *Majmaʿ al-bayān fī tafsīr al-qurʾān* (Qumm: Maktaba Āyat Allāh al-Marʿashī al-Najafī, 1403/1983), 7:101; Ṭabāṭabāʾī, *Mizān*, 15:20.

31. Bukhārī, *Ṣaḥīḥ*, *Kitāb al-qadar*, 1:211, *ḥadīth* 1 and 2. For variants see Muslim, *Ṣaḥīḥ*, *Kitāb al-qadar*, *ḥadīth* 2643 and 2645 (Nawawī's commentary on *Ṣaḥīḥ Muslim bi sharḥ al-Nawawī* (Beirut: Dār Iḥyaʾ al-Turāth al-ʿArabī, 1972), 16:191) For a Shīʿite version see ʿĀmilī, *Wasāʾil*, *Kitāb al-diyāt*, *ḥadīth* 35652.

32. Muslim, *Ṣaḥīḥ*, *Kitāb al-qadar*, 4:2036, *ḥadīth* 2643.

33. Ibid., 4:2038, *ḥadīth* 2644; also, Aḥmad b. Ḥanbal, *al-Musnad* (Cairo: Dār al-Maʿārif, 1377/1985), 4:7.

34. Ibn al-Qayyim al-Jawzīya, Muḥammad b. Abū Bakr, *al-Tibyān fī aqsām al-qurʾān* (Beirut: Muʾassasa al-Risāla, 1994), 337; also, Ibn Ḥajar al-ʿAsqalānī, *Fatḥ al-bārī bi-sharḥ Ṣaḥīḥ al-Bukhārī* (Cairo: Dār al-Kitāb al-Jadīd, 1970), 11:481.

35. Sharaf al-Quḍāt, *Matā tunfakh al-rūḥ fī al-janīn?* (Amman, Jordan: Dār al-Furqān, 1990), 45.

36. ʿĀmilī, *Wasāʾil al-shīʿa*, 19:15.

37. Kulaynī, Muḥammad b. Yaʿqūb al-, *Furuʿ al-kāfī* (Beirut: Dār al-Taʿāruf li al-Maṭbūʿāt, 1413/1993), 7:342; Ibn Bābawayh, Muḥammad b. ʿAlī, *Man lā yaḥḍur al-faqīh* (Najaf: Maṭbaʿa al-Ḥaydarīya, 1957), 4:54.

38. Kulaynī, *Furu' al-kāfī*, 7:347. The use of *diya* as a form of penalty prescribed in this case indicates that the crime is seen as homicide. This signification of *diya* is supported by the lexical sense of the word. See, for instance, major classical Arabic lexicons under WDY: Muḥammad Murtaḍā al-Zabīdī, *Sharḥ al-qāmūs al-musammā Tāj al-'arūs min jawāhir al-qāmūs* (Kuwait: Maṭba'a Ḥukūma al-Kuwayt, 1965–), 10:386; Ibn Athīr, al-Mubārak ibn Muḥammad al-Jazarī al-, *al-Nihāya fī gharīb al-ḥadīth wa-al-athar nihāya* (Qumm: Mu'assasa Ismā'īliyān, 1364/1985), 4:202; *Lisān al-'arab*, 15:383.

39. Qurṭubī *Jāmi' li-aḥkām*, 8:12. Nawawī in his commentary on *Ṣaḥīḥ muslim*, 16:191 and Ibn Ḥajar in his *Fatḥ al-bārī*, being a commentary on *Ṣaḥīḥ* of Bukhārī, 11:481, mention the consensus of the jurists in this regard.

40. Nawawī after commenting on the traditions in Muslim's compilation makes this observation: "The jurists are in agreement that the ensoulment takes place only after four months [of the pregnancy]" (Vol. 16:190–91).

41. Ibn 'Ābidīn, *Ḥāshiya*, 2:370; Ibn al-Humām, Muḥammad b. 'Abd al-Waḥīd, *Fatḥ al-qadīr*(n.p. 1974) 2:495; Qurṭubī, *Jāmi' li-aḥkām*, 12:8; Nawawī, *Sharḥ*, 16:191; Ibn Qayyim al-Jawzīya, *Tibyān*, 337–38; Ramlī, *Nihāyat al-muḥtāj*, 8:416; Mardāwī, *Inṣāf*, 7:386; Ibn Ḥajar, *Fatḥ al-bāri*, 11:481 and 484.

42. Ibn 'Ābidīn, *Ḥāshiya*, 3:176; Ramlī, *Nihāyat al-muḥtāj*, 8:416.

43. Some Ḥanafī jurists maintain that it is permissible to abort immediately after pregnancy when the embryo is in zygotic stage, when no observable evidence about its shape (*takhalluq*) is possible. By this they mean before the spirit enters the fetus. See Ibn 'Ābidīn, *Ḥāshiya*, 2:380; Ibn al-Humām, *Fatḥ al-qadīr*, 2:495; Kāsānī, *Badā'i' al-ṣanā'i'*, 7:325. Among Shāfi'ī jurists Abū Ishāq al-Marwazī and among the Ḥanbalī jurists Mardāwī allow pharmacological direct interruption of pregnancy in the first forty day zygotic stage. See Ramlī, *Nihāyat al-muḥtāj*, 8:416; Mardāwī, *Inṣāf*, 1:386; *Furū'*, 6:191.

44. Most of the Ḥanafī jurists permit abortion at this stage if there is a pressing reason for it. Among these reasons is the one oft-quoted that mentions that if after the pregnancy the nursing mother experiences reduction of her milk which is needed for the child already in existence, then aborting the fetus through pharmacological interruption is allowed (Ibn 'Ābidīn, *Ḥāshiya*, 2:380, 390). On the other hand, the Shāfi'ī and Ḥanbalī jurists allow the abortion without any pressing reason. According to Zarkashī, if a woman finds it necessary to interrupt her pregnancy by taking certain drugs then she is not liable to pay the compensation for abortion to her husband.

45. Generally speaking, this stage is recognized as the pre-ensoulment stage, and majority of the jurists allow abortion at this stage only when necessary. Up until this stage these jurists do not think that the fetus has acquired individuality and personhood which God has forbidden to destroy. The new justification added to the valid excuses to abort is the hereditary conditions. Abortion is permitted under this condition before the first trimester sets in (Ibn 'Ābidīn, *Ḥāshiya*, 2:390; Shirbīnī, *Iqnā'*, 4:129; Mardāwī, *Inṣāf*, 1:386). In the recent rulings if genetic testing reveals medical condition that is detrimental to the child and future generations with certainty then abortion is allowed. However, if the condition can be treated and the fetus can have a normal life with no adverse impact on its future offspring then abortion is ruled out. In other words, the permission is extended only in the area of genetically transmittable

conditions. Excluded in this permission are bodily defects, such as blindness or shortness of limbs, which do not affect the future generation.

46. Ibn 'Ābidīn, *Ḥāshiya,* 3:176.

47. Kulaynī, *Furū' al-kāfī*, 1:281.

48. For the traditions on this subject see: Ibn Ḥanbal, *Musnad,* 5:241; Ibn Māja,*Sunan, Kitab al-janā'iz,* , 1:513, in particular *ḥadīth* 1609.

49. Qurṭubī, *Jāmi' li-aḥkām al-qur'ān* , 12:6; Ibn Qudāma, *Mughnī,* 2:398; Ibn Qayyim al-Jawzīya, *Tibyān,* 351; Ṭūsī, Muḥammad b. al-Ḥasan al-, *al-Nihāya fī mujarrad al-fiqh wa al-fatāwā* (Beirut: Dār al-Kitāb al-'Arabī, 1970), 1:50.

50. Ibn 'Ābidīn, *Hāshiya,* 1:602, 6:591; Ghazālī, *Iḥyā',* 2:53; Ibn Rajab, Aḥmad b. Muḥammad, *Jāmi' al-'ulūm wa al-ḥikam fi sharḥ khamsīn ḥadīthan min jawāmi' al-kalim* (Riyad, Saudi Arabia: al-Mu'assasa al-Sa'īdīya, 1982), 46.

51. Ibn Rushd, *Bidāya,* 2:416; Ibn Qudāma, *Mughnī* 9:539, 556–57; Ibn Ḥazm, *Muḥallā,* 7:30; Ṭūsī, *Nihāya,* 2:803.

52. See detailed comparative rulings on the subject among four Sunni schools in Jazarī, *Fiqh 'alā al-madhāhib al-arba'a,* 5:372–375.

53. Ibn 'Ābidīn, *Ḥāshiya,* 1:602.

54. Ibid., 1:602; Ṣāliḥ 'Abd al-Samī, *Jawāhir al-iklīl* (n.p., 1976), 1:167; Dasūqī, Muḥammad b. Aḥmad al-, *Ḥāshiya al-dasūqi 'alā al-sharḥ al-kabīr* (Cairo: Dār Iḥyā' al-Kutub al-'Arabīya, 1980–), 1:429, Abū Isḥāq al-Shīrāzi,*Muhadhdhab,* 1:138; Ibn Qudāma, *Mughnī,* 2:551.

55. Ibn Nujaym, *Baḥr al-Rā'iq,* 8:389; Kāsānī, *Badā'i' al-ṣanā'i',* 7:325; Ibn 'Ābidīn, *Ḥāshiya,* 5:517.

56. Jazarī, *Fiqh 'alā al-madhāhib al-arba'a,* 5:372. For supporting tradition see: Bukhārī, *Ṣaḥīḥ,* 8:46; Muslim, *Ṣaḥīḥ,* 3:1309.

57. Kharāshī, Muḥammad b. 'Abd Allāh, al-, *al-Sharḥ al-ṣaghīr* (n.p., 1975), 7:33; Ibn Juzayy, Muḥammad b. Aḥmad, *al-Qawānīn al-fiqhīya* (Beirut: Dār al-Qalam, 1977), 227; Zurqānī, Muḥammad b. 'Abd al-Bāqī, *Sharh al-zurqānī 'alā Muwatta' al-imām mālik* (Beirut: Dār al-Kutub al-'Ilmīya, 1990), 8:33; Ḥūt, Muḥammad Darwīsh, *Asnā al-maṭālib fī aḥādīth mukhtalifāt al-marātib* (Beirut: Dār al-Kitāb al-'Arabī, 1983), 4:89; *Nihāyat al-muḥtāj,* 7:389; Abū Isḥāq al-Shīrāzi,*Muhadhdhab,* 2:197; Ibn Qudāma, *Mughnī,* 7:799.

58. Ibn 'Ābidīn, *Ḥāshiya,* 6:591.

CHAPTER 6

1. The Qur'an uses the term *nafs.*

2. Bārr, Muḥammad 'Alī al-, *Mawt al-qalb aw mawt al-dimāgh* (Jedda: al-Dār al-Sa'ūdiyya, 1406/1986), 65–68 correctly identifies the term in its essential signification of "personhood."

3. Imam Zayn al-'Ābidīn, *Supplication Makārim al-Akhlāq,* trans. William C. Chittick (London: The Muhammadi Trust, n.d.).

4. Bukhārī, *Ṣaḥīḥ, Bab al-du'ā' bi al-mawt wa al-ḥayāt, ḥadīṭḥ,* 360.

5. Ibid., *ḥadīth* 362.

6. Dawūd b. Muḥammad al-Qayṣarī, *Sharḥ qayṣarī 'alā fuṣūṣ al-ḥikam* (Tehran: Anwār al-Hudā, 1416/1995), 1:113 writes: "Know that from the point of its substance, its

disengagement from substratum, and its existence the spirit (*al-rūḥ*) belongs to the world of the spirits, disengaged changing in the forms of corporeal body, linked to it, a linkage connected with governing and exercising free disposal, self-subsistent, not in need of it for its survival and for its support."

7. Abū Ḥāmid Muḥammad al-Ghazālī, *The Remembrance of Death and the Afterlife*, trans., intro., notes T. J. Winter (Cambridge: The Islamic Text Society, 1989), 122–23; see also the different views of the Sunni scholars in al-Barr, *Mawt al-qalb aw mawt al-dimāgh*, 37–45.

8. Muḥammad b. al-Ḥusayn al-Ṣaffār, *Baṣā'ir al-darajāt* (Qumm: Kitābfurūshī Islāmīya, 1967), 463.

9. Rāzī, *Tafsīr kabīr*, 21:45.

10. Ghazālī, *Remembrance of Death*, 123.

11. The tradition is related on the authority of the seventh Imam Mūsā al-Kāẓim who describes the embryonic development in the womb as follows: "When God desires to create a sperm drop He inspires the womb to open its entrance to let in the sperm drop . . . Then God sends two maker angels to shape what God wishes to be in the womb. Hence, they intrude in the interior through the vagina until they reach the womb, where there is already in place the ancient spirit (*al-rūḥ al-qadīma*) that has come down through the loins of men (*aṣlāb al-rijāl*) and the wombs of the women (*arḥām al-nisā'*), and blow in the spirit of life (*rūḥ al-ḥayāt*) and survival (*al-baqā'*) endowing the fetus with hearing, seeing, and all other parts of the body and all that it needs from the womb, as God permits it." (Kulaynī, *Kāfī*, 6:13–14, 7:347). It is not far fetched to suggest that the ancient spirit seems to be the DNA that is inherited as part of the biological parent's contribution to the child's characteristics; whereas the second spirit appears to be the innate capacity to perfect oneself by means of the abilities connected with survival.

12. Ibn Bābawayh, *'Ilal al-sharā'i'* (Najaf: Maktaba al-Ḥaydarīya, 1965), 1:107–8, relates a tradition on the authority of the sixth Imam al-Ṣādiq which reads: ". . . Such is the creation of a human being. He is created for this world and the next. Hence, when God combines for him the two it becomes his life on earth because he has forgone the heaven for the sake of the world. Thus when God puts separation between the two, that separation becomes death. The matter reverts to the heaven, and in this way life on earth and death is due to the separation between the spirit and the body."

13. Mullā Ṣadra in his explanation of natural death says: "The basis for this is the freedom of the spirit from its inherent life and abandonment of using the bodily tools gradually until it becomes isolated by itself and frees itself totally from the body so that it can develop into the one commanding an act." Ṣadr al-Dīn al-Shirāzī, *Al-shawāhid al-rubūbīya fī manāhij al-sulūkīya* (Mashhad: Mashhad University Press, 1985), 89.

14. Hishām b. al-Ḥakam asked the Imam al-Ṣādiq if the spirit is other than the blood. The Imam replied: "Yes, the spirit, as I have explained to you, is the substance (*mādda*) from the blood. When the blood becomes cold [upon death] the spirit leaves the body." See: Ṭabarsī, al-Faḍl b. al-Ḥasan al-, *al-Iḥtijāj 'alā ahl al-lijāj* (n.p. 1966), 2:97.

15. See above, Chapter 5, 10–13 for the references in the Sunni and Shī'ite sources. Shī'ite jurists have discussed these criteria in their sections on blood money (*diyāt*), due for destruction of a fetus, inheritance of a fetus, and so on. See, for instance, Muḥaqqiq al-Ḥillī, Ja'far b. al-Ḥasan, *Mukhtaṣar al-nāfi' fī fiqh al-*

imāmīya (Qumm: Mu'assasa Bi'that, 1989), 274 and 239; 'Allama al-Ḥillī, al-Ḥasan b. Yūsuf, *Taḥrīr al-aḥkām* (Qumm: Mu'assasa Ahl al-Bayt, n.d.) 1:278 and 2:174; Ṭūsī, *Mabsūṭ*, 7:200; 'Abd Allāh al-Māmqānī, *Manāhij al-muttaqīn fī fiqh al-a'imma al-ḥaqq wa al-yaqīn* (Qumm: Mu'assasa Ahl al-Bayt, 1984), 530; Aḥmad al-Khwānsārī, *Jāmi' al-madārik fī sharḥ al-mukhtaṣar al-nāfi'* (Tehran: Maktaba al-Ṣadūq, 1936), 5:371; Muḥaqqiq al-Ḥillī, *al-Nihāya wa nukatahā* (Qumm: Mu'assasa Intishārāt-i Islāmī,1987), 3:86.

16. Kulaynī, *Kāfī*, 7:342; Ṭūsī, *Tahdhīb al-aḥkām fī sharḥ al-muqni'a li al-shaykh al-mufīd* (Tehran: Dār al-Kutub al-Islāmīya, 1390/1968), 10:282; Mufīd, Muḥammad b. Muḥammad, *al-Irshād* (n.p., 1962), 119.

17. Kulaynī, *Kāfī*, 6:13-14 and 7:346–47.

18. Ṭūsī, *Tahdhīb*, 10:281, *ḥadīth* 1100 and 1:48, *ḥadīth* 1875; for the opening of the eyes and the ears see Kulaynī, *Kāfī*, 7:345.

19. Ibn Qayyim al-Jawzīya, *al-Tibyān fī aqsām al-qur'ān*, 255.

20. For a detailed examination of various reports and the ultimate conclusion regarding the period of ensoulment, see, for the Shī'ite assessment, Tavakkulī Naẓarī, Sa'īd, *al-Tarqī' wa zar' al-a'ḍā' fī fiqh al-islāmī* (Mashhad: Mu'assasa al-Ṭab' al-Tābi'a li al-Astāna al-Raḍawīya al-Muqaddasa, 1380 Sh/2001), 207–211; for the Sunni assessment, Bārr, Muḥammad 'Alī al-, *Khalq al-insān: Bayna al-ṭibb wa al-qur'ān* (Jedda: Dār al-Sa'ūdiyya, 1415/1995), 359–66.

21. Bārr, *Mawt al-qalb aw mawt al-dimāgh*, pp. 71–82 covers the Sunni views on the criteria and critically evaluates the errors that have crept into the Islamic as well as medical pronouncements of death. For the Shī'ite views see Ṭabarsī, *al-Iḥtijāj*, 2:97; Kulaynī, *Kāfī*, 3:134–35, 3:161–63; Ibn Bābawayh, *'Ilal al-sharā'i'*, 1:309, sec. 261.

22. Tavakkulī Naẓarī, *Tarqī' wa zar' al-a'ḍā'*, 212–16.

23. Rāzī, *Tafsīr al-kabīr*, 30:54, writes: "It is said that life is a description for a person inasmuch as he can learn and act; the matter of death is different. Some say that it is actually a negation of this ability [to learn and to act]. We are of the opinion that this is a description of existence contrary to life and we argue that God, the Exalted says: 'He is the one who created death', because non-existence (*al-'adam*) is not creatable [on its own]. This is the conclusion."

24. Jazarī, *Fiqh 'alā al-madhāhib al-arba'a*, 2:20–21 attributes this distinction and the terminology between "stable" and "unstable" states to the Ḥanbalī and Shāfi'ī jurists. The Ḥanafī jurists distinguish between an observable life beyond the movement following decapitation that leads to living for a day or two and its absence. The Mālikī jurists do not make that distinction at all and simply state the signs that suggest that the animal has reached the death. The Shī'ite jurists make the distinction and discuss different criteria to determine the actual death. See: Ṭūsī, *Mabsūṭ*, 7:203, 6:260, 1:390, 4:124; Ibn Qudāma, *Mughnī*,; Ibn Idrīs al-Ḥillī, *al-Sarā'ir* (Qumm: Dār al-Kutub al-Islāmīya, 1989), 3:96, 108–9; Sarakhsī, Muḥammad b. Aḥmad, al-, *al-Mabsūṭ* (n.p., 1970), 5:12 and numerous other juridical sources mention this distinction between "stable" and "unstable" life.

25. 'Allāma al-Ḥillī, *Qawā'id al-aḥkām fī ma'rifat al-ḥalāl wa al-ḥarām* (Qumm: Manshūrāt-i Rāzī, n.d.), 2:155.

26. Jazarī, *Fiqh 'alā al-madhāhib al-arba'a*, 2:20.

27. Ibid.

28. Khū'ī, 2:19; Ṭūsī, *Mabsūṭ*, 1:390; Shahīd al-Awwal Muḥammad b. Makkī, *al-Durūs al-sharī'a fī fiqh al-imāmīya* (Qumm: Maktaba-yi Ṣādiqī, n.d.) 277; Muḥammad b. Ḥasan al-Fāḍil al-Hindī, *Kashf al-lithām* (Qumm: Maktaba al-Sayyid al-Mar'ashī, 1985), 2:74; Jazarī, *Fiqh 'alā al-madhāhib al-arba'a*, 2:20–22.

29. Shahīd al-Awwal, *Durūs*, 277.

30. Jazarī, *Fiqh 'alā al-madhāhib al-arba'a*, 2:20–21; Ibn 'Ābidīn, *Ḥāshiya*, 6:308–9.

31. Shahīd al-Awwal, *Durūs*, 108–9; Ṭūsī, *Mabsūṭ*, 4:124.

32. A cursory examination of juridical works like Shāfi'ī, *Kitāb al-Umm* (Cairo: Dār al-Wafā', 2001), 3:592–595. and Ibn 'Ābidīn, *Ḥāshiya*, 6:293–294, shows that the Sunni jurists were more interested in physical symptoms of the decapitated animal in determining whether the animal could be consumed by a further ritual act of immolation.

33. Fāḍil al-Hindī, *Kashf al-lithām* 2:75; Najafī, *Jawāhir*, 36:148; Nawawī, *al-Majmū' fī sharḥ al-muhadhdhab* (Dār al-Fikr, n.d.) 9:89.

34. Mullā Aḥmad al-Ardabīlī, *Majma' al-fawā'id wa al-burhān* (Qumm: Jāmi'at al-Mudarrisīn, n.d.), 11:107.

35. 'Allāma al-Ḥillī, *Qawa'id al-aḥkām*, 3:336.

36. Ardabīlī, *Majma' al-fawā'id*, 11:121.

37. Najafī, *Jawāhir*, 36:149.

38. 'Āmilī, Muḥammad Jawād al-Ḥusaynī al-, *Miftāḥ al-karāma fī sharḥ qawā'id al-'allāma* (Qumm: Mu'assasa Āl al-Bayt, 1983), 7:244.

39. Kulaynī, *Kāfī*, 7:8, ḥadīth 7.

40. Ibn Bābawayh, Muḥammad b. 'Ali, *Amālī* (Najaf: al-Maṭba'a al-Ḥaydarīya, 1970), 125.

41. Qāḍī 'Abd al-'Azīz Ibn Barrāj, *al-Muhadhdhab* (Dār al-Fikr, n.d.), 2:463; Ibn Fahd al-Ḥillī, Aḥmad b. Muḥammad, *al-Muhadhdhab al-bāri' fī sharḥ al-mukhtaṣar al-nāfi'* (Qumm: Mu'assasa al-Nashr al-Islāmī, 1407/1987), 4:169–70.

42. 'Allāma al-Ḥillī, *Taḥrīr al-aḥkām*, 2:159.

43. For the Quinlan case see: B. D. Colen, *Karen Ann Quinlan: Dying in the Age of Eternal Life* (New York: Nash, 1976); for Nancy Cruzen there are a number of newspaper articles that provide details of the case. In *Newsweek* (July 23, 1990) Marcia Angell wrote an excellent piece on "The Right to Die in Dignity."

44. Julius Korein et al., "Radioisotopic Bolus Technique as a Test to Detect Circulatory Deficit Associated with Cerebral Death," *Circulation* 51 (May 1975): 924–39.

45. *Al-qarār al-thānī bi-sha'n mawdu' taqrīr ḥuṣūl al-wafāt wa raf' ajhīzāt al-in'āsh min jism al-insān*, in *Majalla al-buḥūth al-fiqhīya al-mu'āṣira*, No. 4, (Feb.–Apr. 1990): 159–60. See also the following note.

46. In several meetings held in Mecca, Jeddah, and Amman under the auspices of The Islamic Juridical Council Muslim jurists of different schools have ruled that once the invasive treatment is intensified to save the life of a patient, it is impermissible to turn off the life-saving equipment, unless the physicians are certain about the inevitability of death. However, in the case of brain death which is caused by irreversible damage to the brain, including loss of spontaneous respiration, the jurists have ruled that if three attending physicians attest to a totally damaged brain that results in an unresponsive coma, apnea, and absent cephalic reflexes, and if the patient can be

kept alive only through external means by a respirator, then the person is biologically dead, although legal death can be attested only when the breathing stops completely following the turning off the life-saving equipment. See ibid.

47. In a detailed study *Marg-i maghzī az dīdgāh-i fiqh va ḥuqūq* (Qum: Intishārāt-i Daftar-i Tablīghāt-i Islāmī, 2001), Dr. Ḥusayn Ḥabībī, physician-cum-ethicist, has contrasted the medical-biological information with the juridical definition of death, and has convincingly argued about the brain being the actual location of the soul, the active principle of life endowed with consciousness. However, the majority of the jurists continue to regard the complete cessation of the heartbeat as the sole criterion for death in the Sharīʿa.

48. It is important to clarify that the religious leaders do not directly make such decisions for the family. Their *fatāwā* (prescriptive rulings) are a source of authoritative information that is utilized by the family or other surrogate decision makers at that critical moment when the patient's severe health condition becomes irreversible.

49. Bukhārī, *Ṣaḥīḥ, Kitāb al-marḍā* , vol. 7, *ḥadīth* 582. The tradition is reported on the authority of the Prophet when he said: "There is no disease that God has created, except that He also has created its treatment."

50. Tawḥīdī, Abū al-Ḥayy, al-, *al-Muqtabaṣāt* (Kuwayt: Dār al-Suʿād al-Ṣabāḥ, 1992).

51. All compilations of traditions like the *Ṣaḥīḥ* of Bukhārī and *Ṣaḥīḥ* of Muslim, have sections that report the Prophet's instructions in the matter of nutrition and its impact on human health. In one tradition he says: "If people eat in moderation, they will have healthy bodies." See: Barqī, Aḥmad b. Muḥammad b. Khālid al-, *al-Maḥāsin* (Qumm: al-Majmaʿ al- ʿĀlamī li-Ahl al-Bayt, 1416/1995), vol. 2, Kitāb al-ma'ākil, Bāb al-iqtiṣād fī al-'akl wa al-miqdārih [The book of foods, section on moderation and quantity of eating].

52. Bukhārī, *Ṣaḥīḥ, Kitāb al-marḍā, ḥadīth* 545.

53. Ibid., *ḥadīth* 548.

54. The principle, as I have elaborated in chapter 2, is regarded as the most important source of all decisions affecting interpersonal relationships. Hence, it can be regarded as the corner stone of social ethics in Islam. In some important ways it resembles in its terms to the principle of nonmaleficence, in particular when distinctions and rules about life-sustaining treatments consider the distinction between killing and letting die, which in turn draws on the act-omission and active-passive distinctions.

CHAPTER 7

1. In January 1994 Muslim jurists and medical professionals gathered in Abu Dhabi to discuss the new medical advancements in the field of organ transplants. One of the critical subjects that was taken up by some scholars was the problem of brain death criteria as distinct from the criteria provided in the Sharīʿa, and whether the religious scholars could endorse the former and allow organ retrieval while the patient was kept ventilated. The interview given by Dr. Muḥammad ʿAlī al-Barr, who is also a first rate scholar of Islamic law and ethics, points out the need to wait long enough to determine brain death before harvesting the transplant organs, because the only way to make sure that the brain functions have ceased permanently is to give more time. See: *Majalla al-ʿĀlam* no. 514 (Jan. 1994): 53–55.

2. Ghazālī, *Remembrance of Death*, 99, 108, 111.

3. Jazarī, *al-Fiqh 'alā al-madhāhib al-arba'a*, 1:533. For the Shī'ite views and their comparison with the Sunni opinions about all issues related to the topic of funerals see: 'Allāma al-Ḥillī, *Muntahā al-maṭlab fī taḥqīq al-madhhab* (Mashhad: al-Maktab al-Markazī, 1421/2000), 7:413–42. There are striking differences between the schools of thought regarding the expression of grief and after burial services. The Shī'ites are inclined to allow more freedom to the bereaved family to hold the commemoration rituals and visitations to the graves.

4. The rights of the body have been taken up in a recent article dealing with the status of the body in Muslim culture in the context of human rights by al-Munṣif al-Wahāybī, "Al-Jasad: ṣūratahu wa ḥuqūqahu fī al-islām," in *Ḥuqūq al-insān fī fikr al-'arabī: Dirāsāt fī al-nuṣūṣ* (Beirut: Markaz Dirāsāt al-Waḥdat al-'Arabīya, 2002), 281–307.

5. Bārr in his interview in *Majalla al-'Ālam*, 54 cites examples in the early history of Muslim warfare in which the Prophet himself engaged in retrieving an eye of his companion, which he brought back to the companion and replanted in his eye socket. In another instance the Prophet replanted a detached hand for another companion. There were also instances of cosmetic surgery to improve the shape of the nose or replace one with a golden nose. According to the famous traditionalist, Nawawī, a bone from the dead was transplanted on the living.

6. Ibid., p. 53–55.

7. 'Abd al-Salām 'Abd al-Raḥīm al-Sukkarī, *Naql wa zirā'a al-a'ḍā' al-ādamīya min al-manẓūr al-islāmī: Dirāsa al-muqārana* (Cairo: Dār al-Manār, 1988), 118.

8. 'Āmilī, *Wasā'il al-shī'a* 2:675, *ḥadīth* 1.

9. Muḥammad Mu'min, "al-Tashrīḥ fī al-ta'līm al-ṭibbī," *Fiqh ahl al-bayt* 1, no. 1 (1995/1416): 81–109, undertakes to provide detailed documentation for the prohibition to perform an autopsy on dead and notes the exceptions to this general prohibition under the present technological advancement in medicine and biological sciences.

10. See the proceedings of the conference on biomedical ethics that took place under the auspices of University of Medical Sciences of Mashhad, March 1990 under the title: *Majmū'-yi maqālāt seminar-i dīdgāh-ha-yi Islām dar pizishkī*, ed. Sayyid Ḥusayn Fattāḥī Ma'ṣūm (Mashhad: Ferdowsi University Press, 1992), especially the last section from pp. 490ff. In this section, the rulings of various prominent Shī'ite jurists on autopsies and related questions are recorded. A similar conference was held in Mecca in 1985 in which the Sunni jurists resolved the permissibility of retrieving organs from the deceased under the guidelines provided by the Islamic Juridical Council. See *Qarārāt majlis al-majma' al-fiqhī al-islāmī*, Eighth Session, 146–49.

11. The case appears in variant forms in the early sources, both Sunni and Shī'ite, that discuss judicial decisions in the form of traditions. For the Sunni ruling on the subject see: 'Izz al-Dīn 'Abd al-'Azīz b. 'Abd al-Salām, *Qawā'id al-aḥkām fī maṣāliḥ al-anām* (Cairo: Dār al-Sharq, 1388/1968), 1:97. For the Shī'ite tradition see Ḥurr al-'Āmilī, *Wasā'il al-shī'a*, 2:674, ḥadīth 4.

12. *Aḥkām amwāt* (Qumm: Intishārāt-i Anṣārī, n.d.), 339–40 cites the opinions of prominent Shī'ite jurists who allow one to open a grave to retrieve an object that belonged to someone and that the deceased had swallowed or was buried with him.

13. Jād al-Ḥaqq 'Alī, "Naql al-a'ḍā' min insān ilā ākhar," *Majallat al-azhar*, no. 10 (July 1983/Shawwal 1403): 1377.

14. Jazarī, *Fiqh 'alā al-madhāhib al-arba'a*, 1:537–38; for the synopsis of the Ḥanafi and other views see Jād al-Ḥaqq 'Alī Jād al-Ḥaqq, "Naql al-a'ḍā' min insān ilā ākhar," *Majallat al-azhar*, no. 10 (July 1983/Shawwal 1403): 1375–84.

15. Jazarī, *Fiqh 'alā al-madhāhib al-arba'a*, 1:539.

16. Muḥammad b. Muḥammad al-Nu'mān al-Mufīd, *al-Muqni'a fī masā'il al-ḥalāl wa al-ḥarām* (Litho., n.d.), 13; for variant traditions that form documentation for this ruling see Kulaynī, *Kāfī*, 3:155; Ṭūsī, *Tahdhīb*, 1:344, *ḥadīth* 1008.

17. Abū 'Amr 'Umar b. 'Abd al-'Azīz al-Kashshī, *Ikhtiyār ma'rifat al-rijāl* (Mashhad: University of Mashhad Press, 1348/1964), 385; 'Allāma al-Ḥillī, *Muntahā al-maṭlab*, 7:410–12.

18. Tavakkulī, *al-Tarqī' wa zar' al-a'ḍā'*, 172–186, investigates in great details all the various positions adopted by the Shī'ite jurists.

19. Būṭī, Muḥammad Sa'īd Ramaḍān al-, *Qaḍāyā fiqhīya mu'āṣira* (Damascus: Maktabat al-Fārābī, 1994/1414), 109–137 discusses issues related to the derivation of benefit from human body, both while alive and after death. On page 133–134 he takes up the new issues that have arisen about the general right of utilizing the cadaver for forensic medicine and for medical education.

20. Abū Dāwūd Sulaymān b. al-Ash'ath al-Sijistānī al-Azdī, *Sunan* (Beirut: Dār al-Kutub al-'Ilmīya, n.d.), 3:212–13, *ḥadīth* 3208.

21. Khū'ī, Abū al-Qāsim b. 'Ali Akbar al-. *Mustaḥdathāt al-masā'il*, printed as an addendum to his *Minhāj al-ṣāliḥīn* (Beirut: n.p., 1393/1983), No. 36 and 37.

22. Kulaynī, *Kāfī*, 7:3, *ḥadīth* 4.

23. Bukhārī, *Ṣaḥīḥ*, *Kitāb al-waṣāya*, 4:46, *ḥadīth* 1.

24. Shāṭibī, *Muwāfiqāt*, 3:318.

25. Ibid., 2:376 takes up the issue of a human's rights while he lives and that the perfection of his body, his reason, and his wealth is in his own hands. Anyone who harms himself and destroys his organs or wealth has acted against God's commandment in the Qur'an that forbids people to destroy their lives. See also 'Abd al-Salām, *Qawā'id al-aḥkām*, 1:130.

26. Khū'ī, Abū al-Qāsim b. 'Ali Akbar, al-, *Ṣirāṭ al-naja fī ajwiba al-istiftā'āt* (Beirut: Dār al-Muḥajja al-Bayḍā', 1416/1995), 353, question no. 971. Jād al-Ḥaqq, "Naql al-a'ḍā' min insān ilā ākhar," *al-Fatāwā al-islāmīya min dār al-iftā' al-miṣrīya* (Cairo: Wizārat al-Awqāf al-Majlis al-A'lā li-Shu'ūn al-Islāmīya, 1980–84), 10:3702–5.

27. Būṭi Muḥammad Sa'īd Ramaḍān, al-,, *Qaḍāyā fiqhīya mu'āṣira*, 131-34 has discussed opinions from all Sunni legal schools on this issue. For the Shī'ite opinions that support the invalidity of such advance directives see Tarakkulī, *al-Tarqī' wa zar'*, 271–78.

28. This ruling creates a tension in dealing with the slave trade. Are those transactions valid? Some authors have undertaken a detailed discussion of the slave trade and have engaged in the usual apologetics defending an institution that Muslim civilization had inherited from Antiquity. See, for instance: Sukkarī, *Naql wa zirā'a al-a'ḍā'*, 68–88.

29. Shāṭibī, *Muwāfiqāt*, 3:376–77. In another section (p. 348) dealing with promoting public good and averting corruption, he explains that assertion of one's self determination (*khīra*) should not lead to oppress others and violate their rights.

30. 'Abd al-Salām, *Qawa'id*, 1:130.

31. Shī'ism and the Mu'tazilite Sunni theology maintain a natural right theory based on natural endowment of reason that is capable of ethical knowledge.

32. For the Sunni accommodation of forbidden rulings that have been permitted when necessary see Muḥammad Na'īm Yāsīn, *Abhāth fiqhīya fī qaḍāya ṭibbīya mu'āṣira* (Amman: Dār al-Nafā'is, 1996/1416), 156–58; For the Shī'ite endorsement of this methodology see al-Sayyid Muḥsin al-Kharrāzī, "Zirā' al-a'ḍā'," pt. 1, *Fiqh ahl al-bayt* 5, no. 18 (1421/2000): 102–4.

33. Kharrāzī, "Zirā' al-a'ḍā'," pt. 1, 105–6, takes up the question of hardship suffered by others in the family because of the unilateral decision of one member to donate an organ. Such acts of altruism based on a person's autonomous decision are culpable in the Sharī'a because of the harm, however unintentional, they can cause to others in the family.

34. Jād al-Ḥaqq 'Alī Jād al-Ḥaqq, "Naql al-a'ḍā' min insān ilā ākhar," *al-Fatāwā al-islāmīya*, 10:3702–15; Sukkarī, *Naql wa zirā'a al-a'ḍā'*, 89 explicitly denies the right of an individual to benefit from his body, even when he recognizes that he has a right of control over it, except in performing services (*'ibādāt*) to God, earning a living by working, and so on. But a right of discretion over an organ or body is absolutely lacking.

35. Kharrazī, "Zirā' al-a'ḍā'," pt. 1, 104–5 takes up the question of the limits on saving the life of another by donating a vital organ. Such a decision cannot be based on an individual's right to self-determination about one's person without fully accounting for one's duties to the members of the family who might be dependent on the donor for their livelihood. This jurist underlines the importance of mutuality in ethical decisions that might harm others inadvertently.

36. I am aware of the fact that, for instance, in the document published in Saudi Arabia on kidney transplants there is a clear distinction made between Saudi and non-Saudi patients in order of priority as recipients of kidney transplants. Such discrimination violates the humanitarian principles of Islam.

37. Kharrāzī, "Zirā' al-a'ḍā'," pt. 2, in *Fiqh ahl al-bayt*, 6, no. 21 (1422/2001), 29–30 explicitly rules that it is permissible to retrieve an organ from a prisoner of war, whether alive or dead, even if there is no permission, because whether living or dead his person is not inviolable. However, retrieving an organ from "protected peoples" (*dhimmī* = Jews, Christians, Zoroastrians) requires their permission, if they are living, as part of the respect accorded to them in the contract. But if it is a dead body, then there is no need for permission, because the contract is terminated upon death. However, if the contract states that their dead bodies will not be desecrated, then it is not permissible to retrieve organs from them, unless their guardians permit it.

38. Kulaynī, *Kāfī*, 6:255; 3:212.

39. For example, Q. 2:145 reads: Say: "I do not find, in what is revealed to me, aught forbidden to him who eats thereof except it be carrion (*mayta*), or blood outpoured, or the flesh of swine. . . ." The prohibition specifically deals with the consumption of carrion rather than its sale.

40. Tavakkulī, *al-Tarqī' wa zar' al-a'ḍā'*, 269.

41. Kāsānī, *Badā'i' al-ṣanā'i' fī tartīb al-sharā'i'*, 7:311–12; 297; 213; 236.

42. Legal scholars representing different Sunni and Shī'ite schools have a variety of opinions on the subject. Hence, they have ruled from permission to prohibition to

donate different organs of the body. For instance, the Ḥanafī scholars have allowed using animal bones for treatment, but have regarded it as reprehensible to use human and swine bone for similar purpose because it is forbidden to make use of both. See *Majma' al-'anhar fī sharḥ al-Abḥar*, 2:525. According to another Ḥanafī scholar, Ibn 'Ābidīn, *Ḥāshiya*, 5:58, human beings have dignity (*mukarram*), regardless of their faith. Hence, even a non-believer has dignity. Consequently, any contract that leads to dishonor him and reduce him to some kind of non-animated existence is non-permissible, actually null and void. Accordingly, the sale of any part that can be separated from him like hair and nails is void and these must be buried.

43. Ibn 'Ābidīn, *Ḥāshiya*, 3:115, Ibn Qudāma, *Mughnī*, 4:304, and other Sunni jurists maintain that it is forbidden to sell any part of the human body; whereas, al-Khū'ī and a number of other Shī'ite jurists maintain the permission to sell all organs of a living person, except eyes. See *Majmū'a-yi maqālāt seminar-i dīdgāh-hāy-i islam dar pizishkī* (Mashhad: Ferdowsī University Press, 1992), 2:510.

44. Sukkarī, *Naql wa zira'a al-a'ḍā'*, 182–83.

45. Qurṭubī, *Jāmi' li-aḥkām*, 1:599–602.

46. Bukhārī, *Ṣaḥīḥ*, 3:169, *ḥadīth* 167.

47. Ibid., 3:174, *ḥadīth* 180.

48. All compilations of the *ḥadīth* relate traditions in praise of the practice of cupping as a valid method of maintaining health and cite numerous instances in the life of the Prophet and his companions as an authoritative precedent. Some traditions approve cupping while a person is fasting since the technique was employed to suck out blood or while on pilgrimage. See, for instance, ibid., 9:227, *ḥadīth* 18.

49. The verse appears in the context of divorce when the woman's rights are explained. One of the situations under these circumstances is if she happens to be pregnant. The verse makes it clear that if she is pregnant then it is the husband's duty to maintain her financially until she delivers, even if this takes full nine months. And, if she is willing to suckle the child, the husband must pay her something in return, according to what is just and fair.

50. Bukhārī, *Ṣaḥīḥ*, 7:15 has a rubric that reads: "Prohibited to you are your mothers who have suckled you [Q. 4:23]: Marriage is prohibited between persons having a foster suckling relationship corresponding to a blood relationship." In the tradition that follows the Prophet declares: "Foster suckling (*al-riḍā'a*) relationships make all those things unlawful which as unlawful through corresponding birth (*wilāda*) relationships."

51. Yūsuf al-Qaraḍāwī, "Bunūk al-ḥalīb," *Majalla majma' al-fiqhī al-islāmī* 2, no. 1 (1986/1407): 385–406 has disagreed with the ancient jurists on the definition of "suckling." According to the Ḥanafī, Malikī and Shāfi'ī jurists, suckling is understood as any milk that gets into the stomach of an infant through the mouth or nose. The prohibition of marriage applies when the milk is given through mouth or nose, because milk given thus contributes to the growth of bone and flesh and is similar to suckling. Some have maintained that milk taken through nose does not lead to consanguinity and consequential prohibition of marriage. Suckling involves sucking (*imtiṣāṣ*) and intimate touching (*iltiṣāq*) which is manifested in motherly kindness which is the main cause for foster relationship. The absence of such closeness in milk-banks rules out the problem of consanguinity. Moreover, if the milk is collected from different donors

then there occurs a doubt in the specific identity of a woman whose milk the child has drunk. In such circumstances, as the Ḥanafī jurists have ruled, suckling the child with this mixed milk does not lead to its prohibition. This is al-Qaraḍāwī's argument. However, this opinion has been challenged by others. A scholarly response has been offered by Muḥammad ʿAlī al-Bạrr, "Bunūk al-Ḥalīb," of *Majalla majmaʿ al-fiqhī al-islāmī*, no 1, 391–406, with an explicit recommendation that there is no need to establish milk banks in the Muslim world. Moreover, all the Sunnī jurists are in agreement that suckling leads to consanguinity and, therefore, it is forbidden without any proper regulation regarding the identity of the child and its relations with other children breastfed by the same woman.

52. Bukhārī, *Ṣaḥīḥ*, 9:121, *ḥadīth* 107; Abū Dāwūd, *Sunan*, 6:98-99, *sḥadīth* 3300.

53. See the detailed examination of this and other opinions among the Sunni jurists in al-Sukkarī, *Naql wa zirāʿa al-aʿḍāʾ al-ādamīya*, 191–206.

54. Nawawī, *Minhāj al-ṭālibīn* (Beirut: Dār al-Fikr, 1978), 1:190; Shirbīnī, *Mughnī al-muḥtāj li-maʿrifa alfāẓ al-minhāj al-* (Beirut: Dār al-Fikr, n.d.) 190–91.

55. See the article by Murtaḍā Ṭāhirī, "Ahmiyat-i bihdāsht-i dahān va dandān az dīdgāh-i islām," in *Majmūʿa-yi maqālāt seminar dīdgāh-hāyi islām dar pizishkī* (Mashhad: Ferdowsi University Press, 1371/1992), 145–59 and the primary sources cited therein. There are numerous traditions in the Sunni and Shīʿite sources that describe the merits of brushing one's teeth several times everyday. The extreme emphasis on personal hygiene, including dental and physical cleanliness, is underscored by requiring ritual washing and recommending brushing one's teeth before each of the five daily prayers. In the sections dealing with ritual purity (*ṭahāra*), the compilers relate various traditions in which the Prophet's own practice serves as the major source of cleanliness and beautification of one's appearance. For instance, Abū Dāwūd, *Sunan*, 1:12–16 relates various occasions during which brushing one's teeth is recommended, and dental cleanliness is regarded as one of the ten natural instincts (*fiṭra*), which include cutting of nails, trimming of beard, and so on.

56. Sukkarī, *Naql wa zirāʿa al-aʿḍāʾ*, 233.

57. Ibn Ḥajar, *Fatḥ al-bārī*, 10:377; Nawawī,*Sharḥ*, 14:106.

58. Ibn Ḥajar, *Fatḥ al-bārī*, , 10:377; Nawawī, *Sharḥ*,, 14:106.

59. Bukhārī has a section with the title "Bāb al-Mawṣūla," which roughly translates as "fixing" one's hair by using false hair. The verbal form in the traditions that criticize the Arab practice of lengthening hair use *ʿaṣala* for treating baldness. See Bukhārī, *Ṣaḥīḥ*, 7:305, *ḥadith* 150–54.

60. Ibid., 10:374.

61. Shirbīnī, *Mughnī al-muḥtāj*, 4:310; Nawawī, *al-Majmūʿ*, 9:41, 44, 45. The Zaydī jurists also maintain the permission. See Shawkānī, Muḥammad b. ʿAlī, *Kitāb al-sayl al-jarrār al-mutadaffiq ʿalā ḥadāʾiq al-azhar* (Cairo: n.p., 1970–), 4:101. See also *al-Fatāwā al-islāmīya min dār al-iftāʿ al-miṣriya* (Cairo, 1982), 7:2505–07.

62. Qurṭubī, *Jāmiʿ li-aḥkām*, 3:1959.

63. Sayyid Yūsuf al-Madanī al-Tabrīzī, *al-Masāʾil al-mustaḥdatha* (Tabrīz: Ismāʿīliyān, 1416/1996), 49.

64. Christina Matta, "Ambiguous Bodies and Deviant Sexuality: Hermaphrodites, Homosexuality, and Surgery in the United States, 1850–1904," in *Controversies in*

Science and Technology: From Climate to Chromosomes, ed. Daniel Lee Klienman, et al. (New Rochelle, NY: Mary Ann Liebert, Inc., 2008), 493–505, examines the frequency of, and justification for, surgeries meant to define male and female.

65. Al-Sayyid Muḥammad al-Ṣadr, *Mā warā' al-fiqh* (Beirut: Dār al-Aḍwā', 1417/1996), 6:133.

66. Joan Roughgarden, "Social Selection versus Sexual Selection: Comparison of Hypotheses," in *Controversies in Science and Technology*, 421–63 describes how biases about gender and sexuality affect both conclusions about sexual selection and the language used to discuss it.

67. Muḥammad Mu'min, *Majma' fiqh-i ahl al-bayt*, rulings in the bulletin published in Qumm, between 1996–98.

68. For detailed discussion on rulings that apply to corrective or cosmetic sex change undergone by an individual see Ṣadr, *Mā warā' al-fiqh*, 134–55.

CHAPTER 8

1. See my essay: "Human Vicegerency: A Blessing or A Curse? The Challenge to be God's Caliph in the Qur'an," in *Humanity Before God: Contemporary Faces of Jewish, Christian, and Islamic Ethics*, ed. William Schweiker et al. (Minneapolis: Fortress Press, 2006), 43.

2. David J. Rothman, "Research, Human: Historical Aspects," in *Encyclopedia of Bioethics*, rev. ed. (New York: Simon & Schuster Macmillan, 1995), 4:2248–58, traces the development of human experimentation in Western civilization. There is no comparable account of such experimentation in Islamic civilization, although there is an explicit recognition of Muslim contributions to medical experimentation even in this article when Avicenna (Ibn Sīnā of Arabic tradition) is quoted by Rothman without any acknowledgement that he was a Muslim, Persian philosopher, and physician when the reference to such a need for medical experimentation in Muslim scientific circles was articulated by Avicenna (d. 1037) on page 2248.

3. Ibid., 2248.

4. It is related on the authority of the Prophet, who is reported to have said: "God has made known disease and cure, and has assigned for every disease a cure. Hence, seek remedy [for the disease] and do not treat [your ailments] by using forbidden [substance]." See: Abū Dāwūd, *Sunan*, 4:6.

5. Major compilations of Muslim traditions devote a section to health and personal hygiene that was practiced by the Prophet and early community. For instance, in Bukhārī, *Ṣaḥīḥ, Bāb mā yudhkaru fi al-ṭā'ūn*, 7:237–40, 44 relates the story of an epidemic in Syria and the discussion among the leaders about the right course of action in dealing with it. The most revealing part of the narrative ends with what the Prophet had taught regarding a place where an epidemic had broken out: "If you hear about it in a region, do not approach it; if you are in the region where it has occurred, do not leave fleeing from it." The latter advice was certainly given to control the spread in other areas, causing greater harm.

6. Hans Jonas, "Philosophical Reflections on Experimenting with Human Subjects," in *Intervention and Reflection: Basic Issues in Medical Ethics*, 7th ed., ed. Ronald

Munson (Belmont, CA: Wadsworth/Thomson Learning, 2004), 45–53, provides a first-rate analysis of the ethical issues involved in human experimentation.

7. John H. Evans, *Playing God? Human Genetic Engineering and the Rationalization of Public Bioethical Debate* (Chicago: University of Chicago Press, 2003), 1.

8. *Al-Istinsākh bayna al-islām wa al-masīḥīya* [Cloning in Islam and Christianity] (Beirut: Dār al-Fikr al-Lubnānī, 1999).

9. Ghazālī, *Mustaṣfā*, 174. Ghazālī's phrase, "Five Purposes" (*al-maqāṣid al-khams*), as discussed in chapter 2, has become an accepted phrase in the Sunni works on legal theory and often quoted in discussions about the principle of *maṣlaḥa*. See Shawkānī, *Irshād al-fuḥūl*, 216.

10. For various Muslim opinions collected from around the world see: Courtney Campbell, "Religious Perspectives on Human Cloning," paper commissioned by National Bioethics Advisory Commission. In addition, for specifically Sunni opinions expressed by their leading religious authorities, see *Al-Majalla: The International News Magazine of the Arabs*, no.894 (30 March–5 April, 1997) and *Sayyidatī*, no. 843, (3–9 May 1997): 62–64. For the Shīʿite opinions besides *al-Istinsākh bayna al-islām wa al-masīḥiyya*, see also Ṣādiq Jaʿfar al-Ḥasan, ed., *al-Istinsākh al-bashārī fī raʾy al-imām al-shirāzī*, ed. (n.p., 1997).

11. The *fatwā* is recorded in *al-Istinsākh bayna*, 305. For discussion, see *Al-Majalla*, no.894, (30 March–5 April 1997): 6.

12. *Sayyidatī*, no. 843, p. 64.

13. Ḥasan al-Turābī, in his opinion on the subject, has pointed out that many scholars have not paid attention to the various scientific facets of the issue, which they need to examine before formulating their responses. See *al-Istinsākh bayna*, 307.

14. Ibid., 63.

15. *Sayyidatī*, 62–63.

16. For instance, see the Catholic opinion expressed by Bishop Ḥabīb Pāshā in *Al-Istinsākh bayna*, 19–21.

17. Much of the information in this section has been collated and compiled from a number of new studies dealing directly or indirectly with religious rulings on human cloning. The main text with which the rulings of other jurists, both Shīʿite and Sunni, have been compared is Muḥammad Saʿīd al-Ṭabāṭabāʾī al-Ḥakīm, *Fiqh al-istinsinsākh al-basharī wa fatāwā ṭibbīya* (n.p., 1999). The other compilations include ʿAbd al-Muʿiz Khiṭāb, *al-Istinsākh al-basharī: hal huwa ḍidd al-mashīyat al-ilāhīya?* (Cairo: Dār al-Naṣr, 1997); Sadiq Jaʿfar al-Hasan, *al-Istinsākh al-basharī*,' (n.p., 1997); Ziyād Aḥmad Salāma, *Atfāl al-anābīb bayna al-ʿilm wa al-sharīʿa* (Beirut, Dār al-Bayārīq, 1996); Aḥmad ʿAmr al-Jābirī, *al-Jadīd fī al-fatāwā al-sharʿīya li-al-amrāḍ al-nisāʾiya wa al-ʿaqm* (Amman: Dār al-Furqān, 1994); al-Sayyid Muḥammad Ḥasan al-Raḍawī, "al-Istinsākh wa ʿamalīyāt al-hindisa al-wārithīya," being the digest of the lectures by al-Ustādh al-Shaykh Muḥammad Sanad, in *Fiqh al-ṭibb wa al-taḍakhkhum al-naqdī* (Beirut: Muʾassasa Umm al-Qurā, 1423/2002).

18. The present discussion was written without taking into consideration the recent scientific discovery reported in the article that appeared on November 22, 2007 in New York Times. Dr. James A. Thompson's laboratory reported a new way to turn ordinary human skin cells into what appear to be embryonic stem cells without ever using

a human embryo. This has certainly eased the ethical concerns over the destruction of human embryos that are raised in this section.

19. See "Position Statement Regarding the Use of Embryonic and Adult Human Cells in Biomedical Research," October 2004, issued by The American Academy of Neurology (AAN) and the American Neurological Association (ANA), in support of the use of human pluripotent stem cells in biomedical research.

20. See, for instance, *Masā'il fī al-talqīḥ al-ṣanā'ī*, in *Masā'il wa Rudūd*, comp. Muḥammad Jawād Raḍī al-Shihābī and ed. 'Abd al-Wāḥid Muḥammad al-Najjār (Qumm: Dār al-Hādī, 1412/1992), 1:99. The opinion is ascribed to prominent Shī'ite jurist, Abū al-Qāsim al-Khū'ī.

21. Ibn 'Ābidīn, *Ḥāshiya*, 6:591.

22. See Muḥammad 'Abd al-Ghaffār al-Sharīf, "Ḥukm al-kashf al-ijbārī 'an al-amrāḍ al-wirāthīya" [The injunction about mandatory investigation of hereditary diseases] in *Buḥūth al-fiqhīya mu'āṣira, Majalla kullīya al-sharī'a wa al-qānūn* (Beirut: Dār Ibn Ḥazm, 1422/2001), first published in *Majalla kullīya al-sharī'a wa al-qānūn* (Azhar University) 18, no. 12 (2000): 236–44.

23. Ibid., 249–50. The author takes up the controversial issue dealing with the exact time of ensoulment and the laws that were passed in the Kuwait parliament based on the medical opinion about hereditary diseases and the parents' right to determine whether to carry the fetus to full term.

24. Raḍawī, "al-Istinsākh wa 'amaliyāt al-hindisa al-wārithīya," 99–100.

25. In their October 1986 meeting the Islamic Juridical Council declared the impermissibility of any form of artificial insemination that did not occur between the husband's sperm and the wife's ovum. See *Qarārāt wa tawṣīyāt majma' al-fiqhī al-islāmī*(Amman, Jordan), no. 34 (11–16 October 1986).

26. Muḥammad al-Sharīf, "Ḥukm al-kashf al-ijbāri," 225–62.

Bibliography

'Abd al-Salām, 'Izz al-Dīn 'Abd al-'Azīz b. *Qawā'id al-aḥkām fī maṣāliḥ al-anām*. Cairo: Dār al-Sharq, 1388/1968.

Abou El Fadl, Khaled. *Islam and the Challenge of Democracy: A Boston Review Book*, ed. Joshua Cohen and Deborah Chasman. Princeton, NJ: Princeton University Press, 2004.

'Abu Isḥāq al-Shīrāzi Ibrahīm b. 'Alī b. Yūsuf al-Firūzābādī. *al-Muhadhdhab fī fiqh al-imām al-shāfi'ī*. Beirut: Dār al-Shāmiya, 1992–96.

Abū al-Qāsim b. al-Ḥasan *al-Gilānī*, known as Mīrza Qummi. *Qawānin al-uṣūl*. Lithograph edition, n.p., 1303/1886.

'Allāma al-Ḥillī, al-Ḥasan b. Yūsuf, *Taḥrīr al-aḥkām*. Qumm: Mu'assasa Ahl al-Bayt, n.d.

———. *Muntahā al-maṭlab fī taḥqīq al-madhhab*. Vol. 7. Mashhad: al-Maktab al-Markazī, 1421/2000.

———. *Qawā'id al-aḥkām fī ma'rifat al-ḥalāl wa al-ḥarām*. Qumm: Manshūrāt-i Rāzī, n.d.

'Āmilī, Muḥammad Jawād al-Ḥusaynī al-, *Miftāḥ al-karāma fī sharḥ qawā'id al-'allāma*. Qumm: Mu'assasa Āl al-Bayt, 1983.

'Āmilī, Muḥammad b. al-Ḥasan al-Ḥurr al-. *Wasā'il al-shī'a ilā taḥṣīl masā'il al-sharī'a*. Beirut: Dār Iḥyā' al-Turāth al-'Arabī, 1391/1971.

Antes, Peter. "Medicine and the Living Tradition of Islam." In *Healing and Restoring: Health and Medicine in the World's Religious Traditions*, ed. Lawrence E. Sullivan. New York: Macmillan, 1989.

Arberry, A. J., *Avicenna on theology*. London: Murray, 1951.

Asadābādī, 'Abd al-Jabbār al-. *al-Mughnī fī abwāb al-tawḥīd wa al-'adl*. Cairo: Maṭba'a Turāthunā, 1361/1942.

Ayoub, Mahmoud. *Redemptive Suffering in Islam: A Study of the Devotional Aspects of 'Ashura' in Twelver Shī'ism*. The Hague: Mouton, 1978.

Azar, Henry A. "Postmortem Sampling in Selected Cases in Lieu of the Traditional Autopsy with Comments on Autopsy and Islam." Unpublished paper. 1994.

Balādhūrī, Aḥmad b. Yaḥyā, al-. *Ansāb al-ashrāf.* Cairo: Dār al-Ma'ārif, 1987.

Bārr, Muḥammad 'Alī al-. *Akhlāqiyāt al-talqīḥ al-iṣṭināʿī.* Jedda: Dār al-Sa'ūdiya, 1987.

———. *Khalq al-insān: Byna al-ṭibb wa al-qur'ān.* Jedda: Dār al-Sa'ūdiya, 1415/1995.

———. *Mawt al-qalb aw mawt al-dimāgh.* Jedda: al-Dār al-Sa'ūdiya, 1406/1986.

Birzilī, Aḥmad b. Muḥammad al-Balwā al-Qairawānī al-. *Mawāhib al-jalīl fī sharḥ mukhtaṣar khalīl.* Tripoli, Libya: Maktabat al-Najāḥ, 1969. Vol. 3.

Bonte, Pierre, and Edouard Conte, eds., *Al-Ansab: la quête des origins: anthropologie historique de la société tribale arabe.* Paris: Maison des sciences de l'homme, 1992.

Bukhārī, Muḥammad b. Ismā'īl al-. *Ṣaḥīḥ.* Beirut: 'Ālam al-Kutub, 1986.

Būṭī, Muḥammad Sa'īd Ramaḍān al-. *Ḍawābit al-maṣlaḥa fī al-sharī'at al-islāmīya.* Beirut: Mu'assasa al-Risāla, 1410/1990; first published, 1386/1966.

———. *Qaḍāyā fiqhīyā mu'āṣira.* Damascus: Maktabat al-Fārābī, 1414/1994.

Campbell, Courtney. "Religious Perspectives on Human Cloning." Paper commissioned by National Bioethics Advisory Commission, 1997.

Chittick, William. *The Sufi Path of Knowledge.* Albany, SUNY, 1989.

Colen, B. D. *Karen Ann Quinlan: Dying in the Age of Eternal Life.* New York: Nash, 1976.

Cragg, Kenneth. *The House of Islam.* Encino, CA: Dickenson Publishing Co., 1975.

Dimashqī, Ibn Badrān al-. *al-Madkhal ilā madhhab imām Aḥmad ibn Ḥanbal.* Beirut: Mu'assasa al-Risāla, 1401/1981.

DuBose, Edwin R., Ronald P. Hamel, and Laurence J. O'Connell, eds. *A Matter of Principles? Ferment in U.S. Bioethics.* Valley Forge: Trinity Press International, 1994.

Evans, John H. *Playing God? Human Genetic Engineering and the Rationalization of Public Bioethical Debate.* Chicago: University of Chicago Press, 2003.

Fāḍil al-Hindī, Muḥammad b. Ḥasan al-. *Kashf al-lithām.* Qumm: Maktaba al-Sayyid al-Mar'ashī, 1985.

Fakhry, Majid. *Ethical Theories in Islam.* Leiden: E. J. Brill, 1991.

———. "The Mu'tazilite View of Man." In *Philosophy, Dogma and the Impact of Greek Thought in Islam.* Brookfield, VT:Variorium, 1994.

First International Conference on Islamic Medicine, *Islamic Code of Medical Ethics.* Kuwait Document, Kuwait Rabi I, 1401 (January 1981), 16–23.

Geertz, Clifford. *The Interpretation of Cultures: Selected Essays.* New York: Basic Books, 1973.

Ghazālī, Abū Ḥāmid Muḥammad b. Muḥammad al-. *The Remembrance of Death and the Afterlife.* Translated with introduction and notes by T. J. Winter. Cambridge: The Islamic Text Society, 1989.

———. *Kitāb al-Mustaṣfā min 'ilm al-uṣūl.* Cairo: Būlāq, 1904–7.

Gillon, Raanan, ed. *Principles of Health Care Ethics.* London: John Wiley & Sons, 1994.

Green, Ronald M., "Theodicy," in the *Encyclopedia of Religion,* ed. Mircea Eliade. New York: Macmillan, 1995, 14:430–41.

Ḥabībī, Ḥusayn. *Marg-i maghzī az dīdgāh-i fiqh va ḥuqūq.* Qum: Intishārāt-i Daftar-i Tablīghāt-i Islāmī, 2001.

Ḥakīm, Muḥammad Sa'īd al-Ṭabāṭabā'ī al-. *Fiqh al-istinsinsākh al-basharī wa fatāwā ṭibbīya.* N.p., 1999.

Ḥakīm, Sayyid Mundhir al-. "Qā'dat nafy al-ḍarar: Ta'rīkh-ha—Taṭawwur-ha ḥatta 'aṣr al-Shaykh al-Anṣārī." In *al-Fikr al-Islāmī* 7 (1415/1994): 264–90.

Hallaq, Wael B. *Authority, Continuity, and Change in Islamic Law.* Cambridge: Cambridge University Press, 2001.

Ḥaram Panāhī, Muḥsin. "Al-talqīḥ al-ṣanā'ī." In *Fiqh ahl al-bayt: Majalla fiqhīya takhaṣ ṣūṣīya faṣlīya* 9:1419, no. 10 (1998): 68–92.

Ḥasan, Ṣādiq Ja'far al-, ed. "al-Istinsākh al-basharī fī ra'y al-imām al-shirāzī." N.p., 1997.

Ḥaṭṭāb, Muḥammad b. Muḥammad b. 'Abd al-Raḥmān, al-. *Mawāhib al-jalīl sharḥ mukhtaṣar khalīl.* Tripoli, Libya: Maktaba al-Najāḥ, 1969.

Haythamī, Aḥmad b. Muḥammad b. 'Alī al-. *Tuḥfat al-muḥtāj bi-sharḥ al-Minhāj.*

Heyd, David, ed. *Toleration: An Elusive Virtue.* Princeton: Princeton University Press, 1996.

Hilālī, Sa'd al-Dīn Mas'ad. "Ijhāḍ janīn al-ightiṣāb fī ḍaw' aḥkām al-sharī'a al-islāmīya: dirāsa fiqhīya muqārana." In *Majalla al-sharī'a wa dirāsāt al-islāmīya* 15, no. 41 (1421/2000): 282–315.

Hodgson, Marshall G. S. *The Venture of Islam: Conscience and History in a World Civilization.* Chicago: University of Chicago Press, 1974.

Hourani, George F. "Ibn Sina's 'Essay on the Secret of Destiny.'" *Bulletin of School of Oriental and African Studies.* University of London, 1966.

———. *Islamic Rationalism: The Ethics of 'Abd al-Jabbar.* Oxford: Clarendon, 1971.

———. *Reason and Tradition in Islamic Ethics.* Cambridge: Cambridge University Press, 1985.

Husaynī, Sayyid Shihāb al-Dīn al-. "Al-talqīḥ al-sanā'ī bayn al-'ilm wa al-sharī'a." *Fiqh Ahl al-Bayt* (Qumm: Mu'assasa Dā'irat al-Ma'ārif al-Fiqh al-Islāmī) 6, no. 23 (1422/2001): 187–90.

Ibn Amīr Ḥāj, Muḥammad b. Muḥammad. *al-Taqrīr wa al-taḥbīr.* Beirut: Dār al-Fikr, 1996.

Ibn Bābwayh. *'Ilal al-sharāyi'.* Najaf: Maktaba al-Ḥaydariya, 1965.

Ibn Ḥajar al-'Asqalānī, *Fatḥ al-bārī bi-sharḥ Ṣaḥīḥ al-bukhārī.* Cairo: Dār al-Kitāb al-Jadīd, 1970.

Ibn Ḥajar al-Haythamī al-Makkī, Aḥmad b. Muḥammad b. 'Alī, *Tuḥfat al-muḥtāj bi-sharḥ al-Minhāj.* Bombay: Muḥammad 'Abd al-'Azīz al-Surtī, 1970.

Ibn Māja, Muḥammad b. Yazīd al-Qazwīnī. *Sunan, Kitab al-janā'iz.* Beirut: Maktaba 'Ilmīya, n.d.

Ibn Manẓūr, Muḥammad b. Mukrim. *Lisān al-'arab.* Beirut: Dār Ṣādir, 1991.

Ibn Nujaym, Zayn al-Dīn b. Ibrahīm b. Muḥammad b. Bakr. al-Baḥr *al-rā'iq: Sharḥ kanz al-daqā'iq.* Cairo: al-Maṭba'a al-'Ilmīya, 1983.

Ibn al-Qayyim al-Jawzīya, Muḥammad b. Abū Bakr. *al-Tibyān fī aqsām al-qur'ān.* Beirut: Mu'assasa al-Risāla, 1994.

Ibn Qudāma, 'Abd Allāh b. Aḥmad. *Rawḍat al-nāẓir wa jannat al-manāẓir.* Riyāḍ: Jāmi' al-Imām, 1399/19.

Ibn Qudāma. *Mughnī.* Cairo: Hajar, 1992.

Ijtihād va zamān va makān: Majmū'a maqālāt (ed. and written by a number of scholars under the supervision of Committee for Investigation of the Juridical Foundations of Imām Khumaynī), 15 vols. (Qumm: Mu'assasa Chāp va Nashr-i 'Urūj, 1384/1995–96).

'Iraqī, Ḍiya al-Dīn al-. *Qā'ida lā ḍarar wa lā ḍirār*. Edited and commented upon by al-Sayyid Murtaḍā al-Mūsawī al-Khalkhālī. Qumm: Intishārāt-i Daftar-i Tablīghāt-i Islāmī, 1418/1997.

Islām wa tanẓīm al-'usra, al-. 2 vols. Beirut: International Planned Parenthood Federation, Middle East and North African Region,1973. The English version *Islam and Family Planning* in 2 vols, 1974.

Istinsākh bayna al-islām wa al-masīḥīya, al- [Cloning in Islam and Christianity]. Beirut: Dār al-Fikr al-Lubnānī, 1999.

Jābirī, Aḥmad 'Amr al-. *al-Jadīd fī al-fatāwā al-shar'īya li-al-amrāḍ al-nisā'īya wa al-'aqm*. Amman: Dār al-Furqān, 1994.

Jād al-Ḥaqq, Jād al-Ḥaqq 'Alī. "Naql al-a'ḍā' min insān ilā ākhar." *Majallat al-azhar*, no. 10 (July 1983/Shawwal 1403): 1375–84.

Jadīd fiqhī mabāḥith. ed. Mawlānā Mujāhid al-Islām Qāsimī. Karachi: Idārat al-Qur'ān wa al-'Ulūm al-Islāmīya, 1409/1989. Vol. 1.

Ja'farī Langarūdī, Muḥammad Ja'far. *Mabsūṭ dar terminologie-yi ḥuqūq*. Tehran: Kitābkhāne Ganj-i Dānish, 1378/1999.

Ja'farī, Muḥammad Taqī. *Rasā'il-i fiqhī*. Qumm: Mu'assasa-yi Nashr-i Karāmat, 1377/1998.

Ja'farzade, Mīr Qāsim. "Dar āmadī bar masā'il-i fiqhī-ḥuqūqī ART." *Bulletin-i tavlid-i mithl va nāza'ī*, Biological and Biotechnological Research Center of Jihād-i Dānishgāhī, no. 7 and 8 (1378/1999).

Jazarī, 'Abd al-Raḥmān al-. *Kitāb al-fiqh 'alā al-madhāhib al-arba'a, Kitāb al-ḥudūd*. Beirut: Dār al-Kutub al-'Ilmīya, 1392/1972.

Jonas, Hans. "Philosophical Reflections on Experimenting with Human Subjects." In *Intervention and Reflection: Basics Issues in Medical Ethics*, edited by Ronald Munson. 7th ed. Belmont, CA: Wadsworth/Thomson Learning, 2004.

Juwaynī, al-Imām al-Ḥaramayn Abū al-Ma'ālī 'Abd al-Malik b. 'Abd Allāh al-. *al-Burhān fī uṣūl al-fiqh*. Cairo: Dār al-Anār, 1400/1976.

Kamali, Mohammad Hashim. *Principles of Islamic Jurisprudence*. Cambridge: Islamic Texts Society, 1991.

Kashshī, Abū 'Amr 'Umar b. 'Abd al-'Azīz al-. *Ikhtiyār ma'rifat al-rijāl*. Mashhad: University of Mashhad Press, 1348/1964.

Khamenei, Sayyid 'Alī. *Pizishkī dar ā'ina-yi ijtihād: Istiftā'āt-i pizishkī*. Qumm: Intishārāt-i Anṣāriyān, 1375/1996.

Kharrāzī, al-Sayyid Muḥsin al-. "Zirā' al-a'ḍā'." Pt. 1, *Fiqh ahl al-bayt* 5, no. 18 (1421/2000).

———. "Zirā' al-a'ḍā'." Pt. 2, *Fiqh ahl al-bayt* 6, no. 21 (1422/2001).

Khiṭāb, 'Abd al-Mu'iz. *al-Istinsākh al-basharī: hal huwa ḍidd al-mashīyat al-ilāhīya?* Cairo: Dār al-Naṣr, 1997.

Khū'ī, Abū al-Qāsim b. 'Ali Akbar. *Ṣirāṭ al-naja fī ajwiba al-istiftā'āt*. Beirut: Dār al-Muḥ ajja al-Bayḍā', 1416/1995.

———. *Mustaḥdathāt al-masā'il*. Printed as an addendum to his *Minhāj al-ṣāliḥīn* Beirut: n.p., 1393/1983.

Khumaynī, Rūh Allāh Mūsavī, *Saḥīfa-yi nūr: majmū'a rahnamūd-hāy-i imām khumaynī*. Tehran: Ministry of Islamic Guidance, 1361/1982.

Khwānsārī, Aḥmad al-. *Jāmi' al-madārik fī sharḥ al-mukhtaṣar al-nāfi'*. Tehran: Maktaba al-Ṣadūq, 1936.

Korein, Julius et al. "Radioisotopic Bolus Technique as a Test to Detect Circulatory Deficit Associated with Cerebral Death." *Circulation* 51 (May 1975): 924–39.

Lane, Edward William. *An Arabic-English Lexicon*, off-print edition. Beirut: Librairie du Liban, 1968.

Madanī al-Tabrīzī, Sayyid Yūsuf al-. *al-Masā'il al-mustaḥdatha*. Tabrīz: Ismā'īliyān, 1416.

Madkūr, Muḥammad Sallām. *Mabāḥith al-ḥukm 'inda al-uṣūliyyīn*. Cairo: Dār al-Nahḍa al-'Arabiyya, 1960.

Māmqānī, 'Abd Allāh al-. *Manāhij al-muttaqīn fī fiqh al-a'imma al-ḥaqq wa al-yaqīn*. Qumm: Mu'assasa Ahl al-Bayt, 1984.

Maqdisī, 'Abū Ya'lā Muḥammad Ibn Mufliḥ al-. *al-Furū'*. N.p., 1962–67.

Mardāwī, 'Alī b. Sulaymān b. Muḥammad al-, *al-Inṣāf*. Cairo: Maṭba'a al-Sunna al-Muḥammadīya, 1955.

Masā'il fī al-talqīḥ al-ṣanā'ī, in *Masā'il wa Rudūd*, comp. Muḥammad Jawād Raḍī al-Shihābī and ed. 'Abd al-Wāḥid Muḥammad al-Najjār. Qumm: Dār al-Hādī, 1412/1992.

Matta, Christina, "Ambiguous Bodies and Deviant Sexuality: Hermaphrodites, Homosexuality, and Surgery in the United States, 1850–1904." In *Controversies in Science and Technology: From Climate to Chromosomes*, ed. Daniel Lee Klienman. New Rochelle, NY: Mary Ann Liebert, Inc., 2008. 2:493–505.

Mayer, Ann Elizabeth. *Islam & Human Rights: Tradition and Politics*. Boulder, CO: Westview Press, 1991.

Moazam, Farhat. *Bioethics And Organ Transplantation in a Muslim Society: A Study in Culture, Ethnography, And Religion*. Bloomington: Indiana University Press, 2006.

Muḥaqqiq al-Ḥillī, Ja'far b. al-Ḥasan. *Mukhtaṣar al-nāfi' fī fiqh al-imāmīya*. Qumm: Mu'assasa Bi'that, 1989.

———. *al-Nihāya wa nukatahā*. Qumm: Mu'assasa Intishārāt-i Islāmī, 1987.

Muḥaqqiq Dāmād, Muṣṭafā. *Qavā'id-i fiqh*. Tehran: Nashr-i 'Ulum-I Islāmī, 1370 Sh/1992.

Mu'min, Muḥammad. *Kalimāt sadīda fī masā'il jadīda*. Qumm: Mu'assasa-yi Nashr-i Islāmī, 1415/1994.

———. "al-Tashrīḥ fī al-ta'līm al-ṭibbī." *Fiqh ahl al-bayt* 1, no. 1 (1995/1416): 81–109.

Muntaẓarī, Ayatollah. *Aḥkām-i Pizishkī*. Tehran: Nashr-i Sāye, 1381 Sh/2002.

Musavi Lari, Sayyid Mujtaba. *God and His Attributes: Lessons on Islamic Doctrine*. Translated by Hamid Algar. Potomac, MD: Islamic Education Center, 1989.

Muslim b. al-Ḥajjāj al-Nisābūrī. *Ṣaḥīḥ*. Beirut: Dār Iḥyā' al-Turāth al-'Arabī, 1972.

Muẓaffar, Muḥammad Riḍā. *Uṣūl al-fiqh*. Najaf: Dār al-Nu'mān, 1966.

Najafī, Muḥammad Ḥasan al-. *Jawāhir al-kalām fī sharḥ sharā'i' al-islām*. 42 vols. Tehran: Kitābfurūshī Islāmīya, 1392/1972.

Nawawī. *Minhāj al-ṭālibīn*. Beirut: Dār al-Fikr, 1978.

———. *Ṣaḥīḥ muslim bi sharḥ al-nawawī*. Beirut: Dār Iḥya' al-Turāth al-'Arabī, 1972.

Nāyibzade, 'Abbās. *Bārvarī maṣnū'ī*. Tehran: Intishārāt-i Majd, 1380/2001.

Naẓarī Tavakkulī, Sa'īd. *al-Tarqī' wa zar' al-a'ḍā'*. Mashhad: Al-Āsatāna al-Raḍawīya al-Muqaddasa, 1422/2001.

Obeyesekere, Gananath. "Theodicy, Sin, and Salvation in a Sociology of Buddhism." In *Dialectical in Practical Religion,* edited by E. R. Leach. Cambridge: Cambrdige University Press, 1968.

O'Flaherty, Wendy Doniger. *The Origins of Evil in Hindu Mythology.* Berkeley: University of California Press, 1976.

Omran, Abdel Rahim. *Family Planning in the Legacy of Islam.* London: Routledge, 1992.

Ormsby, Eric L. *Theodicy in Islamic Thought: The Dispute over Al-Ghazali's 'Best of All Possible Worlds'.* Princeton: Princeton University Press, 1984.

Pellegrino, Edmund, Patricia Mazzarella, and Pietro Corsi, eds. *Transcultural Dimensions in Medical Ethics.* Frederick, MD: University Publishing Group, Inc., 1992.

Qaraḍāwī, Yūsuf al-. "Bunūk al-ḥalīb." *Majalla majma' al-fiqhī al-islāmī* 2, no. 1 (1986/1407): 385–406.

Qarārāt wa tawṣīyāt majma' al-fiqhī al-islāmī (Amman, Jordan), no. 34, (11–16 October 1986).

Qayṣarī, Dawūd b. Muḥammad al-. *Sharḥ Qayṣarī 'alā Fuṣūṣ al-ḥikam.* Tehran: Anwār al-Hudā, 1416/1995.

Quḍāt, Sharaf al-. *Matā tunfakh al-rūḥ fī al-janīn?* Amman, Jordan: Dār al-Furqān, 1990.

Qummī, 'Abbās. *Mafātīḥ al-jinān.* Tehran: Kitābfurūshī Islāmī, 1381/2002.

Qurṭubī, Muḥammad b. Aḥmad al-, *al-Jāmi' li-aḥkām al-qur'ān.* Cairo: Dār al-Kātib al-'Arabī, 1387/1967.

Raḍawī, al-Sayyid Muḥammad Ḥasan al-. "al-Istinsākh wa 'amaliyāt al-hindisa al-wārithīya," being the digest of the lectures by al-Ustādh al-Shaykh Muḥammad Sanad. In *Fiqh al-ṭibb wa al-taḍakhkhum al-naqdī.* Beirut: Mu'assasa Umm al-Qurā, 1423/2002.

Ramlī, Muḥammad b. Aḥmad, *Nihāyat al-muḥtāj ilā sharḥ al-minhāj.* Beirut: Dār Iḥyā' al-Turāth al-'Arabī, 1939.

Raufu, Abiodun. "Polio Cases Rise in Nigeria as Vaccine is Shunned for Fear of AIDS." *British Medical Journal* 2002.

Rāzī, Muḥammad b. 'Umar b. al-Ḥusayn al-. *al-Maḥṣūl fī 'ilm al-uṣūl al-fiqh.* Riyadh: Jāmi'at al-Imām, 1400/1979.

_________. *al-Tafsīr al-kabīr.* Cairo: al-Maṭba'a al Baḥiyya al-Miṣriyya, 1938.

Rispler-Chaim, Vardit. *Islamic Medical Ethics in the Twentieth Century.* Leiden: E. J. Brill, 1993.

Rothman, David J. "Research, Human: Historical Aspects." In *Encyclopedia of Bioethics.* Rev. ed. New York: Simon & Schuster Macmillan, 1995.

Roughgarden, Joan. "Social Selection versus Sexual Selection: Comparison of Hypotheses." In *Controversies in Science and Technology: From Climate to Chromosomes,* ed. Daniel Lee Klienman. New Rochelle, NY: Mary Ann Liebert, Inc., 2008. 2: 421–63.

Rūḥānī, Sayyid Muḥammad Ṣādiq al-, *Masā'il mustaḥdatha.* Qumm: Mu'assasa Maṭbū'a Dār al-Fikr, 1964–65.

Ṣābirī, Ḥusayn. "Istiṣlāḥ va pūyāyī-yi fiqh." *Majalla-yi Dānishkada-yi Ilāhiyāt Mashhad,* no. 49–50 (1379 Sh/2000), 235–86.

Sachedina, Abdulaziz. "Islam." *Encyclopedia of Bioethics* (New York: Macmillan, 1995)

________. "Iran." Coauthored with Dr. Eshraghi. *Encyclopedia of Bioethics* (New York: Macmillan, 1995).

———. *The Islamic Roots of Democratic Pluralism*. New York: Oxford University Press, 2001.

Ṣadr, Al-Sayyid Muḥammad al-. *Mā warā' al-fiqh*. Beirut: Dār al-Aḍwā', 1417/1996.

Ṣaffār, Muḥammad b. al-Ḥusayn al-. *Baṣā'ir al-darajāt*. Qumm: Kitābfurūshī Islāmīya, 1967.

Salāma, Ziyād Aḥmad. *Aṭfāl al-anābīb bayna al-'ilm wa al-sharī'a*. Beirut, Dār al-Bayāriq, 1996.

Sam'ānī, 'Abd al-Karīm b. Muḥammad. *al-Ansāb*. N.p., 1962.

Schimmel, Annemarie. *Mystical Dimensions of Islam*. Chapel Hill: University of North Carolina Press, 1975.

Shāfi'ī. *Kitāb al-Umm*. Cairo: Dār al-Wafā', 2001.

Shahīdī, Mahdī. "Waḍ'iyyat-i ḥuqūqī-yi kūdak-i azmāyishgāhī." In *Majmū'a-yi maqālāt-i ḥuqūqī*. Tehran: Nashr-i Ḥuqūqdānān, 1375/1996.

Shaltūt, Maḥmūd. *al-Fatāwā: Dirāsa li-mushkilāt al-muslim al-mu'āṣir fī ḥayātihi al-yawmīya al-'āmma*. Beirut: Dār al-Shurūq, 1963.

Sha'rāwī, Muḥammad Mutawallī al-. *Al-Fatāwā al-shaykh al-sha'rāwī*, comp. al-Sayyid al-Jumaylī. Cairo: Dār al-Naṣr li-al-tibā'a al-islāmīya, 1981.

Sharīf, Muḥammad 'Abd al-Ghaffār al-. "Ḥukm al-kashf al-ijbārī 'an al-amrāḍ al-wirāthīya" [The injunction about mandatory investigation of hereditary diseases]. In *Buḥūth al-fiqhīya mu'āṣira, Majalla kulliya al-sharī'a wa al-qānūn*. Beirut: Dār Ibn Ḥazm, 1422/2001. First published in *Majalla kulliya al-sharī'a wa al-qānūn* (Azhar University) 18, no. 12 (2000): 236ff.

Shāṭibī, Ibrahīm b. Mūsā b. Muḥammad al-. *al-Muwāfiqāt fī uṣūl al-sharī'a*. Beirut: Dār al-Ma'rifa, n.d.

Shawkānī, Muḥammad b. 'Ali b. Muḥammad al-. *al-Darārī al-muḍi'ah*. Beirut: Dār al-Jīl, 1407/1987.

———. *Irshād al-fuḥūl ilā taḥqīq al-ḥaqq min 'ilm al-uṣūl*. Beirut: Dār al-Fikr, 1412/1992.

———. *Kitāb al-sayl al-jarrār al-mutadaffiq 'alā ḥadā'iq al-azhar* . Cairo: n.p., 1970.

Shirāzī, Ṣadr al-Dīn al-. *Al-shawāhid al-rubūbīya fī manāhij al-sulūkīya*. Mashhad: Mashhad University Press, 1985.

Sind, Muḥammad. *Fiqh al-ṭibb wa taḍakhkhum al-naqdī*. Researched and critically annotated by Muḥammad Ḥasan al-Raḍawī. Beirut: Mu'assasa 'Umm al-Qurā, 1423/2002.

Sīstānī, 'Alī al-Ḥusaynī al-. *Qā'ida lā ḍarar wa lā ḍirār*. Qumm: Lithographie Ḥamīd, 1414/1993.

Soroush, Abdolkarim. *Reason, Freedom, and Democracy in Essential Writings of Abdolkarim Soroush*, trans. and ed. M. Sadri and A. Sadri. New York: Oxford University Press, 2000.

Subkī, Taqī al-Dīn 'Alī b. 'Abd al-Kāfī al-. *al-Ibhāj fī sharḥ al-minhāj:'alā. minhāj al-wuṣūl ilā 'ilm al-uṣūl*. Beirut: Dār al-kutub al-'ilmiya, 1404/1984.

Sukkarī, 'Abd al-Salām 'Abd al-Raḥīm al-. *Naql wa zirā'a al-a'ḍā' al-ādamīya min al-manẓūr al-islāmī: Dirāsa al-muqārana*. Cairo: Dār al-Manār, 1988.

Suyūṭī. *al-Ashbāh wa al-naẓā'ir fī qawā'id wa furu' fiqh al-Shāfi'īya*. Mecca: Maktabat Nizār Muṣṭafā al-Bāz, 1990.

———. *Tanwīr al-ḥawālik: is'āf al-mubatta' bi-rijāl al-Muwaṭṭa'*. Beirut: al-Maktaba al-Thiqāfiya, 1969.

Ṭabāṭabā'ī, Muḥammad Ḥusayn al-, *al-Mīzān fī tafsīr al-qur'ān*. 20 vols. Beirut: Mu'assasa al-A'lamī, 1972.

Tabrīzī, Sayyid Yūsuf al-Madanī al-. *al-Masā'il al-mustaḥdatha*. Tabrīz: Ismā'īliyān, 1416/1996.

Ṭāhirī, Murtaḍā, "Ahmiyat-i bihdāsht-i dahān va dandān az dīdgāh-i islām." In *Majmū'a-yi maqālāt seminar dīdgāh-hāyi islām dar pizishkī*. Mashhad: Ferdowsi University Press, 1371/1992. 145–59.

Taqavī, Sayyid Murtaḍā. "Tahavvul-i mavdū'āt dar fiqh." *Majallah-i fiqh-i ahl-i bayt*, no. 3 (1365/1987): 207–20.

Tawḥīdī, Abi al-Ḥayy, al-. *al-Muqtabaṣāt*. Kuwait: Dār al-Su'ād al-Ṣabāḥ, 1992.

Tom L. Beauchamp and James F. Childress, *Principles of Biomedical Ethics*, 5th ed. New York: Oxford University Press, 2001.

Ṭūfi, Sulaymān b. 'Abd al-Qawī al-. *Risāla fi ri'āya al-maṣlaḥa*. Ed. Ahmad 'Abd al-Raḥīm al-Sāyiḥ. Cairo: Dār al-Miṣrīya al-Lubnānīya, 1413/1993.

Ṭūsī, Muḥammad b. al-Ḥasan al-. *al-Iqtiṣād al-hādī ilā ṭarīq al-rashād*. Tehran: Maktaba Jāmi' Chihilsitūn, 1400/1979.

———. *Tamhīd al-uṣūl dar 'ilm-i kalām-i islām*, being translation of the commentary on al-Sharīf al-Murtaḍā's section on theology in *Jumal al-'ilm wa al-'amal*. Translated by 'Abd al-Muḥsin Mishkāt al-Dīnī. Tehran: Anjuman Islamī Ḥikmat va Falsafī Tihrān, 1358 Sh/1980.

Ullman, Manfred. *Islamic Medicine*. Edinburgh: University Press, 1997.

Wahāybī, al-Munṣif al-. "Al-Jasad: ṣūratahu wa ḥuqūqahu fī al-islām." In *Ḥuqūq al-insān fī fikr al-'arabī: Dirāsāt fī al-nuṣūṣ*, 281–307. Beirut: Markaz Dirāsāt al-Waḥdat al-'Arabīya, 2002.

Wensinck, A. J. *The Muslim Creed*. London: Frank Cass & Co. Ltd., 1965.

Yāsīn, Muḥammad Na'īm. *Abhāth fiqhīya fī qaḍāya ṭibbīya mu'āṣira*. 'Amman, Jordan: Dār al-Nafā'is, 1416/1996.

Zaydān, 'Abd al-Karīm. *Al-Mufaṣṣal: Aḥkām al-mar'a wa al-bayt al-muslim*. Beirut: Mu'assasa Risāla, 1417/1997.

Index